COSMIC GRACE ✛ HUMBLE PRAYER

# COSMIC GRACE ✟ HUMBLE PRAYER

## The Ecological Vision
## of the Green Patriarch Bartholomew I

*Edited by*

JOHN CHRYSSAVGIS

*With a Foreword by*

Metropolitan John (Zizioulas) of Pergamon

WILLIAM B. EERDMANS PUBLISHING COMPANY
GRAND RAPIDS, MICHIGAN / CAMBRIDGE, U.K.

Wm. B. Eerdmans Publishing Co.
255 Jefferson Ave. S.E., Grand Rapids, Michigan 49503 /
P.O. Box 163, Cambridge CB3 9PU U.K.

Printed in the United States of America

08  07  06  05  04  03      7  6  5  4  3  2  1

**Library of Congress Cataloging-in-Publication Data**

Bartholomew I, Ecumenical Patriarch of Constantinople, 1940-
[Selections. English]
Cosmic grace, humble prayer: the ecological vision of the green patriarch Bartholomew I /
edited by John Chryssavgis.
p.      cm.
Includes bibliographical references and index.
ISBN 0-8028-2169-3 (alk. paper)
1. Human ecology — Religious aspects — Orthodox Eastern Church.
2. Orthodox Eastern Church — Doctrines.
I. Chryssavgis, John.   II. Title.

BX337.5.B37213      2003
261.8′362 — dc21

2003052856

www.eerdmans.com

# Contents

Contents

# *Foreword*

One of the questions that the reader of the present volume may naturally ask is, What does the Church have to do with an issue such as the ecological crisis of our time? It is commonly assumed that the protection of the natural environment is a matter that concerns the politicians, the scientists, and the technocrats. The preoccupation of the Orthodox Church and, in particular, her highest authority, the Ecumenical Patriarchate, with such a problem will probably come to many people as a surprise.

The reason for this surprise is twofold. On the one hand, people are used to regarding the Church as an institution devoted primarily, if not exclusively, to "spiritual" matters. Few people would expect from the Church an interest and practical involvement in down-to-earth matters like the environment. This would probably be the case particularly with regard to the Orthodox Church, which is known to Western people mainly for her "mystical" theology, her "spirituality," and her ascetical tradition.

On the other hand, the majority of people seem to ignore or overlook the fact that the ecological crisis is deeply rooted in theology, and it is above all a spiritual problem. It was the merit of the American historian Lynn White to point out for the first time so clearly back in 1967 that the historical roots of our ecological crisis are to be found in Christian theology, particularly in its Western tradition, which led to modern scientific developments marked with a contemptuous and arrogant attitude toward the material world. Christian theology bears, therefore, a historical responsibility for the evil of environmental destruction and should undergo a profound *metanoia* in order to undo the damage it has caused.

Such a *metanoia* or repentance would not be limited to theoretical or doctrinal aspects of the Church's teaching, much as these are necessary and of crucial significance. The Church is called to revise her *pastoral* teaching and work so as to transform the mentality and attitude of modern people, making them realize that the protection of the natural environment is a fundamental religious obligation demanded from humankind by God himself. This means that the Church will have to revise radically her concept of sin, which traditionally has been limited to the social and anthropological level, and start speaking of *sin against nature* as a matter of primary religious significance. In addition to that, the Church must introduce environmental teaching into her preaching, Sunday schools, and other religious forms of education from the lowest to the highest level. The Church cannot be faithful to her mission today without a serious involvement in the protection of God's creation from the damage inflicted on it by human greed and selfishness.

Such considerations and concerns lie behind the decision of the Ecumenical Patriarchate to assume a leading role in the fight for the protection of God's creation. As is evident from the first Patriarchal Message on the Environment issued by the late Patriarch Demetrios in 1989 as well as from the Patriarchal encyclicals and speeches of the present Ecumenical Patriarch Bartholomew, contained in the present volume, the Orthodox Church realizes that without a profound spiritual transformation of the human being there is no hope for salvation of the natural environment from the human interventions that threaten it with destruction, and that in order to achieve such a spiritual transformation *all* religious communities should cooperate, together with scientists, politicians, ethicists, etc. The international Religious and Scientific symposia organized by the Ecumenical Patriarchate aim precisely at such cooperation, and for this reason they constitute a priority in the Patriarchate's activities.

The Orthodox Church's involvement in the protection of the natural environment is a matter of faithfulness to her tradition and to her very nature. Two aspects of her teaching and life testify to this. One is her insistence on the centrality of the Holy Eucharist in Christian existence; the other is her age-long ascetical tradition. The first of these aspects stresses the fact that the human being is the *Priest of Creation* called to take in his or her hands the world as a *gift* and refer it back to the Giver with thankfulness *(eucharistia)*. As the world passes through human hands it is, of course, transformed and cultivated: this is what human labor, including science, art, economy, and so on, does to nature. But in a eucharistic approach, all this labor is justified only insofar as (a) it is *shared* in love with all human beings (= *koinonia,* communion) and (b) it is *referred* back to the Creator with the acknowledgment that human beings are not the possessors of nature, but an organic part of it endowed with the call to lift it up to the One who can give it eternal meaning and life. The ascetic tradition, on the other hand, enables human beings to free themselves from the selfishness that makes them mistake themselves as possessors of creation, and turns them into eucharistic beings.

The reader of the present volume will discover for himself or herself the profound reasons that account for the Ecumenical Patriarchate's involvement in the protection of the environment. The rich introduction by the editor, Fr. John Chryssavgis, will prove an invaluable help in the appreciation of the theological depth and pastoral significance of the work and the word of the Ecumenical Patriarch, a religious leader with true ecological vision.

+JOHN (ZIZIOULAS)
Metropolitan of Pergamon

# *Acknowledgments*

I would like to express my respectful gratitude to His All Holiness Ecumenical Patriarch Bartholomew for his unconditional support throughout and for his paternal confidence in the editorial presentation.

Thanks are also due to His Eminence Metropolitan John of Pergamon for providing the inspiration behind and the theological framework for my interest in this work, as well as to the staff of the Environmental Office at the Fanar for continued and unfailing assistance. In particular, I am grateful to His Eminence Metropolitan Meliton of Philadelphia and His Eminence Metropolitan Tarasios of Buenos Aires for entrusting me with archival material.

It is an honor to include, with the kind permission of Gabriel Pentzikis, the work "Christopsaro" (tempera, 1978) by the renowned contemporary Greek artist and writer Nikos Gabriel Pentzikis (1908-1993) for the cover. There is a folk legend about a fish that found itself outside the sea. It is said that Christ heeded the lament of the fish, lifted it in His hands, and returned it to the ocean. Since that time, the fish bears the fingerprint of Christ on its side. The painting depicts a fish (actually a "John Dory," but "Christopsaro" literally means a "Christ fish") in the water of a baptismal font, surrounded by people — clergy and monastic — in mystical prayer and solemn procession. It reflects many of the themes contained in the introduction and texts of this book: the fish and waters of the oceans, the sacraments and baptism in particular, icons and the cross, the liturgy and prayer, monasticism and asceticism. Like his literature, Pentzikis's art constitutes a visual reflection of all earthly things in light of their mythical and mystical perspective. Deeply resembling Byzantine iconography and even contemporary neo-impressionism, Pentzikis's is a highly transfigurative art that reveals an alternative form and lifestyle, ultimately a transformed world. It manifests the eternal beauty of the world that lasts beyond, and transcends, this ephemeral world. More than this, it is a manifesto of the heart for "a new heaven and a new earth" (Rev. 21:1).

Research for this book commenced during a visit to the archives in Constantinople during the summer of 2001, made possible through "Leadership 100 Endowment Fund." It was completed during a sabbatical semester in the spring of 2002 at Princeton, made possible through the hospitality of a fellowship at the Center of Theological Inquiry. The publication of the book was endorsed partly through the kindness and generous grant received from "The Order of St. Andrew the Apostle/Archons of the Ecumenical Patriarchate in America." I am grateful to Mr. N. Manginas for many of the photographs included in this volume.

Profound thanks are especially due to the editorial team and to the President of Eerdmans Publishing Company, Mr. William Eerdmans, for his spontaneous response and gracious guidance from the very outset of this engagement.

JC

# Introduction

In the past decade, the world has witnessed alarming environmental degradation — with climate change, the loss of biodiversity, and the pollution of natural resources — and the widening gap between rich and poor, as well as increasing failure to implement environmental policies. During the same decade, one religious leader has discerned the signs of the times and called people's attention to this ecological and social situation. The worldwide leader of the Orthodox Churches, His All Holiness Ecumenical Patriarch Bartholomew has persistently proclaimed the primacy of spiritual values in determining environmental ethics and action.

No other church leader has been recognized throughout the world for his dynamic leadership and initiatives in addressing the theological, ethical, and practical imperative in relation to the critical environmental issues of our time as has His All Holiness Ecumenical Patriarch Bartholomew. Patriarch Bartholomew has long placed the environment at the head of his Church's agenda. The Patriarch has developed ecological programs, chaired Pan-Orthodox gatherings and international symposia, and organized environmental seminars for more than a decade.

## Bartholomew: The Green Patriarch

Bartholomew (born Demetrios Archontonis), the current Ecumenical Patriarch of the Orthodox Church, was born on February 29, 1940, in a small village on the island of Imvros, modern-day Turkey. The residents of this island, like the inhabitants of so many other regions of Asia Minor, have been known through the centuries for their profoundly spiritual traditions and pious devotion, and in general for their cultivation of spiritual values. As the young

Demetrios, Patriarch Bartholomew was raised to work the earth of the heart, long before he would be prepared to preserve the green of the environment as Ecumenical Patriarch.

His theological training also attracted the young Demetrios to move beyond the library and to breathe the air of the *oikoumene,* the breadth of the universe of theological communication and ecclesiastical reconciliation. In later years, he would see a similar connection between church and environment:

> For us at the Ecumenical Patriarchate, the term "ecumenical" is more than a name: it is a worldview and a way of life. The Lord intervenes and fills His creation with His divine presence in a continuous bond. Let us work together so that we may renew the harmony between heaven and earth, so that we may transform every detail and every element of life. Let us love one another. With love, let us share with others everything we know, and especially that which is useful in order to educate godly persons so that they may sanctify God's creation for the glory of His holy name.[1]

In 1961, Demetrios graduated from the Patriarchal School at Halki, which for 127 years trained numerous clergymen and theologians of the Ecumenical Patriarchate throughout the world until it was forced to close its doors officially in 1971. This school was to be — and still remains — the venue for numerous meetings and seminars on environmental issues during his tenure as Patriarch. In 1961, Demetrios was ordained to deacon. It was while he served in this office that the young Demetrios also received the monastic name of Bartholomew.

From 1963 to 1968, Bartholomew attended several prestigious centers of scholarship and ecumenical dialogue, such as the University of Munich (Germany), the Ecumenical Institute in Bossey (Switzerland), and the Institute of Oriental Studies of the Gregorian University in Rome (Italy). In the last of these institutions, he received his doctorate in canon law, submitting a dissertation (later published in Greek at Thessaloniki in 1970) on *The Codification of the Holy Canons and of the Canonical Institution in the Orthodox Church.* Subsequent publications covered such subjects as the role of the Ecumenical Patriarchate, the apostolic mission of the Orthodox Church, the tradition and

---

1. See his address at a Scenic Hudson luncheon (November 13, 2000), in Part II below. All quotations from Patriarch Bartholomew in this introduction are taken from the various texts collected in the present volume.

witness of the Church in the contemporary world, theological dialogues with the Roman Catholic Church, and ecumenical relations with other Christian confessions.

Upon the completion of his studies, Bartholomew returned to Constantinople, where, in 1969, he was ordained to the priesthood. From 1972, he served as director of the newly established special Personal Office of Patriarch Demetrios (1972-1991), and in 1973 he was elected Metropolitan of Philadelphia. He attended General Assemblies of the World Council of Churches — even serving as Vice-Chairman of the Faith and Order Commission as well as being a member of its Central and Executive Committees — from 1968 to 1991. These were critical and formative years for the development of the ecological sensitivity of this influential international organization. In 1990, Bartholomew was elected Metropolitan of Chalcedon, the most senior rank among the bishops in Constantinople at the time. And in October 1991, he was elected Ecumenical Patriarch, the most senior of Orthodox bishops throughout the world, "first among equals" among all Orthodox Patriarchs and Primates.

From the moment, and indeed from the very address, of his enthronement, Patriarch Bartholomew outlined the dimensions of his leadership and vision within the Orthodox Church: the vigilant education in matters of theology, liturgy, and spirituality; the strengthening of Orthodox unity and cooperation; the continuation of ecumenical engagements with other Christian churches and confessions; the intensification of interreligious dialogue for peaceful coexistence; and the initiation of discussion and action for the protection of the environment against ecological pollution and destruction.

Perhaps no other church leader in history has emphasized ecumenical dialogue and communication as a primary intention of his tenure. Certainly, no other church leader in history has brought environmental issues to the foreground, indeed to the very center of personal and ecclesiastical attention.

In order for readers to be initiated into the world of the Orthodox Church, and particularly of the Ecumenical Patriarchate, I have chosen to quote extensively below from an address of the Patriarch himself, delivered as an introduction to one of the presentations in this volume.[2]

> The Ecumenical Patriarchate, over which we preside, is an institution with a history of sixteen centuries, during which it retained its see in Constantinople. It constitutes the *par excellence* Center of all the local Orthodox

---

2. See the address by Ecumenical Patriarch Bartholomew at the Foreign Correspondents' Club in Hong Kong (November 6, 1996). This introductory segment has been omitted from the text included in Part II below.

Churches. It heads these, not by administering them, but by virtue of its primacy in the ministry of Pan-Orthodox Unity and the coordination of the activity of all of Orthodoxy. Orthodox Christians on four continents (excluding Africa), which do not fall under the jurisdiction of the autocephalous Churches, fall under the direct jurisdiction of the Ecumenical Patriarchate. The most important of these autocephalous Churches are: the Patriarchates of Alexandria, Antioch, Jerusalem, Moscow, Serbia, Romania, Bulgaria, Georgia, and the Autocephalous Churches of Cyprus, Greece, Poland, Albania, and certain others. Consequently, the Orthodox Churches of Europe, America, and the rest of Asia and Australia, which are not under the jurisdiction of the aforementioned autocephalous Churches, fall under the Ecumenical Patriarchate.

The function of the Ecumenical Patriarchate as the center *par excellence* of the life of the entire Orthodox Church emanates from its centuries-old ministry in the witness, protection, and spread of the Orthodox faith. The Ecumenical Patriarchate has a supranational and supra-regional character. From the lofty consciousness of this fact, but also from a sense of its spiritual responsibility for the development of the faith in Christ of all people, regardless of race and language, were born the new regional Churches of the East, from the Caspian to the Baltics, and from the Balkans to Central Europe, where its missionary activity was extended. This activity already extends to the Far East, America, and Australia, where conditions allow, with absolute respect for the freedom of religious consciousness of all and without resorting to methods of proselytizing. Essentially, wherever there are Orthodox Christian immigrants or natives, a Church is established, and it constitutes a magnet only for those who come freely.

The Orthodox Church is distinguished from other Christian Churches in that it has preserved unadulterated the first and most ancient ecclesiastical tradition and teaching, has avoided innovations and personal interpretations of the Holy Scriptures and dogmas of the faith, and is administered according to the ancient synodical system under local bishops in collaboration with the faithful and successive groups of both local and broader episcopal synods, of which the highest is the Ecumenical Synod, that of the Orthodox worldwide. The basic administrative canons, the details of which are regulated according to local needs, have been determined by the seven Ecumenical Synods. The Church is not managed by regional states in which it resides, although it collaborates in good works when asked to do so.

Within the entire Orthodox Church there is absolute cooperation in good will and mutual respect. Minor human problems that arise are addressed successfully through the application of evangelical spirit. Furthermore, the Ecumenical Patriarchate coordinates ongoing dialogues between Orthodox and heterodox Churches, many of which are progressing propitiously while others move at a slower pace. The objective of these dialogues is the removal of obstacles to the union of all the divided Churches.

As becomes clear from the above, all Orthodox feel that they are constituents of one essentially spiritual community. "When one member suffers, so do all." They feel that they commune in the suffering of their fellow Christians and participate in their joys. Only if one perceives the catholicity of union can one understand the expressions of the Orthodox, which refer to the suffering of the other Orthodox and of the whole world as if they were their own.

## History: Initiatives and Action

The environmental vision and initiatives of the Ecumenical Patriarchate date back to the mid-1980s, when it organized and chaired the third session of the Pre-Synodal Pan-Orthodox Conference, held in Chambésy (October 28-November 6, 1986). Although the decisions of this meeting were not binding, serving only as recommendations, nevertheless the representatives attending the meeting expressed and stressed their concern about the abuse of the natural environment by human beings, especially in affluent societies of the Western world. The meeting also underlined the importance of respecting the sacredness and freedom of the human person created in the image and likeness of God, the missionary imperative and witness of the Orthodox Church in the contemporary world (Sections C and H), as well as the harm wrought by war, racism, and inequality (Sections F and G) on human societies and the environment. The emphasis was on leaving a better world for future generations (Section E).

Thereafter, and especially as a result of the General Assembly of the World Council of Churches held in Vancouver (1983), several inter-Orthodox meetings were organized on the subject of "Justice, Peace, and the Integrity of Creation" and attended by Orthodox representatives. Three significant consultations were held.

The first was in Sofia, Bulgaria (1987). A second consultation, in Patmos, Greece (1988), marked the nine hundredth anniversary of the foundation of the historic Monastery of St. John the Theologian on the island of

Patmos. This attractive and historic island in the Mediterranean would later become the focus of a new initiative of the current Ecumenical Patriarch. However, on September 23-25, 1988, Patriarch Demetrios, under whose spiritual jurisdiction the Monastery lies, assigned Metropolitan John (Zizioulas) of Pergamon as the Patriarchal representative to this conference. The conference, the theme of which was "Revelation and the Future of Humanity," was held on the occasion of this anniversary and organized by the Greek Ministry of Cultural Affairs in cooperation with the local civil authorities. One of the primary recommendations of this conference was that the Ecumenical Patriarchate should assume the responsibility of appointing a particular day of the year as especially designated and dedicated for the protection of the natural environment.

This conference proved to be a catalyst for the direction of many subsequent Patriarchal initiatives on the environment. The Christmas encyclical letter, signed by Patriarch Demetrios, already looked forward to the later Patmos celebrations and symposium of 1995. A third inter-Orthodox consultation was held in Minsk, Russia (1989), while an environmental program was also piloted in Ormylia (1990).

In 1989, the same Ecumenical Patriarch Demetrios, immediate predecessor of Patriarch Bartholomew, who was his closest theological and administrative advisor in these and other matters, published the first official decree on the environment, an encyclical letter sent out "to the *pleroma* of the Church." Because Demetrios was known for his softness and meekness, it seems very fitting that it was during his tenure that the Orthodox Church worldwide was invited to dedicate a day of prayer for the protection of the environment, which human beings have treated so harshly. Demetrios encouraged his faithful to walk gently on the earth, just as he had. This encyclical, proclaimed on the occasion of the first day of the new ecclesiastical calendar, known as the *indictus*, formally established September 1st as a day for all Orthodox Christians within the jurisdiction of the Ecumenical Patriarchate to offer prayers for the protection and preservation of God's creation. Since that time, a similar statement and spiritual reminder have been issued every year, on the first day of September, to Orthodox faithful in North and South America, Western Europe and Great Britain, as well as in Australasia.[3]

---

3. Echoing and citing this appeal by the Ecumenical Patriarchate, and in response to the World Summit on Sustainable Development scheduled for Johannesburg, the central committee of the World Council of Churches passed a resolution (Document GEN 17, 6.2) in its meeting of August 26-September 3, 2002, urging member churches to mark September 1st each year as a day of prayer for the environment and its sustainability. This recommendation was based on a note from its program committee that observed: "Some churches have acted with courage

In the following year (1990), the foremost hymnographer of the monastic republic on Mount Athos, Monk Gerasimos Mikrayiannanites (d. 1991), was commissioned by the Ecumenical Patriarchate to compose a service of supplication, with prayers for the protection of the environment.[4] The Orthodox Church has traditionally prayed for the environment. However, whereas in the past Orthodox faithful prayed to be delivered from natural calamities, beginning on June 6, 1989, the Ecumenical Patriarch was calling Orthodox Christians to pray for the environment to be delivered from the abusive acts of the human inhabitants of this planet. Therefore, most of the prayers composed by Fr. Gerasimos are supplications for repentance, invitations for conversion, and cries of nostalgia for a lost paradise, from which we have been alienated by destroying this world.

A month after rising to the ecclesiastical throne of Constantinople, in November of 1991, the Ecumenical Patriarch initiated and convened an ecological meeting on the island of Crete. The title of the gathering was "Living in the Creation of the Lord." That convention was attended and officially opened by Prince Philip, the Duke of Edinburgh and International Chairman of the World Wide Fund for Nature (WWF).

In the following year, March of 1992, Bartholomew called a meeting of all Orthodox Patriarchs and Primates, who gathered at the Phanar, where the Patriarch resides, for a historic expression of unity in theological vision and pastoral concern. Here, the Ecumenical Patriarch again introduced the topic of the protection of the natural environment and asked all the Leaders of the Orthodox Churches to inform their churches about the critical significance of this issue for our times. The official message of the Orthodox Primates, representing all of the Orthodox Churches throughout the world, acknowledged, approved, and endorsed the Patriarchal initiative to establish September 1st as a day of Pan-Orthodox prayer for the environment.

In the summer of the same year, the Duke of Edinburgh also accepted

---

and vision in advocating for a sustainable earth. The call of His All Holiness Bartholomew I, the Ecumenical Patriarch of Constantinople, to Christians around the world to celebrate September 1st as Creation Day so as to pray for the World Summit on Sustainable Development, stands testimony to the commitment of the churches to the earth."

4. This service was published in 1991 and translated into English by Fr. Ephrem Lash in England. It was among the last services to be composed by Fr. Gerasimos. The translation appeared as "Office of Vespers for the Preservation of Creation" in *Orthodoxy and Ecology: Resource Book* (Bialystok: Syndesmos, 1996). A second English translation of the Vesper Service has also appeared in the United States, entitled *Vespers for the Protection of the Environment* (Northridge, CA: Narthex Press, 2001). The foreword to this translation is included in Part II among the addresses for the year 2001.

an invitation to visit the Phanar and address an environmental seminar at the Theological School of Halki. In November of 1993, the Ecumenical Patriarch returned the visit to the Duke, meeting with him at Buckingham Palace, where they sealed a friendship of common purpose and active cooperation for the preservation of the environment. From that same year, annual encyclicals of September 1st always emphasize the importance of ecological concern and action.

In April of 1994, the Ecumenical Patriarch was invited to the administrative offices of the European Commission, where he delivered a speech with a significant message. It was the first time that someone who was not a state or political leader had been asked to address the European Commission. The influence and impact of the young Patriarch was broadening to secular and governmental levels.

In June of 1994, another ecological seminar was convened at the historical Theological School of Halki. This was the first of five successive annual summer seminars held at Halki on diverse aspects of the environment: "Environment and Religious Education" (June 20-29, 1994); "Environment and Ethics" (June 12-18, 1995); "Environment and Communications" (July 1-7, 1996); "Environment and Justice" (June 25-30, 1997); and "Environment and Poverty" (June 14-20, 1998).

These seminars, the first of their kind, were designed to promote environmental awareness and action inspired by the initiatives of the Ecumenical Patriarchate. They sought to engage leading theologians, environmentalists, scientists, civil servants, and other experts. Speakers have included Church leaders, governmental authorities, scientists and ethicists, academicians and intellectuals, artists and journalists, as well as pioneers of ecological programs worldwide. The participants, who varied in number from fifty to eighty, came from all over the world and represented the major Christian denominations and world religions.

In October of 1994, the Department of Environmental Studies of the University of the Aegean conferred an honorary doctoral degree on Patriarch Bartholomew. This was the first of a series of awards and honorary degrees presented to Bartholomew in recognition of his efforts and initiatives to preserve the environment. The Department of Forestry and Environmental Studies of the Faculty of Earth Sciences at the University of Thessaloniki bestowed a similar honor on the Patriarch in 1997. In November 2000, the New York–based organization Scenic Hudson, one of the earliest and most prestigious environmental groups in the United States, presented the Ecumenical Patriarch with the first international Visionary Award for Environmental Achievement.

In June 2002, Patriarch Bartholomew was the recipient of the Sophie Prize, the most celebrated environmental award in the world.[5] Established by Jostein Gaarder, the well-known author of *Sophie's World,* the Sophie Prize is presented to an individual or organization that has, in a pioneering and creative manner, pointed to and developed alternatives for environmental awareness and action. In the case of Patriarch Bartholomew, the award was presented by the Minister of Environment in Norway during an official ceremony in Oslo. The reasons cited for presenting this award to Patriarch Bartholomew were:

- his pioneering efforts in linking faith to the environment, reminding all people of faith of their direct responsibility to protect the earth;
- his spiritual and practical environmental leadership, managing to raise the environmental awareness of 300 million faithful of the Orthodox Church worldwide and challenging religious leaders of all faiths to do the same;
- his tireless efforts to bring attention to both rights and obligations, criticizing both the over-consumption in the first world countries and the lack of justice that causes growing inequity in developing countries.

The 1999 recipient of the Sophie Prize, Thomas Kocherry of India, made the following remarks about the selection of the Patriarch:

As a religious leader, Patriarch Bartholomew gives meaning to Jesus Christ even today. Through his work, Jesus is still alive and risen. Environmental awareness and social justice go together. His All Holiness has taught the whole world that an institutional church has relevance.

The 2001 recipient, Bernard Cassen of ATTAC in France, observed:

The efforts of His All Holiness in raising environmental awareness . . . as well as exposing the negative impacts of globalization on the poor are examples for other world religious leaders to follow.

In 1994, convinced that any efforts to address the environmental concerns of our times must occur in dialogue with other Christian confessions, other religious faiths, and scientific disciplines, Patriarch Bartholomew established the Religious and Scientific Committee. As we share the earth, so too do

---

5. A further recognition of the Patriarch's inspiration and vision was the 2002 environmental award of the Binding Institute of Liechtenstein in Switzerland (November, 2002).

9

we share the responsibility for our pollution of the earth and the obligation to find tangible ways of healing the natural environment. This ecumenical and interdisciplinary committee is chaired by the Most Reverend Metropolitan John (Zizioulas) of Pergamon, professor of theology at King's College (University of London) and the Theological School of the University of Thessaloniki.

To date, the Religious and Scientific Committee — coordinated by Maria Becket — has convened four international, interdisciplinary, and interreligious symposia in order to study and reflect on the fate of the rivers and seas, which cover two-thirds of the earth's surface. These symposia have gathered scientists, environmentalists, journalists, policy-makers, and representatives of the world's main religious faiths in an effort to draw global attention to the plight of the Aegean Sea, the Black Sea, the Danube River, and the Adriatic Sea. Participants meet in plenary, workshop, and briefing sessions, hearing a variety of speakers on various environmental and ethical themes. Delegates also visit key environmental sites in the particular region of the symposium.

On September 20-27, 1995, the first symposium, "Revelation and the Environment," was convened under the joint auspices of Patriarch Bartholomew and Prince Philip on the occasion of the nineteen hundredth anniversary of St. John's book of Revelation. This scriptural book portrays the destructive impact of humanity on the earth and the seas with vivid language and images that have fascinated a wide variety of readers throughout the centuries.

Traveling on ship through the Aegean and the Eastern Mediterranean, the two hundred participants in this symposium identified the pollution of the world's waters as a threat to the survival of the planet and recommended the creation of a common language for scientific and theological thought in order to overcome centuries of estrangement and misunderstanding between science and faith.

In his opening address, Patriarch Bartholomew noted:

> The Orthodox Church is particularly well represented in parts of the world where "the earth has been hurt" (cf. Rev. 7:3). . . . Conscious of the threat of nuclear destruction and environmental pollution, we shall move toward one world or none.

It is critical to the entire vision of the Patriarch that the first symposium began with an emphasis on and interpretation of the book of Revelation, the closing book of the New Testament. Although in many people's minds the word "apocalypse" would seem to imply destruction and holocaust — which is clearly one aspect of the concept — nevertheless only a literalist and fundamentalist would accept this as the complete interpretation of the term. In fact, "revelation" signifies a vision that evil can be conquered by good, that ugliness can be overcome by beauty. For the book of Revelation is a book of imagination and poetry. The Greek word *(apokalypsis)* implies unveiling; it is an unveiling of possibilities, and specifically of the possibilities of working together for a new heaven and a new earth, for a better environment and world to leave to future generations.

A second symposium, on the subject "The Black Sea in Crisis," was held on September 20-27, 1997, under the joint auspices of the Ecumenical Patriarch and His Excellency the Hon. Jacques Santer, President of the European Commission. This time the symposium undertook a concrete case study, visiting the countries that surround the Black Sea and engaging in conversation with local religious leaders and environmental activists, as well as regional scientists and politicians.

As a direct result of this second symposium, the Halki Ecological Institute was organized on June 5-20, 1999, in order to promote and provide wider regional collaboration and education among some seventy-five clergy and theologians, educators and students, as well as scientists and journalists. This educational initiative marked a new direction in the interdisciplinary vision and dialogue concerning the environment, seeking to implement the principles of the ecological vision determined by the Religious and Scientific Committee by turning theory into practice.

The inaugural session of the Institute was conducted in a forested lakeland area outside of Istanbul and then on the island of Halki in the Sea of Marmara. It was attended by seventy members of the clergy, educational institutions, and media in the Black Sea region. Participants received intensive instruction from a team of international and regional theologians, scientists, educators, and environmental policy professionals. The two-week program included theological and scientific presentations in conjunction with field trips and scientific studies of the specific issues faced in that region. In inviting leaders of the region to send representatives to this Institute, Patriarch Bartholomew wrote:

> It is now our vision to launch a broader educational program. With this vision, we must peer far into the future as we prepare ourselves for a labor that will not end soon, nor can it be conducted easily. We must build on what we have done . . . moving forward in dedication and commitment to our task.

As an adjunct to this program, the Institute simultaneously conducted the Black Sea Environmental Journalists Workshop for approximately twenty print, radio, and television journalists from the six Black Sea nations. The purpose of the workshop was to provide a network for collaborative efforts in the region. The journalists joined the educational workshop for a series of interdisciplinary sessions on topics of mutual interest and concern.

During the second symposium, it became evident that no solution to the ecological collapse of the Black Sea could be found without addressing the degradation of the rivers that flow into that sea. Therefore, a third symposium, "The Danube: A River of Life," was launched in October 1999, under the joint auspices of Patriarch Bartholomew and His Excellency the Hon. Romano Prodi, President of the European Commission. This meeting gathered international and local leaders in the fields of science, religion, and environmental policy, who traveled the length of the Danube River, from Passau, Germany, to the delta of the Black Sea. In the aftermath of the military and ethnic conflict in the former republic of Yugoslavia, the challenge of protecting and restoring the state of the waters and natural environment along the Danube River became all the more critical and urgent. This third symposium focused on the ecological impact of war, urban development, industrialization, shipping, and agriculture.

A fourth symposium, "The Adriatic Sea: A Sea at Risk, a Unity of Purpose," addressed the ethical aspects of the environmental crisis. Held in June 2002 under the joint auspices of the Ecumenical Patriarch and His Excellency the Hon. Romano Prodi, President of the European Commission, this symposium opened in Durres, Albania, and concluded in Venice, Italy. The emphasis during this meeting was on the need to cultivate particular ecological principles and values among peoples in affluent countries and advanced economies as well as among peoples of recovering countries and transitional economies.

Two unique events during this symposium did more than turn a new page in the "book of nature"; they are sealed as memorable occasions in the "book of history." The first of these occurred on June 9, 2002, when the Ecumenical Patriarch celebrated the Divine Liturgy of St. John Chrysostom in the church of St. Apollinare in Classe for the first time in twelve centuries.

Perhaps the most impressive basilica of early Christianity, this church boasts the tomb of St. Apollinare (first bishop of Ravenna) as well as unparalleled sixth-century mosaics. The spiritual reality expressed in these mosaics suggests a sense of eternity and wonder; it is literally a lifting and entry into heaven. The artistic decorations display great originality and innovativeness, depicting the transformation of earth and the correspondence between earth and heaven. In a way never before represented, the Transfiguration of Christ on Mount Tabor is rendered in a completely symbolical manner, with the figure of Christ shown in the form of a cross and the face of Christ at its center, with the voice of the Father replaced by a hand coming out of a cloud and the apostles shown as lambs ordered around the cross (further symbols of sacrifice and martyrdom), and with the entire world shown as beautiful rocks, bushes, and flowers. The overwhelming idea conveyed is that of reconciliation between Christ, humanity, and all of creation. The connection is also clear between transfiguration and crucifixion, between Eucharistic mystery and cosmic resurrection. In his closing address of the symposium, entitled "Sacrifice: The Missing Dimension," Patriarch Bartholomew observed:

> The cross is our guiding symbol in the supreme sacrifice to which we are all called. It sanctifies the waters and, through them, transforms the entire world. Who can forget the imposing symbol of the cross in the splendid mosaic of the Basilica of St. Apollinare in Classe? As we celebrated the Divine Liturgy in Ravenna, our attention was focused on the cross, which stood at the center of our heavenly vision, at the center of the natural beauty that surrounds it, and at the center of our celebration of heaven on earth.
>
> Such is the model of our ecological endeavors. Such is the foundation of any environmental ethic.... The cross *must* be at the very center of our vision. Without the cross, without sacrifice, there can be no blessing and no cosmic transfiguration.

The next day, June 10, 2002, delegates attended the closing ceremony in the Palazzo Ducale, where another historical moment of ecumenical and environmental significance unfolded. There, Bartholomew co-signed a document on environmental ethics with Pope John Paul II, whose presence was communicated via satellite link-up. The Venice Declaration was the first text ever signed jointly by the two religious leaders on ecological issues. The Declaration emphasizes that the protection of the environment is the moral and spiritual duty of all people:

> At this moment in history, at the beginning of the third millennium, we are saddened to see the daily suffering of a great number of people from violence, starvation, poverty, and disease. We are also concerned about the negative consequences for humanity and for all creation resulting from the degradation of some basic natural resources, such as water, air, and land, brought about by an economic and technological progress that does not recognize and take into account its limits....
>
> In this perspective, Christians and all other believers have a specific role to play in proclaiming moral values and in educating people in *eco-*

*logical awareness,* which is none other than responsibility toward self, toward others, toward creation.

What is required is an act of repentance on our part and a renewed attempt to view ourselves, one another, and the world around us within the perspective of the divine design for creation. The problem is not simply economic and technological; it is moral and spiritual. A solution at the economic and technological level can be found only if we undergo, in the most radical way, an inner change of heart, which can lead to a change in lifestyle and a change of unsustainable patterns of consumption and production. . . .

It is not too late. God's world has incredible healing powers. Within a single generation, we could steer the earth toward our children's future. Let that generation start now, with God's help and blessing.

Rome and Venice, June 10, 2002

A fifth symposium, "The Baltic Sea: A Common Heritage, a Shared Responsibility," is planned for 2003 and will concentrate on the disparate resources, economies, and societies of the nine countries bordering on and polluting this northern sea, especially since the end of the Cold War.

## Reading the Statements

The encyclical letters and addresses presented in Part I of this book open with a call to prayer. This entire first section includes the letters written and published by the Ecumenical Patriarch on the occasion of the beginning of the ecclesiastical year, which in the Orthodox Church is commemorated and celebrated as the feast of the *Indictus* on September 1st. The first two encyclicals (1989 and 1990) are signed by the hand of the late Patriarch Demetrios (d. 1991). However, they are an important part of this collection for two reasons: historically, because they mark the initial steps of the Ecumenical Patriarchate toward educating and mobilizing its adherents on environmental issues; and personally, because Patriarch Bartholomew was the closest co-worker and advisor of Patriarch Demetrios. Although Bartholomew himself will always and formally — out of a sense of humility and especially out of a reverence for tradition — acknowledge Patriarch Demetrios, his "revered predecessor" as he will often describe him, recognizing him as the person responsible for the call to prayer for the preservation and protection of the natural environment, in fact Bartholomew has at all times been either behind the scenes or else at the forefront of this unique and pioneering ministry.

14

Thereafter, encyclicals are written and signed by Patriarch Bartholomew every year, with the exception of the years 1991 and 2000. September 1991 marked the death of the late Demetrios, as well as the installation of Bartholomew himself, and no encyclical was circulated during that year. September 2000 marked the special millennial celebrations of the Ecumenical Patriarchate, and once again no encyclical appeared during that jubilee. Nevertheless, even in those two years, environmental issues were not far from the concern of the Patriarch. In 2000, the Patriarch addressed the young people and scholars of his jurisdiction throughout the world, emphasizing critical contemporary issues such as the environment and unemployment. Moreover, as early as 1991, Bartholomew addressed the entire Church with his formal enthronement address of November, which opens Part II of this collection.

This enthronement address is included here for more than merely historical reasons. The address encapsulates and captures the theological vision of a newly elected prince of the Church. Already, from the outset of his Patriarchal service, Bartholomew offers insights and allusions into the hopes and dreams of his promising ministry. More specifically, with reference to the environmental initiatives and actions, the most apparent characteristic of this enthronement address is the mark of humility.

The young Patriarch Bartholomew is able to see the larger picture. He recognizes that he is standing before something greater than himself; he belongs to an "unbroken" succession or chain that long predates him and will long outlast him. He is a part of this tradition and cannot conceive himself apart from this same tradition. Therefore, he speaks of self-emptying (or *kenosis*), of ministry (or *diakonia*), of witness (or *martyria,* a Greek term which also has the sense of martyrdom and suffering),[6] and of thanksgiving (or *eucharistia,* a Greek term which also implies liturgy). He closes the address with the following words:

> Pray for us, all of you, who have come "from the West and the North, by sea and from the East" in order to install us upon this sacred *cathedra* of the Apostle Stachys, as yet another in the long line of his successors. Pray that, faithfully and favorably unto God, we may serve the Lord, this most holy Church, and Orthodoxy under heaven. Pray that we may sustain our people and maintain the privileges and the rights of this most venerable

---

6. Martyrdom is also an important feature of Bartholomew's addresses to the Primates of the Orthodox Churches worldwide (1992 and 1995). The concept of sacrifice is said to be the essential — described as a "missing" — dimension of environmental ethics in the closing address during the fourth international and interreligious symposium (2002).

Throne, which "we sign with great pleasure," as our predecessor to the Throne of Chalcedon, Eleftherios, affirmed at the Fourth Ecumenical Synod. Pray that we may be at all times an instrument of God's will in the service of all humanity. Pray that our Patriarchal tenure may be un-harmed, bountiful, hopeful, unhindered, according to the names and through the intercessions of the Persian martyrs, whom the Church com-memorates today. Pray that the Lord may sustain the Church, strengthen its faith, and bring peace to the world.

Indeed, Bartholomew makes mention of his own spiritual elders, once again referring especially to Patriarch Demetrios as he does on numerous occasions throughout these texts:[7]

> It is our firm hope that, from the heavenly chambers, the prayer of our spiritual father, Metropolitan Meliton of Chalcedon of blessed memory, who offered numerous precious services to the Mother Church, will ac-company and sustain us, as will the prayer of our immediate predecessor, the most gentle Patriarch Demetrios of blessed memory, who embodied the extreme humility of Christ, a humility that this Church "of the poor of Christ" expresses.

The same signature of humility is evident on other levels as well. In the same enthronement address, Bartholomew describes the Ecumenical Patri-archate as a spiritual institution; it is not, he notes, a powerful establishment in secular terms. The same point will be underlined elsewhere, such as in his address in Kathmandu (2000). The emphasis instead is on simplicity — the technical term here in Orthodox theology is asceticism (or the ascetic life).[8] In this respect, specific reference is made to the monastic tradition and par-ticularly to the fact that monks have resided on Mount Athos for over one thousand years. The emphasis in the enthronement address is also on liturgy, which is the source and essence of Orthodox theology and spirituality.[9]

The notion of liturgy leads us into what is perhaps the most distinctive

---

7. See his addresses in Crete (1991), and in Halki (1992 and 1994).

8. This emphasis is found in several texts, such as the opening address of the Black Sea symposium (1997), the address in Santa Barbara (1997), the meditation on the cross (1999), the closing address of the Adriatic symposium (2002), as well as the encyclicals for September 1st in 1994 and 1997; in the latter encyclical, Patriarch Bartholomew states that the ascetic way is the "original commandment" from the moment of the Genesis creation of humanity.

9. The emphasis on liturgy may be found in several of the addresses during the Patmos symposium (1995) as well as in the encyclical for September 1st (1994).

characteristic of Patriarch Bartholomew's vision, already foreshadowed from the day of his enthronement, namely the central and crucial concept of communion. In everything that Bartholomew says and does, particularly in light of the environmental crisis, he is aware that all of the Orthodox must be included.[10] Indeed, not only should all Orthodox Christians be in communion, but also all Christians in general should be in communication. In addition, all religions should be in cooperation;[11] all sciences and disciplines should be committed;[12] all cultures and ages should concur; and even atheists should be seen to contribute in the movement toward the heavenly kingdom. In his welcome address to the third summer seminar on Halki in June 1996, Patriarch Bartholomew noted:

> Unhindered communication among all those concerned with ecological management today is equivalent to the indispensability and the sanctity of prayer.

Bartholomew always defers: to God, to the saints, to his predecessors, to his contemporaries, even to scientific knowledge. The overwhelming sense of humility is, therefore, extended not only upward (before the grace of God) and backward in time (before the face of tradition), but also sideward (before every human face) and downward (before the beauty of the natural world). In other texts, Patriarch Bartholomew will speak of humility before the earth and even of dialogue with nature.[13] This is the way of his Church. It is the way of authenticity. And it is what provides him with an overriding sense also of authority.

It is for this reason that Patriarch Bartholomew considers his prayer for and protection of the environment as an obligation, not as a way of submitting to contemporary fashions or political statements. His commitment to and involvement in environmental issues is not a matter of public relations but of theological conviction. This is very evident in his interviews, found in Part III of this book. It is also apparent in his repeated phrase: "We

10. See also his address to the Orthodox Primates (1992).

11. See his addresses in Italy (1994), his opening address during the Patmos symposium (1995) and before the CEO University in Istanbul (1995).

12. See especially the opening of the Patmos symposium (1995) and the opening address of the Black Sea symposium (1997). On the dangers of isolation from other disciplines, see his address to the Orthodox Primates (1995).

13. See his addresses at the Halki Ecological Institute (1999) and in Novi Sad (1999). In the encyclical for September 1st (2001), Bartholomew underlines the inherent danger in human arrogance over nature.

cannot remain idle!"[14] He makes it clear that he will not cease proclaiming the importance of the environment.[15] It is, he believes, an almost "apostolic commission."[16]

For Patriarch Bartholomew, this commitment is a matter of truthfulness to God, humanity, and the created order. In fact, it is not too far-fetched to speak of environmental damage as being a contemporary heresy or natural terrorism; he condemns it as nothing less than sin![17] The environment is not a political or a technological issue; it is, as Bartholomew underlines in so many of his interviews, primarily a religious and spiritual issue. Religion, then, has a key role to play; and a spirituality that is not involved with outward creation is not involved with the inward mystery either.[18]

I have already noted that this accounts for Patriarch Bartholomew's sense of authority. He offers no apologies for his traditional Orthodox theological background and starting point.[19] He offers no apologies for his criticism of a-religious responses to the environment, whether these derive from scientific or moral sources.[20] In addition, he offers no apologies for his harsh criticism of false technological promises about "progress" and "development."[21] On the other hand, he is quite open about the thirst of western civilization for another worldview and spirituality.[22] In order for readers to appreciate the historical (or cultural) and spiritual (or meta-historical) context within which the Patriarch thinks and speaks, I have included other addresses, which — while not immediately and directly related to environmental issues — nevertheless reveal the perspective from which and the purpose for which the Patriarch is deeply concerned about the environment.[23]

---

14. See the encyclical (signed by Patriarch Demetrios) for September 1st (1989) and Bartholomew's address during the Patmos symposium (1995).

15. See his address at the closing of the Danube symposium (1999).

16. See his opening address of the Black Sea symposium (1997).

17. See his address at the University of the Aegean (1994), the Christmas encyclical (1994), the encyclical for September 1st (1996), the address at Santa Barbara (1997), the message of the Synaxis (1998), and the interviews. For the notion of "spiritual pollution," see his address to the Greek bankers (1999).

18. On the role of religion, see his addresses on the Danube (Bulgaria, 1999) and at the inter-faith meeting (1998). On spirituality, see his encyclical for September 1st (1994).

19. Address to the Orthodox Primates (1992).

20. Encyclicals for September 1st (1992 and 1996), his words at the University of the Aegean (1994), at the Halki seminar (1995), and in Japan (1995).

21. Encyclical for September 1st (1994).

22. See the interviews in Part III, but also his addresses in Italy (1994) and Istanbul (1995).

23. For example, see his addresses at the British Museum (1993) and to the Foreign Correspondents in Hong Kong (1996).

Moreover, he is not afraid to adopt "politically incorrect" language concerning the centrality of the human person within creation.[24] It is not anthropocentrism that is the problem, he would feel; it is *anthropomonism*,[25] that is, the exclusive emphasis on and isolation of humanity at the expense and detriment of the natural environment. Nature is related to people and people to nature.[26] If Bartholomew is radical[27] in the theological articulation of his vision, it is because his worldview is rooted (the literal sense of the word "radical") in his Church tradition.

All of this leads Bartholomew to another dimension of his environmental initiatives, namely his deeply pastoral and compassionate attitude toward those whom he addresses. Whether he is speaking to his colleagues among the worldwide Orthodox Primates (as in his address in 1992), or to individual leaders and churches (as in Galati in 1999), or else to the Orthodox faithful throughout the world (as in all of the encyclicals for September 1st), Ecumenical Patriarch Bartholomew is sensitively, thoughtfully, and gradually educating with his "paternal admonition."[28] He recognizes that, in many ways, although he is firmly rooted in the vine of his Church, yet he is also "out on a limb." He constantly needs to remind his peers and his spiritual children. This is precisely why, as a patient pedagogue, he does not tire in his efforts, even when they appear slow to bear fruit.

Readers will notice an air of repetition, even repetitiveness, in many of the texts that follow. Bartholomew will frequently refer — sometimes in the same phraseology — to his vision, the Patriarchate's initiatives, and the Orthodox theological reasons for these. For instance, there is repeated mention of the encyclicals for September 1st, the summer seminars on Halki, the seaborne international symposia, and the "Bosphorus Declaration." This is not a sign of arrogance, but yet another aspect of humility. Bartholomew knows that he must continually and vigilantly inform his people. I have personally witnessed the way in which, particularly during the international symposia,

24. See his encyclicals for September 1st (1993, 1995, 1997, 1998, 2001), as well as his addresses at the opening of the Black Sea symposium (1997), in Japan (1998), on Halki (1998) and at the opening of the Danube symposium (1999). The various addresses in Norway also stress this factor.

25. This is discussed in various interviews in Part III. See also the address during the presentation ceremony of the Sophie Prize (2002). Against anthropocentrism, see the Synaxis message of the hierarchs (1998). In the Christmas encyclical of 1994, Bartholomew underlines the importance of Christocentrism.

26. See especially his address to the Greek bankers (1999), the encyclical for September 1st (2001), and the interviews in Part III.

27. See his address to the Orthodox Primates (1992).

28. Encyclical for September 1st (1996).

Patriarch Bartholomew will seize every occasion to visit local Orthodox leaders, gently but firmly eliciting their understanding, support, and commitment in the concern for the natural environment. Indeed, the international symposia have had a practical and symbolical value for the visible unity of the Orthodox Church, inasmuch as they have afforded the Ecumenical Patriarch the opportunity of visiting numerous Orthodox churches in the regions.

Bartholomew will invariably relate the environment to a familiar aspect of Orthodox spirituality, namely the icons that decorate Orthodox churches. Symbols are important in Orthodox thought, worship, and life.[29] Creation itself is likened to an icon,[30] in the same way as the human person is created "in the image [or 'icon'] and likeness of God" (Gen. 1:26).[31] Bartholomew invites the Orthodox to contemplate the Creator God through the icon of the created world. Creation is a visible and tangible revelation (or *apocalypse*) of the presence (or *parousia*) of the Word of God.[32] Humanity is called to wonder at creation, but not to worship creation. Otherwise, the natural world is reduced from the level of icon to the level of idol.[33] In the same vein, Patriarch Bartholomew will often refer to human beings as made and intended by God to serve as "priests" within the created world.[34]

Patriarch Bartholomew believes that a particular ethos is called for in our response to the environmental crisis. This ethos is divinely inspired, even commanded, by God.[35] And it is an ethos incarnated, even communicated, by the saints.[36] The saints are those who inform and influence, who reform and instruct the world through their presence and their prayer. They remind us, says Bartholomew, that the personal responsibility and the slightest action of even the feeblest among us can change the world for the better.[37]

Finally, the Ecumenical Patriarch is aware of the reality that environmental issues are intimately connected to and dependent on numerous other social

---

29. See his Christmas encyclical (1994) and the opening address during the Patmos symposium (1995).

30. See his address in Santa Barbara (1997).

31. See his brief remarks in Istanbul (1992).

32. Apocalypse is perceived both as the end (as in the encyclical for September 1st, 1989) and as the epiphany of God (as in the opening address during the Patmos symposium in 1995).

33. See the opening address on the Black Sea (1997), the encyclical for September 1st (1999), and the address to the Greek bankers (1999).

34. See, for instance, his address at the Halki seminar (1992).

35. See his address at the University of the Aegean (1994), his address at the summer seminar on Halki (1995), and his homily in Santa Barbara (1997), but especially the encyclical for September 1st (1997).

36. Encyclicals for September 1st (1997, 1998, and 1999).

37. See especially the encyclical for September 1st (1998).

issues[38] of our times, to which he repeatedly refers in his addresses and remarks. These include such subjects as war and peace,[39] justice and human rights,[40] poverty,[41] and unemployment.[42] Even on occasions when the environment does not appear to be the central issue of a particular address, nevertheless the interconnectedness of the above-mentioned problems with the destruction of our planet becomes profoundly apparent to the discerning reader. It is not by chance that the term "eco-justice" has been coined in ecclesiastical circles to describe this interconnection between creation and creatures, between the world and its inhabitants. We have, in recent years, become abundantly aware of the effects of environmental degradation on people, and especially on the poor.

Before we move on to a brief exposition of Orthodox theological and spiritual perspectives on the environment, a brief word should be said concerning the language of the texts themselves and their translation. The texts and addresses themselves, presented here for the first time in a single collection, are organized chronologically[43] in order to reveal how the Patriarch's environmental thought, vision, and initiatives have developed. Careful effort has been made to revise the translations from the original Greek as well as to edit the texts themselves, significantly though not substantially, with the generous permission and blessing of the Patriarch. The purpose of these editorial changes, sometimes even of textual abbreviations, is to provide greater uniformity and smoother accessibility to a general readership.

Therefore, many names of specific individuals have been removed, except where their inclusion is helpful for the particular context. Titles have been created in order to replace abstract headings. The formal titles and closures of the encyclicals in Part I have been edited. I have incorporated my own

38. See his address at City University, London (1994).

39. See his addresses on peace in Istanbul (1994), at the opening of the Patmos symposium (1995), at the closing of the Black Sea symposium (1997), at the opening of the Danube symposium as well as during its journey through Bulgaria (1999), and in Novi Sad (1999). See also the encyclical for September 1st (1998) and the address to the Greek bankers (1999). Finally, see his addresses on peace and religious tolerance (1994 and 1995).

40. See the foreword for the published proceedings of the summer seminar (1997), as well as his address during the closing of the Danube symposium (1999) and at the Turkish/Greek Business Council (1997). On human rights, among other addresses, see his presentation to the Southern Methodist University (1997).

41. See his encyclical for September 1st (1994), the foreword for the published proceedings of the summer seminar (1998), and his addresses on Halki (1998), in Davos (1999), and to the youth (2000). Especially, see his address to the European Parliament (1994).

42. See his keynote address to the youth (2000).

43. At least by year, although not necessarily by month, for reasons of basic thematic continuity.

title for each of the numerous addresses in Part II, while also adding subheadings within the longer ones. Once again, the purpose of these additions is to encourage readers to see the particular emphases as well as the overall unity within the texts. In Part III, which contains selected interviews and other general comments and remarks, I have chosen particularly relevant excerpts, to which I have again added my own titles.

The language of many of the texts, whether of the encyclicals or the addresses, is often lofty, theological, and even ecclesiastical. For the most part, I have left this tone of solemnity untouched. It is an indication of the importance attributed to environmental issues by the Patriarch as well as a revelation of the profound tradition from which he speaks. However, at the same time, other briefer texts have an air of informality, comprising toasts on the occasion of meals or greetings on the occasion of visits. These have been included in order for readers to recognize the diverse ways in which the ordinary is related to the extraordinary in Orthodox theology and life.

Some of the texts will not immediately appear to bear any direct significance for the environment, relating instead to issues concerning peace and cooperation. They are included inasmuch as they provide the context within which the Ecumenical Patriarch considers environmental issues. Everything that the Patriarch says and does is colored by his keen awareness of and deep concern for environmental issues. There is a sense in which — based on the spiritual tradition of icons, liturgy, and asceticism — the environment is implied in the very silence and prayer of the Orthodox Church. For Patriarch Bartholomew, the created world is part and parcel of our salvation; we shall — and can only — be saved with the environment. Therefore, ecology is very much at the center of his thinking and his action; it constitutes the central place on the altar of his worship, on the desk of his writing, as well as on the agenda of his ministry. This is why, at this point, it may be helpful to consider some of the fundamental aspects of the Orthodox worldview.

## Orthodox Theology and the Environment

### Preliminary Remarks

When we think of the Genesis account of creation, we tend to forget our connection to the earth and our environment. Perhaps it is natural, or perhaps it is a sign of our arrogance, that we tend to overemphasize our creation "in the image and likeness of God" (Gen. 1:26) and overlook our creation from the dust and the dirt of the ground. Our "heavenliness" should not overshadow our "earthliness." If we were to ask people what actually happened on the sixth day of the creation story, on the day before God rested, we might find that many are unaware that we human beings did not get a day to ourselves in Genesis. In fact, we shared the sixth day with the creeping and crawling things of the world (Gen. 1:24-26). We share a binding unity and continuity with all of God's creation.

In recent years, we have been reminded — indeed, in a painful way — of this truth with the extinction of flora and fauna, soil erosion and forest clearance, and pollution of noise, air, and water. Our concern for the environment is not a form of superficial or sentimental love. It is a way of honoring and dignifying our very creation by the hand and word of God. It is a way of listening to "the mourning of the land" and "the groaning of creation." We are called to remember the whole truth about our creation and about the environment. Anything less than the full story, any deviation from the fullness of that truth, is a dangerous heresy.

Speaking about heresy when it comes to appreciating the environment is not too far-fetched at all. Whenever we speak (whether about things in heaven or on earth), we are drawing upon established values of ourselves and of our world. The technical language that we adopt, the particular "species" that we wish to preserve, all depends on the values and the images that we promote or, rather, presume. In the Christian Orthodox tradition, symbols and images play a significant role. When I consider images, I think of the central importance of *icons* (that is, the way we view and perceive creation), and of the *liturgy* (that is, the way we celebrate and respond to creation). I also think of *asceticism* (that is, the way we respect and treat creation).

We tend to call this crisis an "ecological" crisis, and this is a fair description insofar as its *results* are manifested in the ecological sphere. The message is quite clear: our way of life is humanly and environmentally suicidal. Unless we change it radically, we cannot hope to avoid or reverse cosmic catastrophe.

Yet, the crisis is not first of all ecological. It is a crisis concerning the way *we* perceive reality, the way we imagine or image our world. We are treating our environment, our planet, in an inhuman, god-forsaken manner — precisely because we see it in this way, precisely because we see ourselves in this way.

Therefore, before we can effectively deal with problems of our environment, we must change our world-image, which in turn means that we must change our self-image. Otherwise, we are simply dealing with symptoms, not with their causes.

And *causes* are rooted in the way we think, in the paradigms of thought that impel us to pursue a particular lifestyle and particular social, political, and economic interests or needs. The root of the problem, I feel, is religious. The response, then, must also be religious, even if the results will be evident in our economy and justice, in our policy and politics, in our technology and science. This means, however, that as churches we must shift our focus. We can no longer simply be concerned as Christians about a place in heaven for ourselves, and what kind of a place this will be. We must now worry about whether our children will have a place on earth, and what kind of a place this will be.

In classical traditions, human beings regarded themselves as descended from the gods, or from God, and as having a destiny beyond the physical/political/socioeconomic world. They saw themselves as divine beings, created in the divine image. And they looked upon this world, too, as an icon: as soul-full, not soul-less; as animate, not inanimate; as sacred (like them), and not as subject to them. In their experience and in their memory, every leaf, every grain of sand, every bird or star or insect, even the very air that we breathe was regarded as holy, as living. The sap of the trees was as sacred as their own life-blood, indeed was one with their own life-blood. The forests, mountains, lakes, and deserts were not objects for experimentation or resources for exploitation, but a way of life. Trade was life, never a trade in nature itself, never at the expense of nature, never a rape of nature.

The sense of the holy means that everything that lives is holy (William Blake), everything that breathes praises God (Ps. 150:6), the entire world is a "burning bush of God's energies" (Gregory Palamas). And the sense of humility before the whole implies respect toward other people (beyond *me* — the notion of community), respect toward nature (beyond *us* — the shaping of our environment), and respect toward the transcendent (that which is beyond *both humanity and nature.*

This means several things:

- We are a part of a *community.* We are less than human without each other.
- We are a part of the *cosmos.* We are less than human without creation.
- This cosmos is a part of what we call *heaven.* Heaven is less than heaven without this world.

### The World of the Icon and the Icon of the World

Icons, or sacred images, bear a central importance in Christian Orthodox thought and spirituality. The world of the icon offers new insights, new perceptions into reality. It reveals the eternal dimension in everything that we see and experience in our environment. Our generation, it may be said, is characterized by a sense of autism toward the natural cosmos, by a lack of awareness of or communication with the beyond. We appear to be inexorably locked within the confines of our individual concerns, even in our desire to escape from this impasse, with no access to the world outside or around us. We have broken the sacred covenant, the symbolical connection between our selves and our world. And so there is no possibility for intimate communion, no place for mutual enhancement.

The icon restores; it reconciles. It reminds us of another way and of another world. It offers a corrective to the culture that we have created, which gives value only to the here and now. The icon aspires to reveal the inner vision of all, the world as created and as intended by God. Very often, it is said, the first image attempted by an iconographer is that of the Transfiguration of Christ on Mt. Tabor, precisely because the iconographer struggles to hold together this world and the next, to transfigure this world in light of the next. By disconnecting this world from heaven, we have in fact desacralized both. The icon articulates with theological conviction our faith in the heavenly kingdom. The icon does away with any objective distance between this world and the next, between the material and the spiritual, between body and soul, between time and eternity, between creation and divinity. The icon reminds us that there is no double vision, no double order in creation. The icon speaks in this world the language of the age to come.

This is why the doctrine of the divine incarnation, the divine economy, the plan of reconciliation, is at the very heart of iconography. In the icon of Jesus Christ, God assumes a face, an exceeding beauty (Ps. 44:2), a "beauty that can save the world."[44] And in Orthodox icons, the faces — whether of Christ, or of the saints in the communion of Christ — are always frontal. The conviction is that Christ is in our midst, here. Profile signifies sin, a rupture in communication or communion. Faces are frontal, all eyes, eternally receptive and susceptive of divine grace. "I see" means that "I am seen," which in turn implies that I am in communion. This is the powerful experience of the invisible and the immortal, a passing over to another way of seeing, a "Passover," "Pascha."

John of Damascus, the eighth-century champion of icons, reminds us that "[we] do not adore creation; [we] worship the One who assumed creation. . . . God has saved [us] through matter. . . . Because of the incarnation, [we] salute all creation."[45] And in his sermon on the holy icons delivered in the next century, Leontius of Byzantium writes:

---

44. Fyodor Dostoevsky, in *The Brothers Karamazov,* as quoted in Nicholas Arseniev, *Mysticism and the Eastern Church* (Marburg: Student Christian Movement, 1926; repr. New York: St. Vladimir's Seminary Press, 1979), pp. 118-19.

45. *On Divine Images,* chs. 4 and 16.

Through heaven and earth and sea, through wood and stone, through relics and church buildings and the cross, through angels and people, through all creation visible and invisible, [we] offer veneration and honor to the Creator and Master and Maker of all things, and to God alone. For the creation does not venerate the Maker directly and by itself, but it is through [us] that the heavens declare the glory of God, through [us] the moon worships God, through [us] the stars glorify God, through [us] the waters and showers of rain, the dew and all creation, venerate God and give glory to God.[46]

The icon converts the beholder from a restricted, limited point of view to a fuller, spiritual vision, where we see everything as reconciled and as united in a single reality, in Him through whom all things "live and move and have [their] being" (Acts 17:28). For the light of the icon is the light of reconciliation, the light of restoration, the light of the resurrection. It is not the light of this world; it "knows no evening," to quote an Orthodox hymn. This is why icons depicting events that occurred in the daytime are no brighter than icons depicting events that occurred at nighttime. The icon of Gethsemane, for example, is no darker than the icon of Pentecost. The icon of the resurrection is no brighter than the icon of the crucifixion. The icon presupposes, indeed proposes another light in which to see things, a "different way of life," as the Orthodox Easter liturgy reveals. This is a vision that liberates us from every alien vision. It provides for us another means of communication beyond the conceptual, beyond the written, beyond the spoken word. This is the language of silence, of mystery, of the age to come.

As already mentioned, in the icon "I see" means that "I am seen." The last book of the Christian Scriptures is the Revelation of John the Divine. And revelation implies a manifestation of faces, a vocation to become icons. This truth is discerned in the creation of humanity "in the image" of God (Gen. 1:26). As such, the human person exists on two levels, in two worlds, simultaneously. The human person is, therefore, a meeting point for all of creation, a bridge between this world and heaven. In the words of the fifth-century ascetic, Nilus of Ancyra: "You are a world within a world. . . . Look within yourself, and there you will discover the entire world."[47]

In the seventh century Maximus the Confessor described humanity as a "mediator." Like Christ, who is the exact image, the precise icon of the Father, we are called to reconcile, to connect, to heal.

---

46. *Apologetic Sermon III on the Holy Icons,* in *Patrologia Graeca* (hereafter PG), ed. J. Migne, 161 vols. (Paris, 1857-1928), 93:1604.

47. *Epistles,* Book II, Letter 119.

Yet, it is not just humanity that is likened to an icon. The entire world is an icon, a door, a window, a point of entry, opening up to a new reality. Everything in this world is a sign, a seed. "Nothing is a vacuum in the face of God," wrote Irenaeus of Lyons in the second century; "everything is a sign of God." Everything, everyone, contains this dimension, bears this transparency. And so in icons rivers assume human form; the sun and the moon and the stars and the waters all assume human faces, all acquire a personal dimension — just like people, just like God.

And if the earth is an icon, then nothing whatsoever is neutral, nothing at all lacks sacredness. No land is "terra incognita." The Christian is simply the one who discerns and encounters Christ everywhere, the one who recognizes the whole world as the dwelling place of Christ. For if God were not visible in creation, then neither could God be worshiped as invisible in heaven. If God were not tangibly accessible in this world, then neither could God be the transcendent creator of the universe. Unless Christ can be discovered in the least particle of matter, just as in the least of His brethren, then He would be too distant from matter to matter at all. Christians are able to affirm the apocryphal words attributed to Christ: "Lift up the stone, and there you will find me. Cleave the wood, and I am there."[48]

### The World of the Liturgy and the Liturgy of the World

What the Orthodox icon does in space and matter, the Christian Orthodox liturgy effects in praise and time, namely the ministry of reconciliation, the anticipation and participation of heaven on earth. If we are guilty of relentless waste, it is because we have lost the spirit of worship. We are no longer respectful pilgrims on this earth; we are reduced to mere tourists.

The Eastern Orthodox Church retains a liturgical view of the world, proclaiming a world imbued by God and a God involved in this world. Our original sin, so it seems, lies in our refusal to receive the world as a gift of reconciliation, to regard the world as a sacrament of communion. One of the hymns of the Orthodox Church states: "I have become . . . the defilement of the air and the land and the waters." At a time when we have polluted the air that we breathe and the water that we drink, we are called to restore within ourselves the sense of awe and delight, to respond to matter as to a mystery of ever-increasing connections.

By liturgical, however, I do not imply ritual. I mean movement, dyna-

---

48. Quoted in J. Jeremias, *Unknown Sayings of Jesus* (London: SPCK, 1957), p. 95.

mism, and creativity. The world is not static, as Plato might have believed; it is not eternally reproduced, as the classical worldview might propose. It is a movement toward an end, a final purpose, a sacred goal. It is neither endless nor purposeless. It is relational. Think of it as a picture, as an icon: every part of a picture is required in order for it to be complete, from the Alpha to the Omega. If one were to move (or to remove, still more so to destroy) one part of the picture — whether a tree, or an animal, or a human being — then the entire picture would be affected (or distorted, perhaps destroyed).

The truth is that we respond to nature with the same delicacy, the same sensitivity, the same tenderness with which we respond to a human person in a relationship. We have learned not to treat people like things; we must now learn not to treat even things like mere things. We must always think in terms of connections, in terms of communion, in terms of reconciliation. That is our truth as humans within the created cosmos. That is what we are called to "re-member": that we are "members" one of another, "members" of the body of the world. All of our ecological activities are measured ultimately by their effect on people, especially upon the poor.

Therefore, liturgy is a celebration of this communion, of the sense of community, this dance of life. When we enter this interdependence of all persons and all things — this "cosmic liturgy," as St. Maximus the Confessor called it[49] — then we can begin to understand and to resolve issues of ecology and of economy.

Yet our contemporary mechanistic society allows no room for this song of the soul. The prevailing secular, self-centered mentality allows no room for the sacred, the "other-centered" mentality that recognizes that "All this is from God, who reconciled us to himself through Christ" (2 Cor. 5:18). In the breadth of the liturgical worldview, in the air of the liturgy, we recognize that the world is larger than our individual concerns. Indeed, the world ceases to be something that I observe objectively and becomes something of which I am a part — personally and actively. No longer do I feel a stranger, threatened or threatening, but a friend, caring and loving.

In the seventh century, St. Isaac the Syrian described this as "A merciful heart, which burns with love for the whole of creation — for humans, for birds, for the beasts, for demons — for all of God's creatures."[50] And in the late nineteenth century, Fyodor Dostoevsky embraced the same truth in *The Brothers Karamazov:* "Love all God's creation, the whole of it and every grain of sand. Love every leaf, every ray of God's light. Love the animals. Love the

---

49. *Mystagogy* 2 (PG 91:1385).
50. *Mystic Treatises,* Homily 48 (Boston: Holy Transfiguration Monastery, 1986), p. 30.

plants. Love everything. If you love everything, you will perceive the divine mystery in things."[51]

The world in its entirety forms a part of the liturgy. God is praised by the trees and the birds, glorified by the stars and the moon (cf. Ps. 18:2), worshiped by the sea and the sand. There is a dimension of art, of music, and of beauty in the world. This world is the most inconspicuous and silent — and, for all intensive purposes, for most of us, the clearest and most visible — sermon that declares the word of God.

This means that whenever we narrow life to ourselves — to our concerns and our desires — we neglect our vocation to reconcile and transform creation. And whenever we reduce our religious life to ourselves — to our concerns and our desires — we forget the function of the liturgy to implore God for the renewal of the whole polluted cosmos. Our relationship with this world determines our relationship with heaven. The way we treat the earth is reflected in the way that we pray to God.

The liturgy is a "symbol": it is a way of relating, of reconciling (this is the literal sense of the Greek word *symbolon*), of bringing together two distinct, though not unconnected realities. The liturgy offers to God the world, for the life of which God gave His only Son. In this perspective, the direct opposite of the symbolical worldview is the diabolical lifestyle, which excludes heaven from earth, divinity from creation, the spiritual from the material. Yet this way is ultimately alienation, insanity.

Humanity, we now know, is *less than humanity* without the rest of creation. We may go further than this and declare that this world, too, is much more than a reflection or revelation of heaven; it is the fulfillment and completion of heaven. Heaven is *less than heaven* without this world. The earth is not simply a reflection, but a perfection of heaven. The earthly liturgy is not merely a concelebration, but — in what constitutes a sacred and at the same time scandalous truth — a completion of the heavenly dance. Just as we are incomplete without the rest of material and animal creation, so too the kingdom of God remains incomplete without the world around us. How could we ever be thankful enough for this gift?

## The World of the Body in Relation to the Body of the World

Of course, this world does not always feel or look like the completion of heaven. In his letter to the Colossians, St. Paul writes: "In him [Christ], God

---

51. *The Brothers Karamazov* (Harmondsworth, UK: Penguin, 1982), p. 375.

was pleased . . . to reconcile to himself all things, whether on earth or in heaven, by making peace by the blood of his cross" (1:20). Reference to "the blood of the cross" is an indication, for the Christian thinker, of the cost involved. It reminds us of the reality of human failure and of the need for a cosmic repentance. In order to alter our self-image, what is required is nothing less than a radical reversal of our perspectives and attitudes, especially of our practices and lifestyles. There is a price to pay for our wasting: it is the cost of self-discipline, the sacrifice of bearing the cross. The environmental crisis will not be solved simply by sentimental expressions of regret or aesthetic formulations of imagination. It is the "tree of the cross" that reveals to us the way out of our ecological impasse by proposing the solution of (in theological terminology, "salvation" through) self-denial, the denial of selfishness or self-centeredness. It is, therefore, the spirit of asceticism that leads to the spirit of gratitude and love, to the rediscovery of wonder and beauty.

A sermon by the renowned early preacher of the Eastern Christian Church, St. John Chrysostom, is appointed to be read each year on Good Friday. In this sermon, St. John speaks with the same inspiration as he does on Easter Sunday, but this time about the tree of the cross. He says:

> This tree is my eternal salvation. It is my nourishment and my banquet. Among its roots I set my own roots, deep; beneath its boughs I grow and expand; as it sighs around me in the breeze I am nourished with delight.
>
> Flying from the burning heat I pitch my tent in its shadow, and have found a resting-place of dewy freshness. I flower with its flowers; its fruits bring perfect joy. . . .
>
> This tree is sweet food for my hunger, a spring of water for my thirst, clothing for my nakedness. Its leaves are the breath of my life. . . . With its foot resting firmly on earth, it towers to the highest skies, and spans with all-embracing arms the boundless gulf of space between.

Gradually, however, as the sermon progresses, we realize that St. John is not talking about just any tree, but about the very tree of the cross upon which Christ was lifted and crucified, and through which Christ "gave life and animation and strength to all . . . so that all things might be saved [and united and reconciled]."[52]

The cross, then, raises the concept of asceticism. For the connection between our body and our world is intimate and profound. In the third century,

---

52. *Sermon VI for Holy Week* 5 (PG 59:743-44). Cited in Bishop Kallistos of Diokleia, *Through the Creation to the Creator* (London: Friends of the Centre Papers, 1997), pp. 25-26.

Origen of Alexandria believed that "The world is like our bodies. It too is formed of many limbs and directed by a single soul."[53]

There is, as Wendell Berry writes, "an uncanny resemblance between our behavior toward [our body] and our behavior toward the earth. . . . The willingness to exploit one becomes the willingness to exploit the other."[54] If the earth is our very flesh, then it is also inseparable from our story, our destiny, and our God. For "no one ever hates his own body" (Eph. 5:29).

The ascetic way is a way of liberation. And the ascetic is the person who is free; uncontrolled by attitudes that abuse the world; uncompelled by ways that use the world; characterized by self-control, by self-restraint, and by the ability to say "no" or "enough."

In this context, I would define asceticism as:

- traveling light — we can always manage with less than we imagine;
- letting go — we are to learn to relinquish our desire to control;
- opening up — we are called to create bonds, to reunite, to reconcile;
- softening up — how can we make our communities less savage, more inhabitable?
- treading light — we must not hurt, we must stop wounding our environment;
- living simply — not complicating our relationships with each other and with our environment, consuming less;
- simply living — not competing against one another and against nature in order to survive, for the ethics of the risen Christ lie not in "the survival of the fittest" but in His invitation: "Take, eat, this is my body, broken. . . . Drink of this all of you, this is my blood, shed . . . for the life of the world."

Asceticism, then, aims at refinement, not detachment or destruction. Its goal is moderation, not repression. Its content is positive, not negative. It looks to service, not selfishness — to reconciliation, not renunciation or escape. Without asceticism, none of us is authentically human.

Unfortunately, the general impression that people have of asceticism is negative. Asceticism carries with it the baggage of dualism and denial, developed over many centuries, within and without the Christian church. Yet this is not the vision of wholeness that Orthodox spirituality intimates through its

---

53. *On First Principles* 2.1.2-3 (PG 11:183).

54. Wendell Berry, *Standing on Earth: Selected Essays* (Ipswich, UK: Golgonooza Press, 1991), pp. 48-49.

ascetic dimension. The sacramental dimension of the world (earth as created for heaven, and not just for humans) is closely linked with the ascetic dimension (humanity as dependent, not only on God, but also on the world and on the food chain, just like any other creature). This implies that humanity is not the tyrannical overlord — with a license to dominate the earth or to enslave creation — but the servant and minister who kneels to wash the feet of creation, who restores harmony with the rest of the world, who brings "at-one-ment" with the environment, who reconciles with all people and all things.

Let us examine one aspect of asceticism in the Christian Orthodox practice, namely fasting. We Orthodox fast from all dairy and meat products for half of the entire year, almost as if in an effort to reconcile one half of the year with the other, secular time with the time of the kingdom. To fast is:

- not to deny the world, but to affirm the world, and the body, and material creation;
- to integrate body and soul;
- to remember the hunger of others;
- to feel the hunger of creation itself for restoration;
- to hunger for God, rendering the act of eating a sacrament, whereby the table is covered with God's fingerprints (and not just the children's!);
- to remember that we live not by bread alone;
- to be reconciled with one another and the world;
- to fast along with the entire world, for the Orthodox always fast together, never alone or at whim.

To fast is to acknowledge that "the earth is the Lord's and the fullness thereof" (Ps. 24:1). It is to affirm that the material creation is not under our control, is not to be exploited selfishly, but is to be returned in thanks to God, restored in communion with God.

Therefore, to fast is to learn to give, and not simply to give up. It is not to deny, but in fact to offer, to learn to share, to connect with the natural world. It is to begin to break down barriers with my neighbor and my world, to recognize in others' faces, icons, and in the earth the face of God. Anyone who does not love trees does not love people; anyone who does not love trees does not love God.

To fast, then, is to love; it is to see more clearly, to restore the primal vision of creation, the original beauty of the world. To fast is to move away from what I want to what the world needs. It is to be liberated from greed, control, and compulsion. It is to free creation itself from fear and destruction. Fasting is to value everything for itself, and not simply for ourselves. It is to regain a sense of wonder, to be filled with a sense of goodness, of Godliness. It is to see all things in God, and God in all things. The discipline of fasting is the necessary corrective for our culture of wasting. Letting go is the critical balance for our controlling. Communion is the alternative for our consumption. Moreover, sharing is the healing of the scarring that we have left on the body of our world and on the body of God.

## Conclusion

There is a story in an early monastic collection entitled *The Sayings of the Desert Fathers* that relates how the devil once asked a monk, who was sitting and doing nothing: "What are you doing here?" The monk replied: "I am doing nothing, I am simply keeping this place." This reminds me of the divine commandment in the garden of paradise, that we are to "till it and keep it" (Gen. 2:15). Creation seeks neither worship nor contempt from us. Creation seeks but one thing: for us to be truly human, to be truly humble, which implies an identity with the very *humus* of the ground.

At every divine liturgy celebrated in the Orthodox Church, the deacon says: "Let us stand in goodness. Let us stand in awe." As one Orthodox monk once told me, the liturgy is in fact saying to us: "Don't just *do* something; stand there!" Before we can act, or react, or respond, or revise our self-image or our world-image, we must stand still. Let us not forget that it was our doing that got us into this mess in the first place. The sense of "goodness" in the phrase "Let us stand in goodness" reminds me of Peter's words on the Mount of Transfiguration: "Master, it is good for us to be here" (Luke 9:33). Moreover, it leads us back to the words at the beginning of all, in the book of Genesis, when "God saw everything that he had made, and indeed, it was very good" (Gen. 1:31).

PART I

# CALL TO PRAYER: ENCYCLICAL LETTERS

# Messages from Ecumenical Patriarch Demetrios I
## (1972-1991)

## ENCYCLICAL LETTER, SEPTEMBER 1, 1989

*To the Pleroma of the Church: Grace and Peace*
*from the Creator of all Creation our Lord and God*
*and Savior Jesus Christ*

This Ecumenical Throne of Orthodoxy — as protector and proclaimer of the centuries-long spirit of the patristic tradition and as faithful interpreter of the eucharistic and liturgical experience of the Orthodox Church — watches with great anxiety the merciless trampling and destruction of the natural environment caused by human beings, with extremely dangerous consequences for the very survival of the natural world created by God.

The abuse by contemporary humanity of its privileged position within creation and of the Creator's order "to have dominion" over the earth (Gen. 1:28) has already led the world to the edge of apocalyptic self-destruction. This is occurring either in the form of natural pollution, which is dangerous for all living beings, or in the form of extinction for many species of the animal and plant world, or else again in various other forms. Scientists and other scholars warn us now of the danger and speak of phenomena threatening the life of our planet, such as the so-called "greenhouse effect" whose first indications have already been observed.

*In view of this situation, the Church of Christ cannot remain unmoved.* It constitutes a fundamental dogma of her faith that the world was created by God the Father, who is confessed in the Creed to be "maker of heaven and earth and of all things visible and invisible." According to the great Fathers of the Church, the human person is the prince of creation, endowed with the privilege of freedom. Being a partaker simultaneously of the material and the

37

spiritual world, humanity was created in order to refer creation back to the Creator, in order that the world may be saved from decay and death.

This great destiny of humanity was realized, after the failure and fall of the "first Adam," by "the last Adam," the Son and *Logos* of God incarnate, our Lord Jesus Christ, who united in His person the created world with the uncreated God, and who unceasingly refers creation to the Father as an eternal eucharistic referring *(anaphora)* and offering *(prosphora)*. At each divine liturgy, the Church continues this reference and offering (of creation to God) in the form of the bread and the wine, which are elements taken from the material universe. In this way the Church continuously declares that humanity is destined, not to exercise power over creation, as if it were the owner of it, but to act as its steward, cultivating it in love and referring it in thankfulness, respect, and reverence to its Creator.

Unfortunately, in our days, under the influence of an extreme rationalism and self-centeredness, humanity has lost the sense of sacredness of creation and acts as its arbitrary ruler and rude violator. *Instead of the eucharistic and ascetic spirit with which the Orthodox Church brought up its children for centuries, we observe today a violation of nature for the satisfaction, not of basic human needs, but of humanity's endless and constantly increasing desire and lust, encouraged by the prevailing philosophy of the consumer society.*

Yet, "the whole creation has been groaning in travail" (Rom. 8:22) and is now beginning to protest at its treatment by human beings. Humanity cannot infinitely and whimsically exploit the natural sources of energy. The price of our arrogance will be our self-destruction, if the present situation continues.

In full consciousness of our duty and paternal spiritual responsibility, having taken all the above into consideration and having listened to the anguish of modern humanity, we have reached a decision, in common with the Sacred and Holy Synod surrounding us. Accordingly, *we declare the first day of September of each year a day on which, on the feast of the Indiction, namely the first day of the ecclesiastical year, prayers and supplications are to be offered in this holy center of Orthodoxy for all creation, declaring this day to be the day of the protection of the environment.*

Therefore, we invite, through this our Patriarchal message, the entire Christian world to offer together with the Mother Holy Great Church of Christ, the Ecumenical Patriarchate, every year on this day, prayers and supplications to the Maker of all, both as thanksgiving for the great gift of Creation and in petition for its protection and salvation. At the same time, on the one hand, we paternally urge all the faithful in the world to admonish themselves and their children to respect and protect the natural environment. On the other hand, we urge all those entrusted with the responsibility of governing the nations to act without delay in taking all necessary measures for the protection and preservation of the natural creation.

Finally, wishing all good things for the world from our Lord we bestow upon all people our Patriarchal blessing.


# ENCYCLICAL LETTER, SEPTEMBER 1, 1990

*To the Pleroma of the Church: Grace and Peace
from the Creator of all Creation our Lord and God
and Savior Jesus Christ*

A year has passed since we issued a message declaring September 1st of each year as the day of prayers for the protection of the environment. In that message, we called upon the Orthodox faithful and, indeed, upon every man and woman of good will to consider the extent and the seriousness of the problem generated as a result of the senseless abuse of material creation by human beings. On this day, which for the Orthodox Church is officially the first day of the ecclesiastical year, the Orthodox faithful are invited to offer prayers to the Creator of all, thanking Him for the good of His creation and beseeching Him to protect it from every evil and destruction.

The message offered last year continues to echo and to express the inquietude of our Church toward the continuing destruction of the natural environment. For this reason, we considered it expedient, rather than communicating in some other way, to present once again today that same message, unabridged, to our faithful and to all people in order to renew our fervent appeal to all.

Beloved brothers and spiritual children, *use the natural environment as its stewards and not as its owners. Acquire an ascetic ethos bearing in mind that everything in the natural world, whether great or small, has its importance for the life of the world, and nothing is useless or contemptible. Regard yourselves as being responsible before God for every creature and treat everything with love and care.* Only in this way shall we be able to prevent the threatening destruction of our planet and secure a physical environment where life for the coming generations of humankind will be healthy and happy.

May the Creator of all, in His goodness, be the protector and savior of His "very good" creation throughout this New Year. Amen.

# Messages from Ecumenical Patriarch Bartholomew I

## ENCYCLICAL LETTER, SEPTEMBER 1, 1992

*To the Pleroma of the Church: Grace and Peace*
*from the Creator of all Creation our Lord and God*
*and Savior Jesus Christ*

The beginning of the ecclesiastical year, sanctified by the traditional celebration of the *Indictus,* also constitutes a characteristic juncture in the life of the entire creation that surrounds us. This juncture is known, at least to those residing in the northern hemisphere of our planet, as the commencement of autumn; to those living in the southern parts of the world, it is known as the beginning of spring.

Thus, "autumn" and "spring," which to the average person usually signify diametrically opposed factors, actually converge and coincide in the inauguration of the ecclesiastical year as *one entity* established by God.

The faithful, therefore, are able to recognize that, in essence, *beginning and end constitute two aspects of the same created reality, which is bound to march toward its final destination in both "glory" and "infamy." Therefore, we should not allow the shape and rhythm of the present world to frighten us.* In accepting this fundamental truth, we become steadfast and immovable upon the rock of faith. Thus, our sorrowful journey through whatever is "passing" and whatever is "stable" is delivered, at the very outset, from the moral danger that ever lies in ambush, namely, that of elevating ourselves to the whim of power which starts from the ground up or else of sinking impiously into the obscurity of despair out of worldly weakness.

*In the language of the Church Fathers, the human person "stands at the border"* between material and spiritual creation. Humanity is a "borderer"

40

with regard to space and time as well; thus, in "an hour of temptation," one is able courageously to foretaste the "day of salvation."

However, through the sacred correlations mentioned above, creation is by no means at all reduced to a level of irresponsible relativity or relativism. On the contrary, in this way creation emerges in its God-pleasing uniqueness and sacredness. Thus, "summer" and "winter," "light" and "darkness," "greatness" and "smallness," "instant" and "eternal," "material" and "spiritual," "divine" and "human" are proven not to be contrary to each other, but rather to be deeply correlated. For the redeeming will of the benevolent God, who is beyond all things, is realized gradually in time and in space through all of these things.

It is, however, precisely within the framework of the sacred connection and correlation of these ideas that God has not allowed humanity to be a mere *spectator* or an irresponsible *consumer* of the world and of all that is in the world. Indeed, humanity has been called to assume the task of being primarily a *partaker* and a *sharer in the responsibility* for everything in the created world. Endowed, therefore, from the beginning with "the image of God," humanity is called to continual self-transcendence so that, in responsible *synergy* with God the Creator, each person might sanctify the entire world, thus becoming a faithful "minister" and "steward."

It is clear that the concepts of "minister" and "steward" by far exceed the contemporary and internationally accepted ideal of the person called an "ecologist." Usually, we know neither how such an ecologist understands the concept of *oikos* [the Greek word for "house"] nor how that person regards *logos* [the Greek word for "word"]. Today everyone speaks of the dangers facing the "ecosystem" as numbering in the thousands; yet few make any reference at all to the God who "constituted" all things. There are those who anxiously keep records of constantly perishing "deposits" of the main elements of life and movements in nature, again without uttering a word about God, who in His infinite goodwill and beneficence is the "depositor" of all His goods for our use and nourishment. In wisdom God "established heaven and earth," thus abundantly enriching the universe with every kind of source of living water.

At any rate, being God's minister and steward over all of creation does not mean that humanity simply prospers or is happy in the world. This would be crude self-sufficiency and impious minimalism. The main and lasting benefit of these qualifications is that, by using the world in a pious manner, humanity experiences the blessed evolution from the stage of "divine image" to that of "divine likeness." In similar fashion, every other good element of the universe is transformed, by the grace of God and even without human intervention, from the stage of "potentiality" to that of "actuality," in fulfillment of the pre-eternal plan of the entire divine economy.

In addressing these pious thoughts to the faithful of our Church and every person of goodwill, it is our desire, in a manner that is worthy of and pleasing to God, to commemorate and celebrate the inauguration of the *Indictus* as the special day for the protection of all creation. This day was established three years ago by the Mother Holy Great Church of Christ and has now been accepted by all Orthodox throughout the world. Having done so, we should like to take the God-given opportunity to invite and encourage every person, and above all the faithful, constantly to watch over his or her fellow human beings and the world, for the benefit of us all and for the glory of the Creator.

Our words on this auspicious day, and the sacred thoughts that reach beyond these words, are even more timely inasmuch as they are addressed from the sacred center of the Phanar on the occasion of the first and historic assembly of all the hierarchs in active service of the most venerable Ecumenical Throne. Through this sacred assembly the Mother Church seeks more direct cooperation and better coordination by the Holy and Sacred Synod with the hierarchs of the Ecumenical Patriarchate throughout the world, namely with those who shepherd dioceses and those who serve in some other capacity. This assembly of our hierarchy, which the Holy Synod decided to convene on a biannual basis, brings numerous blessings, such as closer communication and communion among brothers who share responsibility, as well as exchange of information and mutual support. It also provides great comfort and encouragement to the children of the Church scattered in the four corners of the earth and represented here by their spiritual leaders. When the faithful around the world from time to time see all of their hierarchy presented and represented as one body, then they recognize it as "divine intervention" against the temptations, sorrows, and dangers in the world and thus feel greater security in God.

Therefore, we fraternally greet the hierarchs that are gathered here from the ends of the earth. And to the rest of the clergy and faithful laity of the Holy Great Church of Christ, those near and far, we pray that the new ecclesiastical year, inaugurated on this auspicious occasion, will be blessed by the Lord, and that His grace and infinite mercy will be with all.

## ENCYCLICAL LETTER, SEPTEMBER 1, 1993

*To the Pleroma of the Church: Grace and Peace*
*from the Creator of all Creation our Lord and God*
*and Savior Jesus Christ*

Together with the other Most Holy Sister Orthodox Churches, we have established September 1st of each year as a special day of concern for and commemoration of the natural environment that surrounds us. Again, this year, we are called to offer wholehearted praise to the Creator of everything both visible and invisible for having placed us as the ones first-fashioned in luscious paradise among all His own creation.

The most fundamental Orthodox doctrine — which addresses impartially the omnipotence, the omniscience, the extreme beneficence, and the wakeful providence of the Creator, as well as the consideration and high regard in general for created beings and matter, with humanity as its crowning point — is indeed the doctrine of the creation of the world *ex nihilo* [literally, "out of nothing"].

Some people contemplate only what concerns the world and recognize the philosophical "web of the Athenians." So they speak with irony of the conviction of faithful believers with regard to creation *ex nihilo*. In challenging this fundamental doctrine, they cite the merit of the corrupted and, in its redundancy, frivolous and refutable notion that "nothing can be amassed *ex nihilo*." The only exception such people accept is that, before there was absolute nothingness in relation to the world, God, as being without beginning or successor, and as being beyond and above space, time, quality, quantity, causal relationship, or dependency, has always preceded and commanded everything.

In his epigrammatic statement that "God is love" (1 John 4:16), St. John the Evangelist attributed to God, who lacks nothing and is without beginning, a compendious and comprehensive name, that of love, which is cardinal to all moral attributes. Therefore, we, who have received the revealed word of God, are justified in believing that everything has been created out of *absolute love* and in *absolute freedom* by God the Maker and Father of all, who, according to St. Paul, calls things from non-being into being (Rom. 4:17).

In contemplating the creation of God within us and around us in this kind of God-given theological perspective, we are certainly justified in being overcome with total optimism, even when the elements of nature are faced with the greatest danger or when history is being gravely distorted. For we recognize that "the souls of the righteous are in the hand of God, and no torment will ever touch them" (Wis. of Sol. 3:1).

Therefore, before any abnormality in nature and history, the first requirement is not so much that we be wise and powerful in order to foresee in timely fashion and deal accordingly with particular earthquakes, floods, or other usually unexpected calamities. Neither is it that we be armed with the provisions of worldly knowledge and science in order to drive back the powers marshaled against us by any enemy or invader. Rather, above all, we must be just, striving at every moment throughout our life to learn the *precepts* of God more perfectly and more profoundly.

This is why it is not incidental that among the first things we do in Orthodox worship is to praise the Lord, invoking Him that we be taught His immovable precepts, which derive from Him only. Never are we so powerful and shielded from every unexpected force as when we chant, as did the youths in the fire described in the book of Daniel, the ode of the beloved: "Blessed are you, Lord, teach me your precepts."

During this period, dear brothers and children in the Lord, we witness international organizations, interstate legislations, and scientific research programs united in jeremiads and lamentations that toll the bell of danger in order that humanity might sober up in time before the coming of mass chaos. Such chaos, they say, would threaten universal order and balance in the various so-called ecosystems, not only of our planet, but also of the entire cosmos. Yet, during this same time, we from the Ecumenical Patriarchate address ourselves first to the conscience of every individual person, inviting people each day and with innocent heart to taste the good things of God, partaking in trembling fear — though, simultaneously, in doxology and joy — of the good things of creation.

Panic has never allowed humanity to render judgments calmly or to balance justly its obligations toward itself, toward the world around, and toward the ever-watchful God above. However, it is precisely these obligations, as they have been coordinated from the very first moment of creation by the just-judging God, which constitute the "precepts" mentioned above. Usually, people speak out and go to great pains to mark and establish *human rights,* which, as a rule, are determined by self-interest and fear and always give rise to powers and demands, which separate persons from groups, from classes, from people.

The precepts of God, on the contrary, are by definition comprehensive and inclusive, as much of a *part* as of the *whole.* This is why, by learning and recognizing them, human beings are rendered, through God's grace, brothers and partakers among themselves. Furthermore, through a eucharistic use of the world, they are rendered partakers of the world and of the infinite love of God, and not consumers, which the atheistic polity or eudemonistic instinct have taught through the hubristic progress of technology.

44

Thus, the first responsibility of the faithful is to examine and study continuously in greater depth the law and precepts of God. Thus, *by becoming cheerful givers and grateful receivers of His wondrous things in this world, we may come to respect the balances of nature set up by Him.*

May the grace of the all-compassionate and all-benevolent God, together with our paternal and Patriarchal blessings and prayers, be with all who fear the Lord.

## ENCYCLICAL LETTER, SEPTEMBER 1, 1994

*To the Pleroma of the Church: Grace and Peace*
*from the Creator of all Creation our Lord and God*
*and Savior Jesus Christ*

On a number of occasions in the ecclesiastical year, *the Church prays that God may protect humanity from natural catastrophes:* from earthquakes, storms, famine, and floods. Yet, today, we observe the reverse. On September 1st, the day devoted to God's handiwork, *the Church implores the Creator to protect nature from calamities of human origin,* calamities such as pollution, war, exploitation, waste, and secularism. It may seem strangely paradoxical that the body of believers, acting vicariously for the natural environment, beseeches God for projection against itself, against its own actions. Nevertheless, from this perspective, the Church, in its wisdom, brings before our eyes a message of deep significance, one that touches upon the central problems of fallen humanity and its restoration. This is the problem of the polarization of individual sin against collective responsibility.

Scripture informs us that if one member of the body is infirm, the entire body is affected (1 Cor. 12:26). There is, after all, solidarity in the human race because, made as they are in the image of the triune God, human beings are interdependent and coinherent. No man is an island. We are "members one of another" (Eph. 4:25). Therefore, any action, performed by any member of the human race, inevitably affects all other members. Consequently, no one falls alone and no one is saved alone. According to Dostoevsky's Staretz Zossima in *The Brothers Karamazov,* we are each of us responsible for everyone and everything.

How does this central problem relate to the matter of protecting the environment against humankind's actions? It has become painfully apparent that humanity, both individually and collectively, no longer perceives the natural order as a sign and a sacrament of God but rather as an object of exploitation. There is no one who is not guilty of disrespecting nature. *To respect nature is to recognize that all creatures and objects have a unique place in God's creation. When we become sensitive to God's world around us, we grow more conscious also of God's world within us. In beginning to see nature as a work of God, we begin to see our own place as human beings within nature. The true appreciation of any object is to discover the extraordinary in the ordinary.*

Sin alone is mean and trivial, as are most of the products of a fallen and sinful technology. Yet, sin is at the root of the prevailing destruction of the environment. Humanity has failed in what was its noble vocation: to participate in God's creative action in the world. It has succumbed to a theory of development that values production over human dignity and wealth over human integrity. We see, for example, delicate ecological balances being upset by the uncontrolled destruction of animal and plant life or by a reckless exploitation of natural resources. It cannot be overemphasized that all of this, even if carried out in the name of progress and well-being, is ultimately to humankind's disadvantage.

It is not without good cause, therefore, that "the whole of creation has been groaning in travail" (Rom. 8:22). Was it not originally seen by God to be good? Created by God, the world reflects divine wisdom, divine beauty, and divine truth. Everything is from God, everything is permeated with divine energy; in this lies both the joy and the tragedy of the world and of life within it. The hymns and prayers in the Office of September 1st, composed by the gifted hymnographer of the Great Church, the late monk Gerasimos of the Holy Mountain, extol the beauty of creation but also remind us of our tragic abuse of it. They call us to repent for our actions against God's gift to us. We have made this world ever more opaque, rendering it ever more tortured. The consequences of nature's confrontation with humanity have indeed been an unnatural disaster of enormous proportions. Is it not, therefore, only right that we Christians act today as nature's voice in raising its plea for salvation before the throne of God?

The Church teaches that it is the destiny of humankind to restore the proper relationship between God and the world, just as it was in the Garden of Eden. Through repentance, two landscapes, the one human and the other natural, can become the objects of a caring and creative effort. However, repentance must be accompanied by three soundly focused principles, which manifest the ethos of the Orthodox Church.

There is, first, the *eucharistic ethos,* which, above all else, means using the earth's natural resources with thankfulness, offering them back to God; indeed, not only them, but also ourselves. In the Eucharist, we return to God what is His own: namely, the bread and the wine. Representing the fruits of creation, the bread and wine are no longer imprisoned by a fallen world but are returned as liberated, purified from their fallen state, and capable of receiving the divine presence within themselves. At the same time, we pray for ourselves to be sanctified, because through sin we have fallen away and have betrayed our baptismal promise.

Second, we have the *ascetic ethos* of Orthodoxy that involves fasting and other spiritual works. These make us recognize that all of the things we take for granted in fact comprise God's gifts, provided in order to satisfy our needs. They are not ours to abuse and waste simply because we have the ability to pay for them.

Third, the *liturgical ethos* emphasizes community concern and sharing. We stand before God together; and we hold in common the earthly blessings that He has given to all creatures. Not to share our own wealth with the poor is theft from the poor and deprivation of their means of life; we possess not our own wealth but theirs, as one of the holy Fathers of the Church reminds us. We stand before the Creator as the Church of God, which, according to Orthodox theology, is the continued incarnate presence of the Lord Jesus Christ on earth; His presence looks to the salvation of the world, not just of humanity but also of the entire creation. The ethos of the Church in all its expressions denotes a reverence for all matter: for the world around us, for other creatures, and for our own bodies.

Hence, our Patriarchal message for this day of protection for the environment is simply that we maintain a consistent attitude of respect in all our attitudes and actions toward the world. We cannot expect to leave no trace on the environment. However, we must choose either to make it reflect our greed and ugliness or else to use it in such a way that its beauty manifests God's handiwork through ours.

The grace and infinite mercy of the Creator of all things and the providence of God be with all of you, beloved brothers and children of the Church.

## ENCYCLICAL LETTER, SEPTEMBER 1, 1995

*To the Pleroma of the Church: Grace and Peace*
*from the Creator of all Creation our Lord and God*
*and Savior Jesus Christ*

With the grace of God, we are called once again to celebrate the beginning of the new ecclesiastical year by making special reference, as was established several years ago, to our responsibility toward creation as it relates to the environment within and around us in general, and more specifically toward what is referred to as the inanimate natural environment.

Within the context of the continuous and ever-developing ecological concern over the years, the Holy Great Church of Christ, the Mother Church, was blessed again this past year of 1995 in convening an international seminar on the environment, which was held on the fragrantly scented island of Halki, in the venerable theological school and monastery of the Holy Trinity. This year's seminar had as its main theme "Environment and Ethics." We took advantage of the opportunity to offer certain appropriate introductory remarks — from the perspective of the Mother Church — regarding the sanctity of creation and the lofty responsibility of the human being created in God's image within the whole scheme of creation.

We take this occasion today as well to remind you of what in the seminar we referred to as a temporal sequence in the production of the various species of creation. This temporal sequence etches in stone our responsibility as administrators of God's creation in the world.

The Fathers of the Church, in a manner fitting to God and in appreciation of the temporal sequence mentioned above, taught that *every species was created before humankind in order for humankind to enter into a full kingdom and serve there as king, priest, and prophet.* We see, therefore, that what might be referred to as the threefold office of the God-man, about which theology speaks at great length, has been extended to humankind from the very outset and by definition from our primeval relationships with natural creation.

What does it mean for us to reign, minister, and teach in the vast expanse of creation? It means that we must constantly study, serve, and pray to transform what is corruptible into what is incorruptible, to the extent that this can be accomplished during our lifetime.

The Church of the Incarnate Word of God continues His redemptive work in a world that is confused and constantly in a state of ambivalence. Therefore, the Church will never cease to remind the world of these fundamental truths regarding the position and orientation of the human person; rather, by word and deed, the Church teaches a way to life.

We, too, from the Holy Great Church of Christ, are striving to fulfill this mission with all our strength. In the context of the celebrations of the 1900th anniversary since the recording of the Apocalypse by St. John on the island of Patmos, we have decided, along with our fellow bishops, to convoke an international ecological symposium. This symposium will sail from Istanbul to the sanctified land of Patmos — where civilizations from the east, west, north, and south have intersected for centuries. Through this means, we shall attempt to reveal more extensively to the eyes of the modern world the magnitude of creation in general, as this was envisioned through God's inspiration by the evangelist of love, St. John the Theologian.

Thus, invoking enlightenment from above upon all men and women, in order that they may live and act toward all creation in a God-loving way, having common and cosmic salvation as their final aim, we pray for peace and undisturbed goodwill for all the earth.

### The Keepsake of Patmos

What does it mean for us to reign, minister and teach in the vast expanse of creation? It means that we must constantly study, serve and pray to transform what is corruptible into what is incorruptible, to the extent that this can be accomplished during our lifetime.

## ENCYCLICAL LETTER, SEPTEMBER 1, 1996

*To the Pleroma of the Church: Grace and Peace*
*from the Creator of all Creation our Lord and God*
*and Savior Jesus Christ*

Praise and thanksgiving and glory unto our God, venerated in the Holy Trinity, who has deemed us worthy to celebrate once more the commencement of the ecclesiastical year and the traditional feast of the new *Indiction*.

At the initiative of our Ecumenical Throne, September 1st has been established, as is well known, as a day of prayer and supplication for the protection of our surrounding natural world. Indeed, this has now become established throughout the entire Orthodox world with the consent and accord of the other Most Holy Sister Orthodox Churches. *We are hopeful that, with time, the rest of*

*Christendom will come to embrace this proposition and request* in order that, before the imminently expiring second millennium in Christ, all Christians may consecrate congruent prayers on the same day. In this way, beginning even now, in every land inhabited by humankind, we may glorify with thanksgiving in the future the all-holy name of our God, Creator of heaven and earth.

It has become an established tradition, as well, that on this auspicious day of celebration our modesty directs anew to the entire congregation of the Church a paternal admonition toward perpetual prayer for our natural environment, stressing in this way all issues deemed timely and necessary.

It is well known to us all that, unfortunately, many such issues arise each year. Naturally, we do not at all overlook the positive efforts made by others on this account. Yet we observe that the ecological problem has become in many respects more complicated and that the ecological darkness has become even more extensive, which is to say that there is still a substantial ignorance in many and a skillful propaganda on the part of the few, who delight in their alliance with the forces of darkness. These facts result in *many fallacies regarding ecology, in purposeful concealment and even distortion of the truth on ecological matters, and, indeed, ecological terrorism in the form of exaggeration or abusive intervention in the natural order of things,* at times even to the point of exercising interstate threat and violence. This has also resulted in the brutal contravention of international agreements on vital ecological issues and the stubborn refusal to accept the financial burdens of elementary and essential ecological discipline as well as a plethora of other violations, which threaten directly the very air that we breathe.

*All of this may be summarized in the sorrowful realization that, despite the painful current experiences and the concerted efforts of many, extremely few positive steps have been made on the arduous path toward a true and stable reconciliation of humankind with our surrounding physical world.*

*This failure is due, mainly, to the insistence of the greater part of humankind on the false understanding that the ecological problem is foremost a matter of logical connections, expressed and materialized through the means and methods of politics, economy, technology, and all other human activities.*

For all these reasons, it is necessary that the Church steadily call to mind the evangelical truth on this matter, namely that all of the above deviations represent a violation of the divine disposition of the physical world, which cannot remain unpunished given the anti-life stance of these deviations. It is, indeed, necessary for the Church to remind us that, on the contrary, the aforementioned and therefore imperatively necessary reconciliation, whenever and wherever it is accomplished, represents *par excellence* a spiritual event. More precisely, the Church reminds us that reconciliation is the blessed fruit of the Holy Spirit, granted to all who freely and consciously partake in the great mystery of divine love, which has followed the creation and constitutes the reconciliation of God, through Christ, with humankind and the entirety of creation.

This reconciliation is understood and experienced within the Church as a settlement: "God in Christ was reconciling the world to himself," not considering their trespasses, as proclaimed by St. Paul, the apostle to the nations (2 Cor. 5:19). This is because all things are derived from God, and in this case God is the source of the renewal of all things, "the new creation," in which we become participants through Holy Baptism, as well as other sanctifying gifts in the life of the Church. They are derived from God, who "reconciled us to himself through Jesus Christ" (2 Cor. 5:18). Moreover, we are all dutifully reminded by the Church that God Himself placed in us "the message of reconciliation" (2 Cor. 5:19), that He entrusted to us Christians the proclamation of the gospel, this joyful message of reconciliation, of the new, loving communion of God with humankind and the natural world.

*Clearly, this is what is most necessary today. This is what is most urgent for the relationship of humankind with the material world: namely, reconciliation* in the aforementioned sense. This reconciliation is not merely to take place in a worldly manner, for our benefit and material gain, or, again, for material prosperity and materialistic welfare. It is to be understood theologically — that is, with humility and repentance, which lead to true participation in the beauty of creation, restored through Christ, with which the goodness of life is connected harmoniously. And this is so because both goodness and beauty share the same source and cause, which is God Himself, who constitutes the brilliant beauty of the most extreme divine goodness and comeliness.

Indeed, beloved brethren and cherished children in the Lord, this is what is truly good: to participate in that divine goodness and beauty so that we, too, may say, according to Dionysius the Areopagite: "We say it is good to participate in beauty; indeed, beauty is participation in that cause which beautifies all good things. This supersubstantial good is called beauty due to the loveliness which it transmits to all beings, to each one appropriately" (PG 3:701). It is from this divine beauty that the commandment derives that we preserve the goodness and beauty within us and around us, as the most exalted gifts of God.

For all these reasons, from this sacred center of Orthodoxy, we salute as very significant the subject chosen for the second Pan-European Ecumenical Assembly, to be held, God willing, in Austria in June of the coming year of our Savior, 1997: "Reconciliation: Gift of God and Source of New Life." The well-grounded expectation that Christians of Europe will dedicate their efforts to the examination of this issue, both separately and in common, fore-shadows many blessings. Among these, we expect a clearer sight of divine beauty in nature and a more decisive involvement of all in its protection and further promotion, through the divine gifts and through the multiple creative forces of humankind.

May the grace of our all-gracious God, who accomplishes this good and concedes this beauty, together with our Patriarchal blessings and paternal wishes, be always with all those who honor His great wonders.

## ENCYCLICAL LETTER, SEPTEMBER 1, 1997

*To the Pleroma of the Church: Grace and Peace
from the Creator of all Creation our Lord and God
and Savior Jesus Christ*

The all-merciful and beneficent God, who created humanity from non-being into being, desired that His beloved creature, the king of creation, namely humanity, might enjoy His "very good" creation. Thus God wanted humanity to enjoy creation from the majestic harmony of the heavenly firmament to the natural beauty of the earthly and marine animals as well as all vegetable life, with all the numerous, harmonious variations revealed on the surface of the world. For, by contemplating the balance, harmony, and beauty of creation, humanity is lifted to a sense of wonder at the supreme perfection of the divine Creator and, consequently, to love and worship Him. In this way, humanity is sanctified and rendered a partaker of divine blessedness, for which it was destined.

However, the enjoyment of earthly and heavenly things was not granted to people without any presuppositions. Such enjoyment had to be the result also of their own voluntary and active will. In this respect, the first-created were given the command to exercise ascetic abstinence in paradise; they were not to eat of a particular fruit. They were also given the command to labor; they were to work and keep the garden wherein they were placed. Moreover, they were given the command to increase and exercise dominion on the earth, in the same sense in which they were to work and keep the earth as an extended earthly paradise.

These commandments surely also apply to us as the successors of the first-created. They do not aim solely or predominantly at protecting nature in itself but at preserving the space within which humanity dwells; creation was made for humanity, and it was made beautiful and productive, serving and supporting every goal in accordance with our divine destiny.

Unfortunately, however, *the fall of the first-created and the deviation from their goal also resulted in the transformation of their attitude toward nature and their fellow human beings. Thus, today we are faced with extremely self-centered and greedy behavior of people in relation to the natural environment. Such conduct betrays their indifference toward natural beauty and natural habitats as well as toward conditions of survival for their fellow human beings.*

In order, therefore, to sensitize people in regard to their obligation to contribute as much as they possibly can to the preservation of the natural environment, even if for their own sake, we dedicated September 1st as a day of prayer for the created order.

Of course, the natural environment also has value in and of itself. Nevertheless, it acquires greater value when contemplated in connection with the human beings who dwell within it. For damage to the environment bears consequences not only for nature but also for humanity, rendering human life less tolerable and beautiful.

According to the Church Fathers, a merciful heart will not only seek the heavenly kingdom and sense that it has no abiding city here on earth, seeking instead the heavenly city; it also cannot tolerate any harm to animals and plants, indeed even to the inanimate elements of nature. Such a person recognizes a value in nature, too, a relative value given by God Himself who created it. Such a spirit should characterize every Christian. We do not limit our expectations simply to this world; nor do we abandon our pursuit of the heavenly reality, namely the divine kingdom. Instead, we recognize that the way that leads to the heavenly Jerusalem goes through the keeping of the divine commandments during our temporary sojourn in this world. Therefore, *we are careful to keep the original commandment to preserve creation from all harm,* both for our own sake and for the sake of our fellow human beings. In any case, respect for the material and natural creation of God, as well as indirectly for all people who are affected by the environment, reveals a sensitivity in human attitudes and conduct that should be characteristic of every Christian.

However, since we can discern that such a spirit does not inspire all people, we beseech the Lord on this day especially that He might illumine them to avoid ecological turmoil and harm. May the Lord, in His long-suffering, also protect us all from the environment that has, because of our sins, revolted. May He spare us from natural destructions that arise from forces beyond our control.

Let us pray, then, and ask the Lord for favorable and peaceful seasons, free from earthquakes, floods, fires, storms, raging winds, and any other natural disaster. May He also spare us from every form of human destruction wrought upon our environment, so that we may live in peace and glorify in thanksgiving our Lord Jesus Christ, who bestows every good thing. May His grace be with you all. Amen.

## ENCYCLICAL LETTER, SEPTEMBER 1, 1998[1]

*To the Pleroma of the Church: Grace and Peace*
*from the Creator of all Creation our Lord and God*
*and Savior Jesus Christ*

The Holy Orthodox Church, accepting that the entire creation is very good, finds itself in a harmonious relationship with the natural world, which surrounds the crown of creation, the human being. *Even though the human being, either as an isolated individual or as collective humanity, is only a minuscule speck in the face of the immense universe, it is a fact that the entire universe is endowed with meaning by the very presence of humanity within it. Based on this assurance, even leading contemporary scientists accept that the universe is infused with the so-called "human principle," meaning that it came about and exists for the sake of humanity.*

Consequently, the response of humanity to its Creator, the all-good God, should have been one of thanksgiving for the abundant wealth that our Maker has placed at our disposal. However, humanity loved creation more than the Creator and did not return its debt to God. Rather, humanity made an idol of creation and desired to be transformed into a wasteful ruler of creation, without any accountability, instead of being a rational and grateful consumer of creation. *Moreover, humanity was often not even satisfied with wasteful manipulation but schemed to use the tremendous forces contained within nature for the destruction of its fellow human beings and the depletion even of nature itself. From the earliest of days, when Cain murdered Abel, at which point humanity altered the staff formerly used for support into a rod of as-*

---

1. This text also served as the basis for remarks of welcome by Patriarch Bartholomew during a colloquium entitled "Monotheism and Environment" organized by the Institute of Religious History and Law of Aix-Marseille University and hosted by the Ecumenical Patriarchate in Istanbul (September 5-8, 1998).

*sault, humanity now tries to use every element as a weapon. Thus, humanity was not satisfied with using elements that God granted in abundance — such as copper, bronze, iron, and so on — in order to produce tools for a peaceful life. Rather, using all the latest scientific discoveries, humanity fashioned from these elements weapons of mass murder and a system of human annihilation.* Unfortunately, humanity continues to make and use these weapons. We therefore see materials of all sorts — gunpowder, nitroglycerine, atomic and nuclear energy, chemical gases, disease-causing bacteria and other micro-organisms — being mobilized and gathered into huge arsenals, to be used as a threat to coerce others into submission but also to annihilate those who do not submit.

Consequently, the rebellion of nature against humanity is hardly a strange coincidence, nor is the continuous exhortation of the Orthodox Church that we should not love the world, which has been led astray from its divine purpose, or things in the world, but that we should love God instead (1 John 2:15). In this way, we are able to enjoy the things of the world with blessing and thanksgiving in Christ, through whom we have received reconciliation (Rom. 5:11).

Nature has rebelled against humanity, which abuses it. Therefore, nature is no longer in perfect divine harmony, the marvelous melody of which comes from the rhythmic orbits of the heavenly bodies and the changing seasons of the year. *Were it not for the good souls of the saints, who uphold the cohesion of the world, perhaps the revenge of nature for the inhumanities we force it to bear would be even more lamentable for those people who improperly use its powers against others.*

In light of the above, on this first day of September in the year 1998 of our salvation, once again dedicated to the natural environment, we invite and urge everyone to convert the tremendous destructive forces that we have accumulated on earth — a planet so small in size, yet so great in evil as well as great in virtue — into creative and peaceful forces.

Unfortunately, the coercion of nature to act destructively against itself and the human race not only derives from the will of certain evil leaders but also is supported by many who deny their own responsibility. It comes from the consenting will of thousands of individuals, without whose psychological support these leaders would not be able to accomplish anything. Consequently, *every living person on the face of the earth has the responsibility consciously to accept or reject what is being done. It is through this acceptance or rejection that one participates in the formation of the predominant will. From this point of view, everyone, even the feeblest, can contribute to the restoration of the harmonious operation of the world. We can do so by being in tune with the forces of the divine harmony and not with those which are badly dissonant and oppose the divine all-harmonious rhythm of the universal instrument, of which each one of us constitutes but one of its innumerable chords.*

Our love for nature does not seek to idolize it; rather, our love for nature stems from our love for the Creator who grants it to us. This love is expressed through offering all things in thanksgiving to God, through whom we, having been reconciled through Jesus Christ (2 Cor. 5:19), enjoy also our reconciliation with nature. Without our reconciliation with God, the forces of nature are in opposition to us. We already experience consequences of this opposition. Therefore, in order to avert the escalation of evil and to correct that which may already have taken place, and in order to suspend the penalty, we are obligated to accept the fact that we need to be responsible and accountable consumers of nature and not arbitrary rulers of it. We must also accept the fact that, in the final analysis, if we use the powers of nature to destroy our fellow human beings, whom we might consider useless, we will have to face the same consequences.

Finally, for all these things, we fervently pray to the Lord God that He may show forbearance for our transgressions; that He may grant us time for repentance; and that He may shine in our hearts the light of His truth. This we ask in order that in our treatment of the environment, and in each of the paths we encounter in life, we may advance in concord with His all-wise, all-harmonious order and decrees. Otherwise, our discordant journey may lead to our demise.

May the grace and infinite mercy of our Lord Jesus Christ be with you all and with all peoples. Amen.

# ENCYCLICAL LETTER, SEPTEMBER 1, 1999

*To the Pleroma of the Church: Grace and Peace*
*from the Creator of all Creation our Lord and God*
*and Savior Jesus Christ*

When Paul the apostle to the nations advised the Thessalonians to "give thanks in all circumstances" (1 Thess. 5:18), he also counseled them to "rejoice always, [and] pray without ceasing" (1 Thess. 5:16-17), thus demonstrating that thanksgiving as prayer and everlasting joy go together and coexist inseparably. Truly, one who gives thanks experiences the joy that comes from the appreciation of that for which one is thankful; thus, from the overabundance of joy, such a person turns toward the giver and provider of all good things received in grateful thanksgiving. Conversely, the person who does not feel the internal need to thank the Creator and Maker of all good things in this very good world, but instead merely receives them ungratefully and selfishly — by being indifferent toward the one who provided these good things and worshiping the impersonal creation rather than the Creator (Rom. 1:25) — does not feel the deep joy of receiving the gifts of God, but only a sullen and inhumane satisfaction. Such a person is given over to irrational desires, to covetousness, and to "robbery and wrongdoing" (Isa. 61:8), all of which are despised by God. As a result, that person will undergo the breaking "of the pride of [his] power" (Lev. 26:19) and will be deprived of the sublime, pure, and heavenly joy of the one who gives thanks gratefully.

*The belief that every creature of God created for communion with human beings is good when it is received with thanksgiving (1 Tim. 4:3-4) leads to respect for creation out of respect for its Creator. However, it does not fashion an idol out of creation itself.* A person who loves the Creator of a given work will neither be disrespectful toward it nor maliciously harm it. Yet, at the same time, that person will surely not worship it and disregard the Creator (Rom. 1:21). Rather, by honoring it, one honors its Creator.

The Ecumenical Patriarchate, having ascertained that the natural creation commonly referred to as "our environment" has to a great extent been maliciously harmed in recent times, has undertaken an effort that strives to sensitize every person — and especially Christians — to the gravity of this problem for humanity and particularly to its ethical and theological dimension. For this reason, the Patriarchate has established September 1st of each year, which is the natural landmark of the yearly cycle, as a day of prayer for the environment. This prayer, however, is not merely a supplication and petition to God for the protection of the natural environment from the impending catastrophe that is being wrought by humankind on creation. It is also a form of thanksgiving for everything that God in His beneficent providence offers through creation to the good and the wicked alike, to the just and the unjust together.

The saints of the Christian Church, as well as other sensitive souls — illumined by the divine light that enlightens everyone who comes into the world (John 1:9), providing that they sincerely and unselfishly desire to receive this light (John 1:11-12) — had great awareness of all evil that comes to any creature of God and, consequently, to every element that makes up our natural environment.

The saints are models for every faithful Christian to imitate, and their sensitive character is the ideal character toward which we all are obliged to strive. However, since not everyone has this same sensitivity, *those who are responsible for the education of others must continually teach them what must be done.* In light of this, we applaud with great satisfaction the proposal of the Committee on the Environment of the Worldwide Federation of Organizations of Engineers, which recently met in Thessalonica during the third international exhibition and conference on "Technology and the Environment," that a binding "Global Code of Ethics" for the environment be drafted.

For its part, the Ecumenical Patriarchate, in addition to proclaiming September 1st as the annual day of prayer for the environment, has successfully organized "Symposium II: The Black Sea in Crisis," in collaboration with other interested parties. As a continuation of this effort, the Patriarchate also established the Halki Ecological Institute, which was held successfully this year. This Institute aims at preparing capable people in the countries and churches surrounding the Black Sea to strive in their respective regions to rouse their leaders and people concerning the danger of the impending death of the Black Sea and the general threat of irreparable and harmful damage to the environment. For this reason, the Patriarchate is currently preparing a third international ecological symposium, this time on the Danube, which is a significant source of pollution in the Black Sea, and which has also undergone enormous ecological alterations and disasters as a result of the recent dramatic bombings.

In addition to the ecological and environmental disasters wrought by humankind, natural disasters have also occurred, such as the recent earthquakes that have struck Turkey. Despite the fact that the consequences of these natural occurrences are often determined by factors for which humans are responsible, the Church fervently beseeches God to show mercy and compassion on human responsibility, and to show His righteousness and goodness both to those who are responsible as well as to those who are not responsible.

The Ecumenical Patriarchate is fully aware that the end of the second Christian millennium has been marked by sad and exceptionally destructive events, which transpired mainly in Yugoslavia and Turkey, but which also continue to occur in varying degrees in other parts of our planet. Humans remain flawed and sinful, and they resist the beneficent influence of the grace of God. For this reason, along with the invitation to all that they respect the natural environment, each for his or her own benefit since it is a gift from God to all humankind, the Ecumenical Patriarchate appeals to everyone to amend their feelings also toward their fellow human beings. Only in this way will the eternal, unchangeable, all-compassionate, and merciful God be able to influence positively the free will of the human person and avert the disastrous manmade activities that are upsetting the balance of the environment.

We recognize that heaven and earth pass away, but the laws of God are eternal and unchangeable as is God Himself. Yet, we also know that the law of God is found in the authority of humankind to determine, to a great extent, the path that our life and world will take.

For this reason, we summon both ourselves and one other to work toward the common good in all areas, and especially in the area of the environment, which in the final analysis includes both our fellow human beings and all of the natural creation.

In closing, we invoke the grace and blessing of God upon everyone who works toward this good; and upon those who out of ignorance or human weakness do evil, we invoke divine illumination and the great mercy of God, that they might come to full knowledge and sincere repentance. Amen.

# ENCYCLICAL LETTER, SEPTEMBER 1, 2001

*To the Pleroma of the Church: Grace and Peace*
*from the Creator of all Creation our Lord and God*
*and Savior Jesus Christ*

The designation of September 1st by the Great Church of Christ, the Mother Church of Constantinople, as a day of prayer for the environment reveals the great significance for humanity of the physical world created by God.

*The double nature of the existence of the human person, consisting of body and soul, or of matter and spirit, according to the "very good" and creative will of God, requires the cooperation of humankind and nature, of person and environment. Without this coordination, the environment is not able to serve humanity according to its destiny, nor is humanity able to avert the disturbance of natural balances and the obliteration of the natural harmony that God created for us.*

*Unfortunately, due to human desire to gain power and wealth, humanity often trespasses the limits of the endurance of nature, subjecting it to maltreatment or abuse.* On other occasions, humanity transgresses against the commandment of God to the first-created to labor and to keep the natural creation, becoming indifferent to the maintenance of its integrity and natural balance.

The result of this behavior is the disturbance of the natural harmony, and the rebellion, as it were, of impersonal nature, which produces phenomena that are the exact opposite to those that serve humankind's normal life. The power that is able to benefit humanity becomes an explosive power of inconceivable destruction. The rivers that are meant to be bearers of life-giving water become carriers of destructive floods. The explosive force of dynamite is transformed from a useful instrument to a power of death and total ruin. Rain is changed from a means of irrigation of plants and the watering of animals to a cause of drowning and uncontrollable currents. Combustion from energy sources and heat becomes a source of atmospheric pollution. In general, *all of nature's resources, designed in their regular operation to provide for humanity's needs for survival, are stretched by humankind beyond their regular limits; this abuse of nature to satisfy human greed and ambition awakens nature's avenging destructive powers.*

The audacity of those who built the Tower of Babel resulted in the disruption of human understanding and communication. In Noah's time, humanity's exclusive turning to the carnal aspect of being, to the exclusion of the spiritual, brought about the purging cataclysmic flood. Since then, God has refrained from using natural disasters to bring humanity back to its senses, as the rainbow symbolizes. Nevertheless, humanity continues to exploit nature in greedy and unnatural ways. As a result, humanity brings about terrible environmental disasters that primarily damage itself. We may recall here such well-known cases as the environmental calamities incurred by nuclear explosions and radioactive waste, or by toxic rain and polluting oil spills. We may also think of the force-feeding of animals so that they will provide more food for us. *All this constitutes an insolent overthrow of natural order.* Indeed, it is becoming generally accepted that the disruption of the natural order has negative effects on the health and well-being of human beings, such as the contemporary plagues of humanity: anxiety, heart disease, cancer, chronic fatigue syndrome, and a multitude of other diseases.

All these bear witness to the fact that it is not God but humanity that causes the contemporary plagues that attack our well-being, since "man is the most disastrous of disasters," as the ancient tragedy puts it. *Thus, if we want to improve the conditions of the material and psychological life of humanity, we are obliged to recognize and respect the natural order and to preserve its harmony and balance; we must avoid causing disarray in the natural order or provoking the destructive powers that are released when ecological harmony is audaciously disrupted.* Nature was created by God to serve humankind — on the condition, however, that humanity would respect the laws that pertain to it and would work in it and protect it (Gen. 2:15).

On this day, dedicated by the Mother Church to prayer for the natural environment, we supplicate the Lord to restore with His divine and almighty power the natural order, wherever human audacity has overturned it, so that humanity might not suffer the tragic consequences of unlawful violations of nature by human actions. We all share the responsibility for such tragedies, since we tolerate those immediately responsible for them and accept a portion of the fruit that results from such an abuse of nature. Consequently, we all need to ask for God's forgiveness and illumination so that we may come to understand the limit that distinguishes the use from the abuse of nature and never trespass that limit.

We wholeheartedly pray that God may reveal this to each one of us and give us the wisdom and strength no longer to transgress these natural limits.

May the grace and the rich mercy of our Lord Jesus Christ, the Creator of all things, who established all natural laws, be with you all, brothers and children in Christ. Amen.

## ENCYCLICAL LETTER, SEPTEMBER 1, 2002

*To the Pleroma of the Church: Grace and Peace*
*from the Creator of all Creation our Lord and God*
*and Savior Jesus Christ*

When the Mother Church declared September 1st each year as a day of prayer for the environment, *no one could imagine at the time (as early as 1990) just how rapidly the natural conditions of the world would deteriorate as a result of harmful human interference or how horrific the consequent damage and loss of human life would be.* Recent floods in Europe, India, and Russia, as well as those occurring during this year and previously in other parts of the earth, all bear witness to the disturbance of the climactic conditions caused by global warming. Such disasters have persuaded even the most incredulous persons that the problem is real, that the cost of repairing damages is comparable to the cost of preventing them, and that there is simply no room left for remaining silent.

The Orthodox Church is a pioneer in her love for humanity and interest in its living conditions. Therefore, on the one hand, the Church recommends that we lead virtuous lives, looking to eternal life in the heavenly world beyond. On the other hand, however, the Church also recognizes that — according to the teaching of our Lord Jesus Christ — *our virtue will not be assessed in isolation from others, but on the basis of applied solidarity with others.* This is characteristically described in the parable of the Last Judgment (see

Matthew 25). In this parable, the criterion for being saved and inheriting the eternal Kingdom is supplying food to the hungry, clothes to the naked, aid to the sick, and compassion to prisoners. Generally, the criterion is offering our fellow human beings the possibility of living on our planet under normal conditions and of coming to know God in order to enter His Kingdom.

This means that the protection of our fellow human beings from destructive floods, fires, storms, tempests, and other such disasters is our binding duty. Consequently, *our failure to assume appropriate measures for avoiding such phenomena is reckoned as an unpaid debt and constitutes a crime of negligence,* incurring a plethora of other crimes, such as the death of innocent people, the loss of homes and crops, and the destruction of cultural monuments and other property.

We pray, therefore, that God will protect us from natural disasters that we cannot avert by our own care and foresight. Yet, at the same time, it is our obligation to engage in the labor of study and the expense of securing necessary measures in order to avoid those disasters which are derived from wrongful human action.

*It is true that the great part of such measures and expenditures cannot be expected of isolated individuals because they transcend their capabilities. Often the needs transcend even the capabilities of individual states, requiring the cooperation of several states or even of the whole world.* Thus, we heartily salute the international consultations on the ecological crisis that are taking place throughout the world or will take place in the future, and pray that they may conclude their deliberations with unanimous decisions on the measures that should be taken, followed by successful and effective implementation of those measures.

Nevertheless, *what contributes most of all to the creation of this ecological crisis is the excessive waste of energy by isolated individuals.* The reduction of wasteful consumption will ease the acuteness of the problem, while the increased use of renewable sources of energy will intermittently contribute to its alleviation. *However insignificant the contribution of any individual may be in averting further catastrophe to the natural environment, we are all called and obliged as individuals to do whatever we can. Only then can we confidently pray to God that He may supply what is lacking in our effort and efficacy.*

We paternally urge everyone to come to the realization of their personal responsibility and to do all that is possible in order to avert global warming and environmental aggravation. We fervently entreat God to look favorably on the common effort of all and to prevent further imminent disasters in our natural environment, within which He ordered us to live and to fight the good fight so that we may inherit the heavenly Kingdom.

PART II

# ADDRESSES AND STATEMENTS

# 1991

The Ecumenical Patriarch Bartholomew I

# ENTHRONEMENT ADDRESS

*Delivered November 2, 1991*

### Continuity and Humility

Venerating the holy, consubstantial, life-giving, and undivided Trinity, obedient to the will of the one Lord as expressed by the Church through the unanimous canonical ballot of the holy brotherhood, and professing the holy Orthodox faith, we assume from the hands of the blessed Demetrios I, great among Patriarchs, the cross of Andrew the "first-called" in order to continue the ascent to Golgotha, the "place of a skull" (Matt. 27:33), in order to be co-crucified with our Lord and His co-crucified Church, and in order to perpetuate the light of the Resurrection.

It is only by so interpreting the canonical ballot of the most respected hierarchy of this venerable Ecumenical Throne, "being caught up in a wondrous state" by the events that surround us in these days (Luke 24:18), that have we accepted the sacred responsibilities of piloting this spiritual ship, the Church of Constantinople, which "was established out of piety and has shown forth shepherds equal to the apostles — indeed, we have unworthily come to be their successor — and which the chief and 'first-called' among the Apostles had as a foundation," as we might say with Symeon of Thessalonica.

Already, with humility, and conscious of our unworthiness, looking ahead to the insupportable cross that we will bear, we seek refuge in the mercy of the Lord and we invoke His grace in order that He might enable us to perfect His power in our infirmity (2 Cor. 12:9).

Indeed, the tremendous concerns that the Archbishop of New Rome assumes and the various temptations and adverse influences with which he must struggle demand that he be experienced in the task of piloting the great ship.

Thus, in self-emptying *(kenosis)*, we approach at this moment the burning and unconsumed bush of the Ecumenical Patriarchate — in and through which we are called to see God — in the service of the mystery of unbroken apostolicity, in the ministry *(diakonia)* and witness *(martyria)* of Orthodoxy, and to the edification *(oikodome)* of Christian unity.

## Thanksgiving and Glory

Speaking for the first time from this Holy See, we say before all else, along with our predecessor among the saints, John Chrysostom, "glory to God for all things."

Then, turning in deep respect and sincere love to the august college of hierarchs of the Ecumenical Throne, to those here and everywhere in the *oikoumene,* to those who have cast their ballot willingly, we offer wholeheartedly our thanks for the truly moving vote of confidence they have placed in our humble person. We affirm again along with Symeon, the holy shepherd of the Thessalonians: "You, therefore, brothers, have accepted me hospitably and have honored me greatly, you have displayed much love. As Paul said, 'you have accepted me as a messenger of God, as Jesus Christ.' You have given yourselves to the Lord, first, and then to me through the will of God; for this I have offered favor to God and am forever thankful."

Hence, we state from the outset that we shall follow the canonical order of our Orthodox Church and respect in particular the venerated Tradition and praxis of the Great Church of Christ. Moreover, firmly convinced by sacred experience of the indispensable value of conciliarity through which the Holy Spirit speaks to the Church, we shall walk the road of service *(diakonia)* to the Church only under her light, within her framework, and in her canonical function, in harmony with our most respected brothers and concelebrants in Christ. In saying this, by no means do we restrict our conviction and intention on this important subject to those things which concern only our Most Holy Church of Constantinople, but we extend this sacred confession and declaration also to all that which concerns the whole Orthodox Church worldwide.

On this auspicious occasion, in which before God and humanity we accept the responsibilities of this ecumenical watchtower, we would like to state that we assume our responsibilities under the protection of the constitution and the laws of the Republic of Turkey. Continuing the age-old tradition of the Patriarchs after the Fall, we shall remain a faithful and law-abiding citizen of our country, as are our spiritual children of the Church here, ministering to God and following the commandment of the Lord by offering honestly and sincerely, rendering unto Caesar what is Caesar's (Matt. 22:21). On this point, we deem it our responsible obligation to state clearly that the Ecumenical Patriarchate shall remain a purely spiritual institution, a symbol of reconciliation and an unarmed force. Exercising the principles of our holy Orthodox faith, safeguarding and conducting itself with regard to Pan-Orthodox jurisdictions, the Ecumenical Patriarchate is detached from all politics, keeping itself far from "the smoky hubris of secular authority." Besides, human power alone, as well as everything else that is human, is nothing else but vanity and delusion of power.

We express our fervent thanks to the honorable Greek government, well represented on this auspicious occasion by its head, His Excellency Constantine Mitsotakis, accompanied by his chosen colleagues. From the height of this Patriarchal Throne, we bless the pious Greek Orthodox people in whose behalf an official Parliamentary delegation is present here.

We also reiterate from this position the thanks of the Ecumenical Patriarchate and our personal thanks to His Excellency the President of the United States of America, who wished to send an official delegation of the White House to our enthronement.

## Pastoral Responsibility

Now, with all our love and affection, we would like to address our flock here with which at this moment we draw up a testament in the Lord. Without any hesitation, we state that we shall be a shepherd to this flock, ready to sacrifice our soul for our sheep. Further, we make the same promise to the entire plenitude of the Holy and Great Church of Christ, in Crete and the Dodecanese, in Epirus and Macedonia, in Thrace and the Islands, to those who abide in the so-called New Regions, in North and South America, in Australia and Europe, that we shall be vigilant in all things and in no way shall we be paternally negligent in serving them from here.

Therefore, to their Eminences, the archbishops and metropolitans, and their Graces, the bishops, those who have been entrusted directly with the shepherding of this most beloved worldwide plenitude of the Mother Church, we extend our embrace of love and peace in Christ as well as the assurance of our close and fraternal collaboration with them, both for the benefit of the flock and in the broader sacred interest of the Throne. We shall convoke gatherings of the entire venerable hierarchy of the Ecumenical Patriarchate in this See as often as possible, for a mutual exchange of information, support, and common projection.

Particularly, we address from this Ecumenical Throne the reverend and most beloved Fathers of the desert, who excel in asceticism on Mount Athos. We affirm that not even for one moment is it conceivable or possible for Mount Athos to exist, continue, and fulfill the age-old most honorable Orthodox monastic tradition without its sanctified links with the Mother Great Church. Therefore, we deem it our duty to do everything for the preservation, prosperity, flourishing, protection, and radiance of the Holy Mountain, always within the canonical order of the Orthodox Church and in the spirit of her hierarchal structure. We ask of the Fathers exactly that which we request of ourselves: the active practice of the two basic monastic virtues, namely, humility and obedience to the Church in fear of God and in faithfulness to their monastic vows. We have nothing more to add in addressing also the historic Monastery of St. John, the disciple of love, on the island of Patmos and the other monastic centers attached to this Throne, which we embrace with equal affection, esteem, and interest.

## Unity and Communion

Proceeding beyond our immediate canonical jurisdiction, we direct our thoughts to the messengers "of the Orthodox Churches which are constituted and illuminated by the one Spirit of Christ." These include: His Beatitude Parthenios, Pope and Patriarch of the great city of Alexandria; His Beatitude Ignatios, Patriarch of Antioch, the great city of God; His Beatitude Diodoros, Patriarch of the holy city of Jerusalem; His Beatitude Alexi, Patriarch of Moscow and All Russia; His Beatitude Paul, Patriarch of Belgrade; His Beatitude Theoktist, Patriarch of Bucharest; His Beatitude Maxim, Patriarch of Sofia; His Beatitude Elias, Catholicos Patriarch of All Georgia; His Beatitude Chrysostomos, Archbishop of New Justinian and All Cyprus; His Beatitude Seraphim, Archbishop of Athens and All Greece; His Beatitude Basil, Metropolitan of Warsaw; His Eminence Anastasios, Metropolitan of Androusa, holding the position of messenger to the Church of Albania; His Eminence Metropolitan Dorotheos of Prague; and His Eminence Archbishop John of Finland. All of these comprise our most beloved brothers and concelebrants at the holy altar of the one and undivided Orthodoxy. Before them, and before the entire Church under the heavens, we confess with boldness and exuberance of spirit our holy and spotless Orthodox faith, the living experience of the Body of Christ, which has extended throughout the centuries, as it emanated from divine revelation and through the Old and New Testaments, as it was transmitted to us by the Lord through the holy spirit-bearing Apostles, as it was formulated in the doctrinal definitions of the holy seven Ecumenical Synods by our God-bearing Fathers, articulated and interpreted by them and the ecclesiastical authors recognized by the Church. In short, we confess unreservedly the faith of the one, holy, catholic, and apostolic Church.

United in this common faith, in the common chalice, and in love, which activates faith, we extend our hand of communion to our venerable colleagues, the Primates, and we promise that, in collective responsibility with them, we shall witness in the midst of a divided world, desiring unity and reconciliation as perhaps never before in history.

## The Ecumenical Witness of Orthodoxy

This witness of Orthodoxy is much more necessary and imperative today, because divine providence has reserved us to behold the rapid and truly world-shattering evolutions and changes in the life of the peoples of the world. These evolutions and changes bring to the contemporary world the hope of a better future, a future of peace, freedom, and respect of human dignity. These rapid transformations have occurred — and are still occurring — mostly in countries and among peoples that are traditionally Orthodox, and therefore it is predominantly the Orthodox Churches that are more influenced by them. It is therefore natural, particularly for the Orthodox Churches, to be called to vigilance, collaboration, and service, so that the results of these developments might indeed be beneficial to humanity, which has suffered greatly in the twentieth century.

Orthodoxy has much, much more to offer the contemporary world. In Orthodoxy, one can find not only the correct faith in the true God but also the correct perception of humankind as the image of God, of the world, and of creation.

We extend the embrace of peace and love to the venerable Primates of the Armenian, Coptic, Ethiopian, and Syrian — both in Damascus and in Malabar — Churches. Their closeness to us in the Orthodox faith leads us today to the active quest, possibly with early results, for the common confession of faith and expression in the common chalice.

From this sacred courtyard we also greet His Holiness the Pope of Elder Rome, John Paul II, with whom we are in a communion of love. We assure him that a very serious concern for us will be the realization of the sacred vision of our late predecessors, Athenagoras and Demetrios, in order that the way of the Lord may be fulfilled on earth for His Holy Church in the reunion of all those who believe in Him through the dialogue of truth. We shall do everything in our power to move in this direction, with fear of God, sincerity, honesty, and prudence. We are convinced that our brother in the West will exhaust all the many possibilities at his disposal in order to cooperate with us in this sacred and holy objective.

Out of a sense of deep esteem in the Lord, we embrace the venerable Primate of the Church of England, the Archbishop of Canterbury George

Carey, and the entire Anglican Communion. Manifesting our intention to continue with faithfulness the long tradition of fraternal relations with the Anglican Church, we express our desire to promote our theological dialogue until we achieve the unity of faith.

In the same spirit, we greet and embrace the Old Catholic Church throughout the world in the person of its venerable Primate, Archbishop Anthony of Utrecht, expressing the sincere wish that the dialogue with his Church may lead us to the glory of Christ.

With feelings of peace and love, we also embrace in Christ all of the other Christian Churches and Confessions, the Lutheran and the Reformed with whom we are in theological dialogue, the Methodists with whom we are in the preparatory stages of dialogue, and every Christian community throughout the world, as many as believe and preach, according to the Scriptures, the crucified Christ and bear the good spirit, that they may partake of the common banquet of the faith in the unity of the apostolic and patristic tradition.

From this sacred See, we further extend a very special greeting in Christ to the World Council of Churches, to the president of the Central Committee who is presently among us, to the General Secretary, its inestimable staff, and to all member Churches. We have been fortunate, over many years and in diverse capacities, to cooperate and struggle along with the Christians of that Council, and to share each other's anxieties in the quest for and the edification of Christian unity as well as for the expression of a Christian position and witness on contemporary problems of humankind. We recognize the Council as an important expression of the ecumenical movement and the schematic function of the ecumenical spirit. The Ecumenical Patriarchate, being one of the founding members of this Council, will not diminish its concern for the good and proper orientation of the Council so that there may not be any departure from its original and principal mission, namely the service of Christian unity. This is the position of all Churches in the East before the World Council of Churches, as our common action on the issues both in Canberra (Australia) and Chambésy (Geneva) has proven. We also greet here among us the honorable Secretary General of the Council of European Churches, of which the Ecumenical Patriarchate is a member; through him, we extend our greeting in Christ to all its member Churches.

Moreover, we shall not be idle in promoting good relations with the major non-Christian religions with the aim of cooperating on the practical level for the safeguard and preservation of the great spiritual and moral values of true civilization and for the rejection of every force that is negative and catastrophic for human personhood.

If necessary, we shall not refuse to *dialogue* also with those who ignore, reject, and even insult God. Rather, we shall transmit to them — indeed, especially to them — the witness of the love of Christ, who left the ninety-nine sheep in search of the one. For Christ was even crucified for this one sheep (Matt. 18:12).

The Great Church of Christ, called from above and from its very beginnings to be a Church of evangelization, cannot deny herself in this regard. She cannot but evangelize and be continually re-evangelized. "And woe to me if I do not proclaim the gospel" (1 Cor. 9:16).

## Youth and Education

We extend our special paternal greetings and our heartfelt Patriarchal blessing to the youth, who constitute not only our future but also our dynamic present, since there is no future without the present. From the Mother Church, we express her and our boundless and sincere empathy with regard to the problems that face contemporary youth throughout the world, considering also these problems to be our own.

We shall by no means neglect the importance of theological studies during the period of our humble Patriarchal tenure. Not only is this the tradition of our Church, but it is also our personal conviction. We shall pursue the promotion of theological studies in order that we might reach an efficacious interpretation of Orthodox tradition in our contemporary era. The Ecumenical Patriarchate must acquire its own means of promoting and proclaiming Orthodox theology. Within this framework, we shall pursue the acquisition of permission from our state authorities for the reopening of our "alma mater," the Theological School of Halki, which was obliged to discontinue operation twenty years ago. Further, the publication of an official ecclesiastical theological periodical of the Patriarchate, as an expounder of its theological thought and unbroken traditions, will constitute a major concern and primary interest of ours.

## Theological Vision and Commitment

Moreover, it is our intent:

- as the successor to the thrones and struggles of our holy predecessors, the Patriarchs of Constantinople, to honor their memory through the celebration of the Divine Liturgy in the venerable Patriarchal Church, beginning with Patriarch Paul the Confessor this coming Wednesday, the 6th of November;

- to reinforce the observance of the special liturgical practice of the Great Church; the promotion of liturgical life, in following the *Typikon* of our Church, will be an object of special concern for us, because this is the center of our Christian existence and life;
- to publish annually a calendar of the Ecumenical Patriarchate;
- to reinforce and make good use of the Patriarchal Institute of Patristic Studies in Thessaloniki, the Orthodox Center of the Ecumenical Patriarchate in Chambésy, the Patriarchal Monastery of St. Anastasia the Pharmakolytria in Chalkidiki, and the Orthodox Academy of Crete;
- to sanctify during the coming Holy Week a new quantity of Holy Chrism, due to the diminishing supply contained in the Myrophylakion of the Patriarchate;
- to reinforce and modernize the support services of the Patriarchate in order that the workload might be less tiring and more productive; the personal piety and ancestral love of the great Angelopoulos family, headed by the honorable Archon Great Logothetis Mr. Panayiotis Angelopoulos, has donated to us "a venerable mansion of Orthodoxy," the new Patriarchal House, functional and beautiful, in which the ministry of the Great Church will continue with even greater results, and from which her voice will proceed full of affection and consolation toward her children throughout the world. To our Great Benefactor and to his beloved family, we express, on this auspicious occasion, the satisfaction and praise of the Church and our people.

Beloved brothers, Fathers, and children in the Lord, "Christ, the true Patriarch of the entire *oikoumene,* to whom all authority has been given in heaven and on earth," according to *The Rudder,* calls the Patriarchs in due time and sends them out as instruments of His eternal ways, as He did with the Patriarchs of the Old Testament. Thus, a Patriarch, according to the imperial definition, "is the living and animate icon of Christ, defining truth through his deeds and words. Paramount for the Patriarch is the salvation of the souls of those entrusted to him, that they may, on the one hand, live in Christ and, on the other, be crucified to the world. Characteristic of the Patriarch is that he be a teacher so that he may calmly and indiscriminately be ranked as one among all, the mighty and the humble alike." If these things concern every Patriarch, what can we say about the Patriarch of this city, which Symeon of Thessalonica characterizes as the founding city of the faith of Christ, the acropolis of Orthodoxy, the city of cities, with its Throne as a most sacred and divine throne of the holy priesthood?

This is the reason for which we entreat, beseech, and supplicate the prayers of all of you, who have readily come together on this joyous occasion, so that we may be deemed worthy by God, from this moment of our entry into the Holy of Holies in order to be totally consecrated to the Lord, to His altar, to His service, and to the service of humanity, to the cross, and to the Church.

## A Church of Martyrs and Saints

Pray for us, all of you, who have come "from the West and the North, by sea and from the East" in order to install us upon this sacred *cathedra* of the Apostle Stachys, as yet another in the long line of his successors. Pray that, faithfully and favorably unto God, we may serve the Lord, this most holy Church, and Orthodoxy under heaven. Pray that we may sustain our people and maintain the privileges and the rights of this most venerable Throne, which "we sign with great pleasure," as our predecessor to the Throne of Chalcedon, Eleftherios, affirmed at the Fourth Ecumenical Synod. Pray that we may be at all times an instrument of God's will in the service of all humanity. Pray that our Patriarchal tenure may be unharmed, bountiful, hopeful, unhindered, according to the names and through the intercessions of the Persian martyrs, whom the Church commemorates today. Pray that the Lord may sustain the Church, strengthen its faith, and bring peace to the world.

It is our firm hope that, from the heavenly chambers, the prayer of our spiritual father, Metropolitan Meliton of Chalcedon of blessed memory, who offered numerous precious services to the Mother Church, will accompany and sustain us, as will the prayer of our immediate predecessor, the most gentle Patriarch Demetrios of blessed memory, who embodied the extreme humility of Christ, a humility that this Church "of the poor of Christ" expresses. We are, finally, assured of the prayer of our respected and beloved parents, whom the benevolent God deigned worthy of witnessing this day.

Again, and many times over, "glory to God for all things."

"God is love." (1 John 4:16)

# ECOLOGICAL RESPONSIBILITY

*Delivered to the Inter-Orthodox Conference,*
*Academy of Crete, November 5, 1991*

It is with much joy and deep satisfaction that we greet the inauguration of this Inter-Orthodox Conference on the protection of the natural environment. The convocation of this conference was a particular desire and hope of our late predecessor, Patriarch Demetrios of blessed memory, who convened it on the decision of the Holy and Sacred Synod, by means of official Patriarchal letters inviting their Beatitudes the leaders of the Orthodox Churches to send representatives. The gathering of such representatives at the Orthodox Academy of Crete for this purpose surely already fills the blessed soul of the late Patriarch with joy. However, it also moves us to offer praise to the Lord and express our warmest thanks to all of you, who have gathered from near and far either as delegates of the Most Holy Orthodox Churches or else as observers from other Churches and confessions and international organizations. We greatly appreciate your favorable response to this initiative of the Ecumenical Patriarchate.

The importance of this conference hardly needs to be stressed. In his message of September 1st, 1989, the late Patriarch Demetrios expressed the deep anxiety of the whole of the Orthodox world and of every responsible thinking person concerning the environmental disaster so rapidly overtaking us, for which our thoughtless abuse of God's material creation is entirely to blame. Already "creation has been groaning in travail together," in the expression of the Apostle Paul (Rom. 8:22), under the boot of human greed. *The responsibility of spiritual and political leaders, as well as of all people in general, is enormous. Orthodoxy, too, must give her testimony.* This conference is invited to contribute in this respect.

We are present in spirit in your deliberations. Furthermore, we bestow on these deliberations our Paternal blessing, praying from our heart that the Holy Spirit will guide your work to full success so that through this means the holy name of the Triune God may be glorified, the bonds uniting the Holy Orthodox Church may be tied more firmly, and the salvation of humanity and the whole of creation may also be furthered.

May the grace and infinite mercy of the Maker of every creature be with you all.

# 1992

View of the island of Patmos with the Monastery of St. John the Theologian

# A COMMON OBLIGATION

*Delivered during the official visit of HRH Prince Philip,*
*Duke of Edinburgh, at the Phanar, May 31, 1992*

It is with great joy and profound esteem that the Ecumenical Patriarchate, in our humble person and on behalf of the Holy Synod, welcomes Your Royal Highness here today to this sacred Center of Orthodoxy. Your visit brings special honor to our Church here as well as to the entire Orthodox Church. We thank you for the effort that you so kindly incurred in order to come here and for willingly responding to the invitation of our predecessor, Patriarch Demetrios of blessed memory, which we very happily renewed.

The bonds between Your Royal Highness and the Orthodox Church are old and deep. Deep and close, as well, are the bonds that for a long time have bound the Orthodox Church, and particularly the Ecumenical Patriarchate, with the Church of England, whose head is Her Majesty Queen Elizabeth II. Your presence here further strengthens these bonds, promoting unity among peoples and among human beings, *a unity of which the contemporary world is in much need.*

### A Unique Witness

We are particularly pleased by the fact that Your Royal Highness is visiting this sacred center after so short a time since the assembly of the Inter-Orthodox Committee was convened on the island of Crete at the Orthodox Academy in order to study the issue of the protection of the natural environment. All of the Orthodox Churches, particularly the Ecumenical Patriarchate, were moved by the fact that Your Royal Highness deemed fit to honor this conference with your participation and to inaugurate its sessions with your inspired address, which was appreciated most deeply by the participants at the conference as it indeed added inestimable meaning to its success. Your visit here offers us the opportunity to express our gratitude for Your Royal Highness's contribution to so delicate and sensitive an initiative as that taken by the Ecumenical Patriarchate.

The sensitivity manifested by Your Royal Highness toward the protection of the natural environment is well known and deeply appreciated by all. As president of the World Wide Fund for Nature International (WWF), you have made an inestimable contribution toward the preservation of nature. This contribution on your part is especially moving to our Church, which considers the preservation of God's creation to be a part of her sacred duty. As you have been made aware from the encyclical message of our predecessor Patriarch Demetrios of blessed memory (dated September 1st, 1989), our Church has designated the first day of September of each year as a day of prayer for the natural environment. It is our hope and prayer that this proposal by the Ecumenical Patriarchate, which has already been accepted by the Primates of all the other Orthodox Churches during their recent assembly, which took place here on the Sunday of Orthodoxy, might be adopted, if possible, by all Christians in general. This would contribute greatly to the establishment, by all believers in Christ, of *a common and unique position* on so critical an issue as the protection of God's material creation.

During Your Royal Highness's stay here, you will have the opportunity to visit, among other points of interest rich in our country's history and culture, the beautiful island of Halki and its Monastery of the Holy Trinity. Our theological school, which we sincerely hope will reopen, functioned there up until some years ago. We look forward with great joy to your visit there, because those participating in the special seminar will have an opportunity to welcome you and to hear you on the issue of the protection of the natural environment. We thank you for this visit.

# THE POWER OF JOINT PRAYER AND ACTION

*Greeting during the symposium at*
*Holy Trinity Monastery, Halki, June 1, 1992*

As the canonical bishop of this sacred monastery, we welcome all of you with great joy and extend to each of you our paternal blessing, invoking the bountiful grace of the Lord upon the work of your gathering here. Prince Philip of Edinburgh, Your Royal Highness's presence among us these days, and especially during this seminar, is a great honor for our Church. Yet, it also offers us the precious opportunity to benefit spiritually from your internationally recognized and deeply appreciated experience and contribution through the efforts that you have made in the area of the protection of the natural environment. Indeed, Your Highness, few have contributed to this vital area as you have. As a church leader, it is our duty to recognize and pay tribute to this contribution by expressing here our own thanks as well as the gratitude of our Church.

The Orthodox Church has many reasons to consider the issue of the protection of the natural environment as exceptionally serious and urgent. Our late predecessor Patriarch Demetrios had earlier stressed the urgency of this whole matter in his encyclical message of September 1st, 1989. Since that time, our brother Primates of the holy Orthodox Churches, during their recent Synaxis at the Phanar, officially expressed their full agreement with the position of the Ecumenical Patriarchate. They proclaimed to all that the entire Orthodox Church has adopted the initiative of the Ecumenical Patriarchate in establishing September 1st of each year as a day of prayer for the protection of God's creation. As we have already said in welcoming you at the Patriarchate, Your Highness, it is our hope that the other Christian Churches will also wish to adopt this initiative of the Ecumenical Patriarchate. In this way, the first day of September of each year may be established by all believers in Christ as an occasion of prayer for the protection of the natural environment.

### Theological and Pastoral Testimony

More specifically, so far as our Most Holy Orthodox Church is concerned, the reasons for our very intense concern for the protection of the natural environment are very deeply felt. This was demonstrated during the Inter-Orthodox Conference convened, at the initiative of our Throne, last November on the island of Crete, which Your Royal Highness also honored with your personal presence and active participation. These reasons, then, for our concern may be distinguished into two basic categories: there are *theological reasons,* reasons of faith; and there are also *pastoral reasons,* reasons of sensitivity toward the world, and the mission and service of the Church in this world.

As to the first category, namely the theological reasons, it is known that the Fathers of the Church always perceived salvation in Christ as relating not only to humanity, but through the human person also extending to all of creation. Our Lord Jesus Christ is the "recapitulation" of all of creation, according to the well-known saying of St. Irenaeus, Bishop of Lyons in the second century. St. Maximus the Confessor, the great seventh-century theologian and Father of the Orthodox Church, was so insistent upon the importance of material creation in the whole divine plan of salvation that he saw the human person as a microcosm and considered salvation in Christ as a "cosmic liturgy" within which all of material creation participates. Moreover, it is indicative of the faith of the Orthodox Church that, at the very epicenter of her life lies the divine Eucharist. This Eucharist is nothing else than a "liturgy," namely a communal act of the people of God, wherein the faithful offer the gifts of creation, the bread and the wine, in order that these may be changed into the Body and Blood of Christ and be returned in thanksgiving to the Creator. Orthodox Christians firmly believe not only that God created the material world but that, through humans, the created world also has, as its destiny, participation in the glory and eternal life of Christ.

Consequently, the final purpose of creation is not its use or abuse for humankind's individual pleasure, but something far more sublime and sacred. It is from these points, then, that the pastoral reasons for the Church's concern for the natural environment emanate. For us Orthodox, every destruction of the natural environment caused by humanity constitutes an offence against the Creator Himself and arouses a sense of sorrow. In relation to the degree to which people are responsible for their actions, *metanoia* — a radical change of course — is demanded of us all. For this reason, each human act that contributes to the destruction of the natural environment must be regarded as a very serious sin. We are talking here about a renewed ethos that must be taught to our faithful. Our faithful must become sensitized to the gravity of this sin and to the need to espouse a corresponding ethos. People must cease regarding themselves as *proprietors of nature* and understand their mission as *priests of creation* who have as their duty the *anaphora* or offering up of the material world to the Creator. In this new ethos, the liturgical and the ascetic tradition of the Church can be of assistance to its faithful.

# SOMETHING IS STIRRING IN OUR CHURCH

*Address at the opening session of the meeting
of Orthodox Primates, the Phanar, March 13, 1992*

With gratitude we offer glory above all to the holy God of our Fathers for having deemed us worthy of manifesting, through this fraternal Synaxis, "the unity of the Spirit in the bond of peace" (Eph. 4:3) and of witnessing to our world the unity, peace, and love that bind us in Christ.

We express our sincere thanks to each one of you, my brothers, for the effort you have undertaken in order to come to this city, rich in history and significance, so that we may accomplish the gathering of the Primates of the local holy Orthodox Autocephalous and Autonomous Churches. Many of you have suggested and proposed such a Synaxis both to my predecessor, the late Patriarch Demetrios, and to us in the recent past.

These suggestions, together with the invitation on my part, as well as the response by all the brethren who were able to accept it, are manifestations of our conviction that *something extraordinary is happening today in the world and in our Church, which lives and moves in the world without belonging to this world* (John 17:16). All of this increases our responsibility as shepherds of the people of God and as, by God's grace, Primates of our local Churches. It imposes even greater vigilance, action, and coordination of our resources, requiring a manifestation, at all cost, of unity, concord, and unanimity to the outside world during this critical and historic moment, in spite of any possible internal difference of opinion, so typical of every family.

## The Power of Tradition

At this moment, the world expects the salvific word of Orthodoxy. The hour has come for Orthodoxy, out of a sense of duty and as a result of her capabilities, to offer that word to the contemporary world. Guided by the holy Scriptures and by sacred Tradition, *we are blessed in the Orthodox Church to treasure the authentic teaching, not only about the Triune God, but also about humanity created in the image of God and about irrational creation.*

Together with the apostles, the martyrs, the Fathers, and the saints from every region and from each era, we confess the apostolic faith that we celebrate particularly when we stand around the Holy Altar offering the divine Eucharist, as we shall do together, with God's help, during the great feast of Orthodoxy. All of us together, as a single body nourished by the Holy Spirit, glorify God the Father of our Lord Jesus Christ in various tongues and in different places "from the rising of the sun to its setting" (Ps. 113:3).

We honor our brothers in the faith who remained loyal to our Lord and Savior during periods of difficulty and even persecution, particularly during recent years. We have been encouraged by their witness. We have been strengthened by their prayers. In troublesome times, God "has not left himself without a witness" (Acts 14:17). May their memory be eternal!

Now, when the clouds and storms have passed, we are called as Primates and as Orthodox Churches to offer our irenic witness to those near and far. Again, our witness will not be easy. Many forces today are working against us in order to reject the reality of God and diminish the dignity of the human person. However, we completely place our trust in the Lord God. We know that His yoke is easy and His burden is light (Matt. 11:30).

Beloved brothers, this present holy Synaxis of ours invites us, at the commencement of Holy and Great Lent, in fear of God, to recall our responsibilities as shepherds of Orthodoxy before peoples and nations for which Orthodoxy constitutes the only hope. Once again, we commend ourselves and each other, our whole life and ministry, and our fellow Christians and Churches to Christ our God. He calls each of us to be the "light of the world" (Matt. 5:14) and the "salt of the earth" (Matt. 5:13), and He exhorts us: "Let your light shine before others, so that they may see your good works and give glory to your Father in heaven" (Matt. 5:16).

## A Critical Presence

If this is true in heaven, and if it is true from the time that the Church began, it is even more valid today, since the Lord gave many of us new opportunities to fulfill His commandment to preach the gospel to all of creation. In many parts of the world, at this very moment, great social and political changes are taking place, and we recognize the deep yearning in the hearts of many people for Christ and His Church. In these times, we believe that the Lord is calling us not only to be vigilant, so as to maintain our faith, but also to have the courage to declare this faith everywhere, that the world may in the end believe (John 17:21) and be saved. *Our times demand prophecy.*

Holy brothers in Christ, our deliberations here have been carefully and meticulously prepared by our plenipotentiary representatives who gathered together at our Patriarchal Metochion in Ormylia, Chalkidiki. To them we express our thanks and pleasure.

One of the topics with which we will concern ourselves here is that of our relations with Christians outside of Orthodoxy in conjunction with the events taking place in the countries behind the former "Iron Curtain." Even as this topic is included on the agenda of our fraternal Synaxis, there also appears to be great interest in this by the non-Orthodox.

Certainly, our communication and our dialogue with our brothers and sisters outside of the Orthodox Church imply neither the acceptance of their doctrinal positions nor the depreciation of the historical teachings of our Orthodox faith. *We humbly consider that dialogues are beneficial in our search for ways to overcome differences and in our effort to enlighten others concerning our positions — without, however, sacrificing anything essential to our faith.* Our Orthodox Church, containing the fullness of truth, also has a corresponding responsibility to contribute to the healing of divisions among Christians.

We recognize the responsibility of our Church, "which, according to the Apostle, has no spot or wrinkle through deviation from the ancient forms, never having accepted or added or subtracted any kind of doctrinal innovation." Nevertheless, sometimes influenced by assaults against the Church, we begin to be shaken in the fulfillment of our responsibility to offer unceasing witness to our faith.

## Articulating the Faith

What can we say about the ecological problem, about missionary activity, about schisms existing in the body of the Church, about the position of Orthodoxy within a united Europe, and about the other topics included in the memoranda that you, my brother Primates, have coauthored and signed? All these are such timely and burning issues, which rightly attract our attention and assume priority among many others, which cannot for the moment be included in the agenda of our sessions here.

On those subjects which have been selected, a lengthy and comprehensive discussion took place in the Inter-Orthodox Preparatory Committee of our Synaxis, which has also prepared, on behalf of us all, the text presented to us. We believe that this text adequately expresses our common positions on the topics to which we have referred, so that it may become the basis for the text of our message to our fellow Christians and to the world, which will be proclaimed in the context of our fraternal liturgical concelebration.

Therefore, let us love one another, so that with one mind we may confess the faith of the apostles, the faith of the Fathers, the faith of the Orthodox, the faith that sustained the universe.

# MESSAGE OF THE PRIMATES

*Message signed and declared*
*in Constantinople, March 15, 1992*[1]

*In the name of the Father and of the Son and of the Holy Spirit. Amen.*

1. Gathered together in the Holy Spirit in consultation at the Phanar, today, the 15th day of March 1992, on the Sunday of Orthodoxy, by the initiative and invitation and under the presidency of the First among us, the Ecumenical Patriarch Bartholomew, after the expressed will as well of other brother Primates, we, by the mercy and grace of God, the Primates of the local Most Holy Patriarchates and Autocephalous and Autonomous Orthodox Churches:

> Bartholomew, Archbishop of Constantinople, New Rome, and Ecumenical Patriarch
> Parthenios, Pope and Patriarch of Alexandria and All Africa
> Ignatius, Patriarch of Antioch and All the East
> Diodoros, Patriarch of the Holy City of Jerusalem and All Palestine
> Alexiy, Patriarch of Moscow and All Russia
> Paul, Patriarch of Belgrade and All Serbia
> Teoctist, Patriarch of Bucharest and All Romania
> Maxim, Patriarch of Sofia and All Bulgaria
> Elias, Archbishop of Metschetis and Tiflis and Catholicos, Patriarch of All Georgia (represented by the Ecumenical Patriarch)
> Chrysostomos, Archbishop of Neas Justinianis and All Cyprus (represented by the Patriarch of Alexandria)
> Seraphim, Archbishop of Athens and All Greece
> Wasyli, Metropolitan of Warsaw and All Poland
> Dorothej, Metropolitan of Prague and All Czechoslovakia
> John, Archbishop of Karelia and All Finland

have conferred in brotherly love on matters preoccupying our One, Holy, Catholic and Apostolic Orthodox Church and have concelebrated the Holy

---

1. The influence of Patriarch Bartholomew in articulating and advancing concern for the environment is apparent in this document.

Eucharist in the Patriarchal Church of the Ecumenical Patriarchate on this Sunday which for centuries has been dedicated to Orthodoxy. On this occasion, we wish to declare the following:

We offer from the depths of our hearts praise in doxology to the Triune God, who deigned us to see one another face to face, to exchange the kiss of peace and love, to partake of the Cup of Life, and to enjoy the divine gift of Pan-Orthodox unity. Conscious of the responsibility that the Lord's providence has placed upon our shoulders as shepherds of the Church and spiritual leaders, in humility and love we extend to everyone of good will, and especially to our brother bishops and the whole pious body of the Orthodox Church, God's blessing, a kiss of peace, and a "word of exhortation" (Heb. 13:22).

My brethren, rejoice in the Lord. (Phil. 3:1)

Be strong in the Lord and in the strength of his might. (Eph. 6:10)

2. The Most Holy Orthodox Church throughout the *oikoumene,* sojourning in the world and being inevitably affected by the changes taking place in it, finds herself today confronted with particularly severe and urgent problems that she desires to face as one body, adhering to St. Paul, who said: "if one member suffers, all suffer together" (1 Cor. 12:26). Moreover, looking into the future of humankind and that of the whole of God's creation, in light of our entrance into the third millennium A.D. of history, at a time of rapid spiritual and social changes, fulfilling her sacred duty, the Church wishes to bear her own witness, giving account for the hope that is in us (1 Pet. 3:15) in humility, love, and boldness.

The twentieth century can be considered the century of great achievements in the field of knowledge concerning the universe and the attempt to subject creation to human will. During this century, the strength as well as the weakness of the human being have surfaced. After such achievements, no one doubts any longer that the domination of humanity over its environment does not necessarily lead to happiness and the fullness of life. Thus, humanity must have learned that, apart from God, scientific and technological progress becomes an instrument of destruction of nature as well as of social life. This is particularly evident after the collapse of the communist system.

Alongside this collapse we must recognize *the failure of all anthropocentric ideologies* that have created in people of this century a spiritual void and an existential insecurity and have led many people to seek salvation in new religious and para-religious movements, sects, or nearly idolatrous attachments to the material values of this world. Every such kind of proselytism practiced today is a manifestation rather than a solution of the existing deep crisis of the contemporary world. The youth of our times have the right to learn that the gospel of Christ and the Orthodox faith offer love instead of hatred, cooperation instead of confrontation, and communion instead of division among human beings and among nations.

3. All of these things call the Orthodox to a deeper spiritual as well as canonical unity. Unfortunately, schismatic groups competing with the canonical structure of the Orthodox Church often threaten this unity. Having conferred also on this matter, we realized the need for all the local Most Holy Orthodox Churches, being in full solidarity with one another, to condemn these schismatic groups and abstain from any kind of communion with them wherever they may be "until they return." In this way, the body of the Orthodox Church might not appear divided on this subject, since "not even the blood of martyrdom can erase the sin of schism," and "to tear the Church asunder is no less an evil than to fall into heresy" (St. John Chrysostom).

4. In this same spirit of concern for the unity of all those who believe in Christ, we have participated in the *ecumenical movement* of our times. This participation was based on the conviction that the Orthodox must contribute to the restoration of unity with all their strength, bearing witness to the one undivided Church of the apostles, the Fathers, and the Ecumenical Councils. It was our expectation that during a period of great difficulties the Orthodox Church would have had the right to count on the solidarity — which has constantly been declared as the cardinal ideal of this movement — of all those who believe in Christ.

With great affliction and anguish of heart, we realize that certain circles inside the Roman Catholic Church proceed with activities absolutely contrary to the spirit of the dialogue of love and truth. We have sincerely participated in the ecumenical meetings and bilateral theological dialogues. After the collapse of the atheistic communist regime by which many of these Orthodox Churches were tremendously persecuted and tormented, we had expected brotherly support, or at least understanding of the difficult situation created after fifty and even seventy years of pitiless persecutions. This situation in many respects is tragic from the point of view of the economic and pastoral resources of the Orthodox Churches concerned.

Instead, to the detriment of the desired journey toward Christian unity, the traditional Orthodox countries have been considered "missionary territories," and thus missionary networks are set up in them and proselytism is practiced with methods that have been condemned and rejected for decades by all Christians. In particular, we make mention and condemn the activity of the Uniates under the Church of Rome in the Ukraine, Romania, East Slovakia, the Middle East, and elsewhere against our Church. This has created a situation incompatible with the spirit of the dialogue of love and truth, which was initiated and promoted by the late Pope John XXIII and the late Ecumenical Patriarch Athenagoras I. It has inflicted a most severe wound on this dialogue that will be difficult to heal. In fact, this dialogue has already been restricted to the discussion of the problem of Uniatism until agreement is reached on this matter.

The same can be said with regard to certain Protestant fundamentalists, who are eager to "preach" in Orthodox countries that were under communist regime. The consideration of these countries as *terra missionis* is unacceptable, since in these countries the gospel has already been preached for many centuries. It is because of their faith in Christ that the faithful of these countries often sacrificed their very lives.

In reference to this subject, we remind all that every form of proselytism — to be distinguished clearly from *evangelization and mission* — is absolutely condemned by the Orthodox. Proselytism — practiced in nations already Christian and in many cases even Orthodox, sometimes through material enticement and sometimes by various forms of violence — poisons the relations among Christians and destroys the road toward their unity. Mission, in contrast, carried out in non-Christian countries and among non-Christian peoples, constitutes a sacred duty of the Church, worthy of every assistance. Such Orthodox missionary work is carried out today in Asia and Africa and is worthy of every Pan-Orthodox and Pan-Christian support.

5. Moved by the spirit of reconciliation, the Orthodox Church has participated actively for many decades in the effort toward the restoration of *Christian unity,* which constitutes the express and inviolable command of the Lord (John 17:21). The participation of the Orthodox Church as a whole in the World Council of Churches aims precisely at this. It is for this reason that she does not approve of any tendency to undermine this initial aim for the sake of other interests and expediencies. For the same reason the Orthodox strongly disapprove of certain recent developments within the ecumenical context, such as the ordination of women to the priesthood and the use of inclusive language in reference to God, which creates serious obstacles to the restoration of unity.

In the same spirit of reconciliation, we express the hope that the progress made in certain dialogues, such as the dialogue with the Oriental Orthodox (non-Chalcedonians), may lead to favorable results once the remaining obstacles have been overcome.

6. Now, at the end of the second millennium A.D., turning our thoughts

more specifically to the general problems of the contemporary world and sharing in the hope but also in the anxieties of humankind, we observe the following:

The rapid progress of technology and the sciences, which provide the instruments for improving the quality of life and relief of pain, misfortune, and illnesses, has unfortunately not always been accompanied by analogous spiritual and ethical foundations. As a result, the aforementioned progress is not without serious dangers.

Thus, in human social life, the fact that only a section of humanity accumulates the privileges of this progress and the power proceeding from it exacerbates the misfortune of other people and creates an impetus for agitation or even war. The coexistence of this progress with *justice, love, and peace* is the only safe and sure road, so that this progress will not be transformed from a blessing into a curse in the millennium to come.

Tremendous are also the problems that come out of this progress for *humankind's survival as a free person* created in the "image and likeness" of God. The progress of genetics, although capable of making enormous contributions to combating many diseases, is also capable of transforming the human being from a free person into an object directed and controlled by those in power.

Similar are the dangers for the *survival of the natural environment.* The careless and self-indulgent use of material creation by humanity, with the help of scientific and technological progress, has already started to cause irreparable damage to the natural environment. Unable to remain passive in the face of such destruction, the Orthodox Church, through us, invites all the Orthodox to dedicate the first day of September of each year, the day of the beginning of the ecclesiastical year, to the offering of prayers and supplications for the preservation of God's creation. The Church also entreats all the Orthodox to adopt the attitude to nature found in the Eucharist and the ascetic tradition of the Church.

7. In view of such tremendous possibilities, as well as dangers, for contemporary humanity, the Orthodox Church hails every progress toward reconciliation and unity. In particular, she hails Europe's journey toward unity and reminds it of the fact that within it live a large number of Orthodox, a number that is expected to increase in the future. It should not be forgotten that the regions of Southern and Eastern Europe are inhabited by a majority of Orthodox people and that the Orthodox have contributed decisively to the cultural molding of European civilization and spirit. This fact renders our Church a significant factor in the molding of a united Europe and increases her responsibilities.

We are deeply saddened by the fratricidal confrontations between Serbs and Croats in Yugoslavia and grieve for all its victims. We believe that what is required from the ecclesiastical leaders of the Roman Catholic Church and from all of us is particular attention, pastoral responsibility, and wisdom from God, in order that the exploitation of religious sentiment for political and national causes may be avoided.

Our hearts are also sensitive toward all those peoples in other continents who struggle for their dignity, freedom, and development with justice. We pray especially for peace and reconciliation in the Middle East, where the Christian faith originated and where people of different faiths coexist.

8. This, in the love of the Lord, we proclaim on the Great and Holy Sunday of Orthodoxy, urging the pious Orthodox Christians in the *oikoumene* to be united around their canonical pastors and calling all those who believe in Christ to reconciliation and solidarity in confronting the serious dangers threatening the world in our time.

May the grace of our Lord Jesus Christ and the love of God the Father and the communion of the Holy Spirit be with you all. Amen.

## ICONS AND RELICS

*Delivered at a dinner in honor of HRH Prince Philip,*
*Duke of Edinburgh, May 31, 1992*

It is with great joy that we welcome Your Royal Highness today to this Center of the Orthodox Church. For you have taken a leading initiative internationally in a God-pleasing campaign for the salvation of our planet and for the preservation of balance in creation.

God created humanity to serve as a king of creation, not for any individualistic exploitation of it that results in destruction, but for the enjoyment of a peaceful and fruitful life in it in harmony with the other creatures, plants or animals. Nevertheless, we have recently experienced a dangerous development, arising from our senseless and often selfish use of natural resources. The environment, as it is presented to us today, appears to resemble the "beast" in the book of Revelation (Rev. 12:4), which waits to devour the newly born child of the woman. The only difference is that the beast of the environment, in a metaphorical sense, expects to devour everyone, and not just the newly born.

If we are to avoid this pressing danger, then we urgently need to restore the proper relation between humanity and the environment. This reconciliation has always been facilitated by the favorable position of nature itself toward humanity, on the one hand, and the means that humanity has at its disposal, on the other.

We often speak about *respect for the human being as the icon of God*. And this is correct. Yet we should not separate this respect from the respect that is due to the whole of the physical environment, because it is obvious that the environment and its inhabitants are in constant and mutual interaction, as we pointed out in our Christmas message.

Allow me, Your Royal Highness, to refer to an example of a contemporary ascetic on the Holy Mountain, who made the following poignant comment: "We venerate the clothing of St. Nektarios, because the Saint used to wear it. *Is it not much more fitting that we should also venerate the flowers and the plants? After all, they enshrine within themselves the energy of God.*" It is because the true monastic has the measure of life that a monk or a nun will never turn either to idolatry or to pantheism. The monastic respects the whole of creation without attributing worship to it. That belongs to God alone.

With these few thoughts we greet once again with great honor and love, and welcome around this table of love, your presence in our midst, raising a toast for good health and many years of Her Majesty, Queen Elizabeth, of Your Royal Highness, and of all the beloved members of the royal family, as well as for the well-being of your noble nation.

# *1993*

Patriarch Bartholomew with Prince Philip, Duke of Edinburgh and Chairman of
World Wide Fund for Nature International, at the 1992 Halki summer seminar

# MNEMOSYNE AND THE CHILDREN OF MEMORY

*Address at the British Museum in London, November 12, 1993*

In Greek mythology, *Mnemosyne,* or Memory, had several children: Clio, Euterpe, Thalia, Melpomene, Terpsichore, Erato, Polyhymnia, Urania, and their leader Calliope. Collectively known as the Muses, they came to be associated with the liberal arts or sciences. However, our expertise lies not so much in the liberal arts as in the spiritual arts. There is one child of Mnemosyne that is no stranger to the Church, and that is Clio, the muse of history. In the Church, Clio appears in two forms: spiritual history, the incarnation of the eternal *Logos,* the Word of God, revealed in the Bible, expounded in Holy Tradition, and immune from time; and secular history, the words of humankind, offered in books whose interpretation changes from generation to generation. The Church protects and defends our spiritual history. But the Church has somehow been marginalized and excluded from secular history — at great cost not only to Greek Orthodoxy but to the entire human family. This is what we wish to talk to you about today — not just about Mnemosyne, but also about its counterpart, Lethe, the river of oblivion.

## An Alternative Vision of History

One might be forgiven, after speaking to the average person, for thinking that the history of Christianity starts with Jesus Christ, moves on with St. Paul at Corinth and Ephesus, continues with the Bishop of Rome, and ends with the Protestant Reformation. Mnemosyne has forgotten Romiosyne! The history and life-giving legacy of Orthodox Christianity have been lost in the waters of oblivion. The reasons for this are complex. They have to do with the predominance of the West since the Renaissance. We must remember that the victor writes history; and Western historians largely believe that the Roman Empire fell in A.D. 476. They play down the fact that Constantine the Great moved the capital of the Empire to New Rome, Constantinople, in A.D. 330. How many of us realize, for example, that all seven Ecumenical Councils of undivided Christianity were held, not in Greece or Rome, but in the East, in what is now Turkey?

What really happened in 476 was that the West was overrun by barbarians and the Greco-Roman civilization that once extended throughout the

94

Empire was shattered. To give some measure of how distant we grew over the centuries, consider the unusual name Western historians gave the Eastern Roman Empire when they "rediscovered" it in the sixteenth century: Byzantium, the pagan, pre-Roman, and pre-Christian name of what was then Constantinople and is now Istanbul.

This was perhaps a logical step for these historians. For centuries after Rome fell, barbarian kings, whose claim to authority was based on force, grabbed at the glorious mantle of Rome to confer legitimacy upon themselves — so powerful did the idea of Rome remain in the popular imagination. The Renaissance was supposed to be a "rebirth" of classical civilization; and to some degree it was. Western scholars created a different name for the New Rome that had not only survived but flourished for another millennium in the East; thus was born the term "Byzantine empire." *We live in a world dominated by the West and by Western ideas. We admire those ideas and admit their power. Yet, there must be a way for us to do this without betraying our own history.* We must summon Clio to speak her truth, which is stronger than any power.

Another factor is at work here. Besides writing history, the West has also long dictated preferences. The interest taken in the Eastern Roman Empire and its Church by Renaissance scholars may have been lopsided, even condescending, but at least we were considered a legitimate field of study. Then came the Enlightenment, which made it fashionable to look down on anything "eastern" or "spiritual." Voltaire called Byzantine history "nothing but declamations and miracles . . . a disgrace to the human mind," while Gibbon described the later Roman Empire as the "triumph of barbarism and religion." The Enlightenment set the stage for the national revolutions of the nineteenth century, and its anti-clerical tone influenced all of them.

Western civilization found it difficult to comprehend the mysticism of the East, which felt the presence of our Lord Christ, the *Theotokos,* the myriad angels and thousands of saints. We must also decry the simplification of Byzantium as "Greek." The Roman Empire was ecumenical. Whether Latin or Greek predominated in Constantinople, it was a multiethnic empire, with the Church willing to use the local language to convey the word of God. Thus were the Slavs and others converted to Orthodoxy and brought into the orbit of our Roman civilization.

And the ecumenical idea, the notion that held together the diverse Christian communities under the rubric of Rome, was reinforced under the Ottomans, whose own empire, let us remember, was also multiethnic and often tolerant. It was Mehmet II, the conqueror of Constantinople, who sought out the greatest ecclesiastical personality of the time, George Scholarios, and enthroned him as Ecumenical Patriarch Gennadios, head of the Rum Millet and spiritual leader of the entire Orthodox world.

## The Role of the Mother Church

The Mother Church was the repository of memory — our Mnemosyne, if you will — during those difficult centuries, and we who continue that tradition today are her children. But let us be clear about this: the memory preserved by the Church during the Ottoman years was not a single ethnic group, whether Greek or otherwise. The memory preserved by the Mother Church throughout the centuries was the memory of an Orthodox ecumenical civilization.

However, in the early nineteenth century, Mnemosyne smiled upon individual ethnic histories while Lethe (or forgetfulness) swallowed up ecumenical Orthodoxy. Almost two centuries later, as the chief representative of the Orthodox *oikoumene* stands here amid some of the greatest monuments of ancient Greece, we have yet to reconcile nationalism and Orthodoxy. The Mother Church believes that before this reconciliation can occur, Mnemosyne must reclaim ecumenical Orthodoxy, the wayward child that we gave up early last century. We must recover our Orthodox faith and heritage and proclaim its virtues.

At this point, we must mention the similar treatment accorded our Muslim neighbors. They, too, have seen their faith dissected and their history disfigured. For this reason, the Ecumenical Patriarchate is a sponsor of "a dialogue of loving truth" between Muslims and Orthodox Christians. We hope to put behind us what is unpleasant while putting forward the best values of humankind. We have a sacred duty, especially in light of our 540 years of coexistence in a predominantly Muslim milieu, to affirm the Christian gospel that we must love God with all our heart and love our neighbor as ourselves (Matt. 22:37-39).

As leaders, we must stand prophetically and work for brotherly and sisterly coexistence among those of different faiths, for the benefit of all. *We must set aside our differences and learn to speak "the truth in love" (Eph. 4:15), as persons created in the image of the one true God.* Entire libraries have been written about nationalism. One curious element of most nationalisms is the way they combine distant memories with new ideas. In art, this combination of old and new is called "postmodernism," and state-builders are certainly "artists" in the most literal sense of the word. The genesis of nationalism involves selective memory; and in the case of the Orthodox countries, nationalism has favored past periods of ethnic glory over the combined splendor of Orthodox civilization.

We lament this imbalance. Without the Church, we of the Orthodox tradition can never have more than a lopsided, skewed, and incomplete view of who we are. The emphasis on national or ethnic heritage has had the effect of fragmenting the family of our ecumenical civilizations — from Russians and Georgians to Albanians and Romanians. This is particularly disturbing because nationalism is a phenomenon with disastrous consequences. The holy Orthodox Church searched long for a language with which to address nationalism, amid the strife and havoc this new ideology created in the Orthodox lands of Eastern Europe for much of the nineteenth century. In 1872, the Holy Synod issued a definitive condemnation of the sin of *phyletism,* saying: "We renounce, censure, and condemn racism, namely racial discrimination, ethnic feuds, hatreds, and dissensions within the Church of Christ." Today, more than a century later, nationalism remains the bane of our ecumenical Church. It is time for us to begin to reconcile nationalism and ecumenicity. They are not mutually exclusive.

That is why the Mother Church has done everything in her power to support, morally and materially, the reemerging Orthodox Churches in Russia and throughout Eastern Europe, especially since the collapse of godless communism. Although these churches are self-governing, they are the daughters of the See of St. Andrew the Apostle. That is why we have spoken out directly against the proselytism by Roman Catholics and Protestants among Orthodox Christians in Ukraine, Slovakia, Romania, and other nations of Eastern Europe — as if these lands had never been Christianized. That is why we convened an unprecedented Pan-Orthodox Council of Synods of the heads of the world's Patriarchal and Autocephalous Orthodox Christians in March of 1992 — an unusual display of Christian solidarity and a return of the ecumenicity of centuries past. That is why we also convened an assembly of the hierarchs of the Ecumenical Patriarchate in August 1992; some eighty bishops came from throughout the world to the Phanar to discuss the status of the Great Church. And, finally, that is why the Ecumenical Throne, in cooperation with the other sister Orthodox Churches, has been preparing energetically for the convening of the Great and Holy Synod of the entire Orthodox Church — the first such gathering of bishops since the last Ecumenical Council, which took place at Nicea in 787.

## The Vision of Ecumenicity

The Ecumenical Patriarchate must play a crucial role in our return to ecumenicity, because the Patriarchate, as the first among equals, is the repository of the memory of "the one, holy, catholic, and apostolic Church." Within our walls, Mnemosyne jealously guards the candle of Orthodox Christianity from Lethe, and in that flickering flame lies the promise of redemption. As long as that candle continues to burn, there is the possibility that someday the flame will again pass outside the Patriarchal church of St. George and will cast its redeeming light throughout the *oikoumene.* That will not happen until lay members of the Orthodox Church — academics, artists, businesspersons, writers, and intellectuals of all nations and ethnic groups — also begin to reevaluate the place of their Orthodox heritage in their identity. And in this, the Orthodox *diaspora* can lead the way; for the *diaspora* lives constantly on the borderline of civilization and is forced to reconsider questions of identity all the time.

There are obvious benefits in this reevaluation for all of us; we will end up with a more balanced and more accurate view of our past and our future. But the benefits extend far beyond ourselves. If we respect our Greek Orthodox inheritance, others will likely respect it, too. We may yet rescue our inheritance, our *parakatatheke,* from the oblivion to which it seems to have been doomed in the West. And in Eastern Europe, we have everything to gain by restoring a more ecumenical view. Those countries which are just now emerging from decades of totalitarianism desperately need the help and leadership of the rest of us. They, too, are the children of the Great Church of Christ, and if we open our hearts and minds to them and include them once again in our *oikoumene,* great things will happen. Fragmentation will give way to unity, Orthodox will greet each other as brothers and sisters, and we will echo the words of the Psalm: "Behold, how good and how pleasant it is for brethren to dwell together in unity!"

## The Primacy of the Spirit

Allow us to reiterate that we do not envision the Ecumenical Patriarchate as another Vatican, nor are we trying to transform it into such. On the contrary, we have stated on numerous occasions that even if such an idea were proposed to us, we would reject it as contradictory to the ecclesiology and traditions of the Orthodox Church. *The Ecumenical Patriarchate does not wish to become a State. It wishes to remain only a Church* — a Church, however, that is free and respected by all — a religious and spiritual institution teaching, edifying, sharing philanthropic ideals, civilizing, and preaching love in every direction. The Ecumenical Patriarchate is the fullness of the church that was founded by the God of love, whose peace "surpasses all understanding" (Phil. 4:7). We "pursue what makes for peace" (Rom. 14:19). We believe that "God is love" (1 John 4:16), which is why we are not afraid, for "perfect love casts out fear" (1 John 4:18).

Indeed, our philosophy can be summarized neatly in the famous words of the Apostle Paul: "Keep alert, stand firm in your faith, be courageous, be strong. Let all that you do be done in love" (1 Cor. 16:13-14). This is *our* faith; this is *our* hope; and this is *our* prayer.

# 1994

Holy Trinity Monastery in Halki, venue of the Halki
summer seminars and the Halki Ecological Institute

# UNITY AND COMMONALITY

*Address to the Plenary of the European Parliament
in Strasbourg, France, April 19, 1994*

We have come among you today with much joy and deep satisfaction, on these official premises of the European Parliament, which in people's minds vividly represents the center of renewed historical efforts to achieve European unification.

We wholeheartedly thank you for the invitation that you extended to us. We thank you, Your Excellency Egon Klepsch, President of the European Parliament, for taking the initiative to invite us. We thank all of you, ladies and gentlemen, members of Parliament, for being present here today. You have the great and historic mission of organizing the unity of the peoples of Europe in peace, justice, and democracy, which means in solidarity and in love. This is a mission that transcends individual limitations and has the power of a communal effort for a better world. We wholeheartedly pray that this mission will continue.

The unification of Europe, to which you have devoted your efforts as representatives of the will of your peoples, is a familiar task to us. We minister to a tradition of seventeen centuries of caring and struggling for the salvation and unity of European civilization. We, the elder Patriarchate of the New Rome–Constantinople, together with the other European axis, Old Rome, have not been able to make this unity visible. We are most deeply grieved by this fact. We continue, however, to pursue in common our witness that a political unity separated from civilization — that is, without the fundamental meaning of human relationships — cannot lead to the achievement of a united Europe. The unity pursued by the peoples of Europe can be realized only as *a unity in the sharing of a common meaning of life,* as a common goal of our human relationships.

It is surprising to observe how the realistic and most deeply democratic organization of the Orthodox Christian Church, with its rather large degree of administrative autonomy and the local independence of its Episcopates, Patriarchates, and Autocephalous Churches, allows them all simultaneously to enjoy a eucharistic unity in faith. Such a model was in fact recently legislated by the European Union under the name of this principle of commonality as the most advantageous method for defining its authority.

In spite of the drastic world changes throughout the history of Europe,

Old and New Rome continue to remain axes of reference and of unity for European civilization. We are referring here to the fundamental meaning of unity, not to some ideological alienation of this concept into religious political doctrines, which often leads to the absolutization of nationalistic and racial particularities.

It is our belief that European unification will not be possible if such absolutes dominate. We are aware that, at this very moment, many of you have put before us and before the Orthodox Catholic Church, which we serve in her senior-ranking diocese, the tragic reality of a horrendous war in our times, in which Orthodox populations of Europe have become embroiled, and where there is fighting among neighboring Christians and people of other faiths.

The Ecumenical Patriarchate and the Orthodox Church generally respect the ethnic traditions and sensitivities of all peoples. However, we most categorically condemn every kind of fanaticism, transgression, and use of violence, regardless of where these may originate. Our persistence in urging the need for free and peaceful communication among peoples, as well as mutual respect and peaceful coexistence among nations, remains unchanged, as we also underscored in the "Bosphorus Declaration" during the Conference on Peace and Tolerance recently convened at our initiative.

## Politics and Poverty

You are the primary contributors to European unification. *It is your obligation as political leaders, especially since you are the ones exercising legal authority, to see to the protection of the weak and every kind of minority,* the safeguarding of freedom of thought and speech, as well as the freedom to move and reside where people's natural, spiritual, and social needs require. In general, it is your obligation to create the kinds of conditions that would allow for the promotion of cooperation and unity among peoples and nations. In conjunction with this, *you have an obligation to lessen or, even more, to remove the inequality of development that is evident between the wealthy "developed" world and the "undeveloped" world. Such inequality endangers the future of humanity and the natural world.*

United Europe must offer not just a plan of unified economic development or a program of collective defense. Present conditions demand a vision for a unified social strategy of peaceful and constructive cooperation for all peoples of Europe. It is a question of civilization. It is an issue of understanding interpersonal relationships. It is a matter of acceptance of one another's national traditions.

## Church and Vulnerability

*The Ecumenical Patriarchate of New Rome–Constantinople, which we humbly represent before you today, does not pretend to bring to this center of European unity political strength, economic power, or ideological claims.* This is not our mission. Permit us to note, however, that our experience through the centuries paradoxically confirms that all power, which continues to stimulate history, is "made perfect in weakness" (2 Cor. 12:9). We submit to you the experience of our recent efforts. Whenever we have made any efforts based on our power or, more properly, beyond our power, out of our concern for ecumenical unity of the Christian churches, *the fruits that we were deemed worthy of receiving were in fact the product of our frailty and not of our force.* In 1920, the Ecumenical Patriarchate, on its own initiative, issued an encyclical addressed to the entire world in order to convene a kind of league of churches, modeled after the "League of Nations," the forerunner of today's United Nations. Through this initiative, and with the cooperation of the Protestant confessions, the World Council of Churches was founded. Here, in spite of existing weaknesses, a certain mutual coexistence of traditions, inter-church aid, and the building of reciprocal respect are generated on the level of a cultivation of consciences.

Similar experiences have resulted from an equally significant initiative of the Ecumenical Patriarchate, namely the inauguration, along with other sister Orthodox Churches, of bilateral theological dialogues with the ancient Oriental Churches, as well as the Roman Catholic, the Old Catholic, the Anglican, the Lutheran, and the Reformed Churches. Perhaps the more senior members among you will remember the historic meeting of our predecessor, Patriarch Athenagoras, with Pope Paul VI, both now of blessed memory, in Jerusalem in 1964. This was the first such meeting of the Primates of Old and New Rome since the Great Schism of 1054. You may further recall the historic mutual lifting of the anathemas between these two churches in 1965 and the exchange of visits between Pope John Paul II and our immediate predecessor, the late Ecumenical Patriarch Demetrios.

We ourselves continue these efforts. Recently, we extended them by attempting an interreligious rapprochement. We convened an international inter-faith conference, under the aegis of the Ecumenical Patriarchate, on the theme "Peace and Tolerance." We are fully aware that the cultivation of a peaceful climate for coexistence and creative cooperation — both among religions and churches and among national states, races, and traditions — demands radical change. Dialogue, international conferences, communication among leaders responsible for drafting legislation, growing closer through goodwill, and abandoning the notion of irreconcilable differences: all these are positive and useful steps; yet they are not enough. The problems of the contemporary world in general, and the problems confronting Europe in particular, demand fundamental reevaluations of our cultural choices. In other words, they presuppose a new cultural model.

## The Issue of Unemployment

Two emphatic paradigms bear special witness to this need. The first is *the tragedy of unemployment,* which plagues Europe today. It is obvious that neither moral counsel nor fragmented measures of socioeconomic policies would suffice to confront the rising unemployment. Indeed, the problem of unemployment compels us to reexamine the self-evident priorities of our society, such as the absolute priority of so-called "development," which is measured solely in economic terms. We are inexorably trapped within a tyrannical need continually to increase productivity and, as a consequence, continually to create newer and larger quantities of consumer goods. Placing these two necessities — of development and of economic growth — on an equal footing imposes the constant need for greater increases in productivity, even while continually restricting the very power of production, namely the human component. Concurrently, consumer needs of this very same human component must constantly increase and expand. Thus, the economy breaks loose from the needs of society, expands without human control, and operates on a model that tries to equate abstract proportions.

Perhaps, as a result of the acute problem of unemployment, it is now time, instead of concerning ourselves with self-centered demands for our individual rights, to prioritize personal productivity within the context of human well-being. Civic leaders must answer the following questions: Who or what will inspire the European of today to give priority to human relationships? What political mandate will convince humankind willingly and joyfully to sacrifice its thirst for consumption and its limitless demand for productivity in order to rediscover the blessing of life in community?

Politics play a critical role in the radical changes in our understanding of human life. However, in people's conscience, such changes are solidified only through the persuasion of experiences conveyed through religious traditions. If the classic and renowned studies by Max Weber, Werner Sombart, and R. H. Tawney hold true in their findings, then at the foundations of contemporary European understandings of work and economics one may find a basic receptivity to Christian theology. If this finding holds true, then *a new concept of understanding work and economy will inevitably pass through some theological revision.* The various ideologies that have circumvented theology in their attempt to find some new concept of work and economy have not brought about any realistic solutions. *Behind the modern impasse of European life hides a theological position.*

## The Radical Issue of Ecology

We believe that similar conclusions may be drawn with regard to a second issue, which is equally critical and distressing in our times, namely *the ecological crisis*. All of us are aware of the nightmarish proportions of this problem as it increases day by day. Permit us to hold to our conviction that *the ecological problem of our times demands a radical reevaluation of how we see the entire world; it demands a different interpretation of matter and the world, a new attitude of humankind toward nature, and a new understanding of how we acquire and make use of our material goods.*

Within the measure of our spiritual capacity, the Orthodox Church and Orthodox theology endeavor to contribute to the necessary dialogue concerning this problem. Thus, at the initiative of the Ecumenical Patriarchate, the Orthodox have established September 1st of each year as a day of meditation and prayer in order to confront the continuing ecological destruction of our planet. Having convened an international conference in Crete, we have further inaugurated a systematic theological study of this problem.

## Being and Acting in Solidarity

*However, our efforts will be meaningless if they remain fragmented.* Therefore, taking advantage of the fact that we are standing here before you, we hasten also to declare that we are prepared to place our modest efforts at the disposal of the European Parliament for any future study and debate concerning a pan-European response to the ecological problem. Permit us to declare the same readiness in reference to the aforementioned problem of unemployment plaguing Europe.

Mr. President, ladies and gentlemen, members of the European Parliament, your gracious invitation has permitted us to share this limited but valuable time in order to communicate personally with you. We feel the overwhelming burden of our responsibility. With our humble words, we have endeavored to review the history and the experience of an institution that for seventeen centuries has functioned and continues to function as an axis for the unity of European civilization. We aspire to continue the tradition of the Ecumenical Patriarchate of New Rome–Constantinople and to continue to preach the Word of God as did the Patriarchs of Constantinople John Chrysostom, Gregory the Theologian, Photius the Great, and a myriad of others, giants not only in the realm of ecclesiastical history but also in European history.

Historical conditions have drastically changed the contemporary world scene. Please accept our presence here as a simple reminder. *We remind you that we exist.* And we continue to minister and to bear witness to the common struggle for understanding and hope worldwide. The metropolitan sees of the Ecumenical Patriarchate throughout all of the European countries, the hundreds of parishes of Orthodox faithful in Central and Western Europe, as well as immigrant and local populations all constitute our flock and are also people of your political constituencies. From outside of the boundaries of the twelve-nation European Union, a great number of other populated nations belonging to the Orthodox ecclesiastical tradition are also following the same European journey. Permit us to express the hope that these peoples will be called soon to participate in the life and institutions of a united Europe.

Through its faithful adherents and under the developing circumstances, the Ecumenical Patriarchate continues, in its ecumenical service, to comprise an essential part of this European civilization. Recognizing that each of you here has particular ideological orientations and personal convictions, we kindly ask that you accept the readiness of the Ecumenical Patriarchate to support you in your efforts for European unification, for a Europe that will exist, not for itself alone, but for the benefit of all the world.

We wish to conclude with a prayer that we Orthodox direct to the Prince of Peace especially during the period of Great Lent: "Heavenly King, strengthen our faith, reconcile the nations, and give peace to your world."

# ENVIRONMENT AND RELIGIOUS EDUCATION

*Greetings at the opening of the first summer
seminar on Halki, June 20, 1994*

By the grace of God, to whom we express our heartfelt gratitude, we are convening this interfaith gathering in this venerable center of Orthodoxy. We are pleased that it is being held within the hospitable environment of this monastery, where our "alma mater," the Theological School of Halki, once flourished. This year marks the 150th anniversary since its establishment.

By the will of God, this conference is the first in a series of seminars that we intend to convene on a yearly basis, here on this amiable and attractive island of Halki *(Heybeliada)*. This conference is convened by formal decision of our Holy and Sacred Synod, which by a separate decision reached during its meeting of June 6, 1989, decreed that September 1st of each year, in addition to being the beginning of the new ecclesiastical year, also be dedicated to the protection of our natural environment.

Through this significant decision, reached under the spiritual guidance of our predecessor, Patriarch Demetrios of blessed memory, we recognize that our Church must become actively involved in addressing the universal problem of the poor management of our natural environment, created by the numerous and unfortunate abuses of nature by humanity. *Human beings were created by God to enjoy sovereignty over nature, but not to exercise tyranny over it. Many sectors of society have now recognized that the ecological problem is directly related to the moral crisis of humanity and that the proper use of nature depends on the perception, position, and practice of human beings in relation to the cosmos.* According to the ancient saying, "Humanity is the measure of all things."

Now that we have been awakened to the impending destruction of nature, and to all that this implies, how has society responded in recent years? We note here the so-called "plans for peaceful coexistence" (between humankind and nature) along with plans for the "development of the environment." All these concerns and actions are of course commendable. As we know, however, they are also limited in their effectiveness, for who will find and apprehend those individuals responsible for forest fires? Who will restrain those who illegally cut down trees? Who will control those unconscionable individuals who pollute our waters, rivers, and seas, and how can this be done? Who can restrain the greedy?

We, the Church, must assist willingly, firmly, and extensively in this pressing and vital concern. We can help by enlightening the conscience of men and women in order to cultivate respect for their fellow human beings and for all created matter. Our goal must be to instill in people a sense of compassion as well as a sense of the fear of God so that they may avoid wrongdoing, vulgarity, impropriety, inhumanity, and especially selfish individualism. Too often those who torch forests, those who illegally cut down trees, and those who pollute our shores are egocentric individuals with hardened hearts, who do so out of greed and for purely utilitarian purposes. A good Christian cannot — rather, a good Christian is by conscience not permitted to — destroy nature and the environment. A good Christian cannot be a source of immoral or destructive acts.

According to Socrates, "virtue is taught." In conformity with our position, therefore, and following much meditation and thought, we have chosen as the theme of this gathering the relationship between religious education and the natural environment. By restricting the discussion of the conference to religious education, we are neither excluding nor underestimating other forms and levels of secular and parochial education. Our goal — and we beseech the attention of the esteemed participants to this point — is to examine and explore ways and means by which we may influence our students in order to sensitize them and awaken their concern regarding this most urgent issue.

## Education and Parish Action

*However, in order that we are not left with empty or vain words, we are of the opinion that our attention must be given to developing programs of practical application.* For example, tree-planting initiatives must be undertaken, just as we have done today, and as we did last December on this island. Groups of students may cultivate gardens, while others can care and tend to forest regions. Along with a series of lectures, seminars should be organized with the express purpose of enlightening students on planting procedures, gardening, and other similar activities. Other groups of children in our secular, parochial, and catechetical schools may adopt vegetable or flower gardens, forested regions, church compounds, abandoned properties, or farm regions cultivated for the common good, as well as areas with natural beauty, which they will care for on a voluntary basis. Their example can serve to sensitize their parents and elders who can then be motivated to do likewise.

We especially advise the clergy and others in parish ministry to encourage and promote love for nature, to care for trees and shrubs as well as church properties and cemeteries. *It is only fitting that love for the environment begins in the church compound, which must be replete with greenery and flowers in bloom throughout all seasons of the year,* "for the Creator of beauty has made them all" (Wisdom of Sol. 13:3).

Such *beauty of nature is the will of God.* Consequently, we are obligated to preserve rather than destroy the environment. Hence, any destruction of nature clearly constitutes sin. We entreat your attention particularly to these final thoughts. As we read the agonizing warnings of conservationists, geologists, biologists, and other specialists who remind us of the great folly of the violation of nature with its foreseeable tragic consequences, we rejoice that you, my beloved speakers and participants, are today contributing to a momentous and monumental task of timely significance for our planet.

"For he did not create [the earth] a chaos, he formed it to be inhabited" (Isa. 45:18). Humanity is therefore obligated not to ravage the earth, creating chaotic conditions with fires and scarcity of water, but rather to develop and enhance it. "You who have nothing to do, plant a tree in the corner of your garden so that others may come and sit there to rest and recollect." These are the words of Adamo, in a timely song with beautiful orchestral rhythm and harmony. It would be worthwhile for our youthful listeners to find it. Let it inspire you, and sing it along with your friends as an indication of your ecological concern. In life, only those divinely and enthusiastically inspired, only those who truly love their environment, are able to create the things of God. "Seedtime and harvest, cold and heat, summer and winter, day and night, shall not cease" (Gen. 8:22). You, our beloved children in the Lord, are contributing to the concern for a proper order and legitimate condition of the cosmos. Cosmos means decoration; it is defined by a love for beauty and decency. May you, therefore, be blessed by God.

### The Least Person Can Make the Greatest Difference

Permit us to confide our thoughts in you. *We do not place much trust in the strong and the mighty, or in people of authority. We believe, rather, in those willing and patient individuals, in those who do not lose sight of their objective,* namely the objective for good. Do not forget the acknowledgment of the ancient Greeks that "drops of water can make even rocks hollow." Many simple people, in various small corners of the earth, with nominal but continuous daily concerns, are able to change the world, even if only slightly, for the better. Today, on the day after Pentecost, we celebrate the Feast of the Holy Spirit. We celebrate the triumph of the few, the weak — at least by human standards — holy disciples and apostles of our Lord, who, empowered by the fire of Pentecost, changed the world some 2,000 years ago, for all time, so that today we are preparing to enter the third millennium after Christ. My brothers and sisters, may we continue primarily to cultivate the field of the soul, but also the garden of our home, so that future generations may reap the fruit of our labor.

# PEACE AND TOLERANCE

*Address to the Conference on Peace and Tolerance*
*organized by the Ecumenical Patriarchate and held*
*in Istanbul, Turkey, February 8, 1994*

Thank you, Rabbi Arthur Schneier, for the great impetus that you have provided for this conference, and for all your work to make it come to pass and to fruition. Your efforts to promote peace, tolerance, and intercultural understanding are deeply appreciated. May God bless you. We share the expression of sorrow that you have expressed for the innocent and defenseless victims of the latest tragedy in Sarajevo, a tragedy that we condemn along with the perpetrators of this act, whoever they may be. We also thank His Eminence and our friend, President Mehmet Nuri Yilmaz, for his invaluable cooperation in assuring the success of this truly historic conference. Greetings also to all of our brothers and sisters from around the world who have come together for this very timely Conference on Peace and Tolerance.

Although we shall focus our remarks on problems in Central Asia and the Caucasus, let us keep in mind that *no member of the human family has a monopoly on malice.* We are all sinners and stand in desperate need of God's grace in our quest for a better world. Yet while some have pointed to the modern "clash of civilizations" as inevitable, the representatives of many of those civilizations have gathered here today in a spirit of brotherhood and harmony. May our Heavenly Father grant us the strength to maintain that fraternal spirit in years to come.

Since the beginning of recorded history, Eastern Europe has been a great crossroads of cultures and civilizations, a vast meeting ground for many and diverse tribes, faiths, and peoples. Sometimes it seems as if our only constants have been conflict and conquest. Paradoxically, however, conflict and conquest have also been the agents of peace. Over the millennia, the empires that took over large portions of the region brought the greatest intervals of peace. From the Macedonian conquest, with its Hellenistic civilization, through the Roman, Byzantine, Ottoman, Habsburg, Russian, and Soviet Empires, peace in Eastern Europe has come, ironically, only at the tip of a sword or the barrel of a gun.

Tolerance did not always come arm-in-arm with peace. *For every example of tolerance, there are many more examples of intolerance.* The peace imposed on Eastern Europe by the conquering empires was relative, and it was always given on the terms of the conqueror. We must understand that and not idealize it. Those empires were shattered with the arrival of Western nationalism during the nineteenth century — and Eastern Europe and the world have never been the same since. Nationalism began as a positive force; it offered a new logic for the construction of democratic states. Nevertheless, nationalism turned out to be a double-edged sword; in the hands of tyrants, it has been destructive — indeed, the most destructive force in human history, killing seventy-five million human beings between 1914 and 1945 alone. We must ask ourselves boldly and honestly: Is it not time to place a rein on the excesses of nationalism?

## History and Nationalism

We are not immune to the forces of history. Neither, however, are we helpless before them. We cannot lament paradise lost, but we must find hope in the kingdom at hand. We must answer the fratricide and fragmentation of nationalism with the brotherly love and integration of ecumenicity. We must teach our people tolerance, which is ultimately based on respect for the sanctity and rights of individual human beings. Indeed, if there is one place where the spiritual and secular universes converge, it is in the individual, in the human person.

Among those of us who place our faith in spiritual institutions, this means that, of all the precepts of our diverse religions, the first principle must be the divine spark in each one of God's children. Among those who place their faith in temporal institutions, this means that, of all political principles, primary emphasis must go not to collective but rather to individual human rights. Indeed, this is one of many areas in which we, as people of faith, have something to teach our secular colleagues. In recent years we have heard some people say that human rights are relative — an unfortunate and potentially catastrophic idea. The human person was created in the image and likeness of God — and there can be no different standard of treatment for those human beings who happen to be Asian, another for Africans, and yet another for Europeans. Culture may be relative, but humanity is not.

The Orthodox Church has long searched for a language with which to address nationalism, amid the strife and havoc that this new ideology created in the Orthodox lands of Eastern Europe for much of the nineteenth century. In 1872, a great synod, held in our Patriarchal Cathedral at the Phanar, in the name of the Prince of Peace, issued an unqualified condemnation of the sin of racism, saying: "We renounce, censure, and condemn racism, namely racial discrimination, ethnic feuds, hatreds, and dissensions within the Church of Christ." Today, more than a century later, extreme nationalism remains one of the central problems of our ecumenical Church. We must answer with deep and uncompromising ecumenicity.

That is why the Mother Church has done everything in her power to support, both morally and materially, the reemerging Orthodox Churches in Russia and throughout Eastern Europe, especially since the collapse of godless communism. Although these churches are self-governing, nonetheless they are the daughters of the See of St. Andrew the Apostle. That is why we convened an unprecedented Pan-Orthodox Council or Synaxis of the heads of the world's Patriarchal and Autocephalous Orthodox Churches in March of 1992 — an unusual and unprecedented display of Christian solidarity, and a return to the genuine ecumenicity of centuries past. During this historic gathering, the spiritual heads expressed deep sadness over "fratricidal confrontation and for all its victims," calling on all religious leaders to offer "particular attention, pastoral responsibility and wisdom from God, in order that the exploitation of religious sentiment for political and national reasons may be avoided."

### Integration and Ecumenicity

Integration must be our watchword, in Eastern Europe as in Western Europe. Today we must follow the Helsinki Accord principle of the inviolability of borders. However, our vision for tomorrow — not only for Eastern Europeans, not only for all Europeans, but for all people — is of a world without borders. There is no good reason why people and goods should not be able one day to move freely between Bitolja and Bucharest, between Trikala and Tirana, between Sofia and St. Petersburg, between Alma-Ata and Ankara. And there is no reason to continue the hatreds that have turned Eastern Europe, and especially the Balkans, into the world's caricature for ethnic conflict.

It was not always that way. Let us remember that less than two centuries ago, there were Greek businesspersons in Odessa and Bucharest, and Albanian enterprises in Egypt. Serbian merchants conducted a lively trade with their Habsburg counterparts. Thessaloniki had a thriving Jewish community. And so on. We must put behind us the divisions and feuds brought about by excessive nationalism. The great empires once united us — but the peace that comes at the tip of a sword is no longer acceptable. As St. Paul exhorts: "If it is possible, so far as it depends on you, live peaceably with all" (Rom. 12:18). The modern way to bring about unity and peace is to extend the European Union — to open our borders to one another, and to let people, capital, ideas, and products flow.

Much has already been achieved in the political world: the General Agreement on Tariffs and Trade, and the Partnership for Peace proposed by American President Bill Clinton. Yet, politicians alone cannot heal the rifts brought about by extreme nationalism. Religious leaders have a central and inspirational role to play. *We must help bring the spiritual principles of genuine ecumenicity, goodwill, and tolerance to the fore. Indeed, this is a way in which we of the cloth may assist our colleagues in government. Our deep and abiding spirituality stands in stark contrast to the secularism of modern politics. The failure of anthropocentric ideologies has left a void in many lives; the frantic pursuit of the future has sacrificed the stability of the past.* As the Council of 1992 stated, these ideologies "have created in people of this century a spiritual void and an existential insecurity and have led many people to seek salvation in new religious and para-religious movements, sects, or nearly idolatrous attachments to the material values of this world."

The famous psychologist Carl G. Jung once said: "Among all my patients in the second half of life . . . every one of them fell ill because they had lost what the living religions of every age have given their followers; and none of them has been really healed who did not regain his religious outlook." Jung knew this in 1959; in 1994, who does not acknowledge it? Communities of faith can balance secular humanism and nationalism with spiritual humanism and ecumenicity — and we can temper the mindless pursuit of modernity with our own healthy respect for tradition. However, we can do this only if we are united in the spirit of the one God, "Creator of all things visible and invisible." Catholic, Orthodox, and Protestant, Jews and Muslims — while we cannot deny our differences, neither can we deny the need for alliance and solidarity in order to help lead our world away from the bloody abyss of extreme nationalism and intolerance. For it is precisely when we disagree that we have the greatest opportunity to demonstrate tolerance.

We at the Ecumenical Patriarchate will continue our efforts to be peacemakers and to light the lamp of the human spirit. We, as the bride of the Risen Bridegroom, wish only to remain a Church — a Church, however, that is free and respected by all. We, like all of you who have gathered here in peace and tolerance, wish to be a religious and spiritual institution, teaching, edifying, serving universal ideals, civilizing, and preaching love in every direction. We assure you, fellow travelers on the road to peace, that we will always work with you — not only in the spirit of peace and tolerance, but, even more, in the spirit of divine love itself. The Ecumenical Patriarchate belongs to the living Church that was founded by the God of love, whose peace "surpasses all understanding" (Phil. 4:7). We "pursue what makes for peace" (Rom. 14:19). We believe that "God is love" (1 John 4:16), which is why we are not afraid to extend our hand in friendship and our heart in love, as we proclaim that "perfect love casts out fear" (1 John 4:18).

Beloved friends, there is more that unites us than that divides us. Let this conference mark a turning point in our history. We have within our grasp the vision of the Psalmist: "Behold, how good and pleasant it is when brothers [and sisters] dwell in unity." We pledge to you today that the Orthodox Christian Church will do everything in her power to fulfill that vision.

## METANOIA: A NEW VISION

*Closing remarks at the Conference on*
*Peace and Tolerance in Istanbul, Turkey, February 9, 1994*

It was with great hope that the Ecumenical Patriarchate sent out the invitation to this conference as a call for peace and tolerance among believers in the one God, in order to cast a new light of understanding on regional conflicts filled with murky mistrust and dark deeds. Responding to the call from our co-hosts, the Appeal of Conscience Foundation and the Ecumenical Throne itself, we have gathered to meet where the continents themselves meet, so that we may confront those who commit wanton killings and spiteful injustices among the world's citizens and begin to speak words of healing to their hardened hearts and, in so doing, to dispel the evils of injustice, conflict, and bloodshed.

We observe that this conference has established among us all — Muslims, Jews, and Christians — a sort of nascent fellowship, wherein thoughts have been exchanged honestly, forging, link by link, a chain of fellowship so that we may finally begin to bind the forces of evil. Our words, freely expressed in plenary sessions, in working groups, as well as in the breaking of bread, have reflected the transforming truth found in the words of St. Francis of Assisi, "where there is hatred, let me sow love." We have discussed frankly and honestly, especially in view of the recent tragedy in Sarajevo, the most dramatic problems in Central Asia, the Caucasus, and the Balkans. We have understood, and hope to understand better, that a distorted history often becomes a myth that justifies the most outrageous nationalism. Indeed, one of our future duties ought to be a genuine effort toward creating, without inflaming passions, an objective history, a true history that enables the *one* to encounter the *other*.

Over the last two days we have experienced a profound yearning for peace and a sincere sympathy that enables us to comprehend one another's tribulations and sufferings. Spinoza said: "Peace is not simply the absence of war." Peace is a divine name; it is the very presence of God, His blessing, His *barakah,* which we must be open to receive. The Lord Jesus Christ promised His followers: "Peace I leave with you; my peace I give to you; not as the world gives do I give to you" (John 14:27).

This spiritual passion for peace places the demand on us that we should no longer seek to justify ourselves by accusing others. Rather, *we require a genuine* metanoia, *a complete change in the way we view the world.* We call on all spiritual peoples of the world to create a Copernican revolution of the spirit that will free the inner universe to no longer gravitate around the ego, be it individual or collective, but around the divine light itself. In so doing, we pastors will teach by our example that God is not the source of vengeance but the essence of love and reconciliation.

Religious people cannot act as statesmen or generals. We can act only when we allow God to act *through* us. God does not act as a typhoon or a tyrant, but as an influx of light and peace that penetrates history through the hearts and minds of men and women. "You have created us for yourself, God, and our hearts are restless until they find their rest in you" (St. Augustine). Such is exactly the task and challenge of this international conference: to open our hearts in order to allow light and peace to pass through us, and through us to the communities of faith where we are called to serve. Thus we may become prophets of peace, peacemakers, who at the conclusion of this Conference on Peace and Tolerance may realize that this new beginning must be based on doing justice, loving mercy, and "walking humbly with [our] God" (Mic. 6:8).

# THE BOSPHORUS DECLARATION

*Joint declaration of the Conference on*
*Peace and Tolerance, February 9, 1994*

I. The participants in the Conference on Peace and Tolerance wish to thank the government of Turkey for the courteous hospitality it has extended to us and for the opportunity to pursue our deliberations on the vital issues of peace and tolerance. The conference wishes to recognize the contributions of President Clinton, President Demirel, Secretary-General Boutros Boutros-Ghali, and all other religious and political leaders who have sent messages of support. In this declaration, we wish specifically to refer to the Berne Declaration of November 26, 1992, which has given us a foundation on which to build. That declaration specifically states that: *"a crime committed in the name of religion is a crime against religion."*

Since November 26, 1992, we have seen many crimes committed in the name of religion, and we, the conference participants, wish to speak out vigorously against them. As recent events have shown, such crimes against humanity continue in Bosnia, Armenia/Azerbaijan, Georgia, and Tajikistan. The cruelties have continued unchecked, and we demand an end to this brutality. We, the undersigned, reject any attempt to corrupt the basic tenets of our faith by means of false interpretation and unchecked nationalism. *We stand firmly against those who violate the sanctity of human life and pursue policies in defiance of moral values.* We reject the concept that it is possible to justify one's actions in any armed conflict in the name of God.

We wish to emphatically remind all the faithful that the Scriptures of all three monotheistic religions specifically speak of peace as a supreme value. "Blessed are the peacemakers, for they shall be called children of God." "Allah summons to the abode of peace." "His ways are the ways of peace."

II. We reiterate that the war in former Yugoslavia is not a religious war and that appeals and exploitations of religious symbols to further the cause of aggressive nationalism are a betrayal of the universality of religious faith. We emphasize the imperative of freedom of conscience and freedom of religion for every minority. We call for an end to the confiscation, desecration, and destruction of houses of worship and of holy and sacred places of whatever religious tradition. We totally abhor and condemn ethnic cleansing and the rape and murder of women and children. We demand the removal of obstacles that prevent humanitarian assistance from reaching those who are suffering.

We condemn the use of force in countries of the former Soviet Union. The conflicts in Georgia, Armenia/Azerbaijan, and Tajikistan must be concluded immediately, and solutions to the outstanding issues must be found by other means.

We recognize that all who are suffering are victims, but we single out specifically the most tragic and innocent victims, the children.

III. We invite our religious communities to embrace children from the areas of conflict in God's love and to extend all possible assistance to the suffering children, to help them find spiritual, psychological, and physical healing. We cannot emphasize enough that spiritual nourishment is a paramount requirement and that religious communities must be supported. We also recognize that the countries suffering from conflict have had a long, dark period of communism where there was little or no spiritual education. We urge all faiths to redouble their efforts at spiritual guidance for those who were so deprived.

We wish to recognize also that tension exists within faiths, and we urge the leaderships of those faiths to bring about peaceful resolutions to the issues that divide them.

IV. The conference participants, like all others who have followed these tragic conflicts, observe with horror the forced migrations of refugees. Millions have experienced or are threatened by forcible displacement. Therefore, we call upon all religious faiths to speak out clearly and consistently against these actions. We condemn those who uproot families from their homes, tear children from their parents, divide husband from wife in the name of false nationalism. We expect all religious leaders to stand fast in the protection of all those threatened by involuntary migration, irrespective of their religious beliefs or ethnic background. We demand that all refugees who have left their home involuntarily be permitted to return with dignity and honor; that the religious communities strengthen their institutions to receive, assist, and protect refugees of whatever faith; that religious and lay relief agencies develop procedures to coordinate their efforts. As long as the conflicts continue we urge all countries to extend temporary asylum to victims, while granting opportunity for refugee status to those who truly seek it; to increase resources for relief; and to work with all people of good faith for the cessation of hostilities.

V. The participants in the Conference on Peace and Tolerance have unanimously agreed to utterly condemn war and armed conflict; to demand that no hostile acts be perpetrated upon any peaceful group or region in the name of a religious faith; to demand the initiation of constructive dialogues in order to resolve outstanding issues between those of different faiths; and to demand the right to practice one's religion in freedom and with dignity.

VI. We have deliberated carefully and are in agreement that wanton killing must stop; that those who continue to perpetrate such heinous acts are criminals; and that, although we have no weapons of war and no armies for combat, we have a greater strength — namely, the strength of spiritual might. We totally condemn those who commit brutalities, killings, rapes, mutilations, forcible displacement, and inhumane beatings.

VII. We, the conference participants, have decided to establish an Appeal of Conscience Conflict Resolution Commission to deal with ethnic conflicts. This commission will be made up of representatives from all faiths and from all countries represented at this conference. The Appeal of Conscience Conflict Resolution Commission will be responsible for informing commission members and for recommending ways and means to deal with the scourge of extreme nationalism and ethnic conflict.

<table>
<tr><td>Rabbi Arthur Schneier,<br>President<br>Appeal of Conscience Foundation</td><td>His All Holiness<br>Ecumenical Patriarch<br>Bartholomew I</td></tr>
</table>

His Eminence Mehmet Nuri Yilmaz,
President of the Office of Religious Affairs
of the Republic of Turkey

His Eminence Cardinal Roger Etchegeray,
President of the Pontifical Council on Peace and Justice and Cor Unum

*The Participants in the Conference on Peace and Tolerance*

## ENVIRONMENT AND CITY

*Remarks upon receiving an honorary doctorate
from City University, London, May 31, 1994*

We are deeply grateful for the honor bestowed on us today, an honor that we accept not on behalf of one individual, but on behalf of the Ecumenical Patriarchate and the entire Holy Orthodox Church, in whose rich vineyard we are privileged to labor. We may toil in this vineyard, we may plant seeds here, we may harvest its fruits, but it is God's vineyard, they are God's seeds, and it is God's fruit. All glory, then, is due to Him.

The company present here today increases the joy we feel in accepting this degree. For we are in the presence of His Royal Highness, Prince Philip; our brother in Christ, the Archbishop of Canterbury; the Lord Bishop of London; the Lord Mayor of London; and, of course, the administration, faculty, and students of this extraordinary university, which serves and enriches London, the largest city in Europe.

We warmly thank His Lordship the Bishop of Stepney for his most kind and generous introduction. Our joy is further multiplied because this honorary degree is being conferred upon us on the momentous occasion of the centenary of City University. One hundred years is indeed a landmark achievement worthy of praise and recognition. We are deeply touched that you have chosen to include us in these celebrations. To you, the esteemed administration, faculty, and beloved students, we extend our heartfelt congratulations and paternal prayers that God, the Giver of Light, may continue to illumine your hearts and minds as you increase in knowledge and wisdom. May God bless you with yet another centenary.

The ancient Greeks believed that human beings could rise to their full potential only within the context of a city. This great university and its talented students are evidence of that ancient wisdom. Nevertheless, increasingly these days, we witness another, darker aspect of life in our cities. We observe children without clothing, food, or shelter; we see people without jobs; we hear of brothers killing brothers; we recognize broken families, broken lives, and broken dreams. Therefore, we ask ourselves: Why? What went wrong? How can this be?

Our first instinct is to doubt the wisdom of the ancients. However, our better instinct is in fact to believe it even more. For, if we truly believe that cities offer great opportunities, we will be driven to discover why it is that so many people are not finding those opportunities. What is missing? What is lacking? The answer, we believe, lies not in knowledge or wealth or political action. It lies simply in faith. Knowledge expands the mind, but faith can open the heart. Wealth builds houses, but faith can move mountains. Politics does the possible, but faith can do the impossible.

*Western civilization has brought about the greatest of human achievements — from medical miracles to people on the moon, from stable democracies to high standards of living. Yet, these have come with a price, and that price is* most evident on the streets of our cities. Politicians and professors alone cannot heal the problems of Western society, be they pornography, pollution, drugs, poverty, crime, war, or homelessness. Religious leaders have a central and inspirational role to play in bringing the spiritual principles of love, tolerance, morality, and renewal to the fore.

This is why we consider this degree such a special honor, for a secular university is bestowing it on a spiritual institution, thus demonstrating that one is not antithetical to the other. Indeed, more than this, it brings our two worlds — of academia and ecclesia — closer together, and for this we are truly grateful to God.

We are convinced that our mission today — namely, that of bringing the healing power of the Holy Spirit to all the children of God — is more vital than ever. The spirituality of the Church offers a different sort of fulfillment than that which is offered by the secularism of modern life. Here, too, there is no antithesis.

## Secular Humanism and Society

*The failure of anthropocentric ideologies has left a void in many people's lives.* The frantic pursuit of the future has sacrificed the inner peace of the past. We need to regain our religious outlook. We must urgently counter the effects of secular humanism with the teaching of the Church on humanity and the natural world and elevate the pursuit of the temporal toward a healthy respect for the eternal by bringing the one into harmony with the other. Moreover, we must repair the torn fabric of society by reminding ourselves every day that the misfortune of some of us affects the fortune of all of us.

Our society resembles the lawyer who asked Jesus: "Teacher, what must I do to inherit eternal life?" Jesus responded: "What is written in the law?" The lawyer said: "You shall love the Lord your God with all your heart, and with all your soul, and with all your strength, and with all your mind; and your neighbor as yourself" (Luke 10:25-27). This led to a further question — one that is extremely relevant to our world today: "Who is my neighbor?" (Luke 10:29). Jesus answered with the story of a man who was robbed and beaten on the road leading from Jerusalem to Jericho. A priest approached that man, and — in much the same way as so many of us step over a homeless person today — crossed to the other side of the road. Then a Levite came by; he, too, avoided the situation by crossing the road. Yet a Samaritan who happened to be traveling down that road was moved to bind the man's wounds, take him to the closest inn, and tend to him. Jesus asked: "Which of these three, do you think, was a neighbor to the man who fell into the hands of the robbers?" (Luke 10:36). When the lawyer chose the Good Samaritan, Jesus simply said: "Go and do likewise" (Luke 10:37).

Today, there is hardly a more important question than "Who is my neighbor?" The future of our world rests on how we respond to this. Sadly, we do not always answer as we should. In Bosnia, where warfare still rages, too many are like the priest in Jesus' parable, crossing the road rather than confronting the situation. In Los Angeles, in London, and in St. Petersburg, too many of our children have been abandoned to the urban warfare of the streets. In South Africa, on the other hand, we have seen millions of our fellow human beings behave like the Good Samaritan. The South Africans are certainly proving themselves true neighbors.

If God would grant us the power to plant just one idea, as though it were a seed, in the fertile minds that are gathered in this great cathedral today — in order, thus, to return the favor for this degree by offering back to this secular institution a simple, yet profound spiritual exhortation — it would be just this: "Go and do likewise." Know that every human being is your neighbor and behave accordingly. Above all else, "love your neighbor as yourself" (Luke 10:27).

# RELIGIOUS EDUCATION
# AND RELIGIOUS OBLIGATION

*From the foreword to the published proceedings
of the first summer seminar on Halki, June 1994*

God, who created the world and humankind, placed those whom he first created in a specially selected garden on the terrestrial globe, according to the teaching of our faith. And He commanded them "to labor in it and to tend it."

The first aspect of this two-part commandment establishes human labor as an obligation ordained by God, giving humanity the capacity of creating while laboring and, thus, of participating to a degree in the creative force of God. This constitutes one of the manifestations of human nature as fashioned in the image of God.

However, according to the second aspect of this commandment, what is recapitulated in the tending of the garden in Eden is the religious and theological basis for the protection of the environment. Tending the garden certainly did not imply protecting it from any assault by some third party (since then there were no such!). Rather, it meant safeguarding it and maintaining it in the same condition as it was given by God to Adam, certainly for his use.

Later, having conformed to the divine commandment to increase and have dominion over the earth, when people in fact did disperse over the entire surface of the planet earth, the commandment to safeguard the earth properly as their habitation understandably spread beyond the confines of the garden of Eden throughout the entire earth.

Thus, today, we are able to say that the Christian religion, the Jewish religion, and the Muslim religion — the latter of which accepts in part the Old Testament as encompassing the declaration of God's will to humankind — are obliged to emphasize to their faithful that *tending the earth and, in general, the worldly environment that we inhabit is a commandment of God. As such, it is a religious obligation.*

This was the theme of the first summer seminar on Halki, entitled "Environment and Religious Education." Upon the initiative of the Ecumenical Patriarchate the seminar was held from June 19-30, 1994, in the holy Patriarchal and Stavropegic Monastery of the Holy Trinity, where the Holy Theological School was housed for a great many years.

# ORTHODOXY AND THE ENVIRONMENT

*Address during the conferral of the first honorary doctorate*
*of the Department of Environmental Studies of the*
*Aegean University, October 1994*

Any effort to connect contemporary environmental pursuits to theological presuppositions seems to be a paradoxical and perhaps eccentric venture. In the minds of most, ecology represents a practical and tangible methodology. In contrast, theology and theological cosmology, and even their terminology, are for most people naturally connected to abstract theoretical pursuits. They refer to associations of doctrines and ideologies that are irrelevant to daily life and its problems.

Contemporary ecology — as a matter of scientific study, but also in the form of crusades and movements for the salvation of our earthly ecosystem — is one of the most characteristic expressions of human interest concentrated on practical goals. The logic of environmental protection is presented as a purely utilitarian matter. If we do not protect our natural environment, then our own survival will increasingly be rendered more difficult and problematic and the very presence of the human race on this planet will be threatened very soon. The danger of degeneration or even of annihilation of the human race is described as imminent.

## The Logic of Ecology and the Logic of Theology

In this way of thinking, the natural environment is conceived as a necessary and sufficient condition for human existence and survival; yet, this condition or context is perceived as utilitarian. The method of thinking is limited to the manner of usage. What is of interest is not the source or cause of the natural reality, nor is any hermeneutical "meaning" sought in the cosmic order and harmony or in the wisdom and beauty of nature. It is of course quite possible that those things which exist in nature were created by some unknown "higher power," or, alternatively, that they are the products of inexplicable "chance" and automatic forces — again without explanation — that exist innately in the very structure of matter. At any rate, the interpretation of any cause or end is not what gives meaning to everything that exists.

Based, then, on such utilitarian logic, contemporary ecological movements demand the definition of rules for the use of nature by humanity. Ecology seeks to be seen as a practical ethic of human conduct in relation to the environment. *Nevertheless, like any other ethic, ecology too provokes us to ask the question: Who is it that defines these rules of human conduct, and with what authority are they defined? What logic renders these rules obligatory? From what source do they derive their validity?*

The rationalism of this utilitarian mentality is perhaps the only answer that ecologists can provide to this question. The correctness of an ecological ethic is derived from and based on its apparent utilitarianism. It is reasonably beyond any doubt that, in order for the human race to survive on this earth, certain conditions are necessary also for the natural environment.

Nevertheless, the rationalism of this utilitarian ethic is precisely what led to the destruction of the natural environment. Humanity has not destroyed the environment out of some senseless masochism. Humanity destroys the environment in an effort to exploit nature, in order to secure more facilities and comforts in daily life. The logic that led to the destruction of the environment is precisely the same logic now as that concerning the protection of the environment. Both of these "systems of logic" approach nature as something exclusively utilitarian. Neither attributes any different meaning to nature. Both exist on the same level of an ontological interpretation of the natural reality — or, rather, a vacuum of deliberate ignorance of any ontological interpretation.

Consequently, the difference revealed by these two "systems of logic" (namely, that which leads to the destruction and that which looks to the protection of the environment) is only quantitative. Ecologists demand a limited and controlled use of the natural environment, a quantitative reduction that will allow its longer use by humanity. They seek a rational limitation of our limitless use of nature. Therefore, they seek a more rational application of a rational system that already exploits nature. They seek a utilitarian restraint of our utilitarian abuse.

Yet, who will define this quantitatively reduced and more correct use of nature within the context of the very same logic? By what measures will this be defined? Although the goal appears to be extremely rational, in fact it is by definition as well as in practice irrational. By definition, it is self-contradictory inasmuch as utilitarianism cannot work against utilitarianism. In practice, it is irrational because the majority of this earth's population does not accept being deprived of facilities and comforts secured for the convenience of a very small minority in "advanced" societies through the destruction of the environment.

In order, then, to meet the demands of ecologists, *another logic is required, one that is able to replace the logic of utilitarianism.* The ecologists' demand must be established on an entirely different basis. For example, it may be rooted in an altruism that is concerned for the survival of future generations, or it may be based on the demand for some "quality" of life that is not measured by consumer comfort and greed. Therefore, we need to find a basis that is not utilitarian but is universally accepted. And it is impossible to define non-utilitarian goals, on which everyone would agree, based on purely rational criteria. We must discern within the human person different needs and a different hierarchy of values. This can happen only when the human conscience acknowledges a different meaning in life and in the world, one that is not exclusively utilitarian.

## A Religious Ethic and Logic

The monotheistic religions preserve an appreciation of the natural reality that is not exclusively utilitarian. According to their traditions, the world is the creation of God. Thus the use of the world by humanity constitutes a practical relationship between humanity and God, since God bestows and humanity receives the natural goods as an expression of divine love.

Two fundamental consequences follow from this understanding.

- First, *the use of the world is not an end in itself for humanity,* but a way of relating to God. If humanity distorts the use of this world into egocentric and greedy abuse by dominating and destroying nature, then humanity is denying and destroying its own life-giving relationship with God, a relationship destined to continue into eternity.
- Second, *the world, as God's creation, ceases to be a neutral object for human use.* The world incarnates the word of the Creator just as any other creation embodies the word of its artist. The objects of natural reality bear the seal of their divine Creator's wisdom and love; they are words (*logoi,* which also implies meaning) of God inviting humanity to dialogue *(dialogos)* with God.

In spite of all this, it is a given historical fact that the contemporary concept of the world as a neutral object that may be used and exploited by humanity for its own individualistic pleasure is a concept that arose and was articulated within the context of Christian Europe. It would take too long to analyze the historical circumstances and theoretical presuppositions that led Christian Europe to replace the relationship between humanity and the world with the understanding that humanity has limitless domination over the world. The reasons for the divergence are not unrelated to the causes that led to the painful Schism in the eleventh century — namely, the severance of Western Christianity from the unified body of the one, holy catholic, and apostolic Church.

It nevertheless remains a fact that the change in human behavior toward the environment today requires a change in meaning, namely a change in the meaning attributed by human beings to matter and nature. Ecology will not inspire any respect toward nature if it is not informed by a different cosmology than that which prevails today in our culture and civilization, if it is not free from a naïve materialism and an equally naïve idealism alike.

## An Orthodox Cosmology

Let us endeavor to outline in brief the potential contribution of an Orthodox ecclesiastical cosmology toward the discovery of a new and different logic. Our superficial remarks will be primarily based on the works of St. Gregory of Nyssa, St. Maximus the Confessor, and St. Gregory Palamas. However, this does not imply that other patristic writers do not contribute substantially to this discussion.

*The fundamental patristic contribution here is the introduction of a third ontological category for the interpretation of existent reality and its principal source. I am referring to the category of divine energies,* which is added to the pair of categories, known as divine essence and divine hypostasis, that prevails in ontological philosophical analysis. Although the starting point of ecclesiastical thought was primarily theological, we shall draw upon the anthropological experience in order to discern analogies that may better clarify contemporary categories of thought.

When we speak of the essence of the human person, we are referring to the common manner through which every person shares in life, in being. We say, then, that the human person is a being that walks uprightly, laughs, thinks, creates, possesses imagination, judgment, willpower, the ability to love, and so on. All these are characteristics of a common human essence or nature.

Naturally, human essence, this universal manner of human existence, cannot exist independently of individual and particular beings. Each individual being realizes the common essence in an actual expression; each person "hypostatizes" the common essence, or constitutes the hypostasis of that essence. Human essence exists only within human hypostasis.

Yet the common features of essence, which are hypostatized by each individual person, are truly existent possibilities, characteristics of the manner in which every human existence is actualized, and here we encounter the notion of the energies or actualization of essence or nature. Each human existence is potentially energized or actualized through its material and spiritual functions, in the expression of its reason, will, imagination, judgment, and so forth.

## An Orthodox Anthropology

Each human individual hypostatizes the common energies of human nature in a unique and unrepeatable manner. Each person has reason, will, imagination, and judgment; yet each person reasons, wills, imagines, and judges in a unique, different, and unrepeatable manner. Consequently, the energies of human nature constitute an ontological reality, not simply because they characterize the common manner of existence among people, but also because they express each person's hypostatic manner of being. The human energies, which are hypostatized within each person, also constitute and reveal the absolute existential otherness and uniqueness of each person.

We come to know a human person, the otherness of that person's existence, by means of the energies through which that person's being is realized and revealed. Therefore, we come to know the composer J. S. Bach by listening to his music; we come to know the artist Rembrandt by means of looking at his paintings. The musical notes of Bach and the paint colors of Rembrandt differ in essence from the human essence of the two artists. Yet, the creative energy of one artist, which reveals the hypostatic otherness and uniqueness of that artist, is also actualized through different essences. The music, colors, writing, marble, and clay actualize the *logos* (meaning or purpose) of the musician, artist, writer, and sculptor. They reveal the person of the artist, his or her existential identity and otherness.

The ontological content of this category of hypostatized energies permits us to attribute the ontological "principle" or beginning of the material world to a personal God. We do not attribute this to the divine essence (which would lead to pantheism), but rather to the hypostatic divine energies. The divine energies reveal the *logos* (meaning or purpose) of God's personal otherness in relation to the world, a meaning that is actualized in matter, yet which remains entirely different from God in essence.

Almost fifteen centuries before the quantum theory was conceived in contemporary physics, Greek ecclesiastical thought confirmed that matter is energy, "a syndrome of rational (or logical) attributes," the created result of the uncreated divine energies. The difference in essence between created and uncreated neither excludes nor hinders the created from being actualized as the *logos* (purpose or word) of the uncreated, from revealing the creative energy and hypostatic otherness of the personal divine *Logos* (or Word) — just as the notes and the colors, while being different in essence from their artists, nevertheless actualize the *logos* (meaning or purpose) of the creative energy and hypostatic otherness of Bach and Rembrandt.

### Human Beings in Relation to Nature

It is only when people regard matter and nature in their entirety as the creation of a personal Creator that the use of matter and nature in their entirety constitutes a genuine relationship and not a domination of humanity over the natural reality. It is only then that we are able to speak of an "ecological ethic," which derives its definitive character not from conventional rationalistic codes of conduct but from humanity's need to love and be loved in the context of a personal relationship. *The logos (purpose or meaning) of the beauty of creation is an invitation addressed by God to humanity, an invitation to a personal relationship and communion with Him. It is a living and life-giving relationship.* In this context contemporary ecology could then become the practical response of humanity to this divine invitation, a tangible participation in a relationship with God.

Is it, however, sufficient to speak of an ontological clarification of the meaning of matter and the world in order to provoke a different relationship between contemporary humanity and the material world? Surely not! In order for humanity to reach the point of responding to nature with the respect and awe with which it responds to a personal artistic creation, this theoretical clarification must become an experiential knowledge and a social attitude. And at this point the role of social dynamics contained within the ecclesiastical tradition and community can be decisive. This transformation can occur only as the ecclesiastical conscience is purified from its estrangement into an ideological structure and prodded from its inactive rest into the preservation of established forms.

The great challenge that the Orthodox ecclesiastical conscience is called to appreciate today is the surprising reality of the contemporary science of physics, the new fascinating cosmology that results from the study of quantum mechanics: namely, the potential of matter as energy, the relativity of space and time as the connection for the presence of matter, and the increasingly clearer anthropocentric purpose of the universe. The language of physics today reveals the universal reality as a *logos* (purpose or meaning) that is actualized and hypostatized only in its encounter with the human personal *logos* (purpose or word).

If there exists a future for the demands of contemporary ecology, then this future is surely based, we would believe, in the free encounter of the historical experience in the Church of the living God with the experiential affirmation of His *logos* (word or purpose) actualized in nature.

# CHURCH AND SYMBOLS

*Christmas encyclical message, 1994*

The Christian Church was revealed — and is constantly being revealed — by the one God, the Almighty Creator of heaven and earth and of all things visible and invisible. These revelations are evident through the human nativity of the consubstantial Word of God. The Church has crossed the narrow confines of Palestine and the Mosaic Law and has ventured out to encounter and dialogue with the world of the Gentiles. Since the beginning, the Church did not hesitate to embrace all that the divine Creator had made in His infinite providence and love. Through the life of doxological worship, particularly through the supreme expression of the divine Eucharist, the very emblems of the Gentile divinities were returned to their natural purity and a new symbolism emerged: *the Christocentric reality of the cosmos and nature.*

In the catacombs of ancient Rome, Christ was portrayed as a pure white lamb, as a fish, or as a vine. The four Evangelists were represented by an angel, a lion, an ox, and an eagle. The Holy Spirit was depicted as a dove ever since the baptism of Jesus Christ in the river Jordan. With the passage of time, the Church became even bolder in making use of nature's symbols in order to decorate the space where the faithful worshiped. The church interior — in fact, liturgy itself — became a miniature icon of the universe, of heaven, earth, the nether world, and the world to come. With the help of these icons we can begin to understand the concepts of sacred space and sacred time.

## Environment and Sin

*While the plenitude of theological vision in Jesus Christ allows the highest doxological offering of the universe to the Almighty, the thoughtless and abusive treatment of even the smallest material and living creation of God must be considered a mortal sin. An insult toward the natural creation is seen as — and in fact actually is — an unforgivable insult to the uncreated God.*

At this particular juncture, the Christian Church, and especially the Orthodox Church, turns its attention toward the "land of the rising sun" and the delicate sensitivity of the spiritual vision of nature found in Buddhism, which has shaped the consciences and souls of the noble Japanese race. It is extremely significant that the Church observes in Japanese life and particularly in Japanese art an overwhelming awareness of and profound respect for the beauty and grace of God's creation. So often Japanese art shows a sensitivity to the temporality and the mystery of the subjects portrayed. Indeed, the realization that the entire visible world has a finite existence, that "it fades like a flower," is for all of us the beginning of the most existential inner searching about what succeeds death.

Orthodoxy has its response: resurrection from the dead, new creation, and "a better and more lasting" existence (Heb. 10:34), for "our citizenship is in heaven" (Phil. 3:20). Nevertheless, the mystery of creation can be appreciated only in faith, without which true knowledge of God would be absolutely unobtainable. This faith has been given "once for all" (Jude 3), just as creation itself was created once for all.

# *1995*

Patriarch Bartholomew planting a seedling donated by
United States President, William J. Clinton, at the
1995 Halki summer seminar

# FUNDAMENTALISM AND FAITH

*Address at the CEO International University,*
*Istanbul, October 25, 1995*

Greetings and welcome to Istanbul, the seat of the Ecumenical Throne of the Orthodox Christian Church. Here, not only the continents meet, but people from all over the world gather to enjoy the mystery, history, and majesty of the Queen City. Today, we are deeply honored to receive so distinguished a group of chief executives. When we first received an invitation from the Chief Executives Organization, we thought for a moment that we were being asked to join. The age qualification was not a problem; and as the spiritual leader of 350 million Orthodox Christians worldwide, we definitely have more than fifty full-time employees. However, we then considered your categories — President, Chairman, CEO, Managing Director, Publisher, or Head Partner. As you can see, there is no listing for Patriarch. Therefore, instead of joining you, we are in fact hosting you here in Turkey.

May we say that, in deciding to meet in this place and time, you have chosen well. As chief executives, one of your duties is to explore new frontiers. The latest great frontier was Eastern Europe, where free enterprise is now taking root. The next great frontier is the Islamic world, and the path to that world begins in Turkey, which is now approaching admission into the European Union.

We are standing today at a crossroads, in every sense of the word. Literally, we are at the crossroads between continents, namely between Asia and Europe. Istanbul is the only city in the world that straddles two continents. Figuratively, we are also at the crossroads between two sometimes antagonistic civilizations, namely between East and West. And metaphorically, we are again at one of the great crossroads in human history, a moment in time when, by the grace of God, a window of opportunity has opened for peace, reconciliation, and unity.

*Some have pointed to the modern "clash of civilizations" as inevitable. Yet we who live at the crossroads disagree — indeed, we are living proof that different cultures and different faiths can coexist in peace.* Although many of you have come to Turkey for the first time, you are surely not strangers to the legacy given to the world by the diverse civilizations and cultures that have blessed this sacred soil. It is in this land that the Creeds which we confess as Christians were first proclaimed. It is on this land that the First Ecumenical

Council established, with the inspiration of the Holy Spirit, the canon that is revered today as the New Testament. It is on this soil that the constitutional and dogmatic framework of the Christian faith was formulated.

We do not deny that tensions and deadly rivalries exist; but we must not deny that it is possible to surmount them. Distinguished guests, we live in an age of wonder and glory. Justice has "run down like waters, and righteousness like an everflowing stream" (Amos 5:24). A tide of tears has washed over our world, and as it recedes it sweeps away much sorrow and pain. The curse of communism has all but disappeared. Palestinians and Israelis have moved toward peace; and Jordan has joined in that effort. In Haiti, the sword of the generals has yielded to the ploughshare of democracy. In South Africa, hatred, intolerance, and violence are giving way to goodwill, democracy, and understanding. For the first time in living historical memory, the people of Northern Ireland are working to solve their problems with words, not weapons.

We have grown accustomed to a steady diet of miracles; we have come to expect them, like the days of the week. We do not ignore the tragedies that continue in Bosnia, Burundi, East Timor, Sri Lanka, and so many other places — far too many other places. Yet, amid the rubble of our tragic century, the heart of humanity is still beating. We must not fail to hear its heartbeat. Amid the gravestones, the human spirit is emerging. We must not fail to notice it. We have been given a rare opportunity. "You have shown your people hard things: you have made us to drink the wine of astonishment" (Ps. 60:3). Somehow, the world is growing weary of bloodshed. It is tiring of fanaticism. It has drunk the wine of astonishment. We must build on this.


## Thirst for the Spiritual


*There is a great hunger for spirituality; there is a thirst for transcendent meaning. We believe that, as we enter the next millennium, religious values, religious feeling, and religious faith are undergoing a massive revival.* Since the Enlightenment, the spiritual bedrock of Western civilization has been eroded and undermined. Intelligent, well-intentioned people sincerely believed that the wonders of science could replace the miracles of faith. However, these great minds missed one vital truth — namely, that faith is not a garment to be slipped on and off; it is a quality of the human spirit, from which it is inseparable. The modern era has not eliminated faith; faith cannot be eliminated any more than love can. The modern era has simply replaced spiritual faith in God with secular faith in humankind.

Today, three centuries after the birth of Voltaire, the pendulum is swinging back. The twentieth century has shown our enormous capacity for creativity. Yet it has also showed our boundless capacity for destruction. We saw seventy-five million human beings killed between 1914 and 1945 alone. In its own fearsome power, humanity also recognized its own awesome fallibility. This alone should move us all to applaud our respective heads of state who are rightly celebrating the fiftieth anniversary of the United Nations.

*There has never been a greater need for spiritual leaders to engage in the affairs of this world. We must take a visible place on the stage, especially because too many crimes today are taking place in the name of faith.* "Beware of false prophets, who come to you in sheep's clothing but inwardly are ravenous wolves" (Matt. 7:15). Although these words come from the Christian tradition, their truth is transcendent. Religious extremists and terrorists may be the most wicked false prophets of all. Not only do they commit horrible crimes against humanity, but they do so in the name of a lie. When they bomb, and shoot, and destroy, they steal more than life itself; they also undermine faith, which itself is the only way to break the cycle of hatred and retribution. International spiritual leaders must play an active role in discrediting such false prophets and in healing the wounds of our people. As Rabbi Hillel asked: "If not us, then who? If not now, then when?"

Last year, in Istanbul, the Throne of St. Andrew convened an international conference on peace and tolerance, which brought together Jewish, Christian, and Muslim religious leaders. The peace and tolerance conference resulted in the now-famous "Bosphorus Declaration," which unequivocally states that "a war in the name of religion is a war against religion." Our Church has had its own experience with such crimes. Today in Turkey, the Patriarchate has earned much popular support, from important national figures right down to the average man and woman on the street. If the Church faces such a threat in Turkey today, it comes not from the State or from the Muslim mainstream, but from the handful of fundamentalists who have appeared on the scene in recent years. We have seen our graveyards and monuments desecrated; we have seen bombs planted in sacred places.

Fundamentalism is a threat, not only to the Ecumenical Patriarchate, but also to the Turkish State itself. Moreover, fundamentalism is a danger, not just in Turkey, but also in Oklahoma City, in Paris, and in Tokyo. The rise of fundamentalism has given greater urgency to the cause of East-West unity. To return to the point that we made earlier, that cause would be served in important ways if Turkey were admitted to the European Union. It would help diffuse East-West tensions, bring about greater global understanding, and undermine the cause of fundamentalists and racists on both sides. Other events could also make a difference. The key environmental event sponsored by the

United Nations, the second Habitat Conference, will take place here in June of 1996. In addition, Turkey's bid to host the Olympics in 2004, if accepted, could prove yet another breakthrough for East-West unity. How marvelous it would be to see the Olympic torch carried from the sacred land of Olympia, Greece, to the holy and historic soil of Turkey. After all, in ancient times, this was the spirit and practice of the Olympic Games — namely, to bring a cessation of all wars and the promotion of "peace on earth and good will to all women and men." In each of the steps that we have outlined, international business has profound interests and will play a critical role.

If Turkey is integrated into the world economy, the gate is opened wider, not only to the Islamic world, but also to the former Soviet republics with strong historic links to Turkey. These Central Asian republics are in need of Western capital and creativity as well as entrepreneurial expertise and ideas. Many other interests would also be served by the integration of Turkey into Europe. It would have a powerful, positive, and stabilizing effect on all of this country's institutions, including, of course, the Ecumenical Patriarchate.

We must put behind us the divisions and feuds of the past. Once, conquest united Europe and Asia; today commerce can achieve the same result. Instead of ships full of soldiers, let us see ships full of cars and computers crossing the Bosphorus. The modern way of bringing about unity and peace is to open our borders to one another and to allow people, capital, ideas, and products to flow.

Much has already been achieved in the political world: the General Agreement on Tariffs and Trade, NATO, the Partnership for Peace, and of course the European Union. Yet neither politicians nor businessmen alone can heal the rifts in our society today. As we said earlier, religious leaders have a central and inspirational role to play; it is we who must bring the spiritual principles of openness, goodwill, and tolerance to the fore. It is our strong belief at the Ecumenical Patriarchate that Orthodox Christians have a special responsibility to assist in an East-West rapprochement. For, like the Turkish Republic, we, too, have a foot in both worlds.

## A View from the Crossroads

We have always lived at the crossroads between East and West; we have witnessed great suffering on both sides, as we see again today in Bosnia. However, we have also witnessed the most extraordinary acts of tolerance, like the welcoming of the expelled Sephardic Jews in 1492 by a Muslim Sultan, and the historic efforts toward peace being made between Muslims and Jews in the

Middle East even as we speak. Another astonishing example of tolerance was exhibited in 1453 by Mehmet II, the conqueror of Constantinople, who actually sought out the greatest ecclesiastical mind of his time, Gennadios Scholarios, and enthroned him as Ecumenical Patriarch, the spiritual leader of the entire Orthodox world.

*We have lived side-by-side with Muslims and Jews, and we have developed close, trusting relationships with both. In the years ahead, even though academic dialogues continue to exist, you will see us strive to establish and enhance a marketplace dialogue between all believers as well.* The Church of peace serves the Prince of Peace, and will do everything in its power to bring about this blessed sense of community. As the American martyr Dr. Martin Luther King Jr. put it: "Love is the only force capable of transforming an enemy into a friend." After all, it was our Lord Jesus Christ who did not merely suggest but commanded us to love our enemies (Matt. 5:44).

However, we will succeed only if we are united with our fellow spiritual leaders in the spirit of the one God, "Creator of all things visible and invisible." Roman Catholic and Jewish, Orthodox and Muslim, Protestant and Buddhist — it is time not only for rapprochement but for solidarity and cooperation in order to help lead our world away from the bloody abyss of extreme nationalism, fundamentalism, and intolerance.

These principles of goodwill and tolerance were reiterated on the sacred island of Patmos last month, in September, when we convened a gathering of the Primates of the Orthodox Christian Churches to commemorate the 1,900 years since the recording of the book of Revelation by St. John the Evangelist. Together, with one heart, mind, and voice, we condemned "all nationalistic fanaticism, as it is capable of leading to division and hatred among peoples; the alteration or extinction of other peoples' cultural and religious particularities; and the repression of the sacred rights of freedom and dignity of the human person and minorities everywhere."

## Peace and the Environment

We at the Ecumenical Patriarchate will continue our efforts to be peacemakers and to light the lamp of the human spirit. We will continue to champion the cause of caring for our environment, which requires *a responsible relationship between God, humanity, and the natural world.* "Love all God's creation," urged Fyodor Dostoevsky, "the whole of it and every grain of sand. Love every leaf and every ray of God's light. Love the animals, love the plants, love everything. If you love everything you will perceive the divine mystery in things."

We shall always work in this spirit of divine love. The Ecumenical Patriarchate is the fullness of the Church that was founded by the God of love, whose peace "surpasses all understanding" (Phil. 4:7). We "pursue what makes for peace" (Rom. 14:19). We believe that "God is love" (1 John 4:16), which is why we are not afraid to extend our hand in friendship and our heart in love, as we proclaim that "perfect love casts out fear" (1 John 4:18).

We came here today in order to embrace you as brothers and sisters. Although we may be of different faiths, we would like to offer you, like a spiritual father, some wisdom that we received from a Muslim mystic and humanist, the renowned Mevlana, who lived in the twelfth century:

> Become like the sun in your compassion and generosity;
> Like the night, cover up the shortcomings of others;
> As the rushing waters, reach out to the entire world;
> During moments of anger, at times of rage, become like a dead man;
> Become like the earth *(humus)* so people can stand firm
>    on your foundation;
> And either become that whom you manifest, or manifest
>    who you really are.

Dear friends, we are convinced that there is more that unites the community of humankind than divides us. It is, as men and women of business like to say, the ultimate "win/win" situation. We have within our grasp the vision of the Psalmist: "Behold, how good and pleasant it is for brothers [and sisters] to dwell in unity!" (Psalm 133:1). We pledge to you today that the Orthodox Christian Church will do everything in her power to fulfill that vision.

## ENVIRONMENT AND ETHICS

*Address at the opening ceremony of the second*
*summer seminar on Halki, June 12, 1995*

Our Holy Great Church of Christ, the Mother Church, justifiably boasts in God for having hastened to be among the first to initiate a complete series of seminars on ecology within the context of her broader ministries in the world. *The Church's efforts, of course, are not to be perceived as simply striding along with modern times. Rather, our concerns are rooted in the deeper conviction that by these initiatives the Church ministers thoroughly and accountably within the primary mission entrusted to her by God in history, namely the evangelization and salvation in Christ of humanity and the natural world.*

Out of this deep-rooted conviction, we humbly believe that, during these distressing times in which contemporary humanity around the world finds itself, although it is by all means a noteworthy and honorable enterprise to speak casually of ecological concerns, there is often the danger of being misunderstood as merely going along with the "trend" of the times, to be seen as trying to impress instead of seeking what actually illuminates relevant problems and contributes to their solutions.

Who can deny that, in spite of the honorable efforts made by various sectors in order to respond properly to the clamoring demand surrounding this issue, too often we compete with each other on the problem of the environment, speaking and babbling rather than thinking and at the same time doing what is right?

This seminar on the environment and ethics, which with God's blessing is being hosted in this renowned Monastery of the Holy Trinity on Halki, is an attempt to restrain precisely this great danger, which silently and perhaps subconsciously threatens to foil much of the theoretical work done on this subject.

Consequently, as our paternal duty, we take this opportunity not simply to give a formal greeting from the Mother Church, one in which we bestow our wholehearted Patriarchal blessing upon the seminar participants who have readily gathered here, but also, purely out of pastoral concern, to address a few thoughts on the topic at hand. In this way, we may perhaps from the onset place a finger on "the mark of the nails" (John 20:25) as we seek a God-pleasing assessment of the obligations and duties of all men and women created in the image and likeness of God toward everything in the created universe within and around them.

### A Divinely Imposed Ethos

Therefore, permit us to state initially that *the truly awesome endowment that we so often voraciously lay claim to within nature — namely, that we are created in the image and likeness of God — by definition predetermines an analogous ethos that is imposed upon us.* Such an ethos is critical for understanding ourselves and each other as well as the microcosm and macrocosm around us.

Only by following this ethos can we truly satisfy God who created "out of nothing" everything that is "very good" (Gen. 1:31).

In other words, this means that humanity, the visible and living image of God in the world, does not have the right to pursue an *ethos* that is ungodly or does not love God. If someone embraces an ungodly ethos, "partakes" of the image but is not a "custodian" of it, he or she also becomes the inciter and chief perpetrator of evil, which God as a fair judge providentially terminates at death, "in order," as St. Athanasius the Great observes, "that evil not be immortalized." On the other hand, the ethos that springs forth from God and bears witness to the unapproachable and unknown essence of God is everywhere and always described as grace, throughout the Bible and God's revelation to us in general, as well as through the teachings of the God-bearing Fathers of the Church.

Speaking in the presence of Christian intellectuals, we have no need to clarify further that the most profound characteristic of the grace of the all-beneficent God is that it is totally free, that is to say, absolutely given and non-reciprocal. We should like to remind you, however, that, in the biblical account of creation, the grace of God is manifested initially as beneficence, goodwill, compassion, philanthropy, and the like. Yet, thereafter, following the fall and apostasy of humankind, God's grace is revealed as mercy, forbearance, expiation, restoration, reinstatement, and adoption.

### Divine Economy and Human Ecology

Nevertheless, we should unequivocally state that, in both instances, the divine will of God was always manifested in the form of law and order, which no one has the right to violate without being punished, since the entire design of the all-beneficent Creator constitutes a unique and indissoluble "divine economy." Thus, whether we speak of natural, moral, or spiritual principles, we acknowledge and emphasize the same infinite grace of God, confident that *the "divine economy" is always the solid support of ecology as a whole.*

All these things are preeminently indicative of the compassion of an omniscient and omnipotent God. And they should certainly and ceaselessly constitute a guiding policy of our own ethos in the world. For, according to Plato, if God "were perpetually to geometrize" (lit., to be the measure of everything in the created world), then it follows that humankind must always read and obey all the laws pertaining to the world.

Within the framework, then, of this pious awareness concerning the world, we should seriously bear in mind also the rudimentary sequence within the entire order of creation in which God in the six days of creation classified everything, as it is known, from the less to the more perfect. Recognizing and acknowledging such an inverse hierarchy, perhaps then we shall respect anew the unquestionable and mystical sanctity possessed by the material world, created before humanity not only for itself as a work of God "created out of nothing," but for the "being" and "well-being" of humankind. Today, we are not being very eloquent when, for the sake of brevity, we characterize the created material world as the "natural environment."

We wish to say a word, in closing, on the famous scholastic axiom of the Western Church, *gratia praesupponit naturam* (i.e., "grace presupposes nature"), upon which essentially the whole of the West built both its past and present theories concerning natural law as well as most of its sociopolitical concerns. This principle will always fall short and suffer injustice as a result of its one-sidedness, especially in regard to fallen creation in general, so long as it is not completed by the supplementary correction *natura praesupponit gratiam* (i.e., "nature presupposes grace"). This corrective balance was appropriately suggested in a relevant study made some time ago by a hierarch of our Ecumenical Throne. For, indeed, it is only within the liturgical conscience of Orthodoxy that the whole of God's creation is illumined and redeemed by divine love.

# RELIGION AND CONSERVATION

*Address at the Summit on Religions and*
*Natural Conservation held in Atami, Japan, April 5, 1995*

It gives us the greatest pleasure to address you today. We are honored by the invitation extended to us by the organizers of the summit and by the hospitality and warm welcome afforded us by MOA International. It is perhaps especially fitting that this, the opening major paper of both sessions of the summit, should be given in memory of Dr. Terumichi Kawai. It was Dr. Kawai's vision that first raised the possibility of this summit. The breadth and depth of the issues to be confronted at this summit reflect the international scope and perception that were the hallmark of Dr. Kawai's work. We had the opportunity of meeting him only once, when he accompanied his father, President Teruaki Kawai, to an audience granted them at the Phanar. We know that the meeting, which revealed areas of profound common concern between us, was also a result of Dr. Kawai's understanding of the need for East and West to meet.

The pairing of concern for the protection of the environment with theological presuppositions may seem a paradoxical and even eccentric enterprise. Ecology is perceived as representing the pursuit of practical and desirable strategies, while theology seems to be a kind of empirically interrelated, abstract, theoretical research. Theological disciplines, which have to do with the association of dogmas and ideologies, seem to have little or nothing to do with the practical aspect of life or religious issues.

Contemporary ecology, whether it involves scientific research or crusading movements for the salvation of the earth's ecosystem, satisfies humanity's need for practical action. Nevertheless, *the rationale behind environmental concerns is often projected purely as a logic of convenience.* If we do not protect the natural environment, then our own survival will become increasingly miserable and problematic. Before long, the very presence of humanity on our planet will be threatened. Day by day, the danger of the degeneration and even the extinction of the human race become more markedly imminent.

### Covenant and Conservation

Within the context of this obvious logic, the natural environment is understood as an essential party in a relationship — one might almost say "covenant" — with humanity for humanity's own survival. It is, however, a one-sided covenant that is comprehended only in terms of the environment's usefulness to humanity. In general, humans are concerned only with how something is to be used. The origin or cause of physical reality is of no concern, nor is the search for a clarified "meaning" of cosmic propriety, harmony, wisdom, or natural beauty. It is possible that the existential matter of nature was created by unknown "powers from above," possibly by inexplicable products of "chance," or even by an equally inexplicable automation, which exists intrinsically in the composition of matter. At all events, it is not the interpretation of cause and aim that gives meaning to existential matter; rather, the meaning of existential matter is confined only to its *utility and advantage* for humanity.

Stemming from this logic of convenience, much of the ecological movement today demands that certain rules be set down for the manner in which humanity is to make use of nature. Ecology aspires to be a practical ethic of human behavior toward the natural environment. However, as in any ethical system, ecology, too, raises the following questions: Who determines the rules of human behavior and under what authority is this ethical system exercised? What logic makes these rules compulsory, and what is the source of their validity? The correctness of an ecological ethic is made evident by its empirical usefulness. It is irrefutably logical that, in order for humankind to survive on the earth, a covenant with the natural environment that subscribes to human survival must be negotiated.

However, such a rationale, founded on the intentional utilization of what is convenient and advantageous, led to the destruction of the natural environment in the first place. Human beings do not destroy the environment because they are motivated by an irrational self-gratification; rather, human beings destroy the environment by trying to take advantage of nature in order to secure more conveniences and comforts in their daily lives. *The logic of the destruction of the environment remains precisely the same as that of the protection of the environment. Both "logics" confront nature as an exclusively utilitarian commodity.* They give it no other meaning. They are motivated by the same interpretation of physical reality.

In this way, the difference between the two "logics" — namely, between that of the destruction and that of the protection of the ecosystem — is ultimately only quantitative. Ecologists demand limited and controlled exploitation of the natural environment — a quantitative reduction — that would permit its greater long-term exploitation. They ask for the rational limitation of non-rational usage — in other words, a kind of consumerist rationalism that is more "ecologically correct" than the consumerist rationalism of today's exploitation of nature. They are, in the final analysis, asking for consumerist "temperance" of consumerism.

Yet, who will determine absolute quantitative "ecological correctness" within the context of a single monolithic logic of convenience? And how will this determination be made? This demand, while appearing to be extremely rational, is, by definition and in practice, irrational. It is self-contradictory by definition because consumerism cannot come into conflict with itself. In addition, it is irrational in practice because the majority of the world's population does not normally and willingly deprive itself of conveniences and comforts. In reality, only a small minority of "civilized" societies has secured these conveniences and comforts through the destruction of the environment.

## A New Theo-logical Logic

If the demands of ecologists are to be recognized as viable, a new logic must be found to replace the logic of convenience. Demands for protection of the environment should be founded on entirely different principles — for example, concern about future generations or pursuit of some "quality" of life that is not judged by consumerist ease or abundance theories. In other words, *demands must be for universally accepted goals whose basis rejects utilization of the environment merely to supply our conveniences.* Moreover, experience has shown that it is impossible for everyone to agree on rational criteria in defining these goals. Therefore, people must come up not only with different demands for environmental protection but also with an entirely new hierarchy of demands. This will be possible only when the meaning of nature in the consciousness of ordinary people changes so that it is not exclusively oriented toward convenience.

Christianity, along with other monotheistic religious traditions, maintains that the physical world is not there exclusively for our convenience. According to these monotheistic traditions, the world is a creation of God. The use of the world by human beings constitutes a practical relationship between humanity and God, since God gives and humanity receives the products of nature as an offering of divine love for the sake of the world. My friends of the Islamic faith tell me that in the Qur'an it is said that all animals live in community and that they are known by and accountable before God (*Sura* 6:38). The Muslim faith also denounces the arrogance of those who treat the rest of creation without respect: "Do you not see that it is God whose praises are celebrated by all beings in heaven and on earth, even by the birds in their flocks? Each creature knows its prayer and psalm, and so too does God know what they are doing. And yet, you understand not how they declare His glory" (*Sura* 24:41).

## Humanity, Covenant, and Ecology

Within this picture of all creation arising from a loving creator God, the question has to be asked: What of humanity? What does our faith say about human beings? The answer is clear and the consequences immense. Psalm 8 addresses this question directly:

> When I look at your heavens, the work of your fingers,
>     the moon and the stars that you have established;

what are human beings that you are mindful of them,
  mortals that you care for them?
Yet you have made them a little lower than God,
  and crowned them with glory and honor.
You have given them dominion over the works of your hands;
  you have put all things under their feet,
all sheep and oxen,
  and also the beasts of the field,
the birds of the air, and the fish of the sea,
  whatever passes along the paths of the seas.

(Ps. 8:3-8)

We have already mentioned how important it is for an agreement or covenant to exist between humanity and creation for the long-term survival of both. This notion of covenant stems from a figure of fundamental importance not only to Christianity but also to Judaism and Islam: the patriarch Abraham. God established with Abraham a holy covenant that confirmed a permanent relationship between him and his chosen people. Jewish scholars say that Judaism sees Abraham as the founder not only of its faith but also of its people. They consider themselves "the people of the covenant." In the book of Genesis, the Lord says to Abraham, "Go from your country and your kindred and your father's house to the land that I will show you. I will make of you a great nation, and I will bless you, and make your name great, so that you will be a blessing" (Gen. 12:1-2).

Christianity sees Abraham's covenant as a forerunner of the new covenant established by Jesus Christ, in which Christian believers become spiritual descendants of Abraham by divine adoption. This is clearly revealed in the hymn known as the Magnificat. It was sung by the Virgin Mary as a song of praise for the gift of Jesus. In this hymn, Mary describes how God will bring down the mighty from their thrones and exalt the humble and meek. He will fill the hungry with good things and send the rich empty away. At the end of her song of praise, she cries: "He has helped his servant Israel, in remembrance of his mercy, according to the promise he made to our ancestors, to Abraham and to his descendants forever" (Luke 1:54-55).

My Muslim friends say that Islam also sees Abraham as the founder of the Kabba at Mecca, and that the Qur'an holds him to be the first true believer and a model for all believers. Central to that covenant is belief in the one God, Creator and sustainer of all that has been, is, and will be. Nothing exists but for the will of God. As the book of Genesis says: "In the beginning God created the heavens and the earth. The earth was without form and void, and darkness was upon the face of the deep, and the Spirit of God was moving over the face of the waters" (Gen. 1:1-2). This reality is echoed over and over again in the Qur'an.

Christianity inherited the Old Testament tradition through the teachings of Jesus, who compared the value of human beings to sparrows, loved and cared for by God. Yet human beings are a hundred times more important (Matt. 6:26). It is also the case that *the sense of humankind being part of a bigger picture, a greater purpose of God, is emphasized equally within both Jewish and Christian texts.* For example, in the Torah, in Genesis 9, the covenant with Noah after the flood is not just made with Noah and his descendants — namely, with the human race alone — but with all life on earth. Similarly, when St. Paul speaks in Romans 8 and in Colossians 1 about the purpose of the life, death, and resurrection of Christ, he does not regard these as affecting only human beings but as occurring for the sake of all life on earth.

### Compassion and Conservation

Ultimately, for Christianity — and, as I understand it, for Judaism and Islam as well — humanity is the most important or most significant species. Nevertheless, with this reality come particular responsibilities. I am told that in Islam this is expressed by the notion of human beings as *khalifas.* A *khalifa* is a vice-regent — someone appointed by the supreme ruler to have responsibility over a given area in an empire. I have been told that the Qur'an uses this term to describe humanity's role. God has given humanity this authority. However, *it is only to be used on God's behalf, not for our own ends and ambitions. Any abuse of this power, any wanton or wasteful use of the world's natural resources, is repugnant to God.*

The belief that God's love underpins the natural world is borne out in the teaching that God Himself is also bound by His love for the world. Therefore, when Abraham stood before God after God declared that He was about to destroy the sinful city of Sodom, Abraham demanded of God that He give justification for this act, saying, "Shall not the Judge of all the earth do right?" (Gen. 18:25). Christianity, along with Judaism and Islam, also acknowledges that *humanity has been given dominion over nature but always within the context of love, justice, and compassion. We live in a tension between the power we have been given and the limits imposed by love and conscience.*

In the Christian faith, we are taught that Christ is part of the creating Trinity of Father, Son, and Holy Spirit. Thus, with St. Paul, we can describe Christ as Creator who emptied Himself of His power and came to earth as a child — as a weak and defenseless child. The Word of God took upon Himself the role of a speechless servant. So at the heart of Christianity is a Creator who becomes a creature; the mighty Lord is born as a child; the Master of all now becomes the servant of all.

One of the most difficult aspects of the teaching of Christianity, and perhaps also of Judaism and Islam, is the belief that we are able to choose to disobey God. Our freedom under God is immense. Our capacity for good is vast. Our capacity for evil is likewise vast. And often this evil comes about because of foolishness, greed, pride, or ignorance. Yet the end result is always the same, namely destruction.

## Communication and Conservation

Two fundamental consequences emerge from the teachings of our traditions. The first consequence is that *the world is not meant to be used by humans for their own purpose, but it is the means whereby humans come into relationship with God.* If humans change this use into egocentric, greedy exploitation, into oppression and destruction of nature, then humanity's own vital relationship with God is denied and refuted, a relationship predestined to continue into eternity.

The second consequence is this: the world as a creation of God is not a neutral object for our use. *The world incarnates the word of the Creator, just as every work of art incarnates the word of the artist. The objects of physical natural reality bear the seal of the wisdom and love of their Creator. They are words of God calling human beings to come into dialogue with Him.*

It is, therefore, a fact that humankind today must change its attitude toward the natural environment. This is a necessary prerequisite for humankind to change the *meaning* that it gives to matter and the world. *Ecology cannot inspire respect for nature if it does not express a different cosmology from that which prevails in our culture today, one that is liberated equally from naive materialism and naive realism.*

Only when human beings confront matter and all of nature as the work of a personal Creator does the use of nature establish a true *relationship* and not a selfish domination of humankind over physical reality. Only then will it be possible to speak about an "ecological ethic," which does not borrow its regulatory character from conventional, rational rules, but out of the need for a person to love and be loved within the context of a personal relationship. The reason for beauty in creation, therefore, is love. It is an invitation from God to humanity; it is a call into a personal relationship and life in commu-

**Creation of the Plants**
Romania, sixteenth century

"Let there be lights in the dome of the sky" (Genesis 1:14)

The Eternal Word and the Created World, Venice, Italy, thirteenth century

**Creation of the Stars**

Greece, twentieth century

*Courtesy: St. Isaac of Syria Skete*

"Let the waters bring forth swarms of living creatures
and birds that fly" (Genesis 1:20)

Greece, twentieth century

*Courtesy: St. Isaac of Syria Skete*

**Creation of Adam**
Bulgaria, seventeenth century

"Adam gave names to all the animals, to all the birds of the air
and all the beasts of the earth" (Genesis 2:19-20)

Meteora, Greece, sixteenth century

**Icon of the Transfiguration**
Ravenna, Italy, sixth century

"Let us venerate the blessed wood of salvation. . . . For today the world is
sanctified. O marvelous wonder! The length and breadth of the Cross is
equal to the heavens. . . . The four ends of the earth are sanctified today"
(The Exaltation of the Cross, September 14)

Wood carving, Athens, seventeenth century

nion with Him, a relation that is vital and life giving. *Contemporary ecology could therefore be seen as the practical response of human beings to God's call, the practical participation in our relationship with Him.*

Is the ontological clarification of the *meaning* of matter and of the world sufficient to prompt a different relationship between contemporary humanity and nature? Of course not. In order for humanity to treat nature with the respect and awe with which we treat a personal artistic creation, the above-mentioned theoretical clarification must become a powerful source of knowledge and must shape society's understanding of the natural world. The Church may play a vital role in these social dynamics, both in maintaining ecclesiastical tradition and in participating in community, so long as it is not too wedded to ideological structure and bureaucracy.

All human beings are caught in the tension between the ability to do the will of God and the ability to rebel. But alongside this tension lies the ability to return to the right path, to follow again the path of God revealed in the Scriptures. This is why we can look upon the present state of the world with comprehension and distress, but also with a sense of hope. With comprehension, because we can see what happens when people forget that this world is not ours but God's; with distress when we see the consequences of injustice and wrongdoing, of pride, foolishness, and greed, which go against the teachings of God. However, most of all with hope, for we believe with confidence that if we turn again to God, God will meet us and bring us home to Himself. By returning to God, we may start again. The past can be forgiven and we can hope — truly and sincerely hope — that things can be fundamentally different.

If there is a future for the ecological demands of our contemporary times, this future is based, we believe, in the free encounter of the historical experience of the living God with the empirical confirmation of His active word in nature.

# REVELATION AND THE ENVIRONMENT

*Address during the official opening of the first
international symposium, "Revelation and the Environment,
AD 95-1995," September 22, 1995*

With the blessing of God, we have assembled like one of the scenes from the book of Revelation. We come from many cultures and peoples, tribes and tongues, nations and faiths. Yet we share a common concern for the future of the planet and the quality of human life and relationships throughout the earth. We are assembled on a kind of latter-day ark, a symbol that would have delighted St. John. As we begin our voyage, the ship confronts us with our essential interdependence. Here, in microcosm, we can see the truth that distress in any part of the ship will soon affect the whole: passengers dining in first class will not for long escape the consequences.

We shall be voyaging to Patmos on the sea of possibility, the sea from which life itself emerged. It is a time of profound cultural change, and at this moment we are mindful of the Spirit of God, which in the beginning moved upon the face of the waters and which continues to move on these waters. We have been drawn together by a memory. Nineteen hundred years ago on the island of Patmos, St. John received the Revelation, which forms the final book of the New Testament. This occasion, however, is not intended to be a simple anniversary or an academic conference about an ancient text. Revelation begins and ends with the good news of the *parousia*, of the coming and the presence of Christ. At the climax of the New Testament, there is no full stop, but only an opening to the work of the Holy Spirit in the future, and the promise of a new creation, *a new heaven and a new earth, a new community in a holy city, a river of life, and a tree with leaves for the healing of nations.* It seemed appropriate to celebrate this anniversary with a conference about our common home, the natural environment. St. John's vision is of a united human family — of every nation and kindred singing a new song.

## The Story of Symbols

Much of the Bible is addressed to those with ears to hear, but the Revelation granted to St. John is also addressed to those with eyes to see. The story is told in symbols and archetypes. The root of the English word "symbol" lies in the

Greek notion of bringing together fragments of truth in order to achieve a more profound understanding than would otherwise be available through mere analysis. Symbols help us to comprehend the relations between our sometimes fragmentary and fugitive perceptions of reality. Great symbols are not devised to illustrate some thesis that we may wish to advance. They arise rather from some deep level of consciousness and are then disclosed to our reason. They have the power to communicate in a way that itself generates energy. Two such symbols have been entrusted to our generation: the "cloud" and the "globe."

In this year of anniversaries, we are all deeply aware of the mushroom cloud that on August 6, 1945, during the sacred Feast of Transfiguration, opened a radically new chapter in human history. The cloud, however, is a symbol also known to the Bible. And, while the mushroom cloud is reflective of humankind's destructive power, it should not be understood in an entirely negative way. For the first time in history, by unraveling some of the forces that lie at the heart of creation, we have acquired the power to destroy all human life on the planet. Because of this, the world community is under threat. *The work that lies ahead for all those who love life is to translate this world community, which exists as an object under threat, more and more into a subject of promise and hope.*

In practice, of course, we extrapolate and anticipate at the same time, in a single act, which is one of the reasons why science and theology need to be in dialogue at this particular moment of transition. Symbols of the end-time combine with what we consider possible to create a field of action and to fill it with either hope or despair. Science saves faith from fantasy. Faith generates the energy for a new world. We face a need to communicate in ways that release healthful energies for restraint and change. Moralizing exhortations about the common good are limited in their usefulness. "Mere appeals to ethical fraternity will never evoke in man that age-old power, which drives the migrating birds across the ocean" (C. G. Jung).

I hope and expect that this conference will increase our understanding of the various ways in which we may perceive and engage with the world around us. Together, as Orthodox Patriarchs, Metropolitans, and Archbishops, we seek your expert counsel, suggestions, and input so that *Orthodox worldwide can better contribute to the common front being forged by intrepid scientists, environmentalists, and theologians who desire not only a pollution-free world, but a "healing of nations" as well.* Indeed, our common future depends on developing a way to perceive and participate in the world that will complement the analytical approach with an ecological awareness of entities in their various relationships.

The statement entitled "Orthodoxy and the Ecological Crisis," published under the aegis of our predecessor of blessed memory, Patriarch Demetrios, reaffirmed that the monastic and ascetic traditions of the Orthodox Church have important insights for us. These traditions develop a sensitivity toward the suffering and beauty of all creation. "Love all God's creation," urged Dostoevsky, "the whole of it and every grain of sand. Love every leaf and every ray of God's light. Love the animals, love the plants, love everything. If you love everything you will perceive the divine mystery in things."

### *Theosis, Metanoia,* and *Enkrateia*

The monastic and ascetic traditions are life-creating traditions, which beckon all to become a new creation in Christ by being born of "water and spirit" (John 3:5), so that all matter, all life, may become sanctified. In order for sanctification or *theosis* (lit. "deification") to become real, there must be a *metanoia,* a conversion or changing of the mind, reflective of the sanctity of tears. It is not a coincidence that a contemporary Christian poet describes the rivers, seas, and oceans as "a gathering of tears" bearing witness to humanity's adventure and struggling journey. So, too, the Fathers of the desert considered "the baptism of tears" as a lofty blessing empowering all men and women who seek "to come to the knowledge of the truth" (1 Tim. 2:4). Therefore, instead of asking for wisdom and strength and holiness, the angels of the desert asked for tears of repentance in their sojourn and struggle for salvation.

*The ascetic tradition also offers a celebratory use of the resources of creation in a spirit of* enkrateia *(abstinence, lit. "a holding within") and liberation from the passions. Within this tradition, many human beings have experienced the joy of contemplation, which contrasts with the necessarily fleeting and illusory pleasure of relating to the world as an object for consumption.*

At the same time, we want to celebrate the resources offered by the international community of scientists and journalists. As we enter the Mediterranean, it is encouraging to recall the achievements of the Med Plan detailed by Peter Haas in his book *Saving the Mediterranean.*[2] It is easy to be cynical about how much impact such a recommendation by scientific experts and others will have on the actions of nation states, but the Med Plan and its development ought to reinforce the urgency with which we seek to build up a network of personal relationships at even higher levels. We hope that this

2. Peter Haas, *Saving the Mediterranean* (Columbia, 1990).

conference and its aftermath will serve as a major contributor to this growing family.

The Orthodox Church is particularly well represented in parts of the world where "the earth has been hurt," to adopt a phrase from the book of Revelation. In a perversion of science, would-be God-slayers have laid waste great tracts of territory. In these countries, the experience of the martyrs, which St. John also aptly describes, is very contemporary. We pray that the energy that comes from giving up life for the sake of God and His Church may flow into a life-giving stream for the benefit of the entire community of humankind.

This brings us to the other symbol that has been given to our generation, namely, the "globe," a symbol that points in this hopeful direction. Because it is more recent, it has sunk profoundly into human consciousness. The earth-rise photograph taken in 1969 from the Apollo spacecraft shows the entire planet sapphire blue and beautiful, as no human being since the dawn of history had ever seen it before. This angelic view is foreshadowed and enlarged in the book of Revelation, when John is shown the heavens opened and contemplates a great multitude out of every nation, rejoicing before the throne of God.

It may be that the choice between life and death that is always being put before us by the Spirit is in our day being translated into a choice between one world or none. Theology and science ought to be partners in this work. We ought not to divide the one reality, but rather seek — as one theologian has expressed it — "peaceful co-existence at the price of mutual irrelevance."[3]

## The Revelation of Hope

We recognize, however, that many people may have doubts about the possibility of any unity between the worldview expressed in modern science and the visionary material in the ancient book of Revelation. How can Revelation's vision of hope, sustained in the midst of passages portraying terrible destruction, be distinguished from a rather unconvincing whistling in the dark to keep one's spirits up in a time of danger and change? One approach is to consider the various ways in which our many languages enable us to contemplate the future in as many different words as possible. We must understand the contrast between the future that is entirely constructed out of past and present, and will itself soon become past, and the future that, beyond our

3. J. Moltmann, *God in Creation* (San Francisco: Harper & Row, 1985).

control, will come upon us. In Greek, *ta mellonta* is what will be, whereas *parousia,* a term frequently used in the New Testament, suggests a future coming.

There is a similar distinction in Latin, derived from this same notion, between *futurus* and *adventus. Futurus* suggests a future entirely constructed out of past and present; as such, it is a stimulus to planning. Futurologists of this school are those who rely on extrapolations from present trends. Often, of course, the collision between trends makes exact predictions impossible. However, there is another problem with this approach to the future. Prolonging and projecting the present endorses present patterns of power and ownership and suppresses alternative possibilities that the future holds. *Adventus,* on the other hand, like *parousia,* alerts us to what is on its way to the present. In the book of Revelation, Jesus Christ is hailed as "the one who is and who was and who is to come" (1:4), when the series might logically have been completed instead by "Him who will be." A sense of the future as *parousia* stimulates the anticipation by which we attune ourselves to something ahead, whether in fear or in hope. These foretastes and symbolic sketches are part of every perception of the unknown, which we explore by reference to ultimate criteria like happiness or unhappiness, as well as life or death.

The climax of our celebrations will be the Divine Liturgy on the island of Patmos. The liturgy is a work that binds human beings together in the Spirit of our Lord Jesus Christ and liberates them to hope and to work for His future coming in the world. Not everyone in this symposium shares the Christian faith. Nevertheless, we trust that we are all here around a common table like the "symposiasts" of ancient times, because we all know that we are on the threshold of a new day. *Conscious of the threat of nuclear destruction and environmental pollution, we shall move toward one world or none. We hope that we are assembled as those who are weary of defining their own tradition principally by excluding others.* For many generations the Patriarch of Constantinople has occupied what is known as the Ecumenical Throne. That title reaches forward to the end-time of the healing of the nations, when there will be communion between God and human beings in a new heaven and a new earth "and death shall be no more" (Rev. 21:1, 4). We pray that this conference may contribute toward mobilizing all people of goodwill in our world and bringing closer together the day foreseen in the vision of Patmos.

# CALL TO ACTION

*Address during the presentation of the results
of the first international symposium, September 25, 1995*

At this moment, we are receiving from your blessed hands the results of the inestimable collected effort of the God-loving participants and speakers of this symposium. And we are deeply moved by the same emotions that fill the liturgical celebrant of the Most High when he receives from the hands of the faithful the bread and wine that are to be consecrated in order that their offerings might constitute immortal nourishment for the whole world.

Therefore, along with their Beatitudes and their Eminences the presiding hierarchs and your honorable persons, we hereby also bless these joyous fruits of your symposium, which by God's grace has drawn to a close. We express our congratulations and gratitude to you all for what has been achieved. We are certain that, from this point forward, your scientific and intellectual vigilance will remain the unswerving compass by which you will guide your colleagues and students to illumined and saving horizons.

During this official occasion, we wish to assure you, on behalf of the Church, that, aware as we are of the significance of your contribution of empirical work in many areas of God-inspired thought and science to the progress and welfare of the world, we shall not cease to pray for your good health and increasing achievement.

In closing, we wish to add one simple observation, which is already known to everyone, namely that the destructive deterioration of the environment is taking on multiple and threatening dimensions. Therefore, we must not be content with verbal protests, but instead we must proceed to continuously stronger and more effective actions, each in his or her own place and position. For pollution is dangerously spreading and rapidly increasing. Indeed, quite possibly and — God forbid — quite probably, according to the calculations of the experts, pollution will become impossible to control. *We cannot remain idle.*

May the enlightenment of the Paraclete always shine in your steps and in your actions within the course of your research and science, for your own benefit and for that of all your fellow human beings and the whole natural world.

# MANNA, MYSTERY, AND MEALS

*Toast at the dinner hosted by the municipality of Patmos
during the first international symposium, September 26, 1995*

Attending this final dinner at this holy hour and on this sacred island, lovingly hosted by the Honorable Mayor, we recall another Mystical Supper which the Lord and Savior shared with His holy disciples, when he said: "I have eagerly desired to eat this Passover with you before I suffer" (Luke 22:15). During the hour of our supper, when the shadow of night approaches and the noise of the day subsides, we are able to confess, talking frankly and in hushed tones.

*At that hour of the Mystical Supper, the beloved disciple, John, lay within the embrace of Jesus; and from that inexhaustible well he was able to draw the living water of sacred theology, through which he quenched the thirst of the entire universe.* There, he received the hidden and living manna. He came to know and to teach love and forbearance. He was vested with the spiritual courage to follow Jesus on the way to the cross.

Indeed, so many holy and sacred things are offered at a holy and mystical supper! And the Lord, recognizing the hunger and thirst of each of us for truth, fellowship, and life, invites us all to His mystical supper. And since he is the friend, not only of that beloved disciple, but also of each and every one of us, He constantly approaches us. He is near to us, knocking at the door: "Behold, I stand at the door and knock; if any one hears my voice and opens the door, I will come in to him and eat with him, and he with me" (Rev. 3:20).

The sacred but, at the same time, also dangerous thing for us is that the Lord is most discerning. He does not force the door of our freedom. And if we do not wish to lose our personal relationship with Him and be excluded from the supper, we must keep both our mind and our senses alert, in order to be able to distinguish the sound of His presence and the word of His Spirit.

If the Lord God, during His mystical supper, grants us freely of the hidden and heavenly manna, that promise of a divinely beautiful life, then at this official banquet, the municipality of Patmos has offered us an abundant table prepared with so much love and delicacy and has also honored us with the Golden Medal of this sacred island.

We are deeply thankful for all these gifts, and for all the other benefits that have been given to us so richly in a variety of ways through the gentleness of the ethos of all the Patmians. We pray that the Lord of glory may send in return upon the beloved mayor and his good co-workers, as well as the guests at this dinner, the pious citizens, those who reside here and those visiting this island, instead of earthly things, the heavenly; instead of temporal things, the eternal; and instead of corruptible things, the incorruptible (from the Liturgy of St. Basil). May the same God make us all worthy to eat and drink together at the table in His heavenly Kingdom. Amen.

# A NEW HEAVEN AND A NEW EARTH

*Toast during the official dinner hosted by His Excellency the President of the Hellenic Republic, the Hon. Constantine Stephanopoulos, first international symposium, September 26, 1995*

Unquestionably, today, the 26th of September, the day on which we celebrate the venerable repose of St. John the Theologian, we are at the height of our celebratory festivities. This morning, by the grace of the Holy Spirit, we assembled, all the presiding hierarchs of the Holy Orthodox Churches of God together with all the faithful, around the holy altar where we offered the bloodless sacrifice. We were fed by the heavenly bread, the food for all the world.

At this solemn hour, having descended to the port of the holy island of Patmos, we are recipients of this abundant dinner, kindly hosted by the Greek government. All of these are blessings from God, gifts of the grace of the sacred Revelation. They are a divine foretaste of endless joy and gladness for all. "He who witnessed the ineffable revelations" saw the holy Jerusalem descending from heaven. There was no need of any sun or moon, since Jerusalem itself was illumined by the glory of God; there was no need of a temple, since the city was, in itself, fully a holy temple. And he heard a voice: "Behold, the dwelling of God is with [people]. . . . He will wipe away every tear from their eyes, and death shall be no more, neither shall there be mourning nor crying nor pain any more" (Rev. 21:3-4).

With this description, St. John assures us that he himself, through the Spirit, had already experienced and enjoyed the "new heavens" and the "new earth" that we anticipate according to the promise of the Lord (2 Pet. 3:13). Similarly, all of us, the faithful, can receive and enjoy this same grace through the celebration of the Liturgy. *If the divine revelation is a liturgical event, then, for the same reason, the Divine Liturgy is a continual revelation that illuminates our whole life.*

## Eucharist, Ecumenicity, and Ecology

Over the last few days, we have not simply been reminiscing about events of the past, occurrences that took place 1,900 years ago. By the power of the Holy Spirit, we have become partakers of this very event, living liturgically this same experience. Through a divine revelation, St. John saw the holy city of Jerusalem descending from heaven, manifesting the glory of God. And we, the faithful, are able to experience the same love of God during the Divine Liturgy. For God "did not cease creating all things until He lifted us up to the heavens and granted to us His future kingdom" (from the Liturgy of St. Basil the Great).

Spiritually, the Jerusalem from on high descends below. *Liturgically, the faithful are lifted up to heaven. Moreover, by the power of the Holy Spirit, all things in conflict come together and receive the gift of the future things.* The things of the past are illumined and everything is gathered in the person of the divine-human Christ, who presides over the one heavenly and earthly liturgy, who is the Alpha and the Omega, as well as the sanctification of our souls and bodies. This same divine-human Lord blesses and sanctifies not only the holy table during the Divine Liturgy, but every material table as well.

In conclusion, we wish to underscore the fact that it was in this place of his exile, while he was held here under tyrannical authority, that St. John the Theologian witnessed the divine revelation and accepted the fullness of freedom. He found and showed us "an open door, which no one is able to shut" (Rev. 3:8), leading us also into infinity and granting to all men and women the potential for freedom.

This proves that the spirit can never be confined. Love can never be conquered, but only conquers, willingly offering itself as a sacrifice for the life and salvation of the world. "This, our faith, is the victory which has vanquished the world" (from the seventh Ecumenical Council). Therefore, the ecumenical mission of the Orthodox Church is found in the truth of love and in the act of service and sacrifice for our fellow human beings. Our leader, our Light and our Shepherd, is the sacrificial Lamb. The beauty and power of love, which is perfected in weakness, sanctifies and brings together the world. Thus, the abrogation of acrimony is achieved, humanity is saved, and the revelation of the essence of life is manifested. Indeed, filled with such divine gifts and graces, we have been truly blessed by the priceless gifts that have been freely bestowed upon us.

## MESSAGE OF THE ORTHODOX PRIMATES

*Message of the Primates of the Orthodox Churches*
*on the island of Patmos, first international symposium,*
*September 26, 1995*

*"Blessing and glory and wisdom*
*and thanksgiving and honor*
*and power and might*
*be to our God forever and ever!*
*Amen."*

(Rev. 7:12)

1. We offer glory, praise, and thanksgiving to our Triune God for once again deeming us worthy, the Primates of the local Most Holy Orthodox Churches by His mercy and grace, to convene at this time "on the island called Patmos" (Rev. 1:9) for the celebration together of the completion of 1,900 years since St. John wrote the sacred book of Revelation, the conclusion of the Church's Holy Scriptures.

Radiantly solemnizing together and concelebrating in the Lord the sacred commemoration of the holy glorious Apostle and Evangelist John, and partaking of the Bread and the Cup of our common faith, hope, and love, it is our desire to direct a message of peace and love to the faithful of our Most Holy Orthodox Church, to all those who believe in Christ, as well as to every person of goodwill so that we may unite with them in listening to "what the Spirit says to the churches" (Rev. 2:11, 17, 29; 3:6, 13, 22) during these critical times.

2. These are indeed critical times, making the responsibility of the Church of Christ, not only to her children, but also to all of humanity in general and to all of God's creation, a somber and multifaceted matter. The apostasy of humankind from God and the effort to deify human power and hap-

piness, the altar upon which everything — our fellow human beings and all the rest of the material creation — is sacrificed, prompt and intensify this crisis, which many characterize as "apocalyptic."

During these times, we believe it is our obligation to underscore what the revelation in Christ means for the progress of humanity, peace, and fellowship of all peoples. It is the responsibility of the Orthodox Churches to contribute in every way possible to the realization and prevalence of these principles throughout the world, by becoming bearers and messengers of the spirit and ethos of the revelation. Therefore, from this sacred place, sanctified by the Evangelist of love, we make an appeal to all — foremost to those who exercise power on earth and those who live in the regions of conflicts and wars — for the sake of peace and justice for all. To this end, we ourselves as Churches are prepared to offer our spiritual and moral contribution wherever necessary.

3. Through this appeal, we wish to make it clear to all — and especially to all those who either deliberately or else out of ignorance present an inaccurate or distorted image of the Orthodox Church — that the Orthodox perception of "nation" in no way contains any element of aggression and conflict among peoples. Rather, it refers to the particularity of each people to maintain and cultivate the wealth of their tradition. In this way, they contribute toward the progress, peace, and reconciliation of all peoples. For this reason, we condemn all nationalistic fanaticism, as it is capable of leading to division and hatred among peoples, the alteration or extinction of other peoples' cultural and religious articulations, and the repression of the sacred rights of freedom and dignity of the human person and minorities everywhere.

4. This message is addressed during a critical point in human history, as we approach the end of the second millennium after Christ and the dawn of the twenty-first century. The Orthodox Church should not leave this to pass without notice, although certainly she is aware that the measuring of time in increments of a thousand years or other units of time is, in essence, merely a convenience. The fact that historical time is measured in reference to Christ calls all those who believe in Christ to notice this historical turning point and to use it as an opportunity to evaluate the great events of this century and to discern the problems and the possibilities of the new century that is dawning.

For these reasons, the Orthodox Church intends to plan Pan-Orthodox celebrations for the jubilee of the year A.D. 2000. During these celebrations the Church will offer doxology to the Lord of history for all that he has given the Church and His world during this fading century. Thus, we shall be rendering "glory to God in all things," according to the saying of a holy Father of the Church, cognizant that His grace, enlightenment, and help will be invoked upon the Church and upon His people at the beginning of the coming millennium.

5. We recall that, for the Orthodox Church, the closing century was full of important events. In various lands, Orthodox Christians suffered cruel and prolonged persecutions. This martyrdom encouraged the Orthodox ethos of an evangelical humility and "the endurance and faith of the saints" (Rev. 13:10), to trust in Him who "went out conquering and to conquer" (Rev. 6:2), with the assurance that along with the life of the cross of Christ comes the experience of the resurrection. The blood of these known and unknown martyrs connects our Church in a special way with the apostolic age.

6. This experience of martyrdom accompanied the theological witness through which patristic theology was renewed and the teaching of the Fathers about the natural world and humankind, and about the sacraments and the Church, was affirmed. The rediscovery and creative presentation of the teachings of the Greek Fathers of the Church, the "language" and spiritual beauty of our icons, the awakening of a missionary conscience, the flourishing of the monastic life, and the rediscovery and appreciation of the spirit of the desert Fathers in conjunction with a fertile dialogue with the contemporary currents of philosophy and science — all these things have made Orthodox theology alive and respected internationally. It is for this reason that we must honor the pioneers of this theological florescence, who through their diligent endeavors led Orthodox theology to a common witness to the modern world, a witness that goes beyond racial distinctions and national boundaries.

7. This creative revival of the spirit of the Church Fathers has helped the contemporary theological and ecclesiastical world not only to renew the life of our local churches in general, but also to offer to the various organizations of the contemporary ecumenical movement and the bilateral and multilateral theological dialogues the witness of "the one, holy, catholic, and apostolic Church." The ecumenical movement, whose activity toward the end of the concluding millennium has been intense and has revived sacred hopes among divided Christians, constituted a wide and significant ground of witness, promotion, and contribution of Orthodox theology. Unfortunately, the crises and deviations observed during the last decades in the bosom of the ecumenical movement impose upon the Orthodox Church a need to resist such deviations and to promote the genuine tradition of the Church. We also consider that Uniatism and proselytism are serious obstacles to the progress of our dialogue with Roman Catholics and Protestants.

8. *During these times of rampant secularization, there is an even greater need to point out and underscore the significance of the holiness of life in view of the spiritual crisis that characterizes the modern world. The misunderstanding*

*of freedom as permissiveness leads to increased crime and to a lack of respect for the freedom of one's neighbor and for the sanctity of life; what is more, it leads to the violation of the natural world and to ecological destruction.* The Orthodox tradition is the bearer of a spiritual ethos that must be emphasized particularly in our times.

9. We offer this Orthodox experience and witness in humility, fully conscious of our responsibility to the *oikoumene,* to all persons and peoples without exception, with respect for the freedom and uniqueness of everyone, in obedience to Him who was slain and by His own blood did ransom the world for God "from every tribe and tongue and people and nation" (Rev. 5:9). The horizon of the Orthodox mission, in spite of temporal difficulties, remains universal; and its direction and expectation remain eschatological.

10. Most especially with regard to the ecological crisis, which for all of us is crucial and threatening, we reiterate through this present message the vigorous concern of the Orthodox Church for the right use of the environment. Already during our previous meeting at the See of the Ecumenical Patriarchate, we expressed this conviction while recording that, by the initiative of the Ecumenical Patriarchate, conferences related to this issue have been organized and September 1st of each year has been designated as a day of prayer for the protection of the natural environment. *Once more, we affirm that we consider this issue eminently threatening, and we call upon all to be vigilant and to take every necessary avenue in order to save and protect God's creation. The Orthodox Church considers humankind to be a steward and not the owner of material creation. This perception is particularly expressed in the tradition and experience of the ascetic life and worship, and above all in the Eucharist. It is imperative today that we all display love and keep an ascetic attitude toward nature.*

11. Thus, the meaning and significance of the Divine Eucharist as the center and as a criterion for the entire life of the Church is obvious. All the holy sacraments and the whole of Church life are centered on and lead to the divine Eucharist. Each Divine Liturgy, celebrated by or in the name of the local canonical bishop, constitutes the axis and the criterion of the entire life of the Church; it reveals the deeper and final meaning of the existence of the whole of creation, namely its communion with the life of the Triune God.

It is therefore apparent that, on the one hand, the Divine Eucharist must always be celebrated in the name of the canonical bishop and with his permission, so that it may be valid and salvific for its participants. On the other hand, the manner of celebration must be proper to its nature and character as an icon of the kingdom and the final meaning of all that exists. It is necessary to say this because serious deviations have been observed at times with regard to the permission given by, and the commemoration of, the canonical bishop in the Holy Anaphora, while the manner of celebrating the Divine Liturgy and worship occasionally shows signs of influences alien to the Orthodox tradition.

12. And now, looking forward in faith and hope to the coming millennium, we call all people to prayer and vigilance in view of the grave problems as well as the great possibilities appearing on the horizon. The achievements of science in almost all areas, and particularly in biology, entail incredible successes, but also dangers. The Church cannot remain indifferent before these prospective developments, since the survival of the human person as "the image of God" is at stake.

13. In the field of broader political changes, the Orthodox Church remains steadfast to the fundamental principle of noninterference in politics. To be sure, the Church cannot be indifferent when political decisions affect the very existence of the Orthodox Churches, in which case she expects that her position will be heard and be taken seriously into account. We consider one such case to be the issue of the future of the Holy Land, both its holy places and its living community, which concerns the entire Orthodox Church and the Patriarchate of Jerusalem in particular. Therefore, any discussion concerning the *status quo* of the Holy Land, which has been secured by international decisions and conventions throughout the centuries, cannot and should not take place without the knowledge or the presence in particular of the Orthodox Patriarchate of Jerusalem, which has resided there for centuries.

14. In the broader field of culture, many have expressed the view that the coming century will bring humanity to "a clash of civilizations" in which the religious elements will be dominant. Such a possibility obliges all religious leaders to show wisdom, prudence, and courage in order that every element of fanaticism and hatred may be eliminated, thereby safeguarding peace in a world that has been tried so severely in wars and conflicts during the century drawing to a close.

15. In a world confronted by all kinds of sects and terrifying interpretations of the book of Revelation, all of us, especially the younger generation, are called to learn and to bear witness, in word and deed, to the fact that only the love of God, of our fellow human beings, and of all His creation offers meaning and salvation to our lives, even during the most difficult periods of history. In spite of its dramatic events, the book of Revelation contains in its depth the gospel of Christ, which reveals to us that human sin and the demonic destructive forces have been and will be defeated by Jesus Christ, the Lord of history, who is "the Alpha and the Omega . . . who is and who was and who is to come, the *pantokrator*" (Rev. 1:8).

From this sacred island of Patmos we address this message to you, beloved ones in Christ, embracing you in His name and bringing to you and all the world the voice of the sacred author of the Apocalypse, a voice of faith, hope, and love. "Behold, the dwelling of God is with [people]. He will dwell with them, and they shall be his people, and God himself will be with them; he will wipe every tear from their eyes, and death shall be no more, neither shall there be mourning nor crying nor pain any more, for the former things have passed away" (Rev. 21:3-4).

The grace of our Lord Jesus Christ and the love of God the Father and the communion of the Holy Spirit be with you all. Amen.

On the sacred island of Patmos, this 26th day of September, 1995, the feast of the holy glorious Apostle and Evangelist John the Theologian.

+The Ecumenical Patriarch Bartholomew, also representing The Patriarch of the Holy City of Jerusalem and All of Palestine Diodoros

+The Pope and Patriarch of Alexandria and All Africa Parthenios

+The Patriarch of Antioch and All the East Ignatios, represented by Metropolitan John of Pergamon

+The Patriarch of Belgrade and All Serbia Pavle

+The Patriarch of Bucharest and All Romania Teoctist

+The Patriarch of Sofia and All Bulgaria Maximos, represented by Metropolitan Gelasios

+The Archbishop of Metschete and Tbilisi and Katholikos Patriarch of All Georgia Elias, represented by Bishop Abraham of Nikortzminta

+The Archbishop of New Justiniate and All Cyprus Chrysostomos

+The Archbishop of Athens and All Greece Serapheim

+The Archbishop of Tirana and All Albania Anastasios

+The Archbishop of Prague and Metropolitan of Czech and Slovakia Dorotheos

+The Archbishop of Karelia and All Finland John

# 1996

Metropolitan John of Pergamon, at the 1996 Halki summer seminar

# COMMUNICATION, COMMUNION,
# AND ENVIRONMENT

*Foreword for the published proceedings of the third*
*summer seminar on Halki held in July 1996, composed*
*in June 2000 in preparation for publication*

The Mother and Holy Great Church of Christ in Constantinople, which protects and proclaims the spirit of the Patristic tradition, has for years now assumed a responsibility for the preservation of the natural environment. The annual summer ecological seminars were organized at the initiative of the Ecumenical Patriarchate in the Holy Patriarchal and Stavropegic Monastery of the Holy Trinity at Halki, with the purpose of studying the ecological crisis in a theological and interdisciplinary manner in order to find appropriate solutions. The seminar that was held July 1-7, 1996, on the theme "Environment and Communication" aimed at the careful consideration of this particular dimension of the subject.

Within creation, all beings, animate and inanimate, communicate with one another and endure the same natural forces, one influencing the other. Nevertheless, the human person is the supremely rational being of communication, endowed with the consciousness of dialogue with one's fellow human beings. This potential of conscientious and rational communication also renders possible the transmission of knowledge, ideas, and sentiments, thereby shaping humanity's stance toward the rest of creation. The transmission today of distorted forms of communication, which look to the transformation of the human person into an individual easily manipulated by a formless and colorless social mass, surely constitutes a phenomenon for concern.

Communication or dialogue comprises the fundamental characteristic of life in the Church. The interpenetration of the three Persons of the Holy Trinity constitutes the ultimate and perfect form of communication. The Church is a body of persons in continual communication with one another. The Holy Eucharist itself, that supreme sacrament of the Church, is the central means of communication between God and humanity in Christ. More particularly, *the offering of creation by humanity to God in an act of thanksgiving constitutes the expression of the greatest ecological ethos.* It is not by accident that the terms used to describe this great mystery are divine Eucharist and divine Communion.

The third summer ecological seminar gathered renowned leaders in the areas of the Church, science, and scholarship as well as communications in order for these to contribute together to a more universal confrontation of the worldwide ecological crisis. Their papers and the recommendations of the groups and workshops serve as a rich resource for the tireless environmental efforts of the Patriarchate but also of every religion and person concerned about the destruction of the creation.

May the grace and boundless mercy of the Creator Lord, whose providence protects all of creation, be with you all.

## CONSERVATION AND COMPETITION

*Address during the tea attended by the religious leaders
of Hong Kong, November 6, 1996*

When closed within a very narrow environment, where they know only those of their own race and religion, people can create within themselves imaginary and deceptive images of others who belong to other races and religions. However, Odysseus, of ancient times, "saw cities of many people and acknowledged their intelligence." He was able to ascertain, as we modern-day Odysseuses are able to ascertain with him, that all of us descend "from one human race," as the Apostle Paul wrote, and consequently, that we are all brothers and sisters.

This brotherhood unites us and at certain times separates us. This happens when we heartlessly treat our siblings unfairly when it comes to dividing up a rich inheritance — namely, this small earth which hosts us and which perpetually moves within the unfathomable universe — given to us by the Father, our good God, who is ever-beneficent and possesses superabundance. For our loving Father has organized everything well in order that this Garden of Eden, our earth, might sufficiently provide for all the needs of those who live upon it. A simple demonstration of the misuse of this abundance would be the voluntary destruction of surplus goods from the developed nations, while other nations suffer a scarcity of goods for consumption, even to a dangerous level. A further example would be the inconceivable waste in terms of labor and money for the production of weapons systems, not to mention the waste created by their catastrophic deployment. Clearly, if all of these efforts were put toward the good of humanity, life on our planet would be much better.

Here in the peaceful and progress-oriented city of Hong Kong, you appreciate efficiency and creativity in human effort, and you well understand the truth of our words. They are the words of a father or brother who beholds with sorrow some of his children destroying one other. He pleads with the rest of his children not to follow the same destructive path, but rather to resolve their differences peacefully through mutual withdrawal. *There is always a solution that is more advantageous than the one that leads to conflict. The obstacle for discovering this solution is not found in our external world, but rather within ourselves, because all our decisions spring from deep inside us.*

We bless your peaceful place. We greet you with love and emotion at the gracious welcome that you have given to us and to our entourage. We wish you health, peace, and progress. May you be a universal example of a peaceful and civilized community, an example of the effectiveness of freedom and of noble competition. For in this blessed place of yours, virtually all of the peoples of the earth meet and work together, coexisting peacefully in spite of their various differences. This is because, among yourselves, you have accepted your neighbor and his or her right to be as he or she is. We would be remiss if we did not note the effectiveness of this attitude, characterized by freedom, mutual respect, and labor.


# ENVIRONMENT AND COMMUNICATION

*Greeting at the third summer seminar on Halki, July 1, 1996*

We have gathered once again for an ecological meeting in this sacred place, the monastery dedicated to the Holy Trinity and the renowned Theological School of Halki, where clergymen and theologians were educated for generations.

*We do not pretend that we have sufficiently cultivated the ground upon which Churches, religious communities, environmental organizations, and scientists can communicate with each other throughout the world about the vital issues of environmental protection. On the contrary, we steadfastly believe that, as we discover more and more the truly unbelievable dimensions of the worldwide ecological problem, a long-term program of complex and concerted studies is required.* In the combined, creative synthesis of their conclusions, we may be able to face more effectively the global threats caused by the irresponsible, if not criminal, behavior of rational human beings toward the non-rational and material creation. In this creation, God has placed humanity from the beginning "in a paradise of delight," not only as sovereign, but also as healer and steward. Our destructive management of creation, besides having a practical impact on the quality of life, assumes a critical, moral dimension that constitutes a profound disrespect toward the Creator.

Moreover, the subject of the environment in general, which is being addressed here today, together with the much discussed issue of communication, is certain to open up very important perspectives for the tasks of this present seminar — for which we rejoice personally and most warmly in the name of the Mother Church.

It is clear that, through these words of greeting for the opening of your deliberations, in no way do we intend to prejudice or even to influence substantially the work that has been planned, since indeed we are not speaking here as one of the experts on the subject. It is rather our desire to express a few general prefatory statements regarding the authoritative position of the Church on the whole subject of environment, especially in relation to the development of increased communication, which is of eminently vital significance for us, for the benefit of the whole of humankind and, ultimately, for the glory of God.

In short, it is sufficient to state that, just as it is important for the various systems of the human body (such as the nervous, digestive, and circulatory systems) to communicate with each other in order to maintain good health, the free operation of communication has the same value and purpose. Hence, the entire physical network of varying biotopes and specific geographical ecosystems will be better served not only through the mutual exchange of information but also by the coordination of activities among all those responsible.

## Communion and Communication

Let us express this same truth in its most spiritual form, and in a manner greatly pleasing to God. Communion with God in prayer, and solidarity and interaction with one's fellow human beings in every real situation, render truly blessed the distribution of all the good things of this present world. In the same way, *unhindered communication among all those concerned with ecological management today is equivalent to the indispensability and the sanctity of prayer.* Ultimately, all things created may be connected eucharistically for the praise of the one Creator and Father God.

With all our soul, and in the true spirit of prayer and service for the whole of humanity along with the whole of creation, we wish that the blessed efforts and tasks of this summer seminar on Halki may bear fruit. We profoundly thank first our respected governmental authorities for the assistance they have provided. Then, we must thank His Royal Highness, Prince Philip, Duke of Edinburgh, who, once more, was well pleased to allow us to place this seminar under our joint aegis. Moreover, we thank all those who sent messages of goodwill for this seminar — in particular His Excellency, the Hon. Bill Clinton, President of the United States, who donated on behalf of the American nation the young tree that we shall plant in a short while as a token of his esteem for the ecological endeavors of the Ecumenical Patriarchate. The expressions of support by these esteemed people demonstrate their strong interest in global environmental problems and indicate humankind's increasing awareness of looming environmental threats. In this, too, communication has played a vital role.

This support also encourages the Ecumenical Patriarchate to continue its undiminished and persistent initiatives to mobilize the moral and spiritual forces of the Orthodox Church in order to realize once more the harmony that existed between humanity and nature, to the glory of the Creator. This is because the Ecumenical Patriarchate continues to observe the rapid deterioration of environmental conditions globally, which frequently results in irreversible changes. However, the Ecumenical Patriarchate sees two hopeful phenomena: first, the international community's adoption of the principles of sustainability in the management of natural resources and a wiser conception of the development process; and second, the growing mobilization of people, and especially of the younger generation, in combating threats and managing the planet in a more sensible way.

In this spirit, the Ecumenical Patriarchate is organizing for the autumn of next year a second symposium on board a ship, with the theme: "Religion, Science, and Environment: An Encounter of Beliefs, a Single Objective." This symposium will focus on the environmental problems of the Black Sea and their solution. The seminar will start on 31 August 1997 from Thessaloniki, the "Cultural Capital of Europe" for that year, and will sail to Istanbul, continuing to Bulgaria, Romania, Ukraine, Russia, Georgia, and returning to Turkey.

Finally, we congratulate the organizing committee of the summer seminar on Halki, and we thank all those who, in whatever way, took part in its realization, along with the participants and speakers who have been kind enough and concerned enough to assemble here. We entreat the divine Creator to bestow His rich illumination upon all; and on everyone here we grant our paternal and Patriarchal blessing.

# CHURCH AND STATE: THE EXPERIENCE OF EASTERN EUROPE

*Address at the Foreign Correspondents' Club*
*in Hong Kong, November 6, 1996*[4]

The most significant world-historical event of the twentieth century was the rise and fall of communism. Both events, the incubation and the decline of what was once called "existing socialism," took place in Russia, where the Orthodox Christian faith was a powerful force for centuries. The beginning of the first communist regime in world history dates to 1917 and was marked by the so-called October Revolution. The fall of the Soviet system, in 1989, occurred in its birthplace, Russia, exactly two hundred years after the French Revolution. It was signaled by demands for "Glasnost" in the management of public life and "Perestroika" of the state from its ruins heaped upon the Soviet lands over seventy years of "existing socialism."

The Orthodox Church has the painful privilege of being the only Christian tradition that coexisted with the communist regime and suffered in its body the cruelty of all manner of religious persecution under that aggressive atheist system, the first to appear in world history and to achieve such success without any resistance.

The French Revolution may have declared atheism and applied it for the first time in history as an official state policy, persecuting the clergy, establishing a worldly calendar, and ridiculing all that is holy and sacred in the Christian faith, but it tolerated the personal practice of religious observance by faithful citizens of the State and instituted religious freedom as a human right; and, despite the many and various measures restricting religious practice, nonetheless

---

4. This address is included here, not so much because of any direct reference to the environment, but because it allows the reader glimpses into the background and context within which the Orthodox Church offers its unique and genuine contribution to pressing environmental issues.

this very first atheistic regime took a position of tolerance and abstention from interference in religion, without resorting to persecution and violence.

## Church and Martyrdom

The secularization proclaimed by the French Revolution and established without violence was accomplished by violent and bellicose means by the Russian Revolution. Atheism was transferred from theory into practice, removing its deceptive facade of mildness to reveal its hideously violent face, moving from ideology into politics, and abandoning peaceful methods in favor of aggressive and violent ones. The first victim of this aggressive atheism was the Orthodox Church. God and history reserved for us Orthodox in this century one of the most *crucifying* experiences of this world. The *persecution,* the *martyrdom,* and the *confession* of faith proved enormously bloody for Christians, and especially the Orthodox, both in the first three centuries and in the twentieth as well. There is, however, a difference.

In early Christian times, all Christians were living in the declining Roman Empire, and thus all Christians were persecuted equally. During the seventy years of the communist regime, however, the preferred and primary victims of persecution were Orthodox Christians, our flock, the faithful people of God of the Orthodox countries. That was where, by tragic coincidence, the newfangled sociopolitical system of existing socialism and its innate aggressive atheism found fertile ground. Anyone wishing to search contemporary world history to find Christian martyrs, confessors, and those persecuted for their Christian faith and lifestyle could safely turn to us and our flock, the much-wounded faithful of the Orthodox countries of Eastern Europe, who have suffered much.

As spiritual leader of these martyrs of contemporary ecclesiastical history, we come today to address you on the subject, "Church and State: The Experience of Eastern Europe" — certainly not in "superiority of speech," but in the fact that we bear, in the historical body of the Orthodox Church, by the mercy of God, all the signs of the harshest persecution over at least seven decades. The Orthodox Church is comprised of millions of faithful, tens of thousands of whom were tortured, killed, exiled, imprisoned, and persecuted in every way. When we speak here of the relationship of the Orthodox Church to the state of Eastern Europe, we mean specifically the coexistence and survival of religion under the communist regime. Thus the subject at hand focuses on the relation of the Church to communism.

It happens that in contemporary history we are the most competent to address such a subject, since we still bear the fresh blood of the martyrs of the Orthodox faith.

We intend to convey to you, through all which we are about to say, something of this martyr experience of our Holy Orthodox Church under communism. In this way the *martyrdom* and the *witness* will be naturally seen together. The martyrdom simultaneously constitutes witness. The deposition of the *witness* instantly becomes an act of *martyrdom*. In this sense at least, not to mention equally painful historical experiences of our Orthodox people, *Orthodoxy happens to be one of the most martyred Churches of contemporary history.*

## Church and State

The first issue facing us when we are "called to account for the hope within us," in relation to the state and especially in Eastern Europe, concerns the official and unofficial position of the atheist regime toward religion and especially Orthodoxy. On this matter, we answer with the following:

The position of the communist regime regarding the Church was always and without exception negative. Under no circumstances was there any deviation or adjustment of position on this issue among the various local communist regimes or even within the varied ideological tendencies within the communist camp.

All held a negative stance toward the Christian faith — the intensity of this opposition to the Church varied, but there was no variation in its essence or content. The leaders and the followers of existing socialism may have differed on many other subjects, but they were always wonderfully in accord on the issue of religion. Christianity was always opposed, although the actual practice of this opposition ranged from neutrality or even indifference to religion to an open and irrepressibly aggressive persecution of both the faithful and pastors, which was turned against even the simple exercise of basic responsibilities of worship.

In certain places, depending on historical circumstances, changes were observed in the anti-religious positions of communist regimes, sometimes improving, but more often worsening. For example, in the Soviet Union, during the Second World War, the great persecutor of the Church, Joseph Stalin, temporarily suspended the merciless religious persecution so that the Orthodox Church would give moral and spiritual support to the Russian people as they confronted the foreign and heterodox invader through the successful execution of the so-called "patriotic war."

In contrast to the few examples of slight relaxation of this antireligious posture, we have many cases of aggravation and changes for the worse. A particularly telling example is Albania, where, around the end of the 1960s, a cruel persecution of religion was announced and pursued with remarkable vehemence, the magnitude of which had never been experienced by the faithful before, even during the first months of the Russian Revolution or the even more miserable years of the Stalinist antireligious rage. There is not sufficient time to relate details of the diligence and maniacal zeal with which the persecuting authorities acted in an effort to eradicate every shred of religiosity.

The relationship between the then hard-line, Stalinist-inspired, Albanian regime and the Chinese communist prototype, with its Maoist ideal of "cultural revolution," along with the contribution of the violent "red guards," might explain why this European country with a socialist regime devoted itself to cruel persecution of religion, while at the same time other satellite states of the Soviet coalition had reduced their atheistic fervor. Perhaps China may have influenced Albania in the hardening of its antireligious politics and acted as a catalyst in the graduation of atheistic ideology from tolerant neutrality to antireligious violence.

## Patience and Expectation

A second issue concerns the position taken by the Orthodox Church in the face of the tempest of atheistic persecution. This is a sensitive point, especially as it relates to the inference of useful experiences, teachings, and potential lessons. From beginning to end, the Orthodox Church remained faithful to the spirit of *martyrdom* and *witness*, with which it is better acquainted than anyone, not only from the early Christian persecutions, but also from the later history of the Eastern Roman Empire, known also as the Byzantine, which survived a host of successive, violent, and continuous persecutions by invaders from both the east and west.

We in the Church have become accustomed from both our faith and our history to live with *patience, persistence,* and *expectation,* which is to say in an eschatological manner, as it is called in theological terminology. We suffer persecution with patience; we persist in our faith; and we expect with hope the Lord of history, the Redeemer and Savior, who is the "slaughtered lamb" "who takes away the sin of the world," the crucified and resurrected Christ, who has suffered for us and with us, according to the fitting expression of St. Maximus the Confessor.

We Orthodox hold a strict neutrality toward every political ideology —

not from indifference, but, on the contrary, from the firm conviction that passing fads and vain notions are imperceptibly interwoven together with self-interest, egotism, and hypocrisy in every ideological configuration of human life. In the final analysis, no political grouping can produce all that it appears to promise or even advocate. Ideology can prescribe and proclaim ideal principles and programs, but its daily political implementation foils every noble intention and honorable effort.

We Orthodox have been taught by bitter but instructive experience of historical reality to disbelieve bold political declarations, and exactly for this reason we do not talk politics, although, of course, we do not deny our responsibilities in accordance with the wise words of an early Christian text, which succinctly describes how all Christians live in their own countries, but as guests, participating as citizens in every way and at the same time enduring everything as foreigners: "Every home land is their own and every home land is foreign" (*Epistle to Diognetus*, ch. 5).

For this reason the resistance of the Orthodox to their atheist persecutors in communist regimes did not take on the form of an organized political campaign, something which in our opinion mistakenly was done in Western Europe in the form of "Christian Democratic Party." We did not engage in a new "crusade" against atheistic communism because we reject all forms of violence, based on the eschatological observation of the kingdom of God, which we foretaste in Holy Eucharist, praying on behalf of both "those who love us and those who hate us," as we Orthodox do at every Divine Liturgy and service of our Church, considering it unacceptable to receive Holy Communion without, above all, love for those who hate us, and working daily in the spirit of *catholicity* and *ecumenicity*, beyond all political arrangements, politicization, or partisanship.

## Eschatology and Ecumenicity

The resistance of Orthodox people to atheism remained exclusively *theological* and purely *eschatological*. It was never transformed into an ideological and political resistance. Nor did we allow any political configuration, parallel to the persecution of communist regimes against us, to establish an "anti-communist front." Even when such a religio-political miscarriage occurred, we denounced it, explicitly or silently, according to the specific historical circumstances and our abilities. Under no circumstances have we allowed the Orthodox faith to slip into any kind of party loyalty or politicization.

Finally, the position of the Orthodox in relation to atheistic communist regimes took on positive content whenever this was rendered possible by specific socio-political conditions and historical circumstances. We have referred already to the Russian example of "patriotic war," when the Orthodox Church overlooked the persecutions of the Soviet dictator and responded to his call to hearten the embattled people. We should also remember the great and practical contribution of Orthodoxy to the promotion and establishment of peaceful coexistence among peoples through interreligious collaboration in the context of the ecumenical movement, and especially the World Council of Churches, of which our Ecumenical Patriarchate is a founding member.

Immediately following the end of World War II and in the midst of the so-called Cold War, the Orthodox Church labored for the peaceful coexistence of the Western and Eastern alliances, responding most positively to the proposal for collaboration with international peace movements as well as with all other international organizations inspired by humanitarianism, without ever taking ideologies into account or one-sidedly supporting the "faithful anti-communists." Above all else, as Orthodox we preserved the *ecumenicity* and *catholicity* of the Christian faith as well as avoiding political alliances and party politics.

The positive response of us Orthodox to all peaceful or patriotic overtures did not lead us to "historical compromise" with or ideological capitulation to communism; nor did it allow deviation from healthy religious sentiment toward foolish nationalistic ambitions or any form of fanaticism. Wherever and whenever we have seen these improprieties and similar deviations from the Orthodox tradition occur, we have hastened to condemn them, stigmatizing vigorously and in every way the abomination of "ethnophyletism" or national racism.

In concluding this address on the relationship between the Orthodox Church and the state in Eastern Europe, and especially atheistic communist regimes, we emphasize and underline the fact that we were persecuted without persecuting. Without cause or provocation we were pursued, but we did not pursue in return. We worked for peace in time of war. We prayed for those who pursued us and wished that each of them would be blessed with the fortune of the "apostle to the nations," who was born as Saul and reborn as Paul, who began life as a fanatical persecutor of Christian faith and ended as an ardent apostle thereof.

A similar miracle occurred in our century with the rise and fall of atheistic communism. Can its history be conceived of as a pale shadow of the conversion of Saul into Paul? Would not, perhaps, such an image be somewhat bold? Even if that were the case, and we retain great reservations about paralleling a personal religious conversion to a world-historical shift of a sociopolitical nature, we nonetheless wish to emphasize, exalt, and promote the message of hope contained in both cases.

As Ecumenical Patriarch we wish to convey this message of hope to all of you, the representatives of the communications media, and to request that you, too, each according to your own measure, become apostles of hope through the power of the pen and of the image, through radio, television, and all other electronic media, inspired by the example of vindicated hope provided by the Orthodox Church in Eastern Europe in this presently expiring twentieth century.

# BEAUTY AND NATURE

*Address at Sydney Town Hall, Australia, November 26, 1996*

Sydney is the oldest, most populated, and most attractive city of the fifth continent; and it is a most significant center of social, financial, and cultural life in Australia. Yet, by the standards of the Old World, it is a relatively new city. Nevertheless, we can discern in this city architectural tradition and urban planning, a cultural tradition, a tradition of freedom, and harmonious and ordered coexistence of its inhabitants. Each ethnic community is granted the opportunity to be organized and to develop based on their religious convictions and the cultural particularities in the context in which they live, for the good of Australian society as a whole. . . . This is why Orthodox Christians are able to live comfortably within the tolerant and liberal Australian society and also to contribute to it.

Coming from a rich tradition such as ours, and encountering here the mayor of the largest city in this free country, we feel that we share the same spirit. Therefore, we pray that the Lord will bless your efforts for the beautification of the city. May the development of the urban area and your city planning be rendered still more humane, applying modern technology in ways that are beneficial to humanity and harmless to the environment, and creating new spaces that will cultivate and promote the cultural activities of your citizens.

## Humanity and Nature

The Ecumenical Patriarchate, too, has a particular interest in the preservation of ecological balance. Creation is a gift from God to humanity, a companion and servant in the daily needs of humanity. It has been given to us in order to live in harmony with it, use its resources with measure, and cultivate and preserve it, in accordance with the Old Testament command to "till it and keep it" (Gen. 2:15). Within the unimpaired natural environment, humanity discovers spiritual peace and rest; and in humanity that is spiritually cultivated and possesses the grace of God and inner peace, nature recognizes its lord and companion. The Orthodox Church has always encouraged humanity to respect the works of God, while the saints are considered the best friends of creation.

This is why we rejoice at being in Sydney and in observing the ecological balance here. You live in one of the most beautiful cities of the world in the midst of incomparable natural beauty. Your efforts toward a harmonious development of the urban area with the surrounding natural environment are admirable. We pray that the city of Sydney will grow with the same respect and attention that creation deserves, so that it may continue to be, even for those who come after us, a place of spiritual comfort and an opportunity to glorify the Creator.

We have been deeply gladdened by our visit to Sydney, and we have admired the dynamism and order of its society, which respects humanity as well as the environment with its buildings and architecture. Technology has been applied here with discernment. We have enjoyed the natural beauty as well as the human simplicity and warmth.

# 1997

A traditional welcome with bread and salt for Patriarch Bartholomew at Odessa,
during the Black Sea symposium (1997)

# THE ECOLOGICAL CRISIS

*Toast during the official banquet, second international symposium,*
*Batumi, Georgia, September 21, 1997*

The contemporary ecological crisis in its diverse forms has been character-ized as, and indeed is, the most immediate threat not only to the functional balance of our ecosystem but also to the continuation of life on our planet. The hole in the ozone layer, the greenhouse effect, the pollution of the atmo-sphere, the defilement of the terrestrial and underground water-table, and many other phenomena bearing on the contemporary ecological problem throughout the world have already been pointed out at the international and local level, both by international organizations and by informed, sensitive lo-cal representatives, both governmental and other.

The impressive presence and the warm reception accorded to the inter-national ecological symposium by the political, religious, and intellectual leaders of the lovely city of Batumi give expression to the pain of our com-mon concern over this problem that is ongoing and universal, yet has unique consequences in every particular place and for every particular people. The impressive response, however, of the people to this initiative of the interna-tional ecological symposium confirms not only the wider consciousness of the tragic dimensions of the environmental crisis, but also the people's wholehearted disposition to contribute in every useful way toward the pro-tection of their environment.

The beautiful city of Batumi and its surroundings have long been a ma-jor crossroads of peoples, religions, and cultures. Commerce, in previous times, and thriving industry in more recent years, were influenced to a great extent by the city's natural link with the Black Sea, which was indeed a "hos-pitable sea" for all the people of the North and the South, the East and the West. Today, the beautiful coastline near the city, which becomes crowded with thousands of tourists during the summer months, is in danger of losing its attraction because of the dangerous pollution of the Black Sea, into which radioactive and other harmful waste is emptied, not only from countries sur-rounding the Black Sea coast, but even from those further afield.

The dumping of radioactive and other kinds of waste into the Black Sea is continuous and uncontrolled, and the Black Sea is in danger of being la-beled as the most polluted sea in Europe. This pollution will have particularly dangerous consequences, not just for the peoples of the entire Black Sea area, but for the whole Eastern Mediterranean, unless the necessary measures are taken quickly for its vital protection. The uncontrolled influx of radioactive and destructive waste-matter, primarily from countries to the north and the west, with the major rivers as the principal channels, combined with the impossibility of their disposal through the very small and shallow outlets of the waters of the Black Sea, have rendered the deeper sections of its sea bed a dangerous depot of the waste of the countries of Central and Eastern Europe.

## A Cry of Agony

The theme of this international ecological symposium is a responsible cry of agony for the visible danger of total catastrophe for the Black Sea, that natural source of life for all the peoples of the Black Sea region. The undertaking of the symposium by ship, with scientific reports presented by eminent scientific personalities, provides important benefits: it gives us a living link with the problem while we hear about necessary proposals for its solution, and it gives us contact with the appropriate political and intellectual leaders of the Black Sea region, who live with the painful consequences of this continuously aggravated environmental crisis and who are willing to join us in the attempt to overcome the threat of disaster.

The formulation of the main theme of the symposium is in the form of a question. Obviously, this is not because the eventual danger is uncertain, but because *our cooperation for the aversion of the danger must be constant and must be proclaimed in every quarter as a cry of agony for the future* of the peoples of the Black Sea region. In this common effort, science will offer the correct processing of the necessary proposals for the control of the influence of radioactive and other polluted waste; religion will challenge the common conscience of every believer, reminding us of our personal responsibility before God for guarding the integrity of divine creation; and the political leadership of the peoples will support, through every useful means, the protection of the natural resources of life for all the peoples of this region.

Scientists observe that the Black Sea is in danger; political leadership becomes receptive to messages concerning the dangerous threat; and the peoples live out the tragic consequences of pollution in their everyday lives. The reversal of this crisis will undoubtedly be difficult, because it has become too much caught up in the vicious cycle of a consumerist idea of the link between humanity and the ecological environment; but it is more necessary than ever, even if many years of hard struggle are needed. The cooperation of religious leaders with all the others here, using all the means at their disposal, for the effective confrontation of this serious problem will give to concrete proposals the dynamism of the faith of the peoples involved for the protection of the ecosystem from the plundering mania of contemporary humanity.

# PROMPT AND PROPER RESPONSE

*Greeting on arrival at Novorossisk for the*
*second international symposium, September 22, 1997*

An international symposium in which distinguished representatives of religion, science, and the competent organizations for the protection of the environment participate could be characterized as an opportune initiative for greater conscientiousness concerning the dangerous dimensions of the modern ecological problem. However, this international ecological symposium, which has as its main topic the recognized danger of the destruction of the Black Sea, assumes special importance since it analyzes through well-founded reports the destructive factors of this specific problem and proposes specific solutions for its timely confrontation. At this symposium, the theoretical declarations of international organizations dealing with the seriousness of the modern ecological crisis come into contact with the particular dimensions of the problems of the Black Sea, the correct confrontation of which calls for the immediate move from theoretical accounts to practical proposals for its prevention or cure.

The visit to this splendid city of Yalta offers a representative picture of the exceptional importance of the Black Sea for the life of the peoples of the area around it, while at the same time making more tangible the threat of the results of this proven ecological crisis for subsequent generations. It is now commonly agreed in science that the correct confrontation of a problem must be preceded by the correct description of all the factors that bring it about. The presentations of the specialist speakers at the symposium are describing with characteristic completeness the causes of the problem and submitting well-founded proposals for its timely and effective confrontation.

Nevertheless, in the final analysis, *all the disturbing descriptions of the causes that have turned the Black Sea into a storehouse of radioactive and other waste materials from the countries of Central and Eastern Europe, as well as all the proposals for the confrontation of the problem, hold humankind responsible.* This is the tragic reality of the problem. The arrogant apostasy of humanity from its relationship with our divine Creator's creation is the deeper reason behind the presumptuous and improper exploitation of the ecological environment. Now the painful consequences of this apostasy for human life itself and for life on our planet, as indicated by the anxious declarations of all the responsible international organizations, render essential the restoration of humankind's inner spiritual equilibrium, so that we may become more fully aware of the threat.

## Passive Observers or Active Participants?

The imminent danger of the destruction of the Black Sea, as has been described with tragic clarity in the addresses of the specialist speakers and in the interventions of the distinguished members of the symposium, constitutes what is perhaps the most characteristic confirmation that human beings, with their arrogant preference for violent submission of the natural environment, have eventually become timid and ineffective observers of the tragic results of their choices. The purpose of our symposium is to evaluate the conclusions of science and the principles of religion for the restoration of the genuine relationship of humanity with the natural environment, in order to assume personal responsibility for the specific problem of the Black Sea and more generally the problems of our planet.

The warm reception accorded to our symposium by the civil and intellectual leadership of the beautiful city of Yalta constitutes not only a significant encouragement for our initiative but also an expression of active participation in the struggle to save the Black Sea. If all the cities of this region support the final proposals of the symposium with consistency and firm resolve, then our hopes will not be disappointed, and the Black Sea will become a credible commendation for confronting other, similar ecological crises.

# HISTORY AND PERSPECTIVE

*Address to the Turkish/Greek Business Council
and the Young Businesspersons Association, May 26, 1997*

I am pleased to address this prominent body of Turkish and Greek business-persons, who have come together in the spirit of peace and brotherhood to cultivate and promote some noble ideals, which do indeed make a difference in the quality and substance of life, and to which all of us here in various walks of life and from various disciplines and beliefs are called to serve for the good of the human race.

Three days from today, Turks and Greeks alike, each in their own way, will mark the 544th anniversary of the Fall of Constantinople. The poignancy of this historic occasion is that what was a victory for some and a loss for others still rings fresh in the consciousness of both, as though the Fall happened only yesterday. *While it is emotionally difficult to put the past behind us, we must at least be willing to put things into proper perspective.* For more than half a millennium our paralleled history has been marred by strife, suspicion, and animosity.

You might ask why I bring this delicate subject up here and now. And as you are not children; as you are well educated, objective, and open-minded; as you are able to anticipate the deeper meaning lying beneath the historic event, I would be obliged to answer that while we linger in the past, while we keep old wounds alive, while we continue to argue over who did what to whom and when and why, other nations have left us behind and have moved forward.

Sir Winston Churchill once observed that the problem of the Balkan nations was that they have too much history. Was he right? To a point, perhaps, since history to each of us is often so glorious that we are easily transfixed and even hypnotized by it. I cannot imagine that Churchill himself was so dispassionate about the history of the British Empire. Nevertheless, perhaps now is the time to accept history maturely, objectively, fearlessly, and with an open heart, so that we can enter the new millennium soon to dawn upon us free of the heavy burden of hatred.

## Enmity of the Past

There are some who say that national and ethnic tensions and enmity are not a matter of choice, that historic hatreds are an inevitable product of human history, and that whenever people of different faiths, cultures, and civilizations face one another, they inevitably clash.

I, personally, beg to differ. *Hatred is a choice — a very bad choice —* and anyone who doubts this needs only to remember the World Wars and all the other wars of this century, which cost millions of precious lives. These were wars that could have been avoided and lives that could have lived their natural course. Nevertheless, following World War II, hatred *did not* prevail. Led by the United States, the allies began to rebuild Germany and Japan, the Marshall Plan ensured freedom and democracy in Western Europe, and the Truman Doctrine, whose fiftieth anniversary we celebrate this year, extended support to Turkey, Greece, and elsewhere. These policy decisions stand among the most significant ever made. And they succeeded for one simple reason: they placed a higher value on the future than on the past, on love than on hatred.

Turks and Greeks have sinned against each other. Even worse, like children, they have kept score of the pain and losses suffered. As a man of God, I feel it is within the realm of my pastoral responsibilities to admonish anyone willing to listen that we are all sinners and to exhort them to acknowledge that the fullness of time has come when we must confess our sins and put them behind us. I cannot accept what some say, that Greeks and Turks cannot get along any better than cats and dogs (if you will pardon the expression; it is not mine), that this is how it has always been, and that our enmity is a natural one. In the first place, we are all members of the human race, not the animal kingdom. And in the second, enmity is not something natural; rather, it goes contrary to the image and likeness of God in each and every one of us.

## Unity in the Present

We know that Greeks and Turks are capable of rising above their differences. We have seen this happen during the course of modern history — indeed, it happened at a time when the wounds of the two countries were still very fresh, in 1930, when Greek Prime Minister Eleftherios Venizelos and Turkish President Mustafa Kemal Ataturk shook hands and signed an alliance between the two countries.

The lesson is clear: to be able to face the future, we must loosen the emotional knot of the past, while neither forgetting nor belaboring the unchangeable and undeniable events of history. To do this, however, takes great courage and faith, the kind of courage and faith that marks great civilizations and progress, the kind of courage and faith that you as leaders in the business world possess.

You know the history of our two peoples well. You know the bad blood that exists at certain times and on certain levels. You know that the response must be bold and decisive, and that you may even be criticized, perhaps even vilified, for participating in this effort. And yet, you are here — here to say that our children and our children's children must not grow up feeling the hatred that has poisoned our relations for so many generations. You are here to risk everything for peace, where others would rather risk everything for war. And why? Because you acknowledge that nothing was ever gained by hating; rather, too much has been lost and the price has been too high. From your perspective, among these losses one must count the economic prosperity of Greece and Turkey. While both countries have great economic potential, both have allowed military rivalry to take a heavy toll on their budgets; both have forsaken the huge economic boost that the Balkans would provide should Greece and Turkey forge closer ties of friendship and trade.

Imagine if we were a thriving cooperative and peaceful region again, as in the days when the Byzantine Commonwealth was at its summit. Historians point out that the merchants of the East thrived at a time when the West could barely make ends meet. In fact, the Byzantine currency — the gold solidus or bezant — held its value for seven centuries, thus making it the most stable currency in history! Less than a century ago, in the multicultural, multinational Ottoman times, there were Greek businessmen in Odessa and Bucharest, Albanian enterprises in Egypt, Serbian merchants conducting lively trade with their Habsburg counterparts, and a thriving Jewish community in Thessaloniki. So, just as in those times, why not today? Imagine what our region could do today given the many God-given talents and resources our peoples possess.

In fact, goods do move freely between Bitolja and Bucharest, between Trikala and Tirana, between Sofia and St. Petersburg, between Alma-Ata and Ankara. Of course, free trade also ensures exchange in culture and the arts, promotes understanding and tolerance among religions and traditions, and elevates the dignity of humanity nearer to the sublimity intended by our common Creator. There is no reason to continue the divisions and enmities that have made Eastern Europe, and particularly the Balkans, the world's stereotype for ethnic conflict.

## Maturity for the Future

It was not always that way. Let us therefore draw from our experience and maturity and put behind us the divisions and prejudices of the past. Once, only conquest united Europe and Asia; today, so much else, including commerce, can achieve the same result. Instead of ships full of soldiers, let us see ships full of produce crossing the Bosphorus. Instead of military strategies and men on the battlefield, let us see genius in the realm of arts and science. Instead of casualties, bloodshed, and victims, let us see life lived to its fullest! You, as businesspersons and industrialists, are in a unique and privileged position to set the example for other countries. You can inspire them with your own vision and resolve. *You can be the ones to move mountains!*

The way of bringing this about today is through unity and peace, open borders, and a far-reaching European Union in which people, capital, ideas, products, cultures, and religious preferences and ideologies flow freely and unimpeded, without fear and trepidation; an inclusive European Union in which peace, democracy, justice, human rights, mutual respect, and all other values — spiritual and moral — are the bedrock, the consciousness, and the future. *This is the soul of a united Europe.* In this united Europe *there is a place for Turkey.* Greece, as Turkey's closest neighbor, can work toward this aim.

As Enrico Vinci, the former Secretary General of the European Parliament, pointed out: "The European Union cannot and must not close its doors. Its expansion is a historic necessity and is the product both of the changes that have taken place over the last years and of the phenomenon of the dismantling of boundaries and obstacles to the free movement of ideas, trade, capitals, and services." The Ecumenical Patriarchate looks forward to the day when a United Europe will include not just the one neighbor, but both of them together, working side by side. It was General De Gaulle who said: "C'est la géographie qui commande" (It is geography that commands).

Much has already been done and is being done to foster reconciliation and economic cooperation between Greece and Turkey: the positive remarks by Foreign Minister Pangalos in March during a visit to Washington; the attendance of Chief of Staff General Ismail Hakkl Karadayi at the recent Greek Independence Day celebrations in Ankara; the meetings between Deputy Foreign Minister George Papandreou and Undersecretary Onur Oymen in Malta, and Chief of the National Defense Staff General Athanasios Tzoganis and General Karadayi in Brussels; the European Union initiative on the Aegean problems, coordinated by Dutch Foreign Minister Hans van Mierlo; the Black Sea Economic Cooperation Forum recently hosted by Turkey; the upcoming meeting of Balkan Foreign Ministers, which will be hosted by Greece; the meeting of Greek and Turkish students within the framework of the European Forum of Students (A.E.G.E.E.), which has created an atmosphere of hope for future generations; and, as recently as yesterday, the bold and estimable initiative of my friends Mr. Rahmi Coc and Mr. Sarik Tara to bring about the first meeting of Greek, Turkish, and Greek and Turkish Cypriot businessmen, which we learned met yesterday in Istanbul. We highly commend this historic initiative and encourage the partners involved to continue their efforts. Nevertheless, in this and in the other areas mentioned above, much more needs to be done.

## A Global Vision

We wholeheartedly embrace an affecting statement by Secretary of State Madeleine Albright, which we would like to repeat to you today. Madame Albright said: "We desire to see Greece and Turkey live and cooperate against those who threaten the civilized world through acts of terrorism, the expansion of nuclear arms, the destruction of the environment, and narcotics."

Although many of the initiatives and challenges mentioned above are led by political leaders, politicians alone cannot heal the rift between Greece and Turkey. We all have a role to play if this rapprochement is to be successful. We no longer live in a time of provincialism, but, again as Vinci has said, "in *a time of globalism in the making*." The Greek and Turkish economies absolutely must cooperate because the "world financial battles are ruthless," and together they must confront the fierce competition and antagonisms rampant in the financial world today. Certainly, you as business leaders are uniquely positioned to articulate the real costs to Greece and Turkey of keeping ancient animosities alive. You can help our peoples focus on real problems, like the balance of trade with each other. We shall help by setting an example of how not to dwell on the balance of sins against each other. You can channel the two nations' competitive efforts away from the battlefield and into the free market, filling orders instead of graves, and we shall concentrate on the spiritual substance of the human person, who, with God's help, can find the will to succeed at peace and reconciliation.

We religious leaders are aware of our weighty responsibilities. We shall make it unequivocally clear that the spirit and the letter of those books which each holds as holy and sacred support the idea of reconciliation in good faith among rivals. The Qur'an, for example, calls for a fierce response to enemies, but it always leaves a door open to peace, as in the following passage:

Prepare you against them what force and companies of horse you can, to make the enemies of God, and your enemies, and others beside them, in dread thereof. . . . But if they incline to peace, incline you to it too, and rely upon God; verily, He both hears and knows. (*Sura* 8:60-61)

Elsewhere the Qur'an speaks beautifully of a common bond and reward:

Verily, those who fear God shall dwell amidst gardens and springs: "Enter you therein with peace and safety!" And we will strip whatever ill feeling is in their breasts, as brethren on couches face to face. (*Sura* 15:45-47)

We are both God-fearing peoples, are we not? The greatest challenge we face today comes from the so-called Godless society, from those who leave no room for God in their daily lives. The Christian gospel heralds a similar message of peace, mercy, reconciliation, and the rewards of God:

If any one says, "I love God," and hates his brother, he is a liar; for he who does not love his brother whom he has seen, cannot love God whom he has not seen. (1 John 4:20)

Likewise, a message is also directed to those who make peace:

Blessed are the merciful, for they will receive mercy.
Blessed are the pure in heart, for they will see God.
Blessed are the peacemakers, for they will be called children of God.
(Matt. 5:7-9)

## Children of God

We are proud to say that whether you are Christian, Muslim, or Jew, your efforts to reconcile Greeks and Turks make you children of God. Go forth from here and spread the word that hatred must cease; that "the person who does not love does not know God, for God is love"; that that which unites us is greater than that which divides us; that, in the words of Dr. Martin Luther King Jr., "We must learn to live together as brothers, or we will perish together as fools."

We at the Ecumenical Patriarchate understand this and have taken steps to work toward this aim. In 1994, along with the Appeal of Conscience Foundation, we sponsored the Peace and Tolerance Conference, which issued the now often cited "Bosphorus Declaration." In early June, at our invitation, we are hosting here in Istanbul the tenth international academic meeting between Christians and Muslims. And we shall continue our efforts to be peacemakers and to light the lamp of the human spirit. We, as a Church free and respected by all, shall continue our work as a religious and spiritual institution to serve God, to preach love, and to minister to our neighbor who is created in His image and likeness.

"We pursue what makes for peace" (Rom. 14:19), and that is why we are not afraid to extend our hand in friendship and open our heart in love. For us, "perfect love casts out fear" (1 John 4:18).

Many if not most of you are known to me personally, and I shall boldly but confidently suggest that all of us in this room share the same objective; therefore, I exhort you, in the name of humanity, inspired by our common God, be fearless, be persistent, be persuasive, knock on every door; for wherever you go, you go in God's name. As peacemakers, you bring the message of reconciliation. As people of courage and conviction, you have made a choice — the right choice — to rid our peoples of hatred and to promote friendship. As people of vision, you see a bright future economically, but also one that expands the cultural, political, and spiritual horizons of our world.

# ENVIRONMENT AND JUSTICE

*Welcome address at the opening of the fourth*
*summer seminar on Halki, June 25, 1997*

It is a well-established fact that care for the environment of our human family and concern regarding ecological matters constitute a most urgent matter for each and every human person. With every passing day, the danger threatening the survival of life on this beautiful planet becomes more apparent. Today, a host of international organizations, governments, and leading non-governmental bodies are sending the same message, in no uncertain terms, that they are bearing down on the very visible danger that is posed by the real disturbance in the ecological balance. Each has set forth proposals for the prevention of the certain destruction of our planet of which we have been forewarned.

For this reason, the Ecumenical Patriarchate, the Mother Church, has taken this initiative and joined its own voice to those of many others and has taken diligent and incisive action for the protection of the environment, inasmuch as our material world is first and foremost a spiritual organism. The Church is compelled first by its love in Christ for our endangered fellow human beings, and also by its responsibility not only to teach the faith, but to practice it (James 2:14-17).

So it is that, as in many other matters of faith, the Church risks being condemned as indifferent unless it speaks out appropriately with the "word of truth." Failure to do so would result in opening the field to other voices, and it could sometimes result in the consequence that we, believers in Christ, might not even recognize what our own faith teaches about these issues.

Therefore, we are acting out of love and a sense of responsibility, in order that we may speak the truth and be of service to our fellow human beings. Part of our contribution to these efforts is the annual organizing of these environmental seminars here in the sacred monastery of the All Holy Trinity at Halki. The theme of this year's seminar is "Environment and Justice."

At first glance, these concepts might appear unrelated, but they are most certainly worth a closer look. In Holy Scripture, justice does not have only or principally the current meaning of the dispensation of justice, namely of justice being served. Justice carries the more extensive and comprehensive sense of virtue, such as is expressed in the well-known aphorism of Aristotle: "Every virtue is contained in justice." The just person does more than merely comply with the law; the just person bears within himself or herself a higher conception of justice, namely of the perfect relationship of all things to one another. Thus, the just person is virtuous in every respect. For example, Holy Scripture describes as just those who show mercy all the day long and freely give of themselves, without any legal obligation. Likewise, Scripture portrays St. Joseph the Betrothed as being a just man, namely as being virtuous in all things, precisely because at the moment that he thought the all-holy Virgin was guilty of illicit union (the result of discovering her pregnancy), he did not wish to make an example of her or subject her to the punishment prescribed by the law, which was death by stoning.

*If justice is identified with this correct understanding, then it becomes immediately apparent that the contemporary acute ecological problem has its root precisely in the lack of justice, in the lack of that comprehensive virtue of possessing all virtues.*

## Repentance and Restoration

Humanity freely departed from this virtue of justice when, at the prompting of the serpent, Adam declared his autonomy from God and thereby overturned the relationship of love and trust with God. As a result, we came to sense our own vulnerability; we began to know remorse, to hear the approaching footsteps of death; and since that time we have been filled with fear and anxiety (Gen. 2:9-11). Recall how Adam was called by God to account for his disobedience. Instead of humbling himself and seeking forgiveness, he placed the blame on God Himself, claiming that Eve was the cause, that helper whom God had provided for him. Thus, Adam lost the opportunity for repentance and for the restoration of love that would have absolved him from the fear of living the remaining years of his life in the inherited fear that has endured in every generation since.

From that time, humankind has been engaged in the titanic, if not Sisyphean, attempt to reclaim through its own efforts the power of kingship over creation, which was forfeited by this disobedience. Humankind arrogantly struggles through its own means to establish itself as God, to acquire for itself the very powers of divinity. Quite obviously, we have not succeeded in obtaining our desire. Surely there are many and varied passions of humankind that impel us to differing actions. Yet, beneath them all, one discovers our basic fear and fundamental uncertainty about the future. Consequently, we struggle to find substitutes for the real hope and reassurance by which we can achieve security. Unfortunately, these efforts fail to establish us on the only true and firm foundation, which is Christ, for only trust and love for Him can cast out fear.

Thus, we see humanity striving to shore itself up by accumulating wealth and by manufacturing weapons to seek revenge and often to destroy one's fellow human beings as an enemy, real or imagined. We contradict ourselves by exterminating certain creatures as being bothersome while affirming that these same beings protect us from others that are even more dangerous. *Humanity has not only sought to take from the natural world that which is necessary for its own stability and survival, but often seeks to satisfy its perceived and ultimately false psychological needs, such as the need for self-display, luxuries, and the like.* Twenty percent of humanity consumes eighty percent of the world's wealth and is accountable for an equal percentage of the world's ecological catastrophes. One cannot characterize this situation as just; and what is more, this injustice has had a direct impact on the ecology of the environment. However, it is plain that this numerical minority of financially powerful people is not the only cause for the ecological ruin of our planet. Every person ruled by instinctual fears attempts to exploit and loot nature. Consider the willful scorching of the earth, over-fishing, wasteful hunting, excessive and dangerous overuse of resources, and other similar "injustices" against the ways of nature, which share in the responsibility for the ecological crisis.

During the course of this seminar, you will have the opportunity to study these issues in detail. We wish to convey to all of you participating here our heartfelt welcome, together with our paternal prayer that you might worthily actualize the possibilities available to you during the course of this seminar. We encourage you to exhaust the present theme, which we have raised here in a few points, to stimulate your minds by engaging your work from every perspective and by gleaning ideas and hypotheses that are useful for all of humanity. It is indeed just for each of us to shoulder the burden of his or her own responsibility and not to remain silent, thinking that others will take charge and be liable and that we can remain an isolated, insignificant factor. Only if there is "just" comprehension by each of us of our responsibility to work together — all of us — in a universal effort will we be able to hope for a better world.

# JUSTICE: ENVIRONMENTAL AND HUMAN

*Foreword to the published proceedings of the*
*fourth summer seminar at Halki held in June 1997,*
*composed in June 2000 in preparation for publication*

For the Orthodox Church, the worldwide ecological crisis constitutes the expression of a more comprehensive crisis of the human race and concerns all of the critical issues faced by humanity. The crisis faced by creation cannot be examined exclusively from the perspective of the numerous and undoubtedly beneficial branches of science and technology. In order to secure long-term solutions and avoid repetition of errors of the past, we are obliged to study the ecological crisis, too, in light of the more general moral crisis.

One of the more fundamental problems that constitute the basis of the ecological crisis is the lack of justice prevailing in our world. By justice we mean not only the legal correspondence of giving and receiving, of transgressions and consequences, of offering and reward, but the more inclusive virtue that lies beyond the narrow fulfillment of obligation. The liturgical and patristic tradition of the Church considers as just that person who is compassionate and gives freely, using love as his or her sole criterion. *Justice extends even beyond one's fellow human beings to the entire creation. The burning of forests, the criminal exploitation of natural resources, the gap between the wealthy "north" and the needy "south," all of these constitute expressions of transgressing the virtue of justice.*

With the ultimate goal of studying the ecological crisis comprehensively from the viewpoint of justice, the fourth annual summer ecological seminar was held June 25-30, 1997, in the Holy Patriarchal and Stavropegic Monastery of the Holy Trinity at Halki, with the general title: "Environment and Justice." It is clear from the proceedings that this seminar succeeded in an interdisciplinary approach of the subject. Participants also included representatives of the Orthodox Church; of other Christian confessions; of other religions; governmental authorities; and environmental, scientific, and forensic experts — all of whom provided invaluable resources for those who are interested in just solutions to the ecological problem that challenges humanity today. May the grace of the Creator of all the creation, our Lord and God and Savior Jesus Christ, be with you all.

# CREATOR AND CREATION

*Address at the opening of the Black Sea symposium
(second international symposium), September 20, 1997*

Among many prevailing misconceptions is the idea that religion in general, and Christianity in particular, is interested only in life after death, as if by struggling to divest oneself of a material body one might be changed into a liberated spirit, as Plato taught. However, leaving the arguments of other religious teachings and philosophical schools to their own adherents, we will focus here on the Eastern Orthodox Church, in recognition of our responsibility.

*It is a qualitative element in our faith that we believe and accept that the Creator, who loves us, fashioned humankind in its psychosomatic reality and also fashioned the material universe according to His image and likeness, mak-*

*ing it and us "very good."* Consequently, we stand far from any dialectical opposition of matter and spirit, body and soul, or the present world and metaphysical reality. We reject this Manichean perception and live in harmony in ourselves and in harmony with the material and spiritual world within which we live and move and have our being. We live in harmony with God, the Creator of all things, and with all things that He has created.

Obviously, we recognize a certain hierarchy in the created order, and we accept a gradation of proportionate value in the harmony of creation, inasmuch as the omniscient Creator has arranged all of creation in the fullness of His love. Even when we cannot know the specific reason for the creation and existence of an objective reality, or even the property of a physical law, we can still be absolutely certain of one supreme *Logos*, who has established and apportioned all things with immanent rationality. It is for this reason that we hesitate to opine that human remedies, which interfere with the natural order, are better than those found in the natural conditions provided by God. However, it does not follow from this that we consider the natural order to be an intangible "taboo," for we possess the commandment of God that we should have dominion over the earth.

### Environment as Home

We should focus our attention from the outset on the proper limits of our interventions, such as they are, and on consideration of what might be considered appropriate interventions. We can speak in a positive manner and without hesitation about these things. *In describing the appropriate limits of our interventions in the natural world, in each particular instance we stand on a razor's edge, which itself is a measure of our own spiritual condition.* Our answer presupposes a careful weighing of innumerable factors with prudence and dispassionate discernment. Unfortunately, this is rare, much as our own virtue is rare.

The first part of the word "ecology" is derived from the Greek word *oikos*, meaning our "home." There is more to our "home" than people, land, water, plants, and animals. That is the spirit of the term. Yet people rarely take time to look at the beauty of this world or to feel the spiritual connection between our surroundings and us. In order to change our behavior toward the "home" we all share, we must rediscover spiritual linkages that may have been lost, and reassert human values in our behavior.

## Humanity and Nature

And so we stand before nature, or the "environment," affirming its worth just as the Creator of all things did when He characterized it as "very good." *However, at the same time, we face the reality of the hierarchy inherent in the design of the cosmic plenitude, both the material and the spiritual, and we assign it to its proper place. We do not make of nature an absolute value, nor do we deny it to the point of absolute negation.* Nature exists for the service of humanity according to the material side of our nature; it is not humanity that exists for the sake of nature.

With this understanding, the core of our concerns for the Black Sea and the environmental dangers threatening it is focused on those people who live in the surrounding regions of the Black Sea, and not on the Black Sea in itself. We are interested in preventing the Black Sea from becoming an environmental catastrophe. Therefore, we declare that our most vivid concern is for our fellow human beings who dwell in this region and who may not be aware of the danger that threatens their life, health, and livelihood through the disruption of the natural ecological balance of the Black Sea.

The Black Sea is a remarkable place with a long history, both natural and human. Unlike other seas on our planet, it was formed comparatively recently, when the waters of the Mediterranean broke through the Bosphorus valley, flooding a vast low-lying freshwater lake, some seven or eight thousand years ago. People living in primitive settlements must have watched this great event, as a salty cascade surged down the valley to give new life to the new sea. Subsequent generations have admired the beauty of this sea, enjoyed the fish it provided, and sailed its waters. Different civilizations have come and gone, but always the sea seemed immutable, governed by the "everlasting covenant between God and every living creature upon earth" that was proclaimed in the book of Genesis after Noah and his Ark survived the mighty floodwaters. Now, almost as dramatically as it was formed, changes are taking place in it: fish are disappearing, crystalline waters are becoming choked with green algae, beaches and harbors are badly polluted, and the Black Sea's beauty is soiled by the hand of humankind.

We are deeply concerned for the daily life of the people in this region, for it too is a gift of God, "very good" indeed, and destined to be used as a starting point for an eternal life, continuing beyond the grave into the infinite, when the bodily substance of our nature is transmuted into a spiritual reality.

## Ascesis and Consumption

To ensure the furtherance of natural life, we consider ascetic self-denial to be necessary and the reduction of many material pleasures to be beneficial. However, such deprivation should certainly be a voluntary and conscious decision, and not something imposed by external constraints and consequently without ethical merit. Therefore, from this perspective, we join forces with all those who are concerned for the sustainability of those material goods necessary for survival, but we do not approve of overproduction, irrational exploitation, and greed. We seek and urge the patristic and Aristotelian sense of moderation and balance and would dissuade you from forming an idol of wealth as much as from reducing wealth to an evil in itself. For wealth is the accumulation of the abundance of human labor and natural resources. Wealth is both valued and reviled in an ethical sense, according to the manner of its concentration and the manner of its use.

*It is obvious that the rapacious exploitation of natural resources, which derives from greed and not from extraordinary circumstances of need, entails a debilitation of nature to the extent that it cannot renew its own productive powers.* Such exploitation is as unethical as it is irrational, given that, as is observed sociologically, a lack of ethics coincides with a lack of intelligence to an astounding degree, because someone who is truly intelligent understands the injurious nature of bad character. Again, it is equally evident that the utilization of concentrated wealth for selfish purposes, for one end or another, for good or bad, is ethically disdainful. Rather, surplus human wealth and natural resources should be held in trust and used to improve the quality of life in human society in various areas, including education, public health, and the development and enrichment of the spiritual life. This justifies wealth as a shared property, expended for the common good, even if it is managed by only one part of human society.

The Orthodox point of view and teaching are that the environment was created so that we might evolve and develop within it in body and soul. In addition, we ought to observe the divine law and do those things that are useful and reasonable for our self-sufficiency, and not practice any kind of hoarding. If there should happen to be an excess, without draining nature dry, this ought to be employed again for the common good. Thus, religion propounds eternal truths and maintains sensitivity to all members of society because of the danger of falling away from those same truths.

## Science, Politics, and People

It is at this point that the work of science begins, for science observes the situation and certifies the problems; proposes measures that would stave off the worsening of the situation; and organizes the effective application of these measures. Not infrequently, whenever science considers it possible through the measures at hand, it also proposes the restoration of the destroyed elements in the environment.

This symposium gathers, as its title declares, representatives of religion and science. All of you enjoy the blessings of the Holy and Great Church of Christ and, we can most certainly assure you, our own love and prayers; you enjoy the patronage of the President of the European Commission, His Excellency Jacques Santer. The subject of this symposium is of interest to many peoples and their governments. The circumnavigation of all those interested countries as the venue for this symposium constitutes a conscious decision, aimed at sensitizing individuals and whole peoples to the significance of the region of the Black Sea for their life. Environmental change and destruction on such a vast scale, through the thoughtless contribution of many, wreaks havoc over a long period of time and in all directions. The redress of such circumstances is a most onerous task, requiring the cooperation of all concerned parties. That is why it constitutes a challenge to the ethical and social conscience of us all.

The Black Sea is spoiled and its biotope destroyed because of the indifference of countless people, each of whom contributes to a greater or lesser extent to the unfortunate result. *A ship's captain, for example, protected by the fact that it is not easy to prove that he discards his ship's polluted waste into the sea, is as responsible as the person who lives far from the coastline, but who discards personal destructive waste into the river, which ends up in the Black Sea.* Unless everyone is made sensitive to the harmful nature of such actions, it is almost impossible for any endeavor to improve the situation to succeed.

## The Role of Religion

It is precisely here that the fundamental role of religion is revealed. Religion can inspire the behavior of every individual; it also plays a strong role in influencing the thought and actions of groups and mass movements.

The fact is that the terrible condition of the Black Sea region results from the contribution of many people, some of whom may hardly be aware of their own responsibility, because their contribution to the overall result is relatively minor. If this problem is going to be overturned, everybody's cooperation will be required; in other words, it is absolutely necessary to achieve a social ethic and a common effort. Every deed that benefits others also benefits us.

This sense of a common fate — the polar opposite of the widespread individualistic and self-interested attitude, which is shortsighted in its appreciation of the world — is a basic teaching of the altruistic Christian faith, and especially of Orthodoxy. Without it, facing problems such as those of the Black Sea would be impossible.

*Surely there are not many people today who are ignorant of the influence of prevailing ideas and beliefs on our lives. To make new ideas prevail we must focus on winning adherents and spreading those ideas.* With this in mind, we also seek through this symposium to activate for the common good the dormant sense of responsibility that exists in each individual and among every people. In this way, the aim of a healthier Black Sea may be more easily achieved for the benefit of all humankind.

We are deeply pained by the suffering that, because of human indifference, keeps piling on our fellow human beings. We call on every conscience to awaken! We know that our beloved fellow participants' consciences are already sensitized, and we call you to a virtual apostolic commission: to spread the word about the necessity for a common confrontation of these problems.

We would like to express our thanks, first, to all of you for being here, each for your own personal reasons, and thus showing a commitment to a cause dear to our heart. Thanks to all whose organizational skills have made this symposium possible. Thanks to all those who have contributed, whether with resources, time, effort, or in other ways, and above all, thanks to God for bringing us together in this place and at this time so crucial to the future of the Black Sea in particular and of humankind in general.

# WORSE THAN THE PLAGUES OF PHARAOH

*Toast during the banquet in Constanza,*
*second international symposium, September 26, 1997*

With exceeding joy, we find ourselves around this hospitable table during this glad hour, enjoying the riches of your bountiful welcome, which you have offered to all of us unsparingly, both clergy and lay people, rulers and citizens, on the occasion of this international and interreligious symposium on religion, science, and the environment, focusing on the theme "The Black Sea in Crisis." As an expression of our sincere and warm thanks for all that you have offered to us and our companions, please accept these few thoughts concerning the burning issue with which all of us are preoccupied during this conference.

One of the most urgent problems of our era is that of the environment, because, for the first time in the history of humanity, nature is threatened together with humanity in a definitive and irreversible manner. *The new element, which elevates the ecological problem to a level above that of the plagues of Pharaoh, is the irreversible character of many of the catastrophes that are occurring.* The ills afflicting the environment are difficult to correct, and for that reason it is essential for us to take preventative measures.

Our common responsibility for nature constitutes the starting point of every concern about ecological matters. Believers and unbelievers, religious people and atheists, regardless of sex or nationality, social position, economic situation, political standpoint or position on world theory — all are equally affected by the destruction of nature. For this reason, precisely, all of us without exception fully bear the responsibility for indifference in the face of the ecological threat. All of us are affected by the destruction of the natural environment and, without exception, we should all assume our responsibilities and undertake initiatives. All of those who violate nature are perpetrators today and tomorrow become victims of their own violence.

### Response to Earth, Return to God

In participating in the effort to protect nature, the Ecumenical Patriarchate does not go as far as to idolize it, but tries to make conscious responses so as to conform to the divine commandment to labor and to preserve the environment in which God placed humanity. One criterion of environmental behavior for us is the liturgical ethos of the Orthodox tradition. This ethos is summarized, as it were, in the eucharistic proclamation: "As we offer to you your own of your own — in all things and for all things — we praise you, we bless you, we give thanks to you, Lord, and we pray to you, our God." *We do not despise God's gifts, among which is the "very good" creation. Rather, we offer this gift back to God with awe and due respect.*

Gift (*doron*, in Greek) and gift in return (*antidoron*, in Greek) are the terms by which it is possible to signify our Orthodox theological view of the environmental question in a concise and clear manner. Nature is the *doron* of the Triune God to humankind. The *antidoron* of humankind to its Maker and Father is the respect of this gift, the preservation of creation, as well as its fruitful and careful use. The believer is called upon to celebrate his or her daily life eucharistically, that is to say, to live and to practice daily what he or she confesses and proclaims at each Divine Liturgy: "We offer to you your own of your own, in all things and for all things, and we give thanks to you, Lord!" *Doron* and *antidoron* comprise the realized eucharistic conduct of the Orthodox Christian, which is prefigured in an exemplary manner in the liturgical practice.

The ecclesiastical ethos is the best measure for preventing ecological disaster today. It is precisely in this sense that we are participating most vividly in the environmental movement of our own times on a worldwide as well as on a regional basis, just as in the present symposium around the coastal areas of the Black Sea, under the eloquent subtitle: "The Black Sea in Crisis."

Therefore, we offer a toast to the preservation of the Black Sea from the imminent threat against it, for the good of humankind, praying that everyone will understand the good reasons for offering it back, pure and alive, in gratitude to our Lord Jesus Christ, who first offered it to us.

# REENVISIONING ECOLOGICAL HISTORY

*Address during the closing of the*
*international ecological symposium in Thessaloniki, Greece*
*(second international symposium), September 28, 1997*

With God's grace, the scientific and religious symposium, which has lasted for a number of days on board this ship, and which has dealt with the ecological dangers to the Black Sea around which we have sailed, has successfully come to an end. The detailed and erudite papers that we have heard, the positive responsiveness of the people around its shores and of governments and Churches, and the proposals discussed and the conclusions reached all give us the hope, if not the certainty, that the symposium has achieved its aim.

We thank all those who have contributed in various ways to the successful conduct of the symposium. We thank His Excellency Jacques Santer, President of the European Commission, under whose patronage, together with that of the Ecumenical Patriarchate, the symposium was organized; the distinguished participants who comprised the key to its success, chaired by His Eminence Metropolitan John of Pergamon, our beloved brother in Christ; the Honorable Chairman of the Organization for "The Cultural Capital of Europe — Thessaloniki 1997" and all the members of its Board of Management, and especially its Deputy Chairman, Mr. Demetrios Salpistis; and the ANEK Shipping Company, its experienced captain, and the helpful crew of the ship *Eleftherios Venizelos,* on whose account the journey was accomplished with every convenience. We also thank the religious and civil leaders of the countries along the shores of the Black Sea who, together with their peoples, gave us the warmest of welcomes. Above all, we thank the most high God, who made us worthy to exercise the talent given by Him to each of us for the common good.

The first page in the history of saving the Black Sea from ecological devastation has been written. Consciences have been sensitized, and resolutions have been made. Now these intentions must be put into practice. The baton has been passed, and each of us returns to his or her own main occupation. This does not mean that we abandon the problem. Rather, we will remain watchful and ready to offer every assistance.

We will not focus on the accounts of the proceedings and their conclusions at this festal closing session. Instead, we wish to turn our attention within, to ourselves. For, as human beings, we are both the cause of the various ecological problems and the receiver of their results. Yet, it ought not to escape our attention that we are ourselves an "environment" for our fellow beings. *Each of us, as a dweller in the wider ecosystem, is in this respect part of the environment for our fellow human beings.* We are human, it is true, but also part of the environment. As a result, it is not sufficient that we secure good treatment of the natural ecosystem, which surrounds humankind, and with which we usually concern ourselves. It is also imperative that we secure peaceful and compassionate human behavior, behavior that makes for harmonious human relations. Unfortunately, the ecological problems relating to the natural environment are usually provoked by human actions; but despite the seriousness of this fact, it is, comparatively speaking, frequently of less importance than all the ills that human beings perpetrate against each other.

## Rewriting the Ecological Story

Ecological adulteration is an imminent danger, a danger threatening both nature and humankind. Unfortunately, however, human beings are frequently a threat — and even a direct cause of catastrophe — to their fellow human beings as well. Both history and our daily lives are full of persecution, oppression, genocide, execution, destruction, and plundering of man by man. Thus, *the damage to nature that results from greed and indirectly harms the members of human society is not the only serious problem. The direct harm human beings bring upon fellow human beings, resulting from various inhumane motives and developing within diseased and fanatical souls, should also be the focus of our attention.* Consequently, we ought to turn our attention to the ways in which people form the environment of their fellow human beings, creating for them good or, occasionally, unbearable conditions of life, and to investigate in what ways we can improve the conditions in which human beings live together.

With full awareness, we have sidestepped the issue of the environment. However, if we do not change within ourselves the attitude of our heart toward our fellow human beings — moving from an attitude of indifference or even enmity to an attitude of friendship, cooperation, and acceptance — then we will achieve nothing in the confrontation of the ecological problems of worldwide interest.

In hope that the heavy clouds of human conflict will be dispelled, and daily offering fervent prayers for this cause, with gratitude and paternal love we bid farewell to the beloved participants of this symposium. And we entreat the Lord to protect and shield you all during your return journey and throughout all the days of your life that lie before you.


## UNITED AS NATIONS

*Address during the United Nations luncheon at Le Cirq Restaurant,
New York City, October 27, 1997*


As leaders of the international community, you have an awesome responsibility to ensure peace throughout the world. As the successor to the Apostle Andrew, the first-called disciple of Jesus Christ, we too have a similar responsibility. We are charged by Christ to preach the message of peace, hope, and love. We do this recognizing that our message must be set within the realistic context of people's lives. We are committed to the universal cause of freedom, religious and political self-determination, and justice.

We have spoken today with the Secretary General of the United Nations, the Hon. Kofi Annan. We thank him for his warm welcome. We look forward to working with him on all issues that touch upon the fundamental message of our Lord's commandment to love one another. We believe that our contribution is valuable, since we represent the 300 million communicants of the world's Orthodox Christians who span the planet's many continents.

Certainly, the United Nations has recognized the increasing importance of religious communities in the conflicts that have marked the post–Cold War world. *It is a tragic fact that religion has contributed to cycles of violence and fragmentation between and within nation-states, before and since the end of the bipolar international order. However, it is also true that the end of bipolarity has produced new social and political circumstances. Recently, religious entities have directly cooperated with temporal powers in developing principles, language, and concrete policies premised on the rejection of categories of power that lead to separation, exclusion, disintegration, and conflict.*

During the mounting chaos that was part of the implosion of Albania during much of 1997, the Orthodox Church of Albania was the first voice in civil society to call upon all citizens to refrain from acts of violence. Since 1991, the country's Orthodox leadership has worked steadily and closely with its Muslim counterparts.

In Turkey, the Ecumenical Patriarchate has led the way in its efforts to promote interfaith tolerance, by convening the Conference on Peace and Tolerance among Christians, Jews, and Muslims. This forum produced the "Bosphorus Declaration," whose signatories condemned all religious violence and proclaimed that crimes in the name of religion are crimes against all religion. Similarly, and only recently, the Greek Orthodox Church in America inaugurated an official dialogue with Muslim leaders in America. On a global scale, the International Orthodox Christian Charities (IOCC) is a transnational non-governmental organization. This organization, very dear to our hearts, is vigorously opposed to proselytism. It is committed to interfaith cooperation, via philanthropic and welfare projects, for improving literacy and life expectancy, as well as for combating infant mortality and disease.

## United as Inhabitants of the Earth

*The Ecumenical Patriarchate has worked to promote awareness of the global ramifications of environmental issues. We see this divinely inspired work as integral to the goal of world peace.* We shall continue our yearly seminars on environmental issues on Halki and our other initiatives elsewhere.

We mention these positive examples of the Orthodox Church's involvement in worldly affairs in order to underscore the fact that our faith offers a rich set of resources useful in promoting the United Nations' noble agenda of conflict resolution and peace building. Unfortunately, the unique resources of the Orthodox Church remain relatively unknown to and, therefore, underutilized by the United Nations. This situation has led to certain situations where Orthodoxy has not had the support it might have had, support that would have assisted the Church's message of love to prevail in the face of historical animosities.

As the Mother Church of Orthodoxy, the Ecumenical Patriarchate of Constantinople is ready to expand all its efforts to rebuild the moral and ethical well-being of long-suffering peoples everywhere. We say this without any intention of transgressing the fundamental rights of spiritual self-determination. However, we would hope that the West might also make an effort to understand the unique hardships that the Orthodox Christian East has suffered during many long decades of persecution. We ask that non-coercive aid programs be extended to Orthodox Christians in areas where they are recovering from decades of repression and persecution.

We believe that Orthodoxy's rich creation theology rests on the assumption that the entire cosmos is an integrated whole. The Orthodox Church's theological and existential goal of the integrity of all creation is consonant with the United Nations' goal of peace building. Orthodoxy's understanding of the human being as person, as a microcosm of the cosmos, assumes that our humanity is existentially meaningful only through free and conscious engagement in relation with others. The Ecumenical Patriarchate is committed to transforming the human condition. Our vision of freedom is relational, and it is consistent with UN efforts at transforming post-conflict situations by restoring the torn fabric of individual and community life.

The Orthodox Church transcends linguistic, ethnic, and national divisions. Our Holy Orthodox Church is modeled on the Trinitarian principle of unity-in-diversity, whereby heterogeneity and uniqueness are fundamental aspects of our humanity. The Church's experience is comparable to the UN itself, an entity whose unity is the result of the diversity of its membership.

Dear co-workers in the vineyard of peace, our presence here today is meant to reaffirm the commitment of the Holy Orthodox Church to the UN agenda. We humbly observe that our Church is capable of offering much that could better the health of the UN family.

We exhort you to assume the responsibility, which has been given to all of us by God, our Creator, to renew collectively our commitment to restoring peace, justice, and the integrity of all creation. We ask you to consider the creative gifts of the Orthodox Christian community as a resource for change, and we respectfully offer you the spiritual resources of the Ecumenical Patriarchate.

## BEYOND ARID INTELLECTUALISM

*Address during Convocation, on being presented
with an honorary degree at the Fletcher School of Diplomacy,
Tufts University, Boston, October 29, 1997*

We are deeply grateful for the honor you are bestowing on us today. We accept this honor, not as an individual, but on behalf of the Holy Orthodox Church's over 300 million communicants, whom we humbly serve as Ecumenical Patriarch. Receipt of this honorary degree, a doctorate of international laws from Tufts University, encourages our reflection as well as gratitude. We are heartened by the message of hope, optimism, and willingness to serve reflected in the conferral of this honor. Likewise, we are sobered by the challenges and the as-yet-unrealized potential that this degree brings to mind.

Dear friends, it is only appropriate that an institution such as Tufts University, with its long and successful history of combining intellectual creativity with constructive activism, should make the decision to confer this degree on us and, in so doing, on the Mother Church of Constantinople. Your university's history demonstrates recognition of the importance of moving beyond arid intellectualism, which results in excesses of rationalism and one-dimensional secularism.

Tufts University is an authentic model of the academy as lived from antiquity until the high Middle Ages. Tufts University has remained loyal to the classical ideal of the university as an environment in which the noble pursuit of truth imposes no boundaries on the human intellect and spirit. This is witnessed by the diversity of your institution's programs in a number of disciplines and professional areas. These include veterinary sciences, medicine, engineering, international relations, physics, religion and philosophy, and the arts. In short, we understand your conferral of this honorary degree as a shining example of your university's self-perception as an icon, as a door or threshold that invites students to pass into a place where their pursuit of truth takes them on an adventure of inquiry into things both secular and sacred.

Our presence here today reflects Tufts' commitment to education as a voyage of discovery into truths reflected in the universe of both spiritual and temporal realities. We are also encouraged by the lived expressions of your commitment to education as a mission of service and activism. Again, in their willingness to serve, the faculty, students, and alumni of Tufts University have demonstrated an extraordinary awareness of the spiritual aspects of our humanity. More specifically, you also recognize religion as a profound and powerful force for peace and reconciliation in the world.

Indeed, one of your university's flagship schools, The Fletcher School of Law and Diplomacy, is a brilliant exemplar of the view that the path to global peace involves, or rather demands, visionary leadership and daring policy initiatives. In this respect, the Fletcher School of Law and Diplomacy represents a holistic philosophy of education that characterizes Tufts University as a whole.

Your university stands at the forefront of scholarship and policymaking in international affairs, precisely because of the recognition that the world's great religions offer incredible resources. Whether through individual leaders, communities, or ideas, these resources must be incorporated in the efforts to secure the ideals of the late twentieth century.

## The Role of Orthodoxy

Dear friends, we accept today's honorary degree in full awareness of the responsibility that accompanies a doctorate in international laws from a university such as Tufts. By the same token, we offer up the holy, catholic, and apostolic Orthodox Church, as uniquely endowed with worldwide and historical experiences, exceptionally suited to meeting the challenges of global peace on the eve of the new millennium.

However, in humbly offering ourselves to this service, we also exhort you to help create the possibilities for Orthodox Christianity to contribute to this process of building peace. Sadly enough, Orthodox Christianity — despite its more than 300 million communicants in countries as far apart as the United States, Panama, Israel, Kenya, Greece, Turkey, Russia, Ukraine, Korea, Australia, Japan, and many others; despite its unbroken continuity of tradition with the Church of Christ; despite its survival through systematic persecution in former communist countries over the better part of this century — remains largely unknown to scholars, even to those well versed in the Western

Christian Churches, as well as in the four world religions of Judaism, Islam, Hinduism, and Buddhism.

Equally discouraging is the fact that, despite the richness of Orthodox Christian theology and the reemergence of the institutional Orthodox Church in Eastern Europe, policymakers involved in traditional diplomacy, and non-governmental organizations involved in efforts at conflict resolution, have failed to tap the Orthodox Church's potential for community building and reconciliation.

Clearly, our presence here today indicates that Orthodox Christianity is not terra incognita for the scholars and practitioners who make up the Tufts University family. However, our optimism about your recognition is necessarily tempered by the realities just mentioned. We are aware of the challenges associated with introducing Orthodoxy into the rich scholarly debates begun in the intellectual tradition of Max Weber. We are cognizant of even greater challenges related to educating policymakers about the democracy-building and peace-making potential of Orthodox Churches across the globe.

However, above all, as believers in the God-given possibility for the salvific transfiguration of every member of the human race, we have confidence in the unique contributions that the ideas and praxis of the Holy Orthodox Church can offer toward peace in our time and our common future.

As the Ecumenical Patriarch, the "first among equals" of all the Orthodox Churches, we would like to take a few moments to share with you some of the most crucial, yet not fully known and thus not fully accessed, strengths of the Orthodox Church. We have much to contribute to the efforts of teachers, researchers, and policymakers who are committed to making religion a force for the prevention and resolution of conflicts that continue to undermine the security of human societies.

### Three Fundamental Principles

We suggest to you three particular strengths of Orthodox Christianity, which our Church can bring to bear in cooperation with these efforts. We accept the reality of the nation-state, but we categorically reject systems of repression and oppression, premised on parochial nationalism, fragmenting communalism, and aggressive expansionism.

We begin with the first strength, which is Orthodox Christianity's conception of *the human being as person,* such that personhood is an ontological category of being. This theological thinking is deeply rooted in our tradition, which understands God as a Trinity — a community, if you will — of divine persons. The human being, as an existential reality, can be a person only when living in freedom. Only in conditions in which the full range of possibilities is open to our free and conscious choice are we able to transform our temporal reality and our selves into the image of the divine kingdom. Our humanity is realized through the free act of relationship with others. Personhood is a free act of communion that makes heterogeneity and uniqueness fundamental aspects of our humanity.

In addition to its conception of personhood, Orthodox Christianity brings a second strength to efforts at international peacemaking and reconciliation. Specifically, *Orthodox Christianity is a way of life* in which there is a profound and direct relationship between dogma and praxis, faith and life. This unity of faith and life means that the reality of the eternal truths lies in their experiential power, rather than in their codification into a set of ideological constructs. Furthermore, the equal importance of creed and experience points to an understanding of holy tradition as the living continuity of the personal encounter of humanity with God.

Third, and finally, Orthodox Christianity understands *the inherent character of all creation, both humankind and the physical or natural environment, in terms of its original and potential integrity.* Since the inherent character of all creation lies in its whole and unified integrity, an integrity that has been disrupted by the destructive actions of humankind, the salvation of all creation can come only through the restoration of the innate harmony expressed in the divine kingdom.

## Holistic and Global

Dear friends, you may wonder what relevance these three concepts — of personhood, of a way of life, and of integration — have for peace in the international scene. You may argue that these three concepts are nothing more than theological abstractions divorced from the hard realities of a world marred by abominations committed in the name of religion. You may consider these concepts hypocritical meandering in the face of the economic blight, political charlatanism, cultural discrimination, military savagery, and environmental pollution that destroy individuals, villages, cities, nations, and regions with almost inconceivable regularity in our world and in our time. Indeed, you may wonder why it is that we have presented these three concepts as the potential strengths that the Holy Orthodox Church brings to the processes dedicated to encouraging order, to providing meaning, and to promoting justice in the international arena.

Yet, we would submit that each of the three concepts suggests common points of solidarity between the Orthodox world and the increasingly transnational community of peacemakers. Specifically, the principles of freedom and relational being make Orthodoxy's conception of personhood fully compatible with democratic norms regarding individual human rights. Moreover, the heterogeneity and dynamism of personhood reinforce secular principles encouraging toleration for differences within society, rather than defensive reaction against otherness. Debates over multiculturalism within the context of the United States, as well as efforts to craft new constitutions in the multiethnic societies in southeastern Europe, would be enriched by attention to Orthodoxy's vision of the person.

Likewise, Orthodox Christianity's definition of religion as a way of life opens up an entirely new role for tradition in our late modern or postmodern world, a role wherein tradition provides for fluid changes rather than destabilizing rupture in societies undergoing all forms of modernization. Equally important, the unity of doctrine and praxis means that holy tradition is a continual, reiterative experience of truths that are "inwardly changeless . . . constantly assuming new forms, which supplement the old without superseding them," to quote Bishop Kallistos Ware. Orthodox believers can experience their faith in a variety of local, national, and regional contexts, rather than reacting defensively against homogenizing global tendencies of liberalizing, pluralist changes. *The seamless quality of the Orthodox unity of belief and practice also means that each person experiences his or her faith in both the public and private spheres, in a myriad of cultural contexts, through all types of activity, rather than through the narrow mechanisms of political power. From the Orthodox perspective, religion as a way of life eschews political institutional power.* In fact, the Mother Orthodox Church of Constantinople is a signatory, on behalf of all Orthodox Churches around the world, to the "Bosphorus Declaration" of 1994, an interfaith document that condemns all crimes in the name of religion as a crime against religion itself.

Finally, the holistic character that marks the Orthodox conception of the sanctity of creation is strikingly consistent with the international community's emphasis on reconciliation. Social scientists and government policymakers, scholars and practitioners, and all those individuals and groups concerned with describing, analyzing, and managing our current system of international relations would do well to look to Orthodox Christianity's theology of creation. It is a model for how human beings can accept responsibility to participate intentionally as "co-creators" with the Creator, reconciling humanity with itself, and ending the alienation of humanity from the natural environment. Members of the policy, academic, and media communities who are genuinely interested in redefining the tools, constructs, and perceptual landscapes that currently affect conflict resolution and peacemaking would do well to look to an Orthodox theologian, the late Nikos Nissiotis, for an insightful formulation of peace as the restoration of the original integrity of the cosmos. For Nissiotis, peace is "principally a hard process of reconciliation in and with one's self and with the whole of creation."

## A Final Pledge

Dear friends, we close with a pledge. The Ecumenical Patriarchate will do all in its power to live up to the responsibility attendant with the honor that you have bestowed upon us today. Toward this end, and in keeping with the venerable tradition of this university's contributions to international law and diplomacy, we humbly pledge to "pursue what makes for peace" (Rom. 14:19). We also pledge that the Orthodox Church will undertake its entire work for global peace and international reconciliation through the "perfect love, which casts out fear" (1 John 4:18). Moreover, within the context of Tufts University, as an institution committed to knowledge as the quest for truth, we pledge to enliven the truth-seeking journey of the scholars, students, and alumni of the Tufts community, with the beliefs and public works of the Holy Orthodox Church.

We match our closing pledge, dear friends, with an entreaty to you. In the name of the rigorous standards of international law and the codification of human rights for which the Fletcher School has become a standard bearer, we entreat you to renew your pledges on behalf of global peace, reconciliation, democracy, and freedom. Your pledge demands that you endeavor to bring the rich intellectual tradition of Orthodox Christian thought — long hidden behind the curtains of captivity — into today's academy, into its scholarship, research into international relations, conflict resolution, and security studies.

The painful and joyful experiences of the Ecumenical Patriarchate of Constantinople seal our pledge to uphold the principles of the honorary doctorate that you have conferred on us today. For the same reason, we ask that you work to alleviate the suffering of the Orthodox Church and all other individuals and groups persecuted because of their quest for truth. We exhort you to enliven your knowledge through a life of service to the peaceful reconciliation of all creation.

## SPIRITUALITY AND HUMAN RIGHTS

*Address during the conferral of an honorary doctorate
at Southern Methodist University, November 5, 1997*

We thank you for your warm hospitality and for the supreme honor of this degree. We feel as though you have conferred it, not so much upon us, but upon the entire Orthodox Christian Church, which we lead as Ecumenical Patriarch. As the Ecumenical Patriarch, we bear the sacred responsibility of guiding the faithful of the Greek Orthodox Archdiocese of America in their spiritual growth and development. This holy Archdiocese is celebrating seventy-five years of growth and progress this year. We are proud of the accomplishments that the faithful have made in America.

As the Ecumenical Patriarch, we also have the privilege of serving as the senior brother among the leaders of the worldwide Orthodox Church. The origin of our position as Ecumenical Patriarch reaches back to the very beginning of Christianity. We are the 270th successor to the Apostle Andrew, the "first-called" disciple of Jesus Christ. By the mercy of God, this spiritual authority and ministry have been entrusted to us. It is the authority of Jesus Christ passed on in unbroken continuity from the time of His earthly sojourn to the present hour. This authority is at the heart of apostolic succession. It is the pearl of great price that God calls us to guard; and at its heart is the great commandment of Christ to love one another. Our relationship as a community of believers is founded on this very commandment of love.

*The Christian message of love has been marginalized by the rise of modernity in the post-Enlightenment world.* Often, the message of love is seen as simplistic, too naive to matter in a complex secular society. The hallmark of modernity is that social empowerment is centered upon the individual's self-conscious understanding of his or her place in the world. Human rights are seen as an outgrowth of individual rights, rights that have been described in increasingly secular terms, at least since the Enlightenment.

Contemporary society is puzzled by, and often is in conflict with, an interpretation of human rights that is centered upon a religious understanding. American culture is bifurcated into two broad camps, which are separated by differing religious sensibilities. Inflexible religious extremism limits human rights to narrow categories of norms determined by human interpretation of the divine will. Such extremism is the dangerous prelude to religious fanaticism and persecution. We reiterate our deeply held belief that violence in the name of religion is violence against all religion.

## Secularism and Human Rights

Secular American culture allows that human rights are God-given, but the relationship between God and humanity is always seen as personal, private, without any visible or public sign. Such a relationship is enshrined in the American Constitution and in the Bill of Rights. These are indeed noble documents, and they are fundamental to the world's understanding of democratic principles. However, as noble and necessary as these documents are in the global culture's vision of individual and human rights, they are also rationalist constructs. They do point to a human relationship with the Divine, by suggesting that basic rights are divinely ordained. However, they do not aspire to manifest within individual lives the complex spiritual relationship that we believe is the ontological reality of human existence. They prefer a mechanistic sense of order rather than a spiritual experience of the Divine. The mystery of faith is fundamental to the human spirit, for it allows individuals to perceive their inner life as something more than the temporary conjunction of biology and electrical impulses.

Our faith seeks to understand the entire cosmos, and everything within it, as a seamless garment of God's vast creation. The individual exists, not separate from the rest of creation and fellow human beings, but in constant relationship to the ontological plenitude. It is this constancy of relationship that informs an individual's understanding of personal existence as being grounded in the created order. With this grounding, one is able to value oneself in the context of the cosmos. One's validation rests on God's love for the creation and not on the vagaries of mere human guarantees. It is in this relational context that a just society may be founded and sustained. We believe that a just society is proof of God's will at work in humankind.

God's will is made manifest through those who conform their will to God. For Orthodox Christians, Jesus Christ is the perfect model of humanity acting in perfect concord with God's will. We believe that Jesus Christ is both perfect God and perfect man. He is the guide and the ultimate end of the perfect union of the Divine with the human, and of the uncreated with the created. Through Christ's example, suffering, death, and resurrection, the entire created world has been transformed and is being transformed. Since God's love gave us His Son, the preexistent Word of God incarnate, we believe that the entire natural world and humankind are being transfigured by God's love.

*As we receive the message of Christ's commandment to love one another, we become agents of change in the world.* We are transformed, moving "from glory to glory" in a process of deification (or *theosis*). Orthodox spirituality understands this process as one that is not merely individual, but primarily corporate. Society, too, becomes transformed. We affect everyone and everything that we touch by example and through our actions in this world.

The free will to choose to center our actions, our hearts, and our minds upon God is the image of God at work in our lives. We are created in God's image, and our free will to choose between good and evil is proof of that truth. The image of God within us is freedom. Since all human beings are created in the image and likeness of God, freedom is an inalienable right of the human being. It is inalienable from being human.

Faith in God, faith in God's iconic presence within humanity, is the source and guarantee of freedom. There can be no true freedom without faith in God; for, without God, freedom has no ontological reality. When freedom and human rights are threatened, or even curtailed by the evil that human beings perpetrate, faith in freedom is still possible.

### Human Rights, Other People, and Material Creation

Orthodox spiritual teaching assures us that Orthodox Christians must always respect the human rights of others. If we do not respect those rights, then we have desecrated the image of God inherent in all human beings. It is the responsibility of religion to guide persons toward God, that they might seek justice in love for one another. We see spirituality, the relationship of the individual to God, to be fundamental to the realization of freedom — the freedom of the individual to express his or her personhood, as well as the faith that is necessary to affirm the personhood of others.

The seamless garment of God's creation places the human person at the nexus of the Creator's union with His creation. *Divine and human meet in every human being and in every detail of this created world.* The individual is the window of God's will in the creation. Our faith is the guarantee of our spiritual freedom, and that freedom guarantees our physical freedom in the world. Freedom is the key to the transformation of the world, the key to guaranteeing human rights as fundamental to humanity's existence. Faith assures us that freedom is more than government polity. Faith assures us that the denial of freedom is contrary to a higher authority whose law is always benevolent, for God's commandment is to love one another.

It is our prayer to the almighty God that all human beings may enjoy the fullest measure of freedom. We affirm that their rights are an inherent element of Orthodox spirituality, a dogmatic truth of the relationship between Christ and humanity. We pray that the Lord will grant peace and enlightenment to all who seek God in their hearts and minds, that they might faithfully keep the commandment to love one another.

We thank you once again for this honor. We shall cherish it as a sign of your commitment to ecumenical understanding and cooperation. We invoke upon this university, and upon all those who labor in it, the grace, peace, and infinite mercy of God.

## BEAUTY AND NATURE

*Homily at the fiftieth anniversary
dedication of St. Barbara Greek Orthodox Church
in Santa Barbara, California, November 8, 1997*

As your Ecumenical Patriarch and spiritual father, we find ourselves in your city to participate in this joyful and moving celebration of the fiftieth anniversary since the founding of your church. This Orthodox parish and community has been a vibrant participant in the life of a city that takes great pride in its striking natural beauty and in its exemplary ecological sensitivity. You have shown your commitment to your neighbors today by sponsoring this symposium on the sacredness of the environment and on our responsibility toward God's creation. What place could be more appropriate for ecological awareness than the Greek Orthodox Church of St. Barbara, in this historical and luminous city of Santa Barbara?

This city combines the mountains, the forests, the valleys, and the waters, all praising their Creator in a divine symphony. This church edifice stands with imposing dignity at the top of this holy and sacred hill. Your altar is dedicated to the Great Martyr Barbara, whom we shall commemorate next month. She is renowned for her miraculous powers of healing the sense of sight. The vision of light is considered to be the most significant of human experiences. The sense of sight was regarded as the most profound sense in the classical Greek philosophical and patristic world. *Truth is beheld; it is not understood intellectually. God is seen; He is not examined theoretically. Beauty is perceived; it is not speculated about abstractly.*

In the brief service just held, we were reminded of how, when God made the heavens and the earth, He said: "Let there be light" (Gen. 1:3). He made the waters, the land, the sky, and the living creatures. "And God saw that it was good [*kalon*]," which literally means "beautiful." This beauty is, first and foremost, the beauty of divine sacredness, a self-revelation and self-realization of God, who invites us to share in and to enjoy that beauty. For everything that lives and breathes is sacred and beautiful in the eyes of God. The whole world is a sacrament. The entire created cosmos is a burning bush of God's uncreated energies. And humankind stands as a priest before the altar of creation, as microcosm and mediator. Such is the true nature of things, or, as an Orthodox hymn describes it, "the truth of things," if only we have the eyes of faith to see it.

Realistically, we also know that this vision has been blurred, the image has been marred, by our sin. For we have presumed to control the order of things and have therefore destroyed the hierarchy of creation. We have lost the dimension of beauty and have come to a spiritual impasse where everything that we touch is invariably distorted or even destroyed. Nevertheless, through the divine Incarnation, our sight is once again restored, and we are once more enabled to discern the beauty of Christ's countenance in all places of His dominion and "in the least of these," our brothers and sisters (Matt. 25:40). When "the Word became flesh" (John 1:14), we were endowed with new eyes, new ears, new senses altogether, in order to see the invisible in what is visible, and in order to experience the uncreated in what is created.

### Creation and Icons

This same truth is revealed in the iconography of our Church. Icons are a necessary expression of the world's sacredness. "Standing inside the Church, we think that we are in heaven," as one hymn states, because the Church is the embodiment and sanctification of the whole world, while the created world is called to become the Church. Icons break down the wall of separation between the sacred and the profane, between this world and the next, between earth and heaven.

We are called today to rediscover this iconic dimension of creation. And this is what distinguishes us as Christians and our awesome responsibility for the survival of our environment. In the Church, then, "through heaven and earth and sea, through wood and stone, through relics and Church buildings and the Cross, through angels and people, through all of creation, both visible and invisible, we offer veneration and honor to the Creator and Master and Maker of all things, and to Him alone."

*All things are sacramental when seen in the light of God.* In the Great Doxology that we just chanted, we prayed that "in His light we may see light, for He is the one who has shown us the light." And this beautiful building, with its traditional Byzantine architecture and refreshing Mediterranean setting, is a symbol of that original beauty that was restored to us in Christ.

Let us open our eyes to see the world that God has made for us. Let us walk gently on the ground that so patiently tolerates our behavior. Then, as children of God, we can liberate the whole creation. Nothing less is expected of us. Nothing less dignifies us or the world around us. And nothing less is worthy of our high calling in Christ Jesus, who is adored and glorified with His eternal Father, and the all-holy, good, and life-creating Spirit, now and forever, and unto the ages of ages. Amen.


## A RICH HERITAGE

*Address during the environmental symposium
in Santa Barbara, November 8, 1997*


It is with deep joy that we greet all of you, the honorable delegates and attendees of this blessed symposium on the sacredness of the environment. Here in this historical city of Santa Barbara, we see before us a brilliant example of the wonder of God's creation. Recently, that God-given beauty was threatened by an oil spill. We are proud that the effort to restore the damaged beauty of Santa Barbara's seas was led, among others, by Orthodox Christians, Dan and Candy Randopoulos.

The Ecumenical Throne of Orthodoxy, as preserver and proclaimer of the ancient patristic tradition and of the rich liturgical experience of our Orthodox Church, today renews its long-standing commitment to healing the environment. We have followed with great interest and sincere concern the efforts to curb the destructive effects that human beings have wrought upon the natural world. We view with alarm the dangerous consequences of humanity's disregard for the survival of God's creation.

It is for this reason that our predecessor, the late Patriarch Demetrios, of blessed memory, invited the whole world, together with the Great Church of Christ, to offer prayers of thanksgiving and supplication for the protection of the natural environment. Since 1989, every September 1st, the beginning of the ecclesiastical calendar, has been designated as a day of prayer for the protection of the environment, throughout the Orthodox world.

Since that time, the Ecumenical Throne has organized an Inter-Orthodox Conference in Crete in 1991 and convened annual ecological seminars at the historic Monastery of the Holy Trinity on Halki, as a way of discerning the spiritual roots and principles of the ecological crisis. In 1995, we sponsored a symposium that sailed the Aegean to the island of Patmos. The symposium "Revelation and the Environment, A.D. 95 to 1995" commemorated the nineteen hundredth anniversary of the recording of the Apocalypse. We have recently convened a transnational conference on the Black Sea ecological crisis, which included participants from all nations that border that sea.

In these and other programs, *we have sought to discover the measures that may be implemented by Orthodox Christians worldwide, as leaders desiring to contribute to the solution of this global problem. We believe that through our particular and unique liturgical and ascetic ethos, Orthodox spirituality may provide significant moral and ethical direction* toward a new awareness about the planet.

## Liturgy and Life

We believe that Orthodox liturgy and life hold tangible answers to the ultimate questions concerning salvation from corruptibility and death. The Eucharist is at the very center of our worship. *And our sin toward the world, or the spiritual root of all our pollution, lies in our refusal to view life and the world eucharistically, as a sacrament of thanksgiving, as a gift of constant communion with God on a global scale.*

We envision a new awareness that is not mere philosophical posturing, but a tangible experience of a mystical nature. We believe that our first task is to raise the consciousness of adults, who most use the resources and gifts of the planet. Ultimately, it is for our children that we must perceive our every action in the world as having a direct effect upon the future of the environment. At the heart of the relationship between humanity and environment is the relationship between human beings. As individuals, we live not only in vertical relationships to God, and horizontal relationships to one another, but also in a complex web of relationships that extend throughout our lives, our cultures, and the material world. Human beings and the environment form a seamless garment of existence, a complex fabric that we believe is fashioned by God.

People of all faith traditions praise the Divine, for they seek to understand their relationship to the cosmos. The entire universe participates in a celebration of life, which St. Maximus the Confessor described as a "cosmic liturgy." We see this cosmic liturgy in the symbiosis of life's rich biological complexities. These complex relationships draw attention to themselves in humanity's self-conscious awareness of the cosmos. As human beings, created in the image and likeness of God (Gen. 1:26), we are called to recognize this interdependence between our environment and ourselves.

In the bread and wine of the Eucharist, as priests standing before the altar of the world, we offer the creation back to the Creator in the context of a mutual relationship to Him and to each other. Indeed, in our liturgical life, we realize by anticipation the final state of the cosmos in the kingdom of heaven. We celebrate the beauty of creation and consecrate the life of the world, returning it to God with thanks. We share the world in joy as a living mystical communion with the Divine. Thus we offer the fullness of creation at the Eucharist, and receive it back as a blessing, as the living presence of God.

## The Ascetic Way

Moreover, there is also an ascetic element in our responsibility toward God's creation. This asceticism requires from us a voluntary restraint, in order for us to live in harmony with our environment. *Asceticism offers practical examples of conservation.* By reducing our consumption — what in Orthodox theology we call *enkrateia* or self-control — we seek to ensure that resources are left for others in the world. As we restrain our will, we can demonstrate a concern for the third world and developing nations. Our abundance of resources will be extended to include an abundance of equitable concern for others.

We must challenge ourselves to see our personal, spiritual attitudes in continuity with public policy. *Enkrateia* frees us from our self-centered neediness so that we may do good works for others. We do this out of personal love for the natural world around us. We are called to work in humble harmony with creation and not in arrogant supremacy over it. *Asceticism provides an example whereby we may live simply.*

Asceticism is not a flight from society and the world, but a communal attitude of mind and way of life that lead to the respectful use, not abuse, of material goods. Excessive consumption may be understood to issue from a worldview estranged from self, from land, from life, and from God. Consuming the fruits of the earth in an unrestrained manner, we become consumed ourselves by avarice and greed. Excessive consumption leaves us emptied, out of touch with our deepest self. *Asceticism is a corrective practice, a way of metanoia, a vision of repentance.* Such a vision will lead us from repentance to return, the return to a world in which we give as well as take from creation.

## Repentance for the Past

We invite Orthodox Christians to engage in genuine repentance for the way in which we have behaved toward God, toward each other, and toward the world. We gently remind Orthodox Christians that the judgment of the world is in the hands of God. We are called to be stewards and reflections of God's love by example. Therefore, we proclaim the sanctity of all life; the entire creation is God's and reflects His continuing will that life abound. We must love life so that others may see and know that it belongs to God. We must leave the judgment of our success to our Creator.

We lovingly suggest to all the people of the earth that they seek to help one another to understand the myriad ways in which we are related to the earth and to one another. In this way, we may begin to *repair the dislocation that many people experience in relation to creation.*

We believe deeply that many human beings have come to behave as materialistic tyrants. Sadly, those who tyrannize the earth are themselves tyrannized. Rather, we have been called by God to "be fruitful and multiply . . . and have dominion" in the earth (Gen. 1:28). Dominion here is a type of the kingdom of heaven. Thus St. Basil describes the creation of humanity in paradise on the sixth day as resembling the arrival of a king in the palace. Dominion is not domination; it is an eschatological sign of the perfect kingdom of God, where corruption and death are no more.

## Environmental Sin

*If human beings were to treat one another's personal property the way they treat their environment, we would view that behavior as anti-social and illegal. We would impose judicial measures necessary to restore wrongly appropriated per-*

*sonal possessions. It is, therefore, appropriate for us to seek ethical and even legal recourse where possible, in matters of ecological crimes.*

*It follows that to commit a crime against the natural world is a sin. For human beings to cause species to become extinct and to destroy the biological diversity of God's creation; for human beings to degrade the integrity of the earth by causing changes in its climate, by stripping the earth of its natural forests, or by destroying its wetlands; for human beings to injure other human beings with disease; for human beings to contaminate the earth's waters, its land, its air, and its life, with poisonous substances — all of these are sins.*

In prayer, we ask for the forgiveness of sins committed both willingly and unwillingly. And it is certainly God's forgiveness that we must ask for causing harm to His own creation. In this way, we begin the process of healing our worldly environment, which was created by God and blessed with beauty. Then we may also begin to participate responsibly, as persons making informed choices, both in the integrated whole of creation and within our own souls.

## Environmental Ethics

In just a few weeks the world's leaders will gather in Kyoto, Japan, to determine what, if anything, the nations of the world will commit to do in order to halt climate change. There has been much debate back and forth about who should and should not have to change the way they use the resources of the earth. Many nations are reluctant to act unilaterally. This self-centered behavior is a symptom of our alienation from one another and from the context of our common existence.

We are urging a different and, we believe, a more satisfactory ecological ethic. This ethic is shared with many of the religious traditions represented here. All of us hold the earth to be the creation of God, where He placed the newly created human "in the garden of Eden to till it and keep it" (Gen. 2:15). He imposed on humanity a stewardship role in relationship to the earth. *How we treat the earth and all of creation defines the relationship that each of us has with God. It is also a barometer of how we view one another.* For if we truly value a person, we are careful about our behavior toward that person. Yet, the dominion that God has given humankind over the earth does not extend to human relationships. As the Lord said, "You know that the rulers of the [nations] lord it over them, and their great ones are tyrants over them. It will not be so among you; but whoever wishes to be great among you must be your servant, and whoever wishes to be first among you must be your slave; just as the Son of Man came not to be served but to serve, and to give his life a ransom for many" (Matt. 20:25-28).

It is with that understanding that we call on the world's leaders to take action to halt the destructive changes to the global climate that are being caused by human activity. And we call on all of you here today to join us in this cause. This can be our important contribution to the great debate about climate change. We must be spokespeople for an ecological ethic that reminds the world that it is not ours to use for our own convenience. It is God's gift of love to us, and we must return his love by protecting it and all that is in it.

We congratulate all those who initiated, organized, addressed, and participated in this important symposium. It is our fervent and sincere prayer that this will become a focal point for further theological reflection and practical action throughout the parishes of this Holy Archdiocese of America, all the Orthodox Churches in this great land, and all Americans of goodwill. We are especially thankful for the presence of Secretary Bruce Babbitt and the commitment that President Clinton and Vice President Gore have made toward sound ecological policy.

The Lord suffuses all of creation with His divine presence in one continuous legato from the substance of atoms to the mind of God. Let us renew the harmony between heaven and earth and transfigure every detail, every particle of life. Let us love one another and lovingly learn from one another, for the edification of God's people, for the sanctification of God's creation, and for the glorification of God's most holy Name. Amen.

# *1998*

Patriarch Bartholomew with the Hon. Bruce Babbitt (Santa Barbara, 1997)
*Photo courtesy of St. Barbara Church, CA*

# ENVIRONMENT AND POVERTY

*Greeting at the commencement of the fifth
summer seminar on Halki, June 14, 1998*

It has already been four years since the Holy and Great Mother Church of Christ took up the initiative to hold a series of summer ecological seminars in this ancient and holy monastery. The fifth of these seminars commences to-day. Although five successive seminars are not sufficient to allow us to say that they have become an established institution, we are able to say that the timeliness and the acuteness of the ecological problem, whose solution cannot be immediately predicted, demand an increase and not a reduction of our efforts. Thus, what is needed is to expand and not to curtail the offerings of these seminars, which, God willing, would consequently result in their consolidation.

As is known, the topic of the first ecological seminar that took place here, in 1994, was "Environment and Religious Education." The following year the seminar was concerned with the topic "Environment and Ethics." The presentations and reports of both these seminars have already been published in English and are available to all who desire to acquire them. The third successive seminar had as its topic "Environment and Communication." The fourth concerned itself with the topic "Environment and Justice." The topic of this present fifth seminar is "Environment and Poverty."

As is apparent from this list of topics, the center of our concern focuses on the human person, who indeed lives within a specific terrestrial and natural environment. For the environment receives its worth from — and receives its name in relation to — a distinct focal point, which it surrounds. This focal point is, in essence, humanity, or otherwise the human biotope — not unto itself, but as a human ecosystem, since humanity, of course, does not live nor is it able to live by itself in nature. Human beings live simultaneously and collaterally in this system, together with the multitudes of living plant and animal organisms, each of which thrives or, better, survives in specific environmental circumstances. *Humanity is dependent on a natural ecosystem in which the needs of all the living organisms that coexist are well balanced and served by each other. The disturbance of this balance within the ecosystem renders the survival of certain types of life difficult; the extinction of certain organisms causes further disproportion in the ecosystem or the asymmetrical growth and development of other organisms.* Many organisms then find it difficult or impossible to meet their needs, which soon results in their death. This can often be seen where habitats have been laid waste; a significant change of habitat leads to the destruction of one ecosystem and its replacement by another, usually inferior, one.

## Hybris and Nemesis

In ancient Greek thought, immeasurable growth and excessive development are sometimes characterized as *hubris* — coinciding with elements of haughtiness and disrespect — while the consequence of this is brought on by *nemesis*. In Christian terminology we speak of sin, whose basic root or source is human pride, and whose wages are called, in one word, "death" (Rom. 6:23).

The topic of this year's seminar presents us with an inquiry about the meaning of the term *poverty*. The fact that the term *poverty* is in contradistinction to the term *wealth* immediately guides our thoughts in the direction of ethics or deontological study — namely, the study of our moral and ethical duty and obligation.

In the purely biological sphere, where the selection of the good or the bad occurs naturally, we speak of sufficiency and insufficiency as an objective condition, independent of the will of the subject, and therefore a neutral ethic. For example, we might discuss whether nutrients are sufficient or insufficient in certain ecosystems, but we do not consider the living beings existent in those systems responsible for those conditions.

However, in any human society, when some members grow wealthy or otherwise live over and beyond sufficiency — that is to say, they possess more than they need — while at the same time others in society have less than the basic necessities that they require to survive, we begin to ask what the reason may be for this unbalanced distribution of wealth. We start to wonder if the totality of available goods is sufficient for the totality of the needs. We question whether this unbalance is the result of greed and abuse of power on the part of the wealthy, since they are in possession — without real necessity — of the portion belonging to those who are lacking the basic necessities of life.

As we can see, the topic of poverty has many aspects and dimensions, and the appreciation and discernment of all these issues exceeds the limits of the present seminar. All of human history has unfolded as a struggle to extend human power, both personal and collective, over the material goods of the earth, and why this is so has perplexed philosophers and others for centuries. Why does humankind engage in this mad frenzy for the exclusive control of goods, which should be sufficiently available and shared by all?

## Reality and Ideal

For the duration of the present seminar, we shall confine ourselves to the investigation of the connection between the environment and poverty. Based on what we have said above, this specific topic may be studied from two possible points of view: namely, the objective and the deontological. We see the objective point of view in research into the sufficiency or insufficiency of goods that are naturally produced or that are produced by humans in order to satisfy human requirements. Let us set aside for now the economists' rhetoric about the boundlessness of human needs; such talk does not concern natural, physical needs but psychological or spiritual desires. As the Church, *we cannot sanction the boundless "needs" and desires of the diseased human soul that are caused by greed,* but can sanction only those needs which are genuine or natural (and in conformity with the common good). If we compare the available means of production with the level of realistic needs — namely, those needs which are both naturally and ethically justifiable — then we will be able to confirm with much astonishment that the earth is capable of nourishing and generally satisfying all of these needs for the totality of its population.

The pessimistic theories of those who support opposing views have not been proven true. On the contrary, it has been proven that, through technological and scientific progress in general, overabundant cycles of surplus crops have been achieved to the point that problems do not center on the lack of material earthly goods but rather on their overabundance. Certainly, production levels have not yet been adequately balanced; certain regions have an overabundance while others suffer because of deficiency. Nevertheless, this is not because balance is impossible to achieve but because of the lack of human will and desire to do what ought to be done, the lack of moral awareness, organization, and cooperation. In reality, this is an ethical or deontological problem, and not a natural one.

Perhaps pessimists will raise certain objections, but we are of the opinion that these objections do not stand. Especially with regard to the industrial manufacture of goods, it is very clear that the possibilities are great: the world's industry could definitely produce enough to satisfy all human material needs. With regard to natural goods and products, the information at hand suggests that there is a surplus of goods in technologically advanced countries. This fact indicates that, through the use of modern methods and technology, the quantity of natural and manufactured goods could readily be increased to meet the needs of all peoples of the earth — if the human will exists to do so. Consequently, this objective analysis leads us to the conclusion that the problem of the distribution of wealth is the result of selfish and inappropriate human behavior, and not because of the lack of natural resources.

## Mercy and Charity

We now come to the second point of view, the deontological or ethical view of this topic. The relevant positions and teachings of the Orthodox Church on these matters are, we believe, well known. *The spiritual leadership of the Church, as well as every member who belongs to the Church, must sense that the needs of the least of the brothers and sisters of the Lord are their own needs, and they should work toward the satisfaction and fulfillment of those needs.* The commandments of our Lord and the holy Apostles in regard to this issue are numerous. Consider the beatitude "Blessed are the merciful, for they will receive mercy" (Matt. 5:7); the beautiful parable of the last judgment, in which the primary criterion of judgment will be the loving behavior, or the lack thereof, of one human being toward one's fellow human being (Matt. 25:31-46); the words of the Apostle James, the brother of the Lord, who wrote that "religion that is pure and undefiled before God, the Father, is this: to care for orphans and widows in their distress, and to keep oneself unstained by the world" (James 1:27); and likewise "if a brother or sister is naked and lacks daily food . . . and you do not supply their bodily needs, what is the good of that?" (James 2:15-16). These are just a few examples of the positive Christian obligation to relieve the needs of one's fellow human being. Inversely, the explicit condemnation of greed as idolatry (Col. 3:5); the proclamation of the Lord concerning the difficulty of the rich in entering the kingdom of heaven (Matt. 19:23); the assertion that the desire to acquire material goods and pleasures is the reason for wars (James 4:1-2) — these are but a few examples of the ethical unworthiness of the possessive ideology of the secular mind-set.

This is how the Christian *phronema* finds itself close to the natural order of things, which, through the mouth of the Lord, is offered to humankind as the example of how to live: "Therefore I tell you, do not worry about your life, what you will eat or what you will drink, or about your body, what you will wear. . . . For it is the Gentiles who seek for all these things" (Matt. 6:25, 32). Christians believe that God, who feeds and clothes even the flowers of the field and the birds of the air, will also give us what we need. This exhortation to trust in divine providence — that is to say, to have faith in God's love and concern for us — does not revoke our obligation to work and produce that which is necessary. Moreover, it also condemns lack of faith and avarice, as well as excessive worry about this topic. The neptic Fathers, without despising material goods, but through the grace of ascetic struggle learning to forsake many of them, and preaching by the mouth of Abba Isaac the Syrian, declare that "it is clearly known that God and His Angels rejoice in caring for what is necessary, while the devil and his co-workers rejoice in resting" (*Sermon* 27).

### Wanting and Wasting

This is how a Christian is guided toward a balanced use of the material goods of creation in temperance and contentment (1 Tim. 6:6-8), traveling the royal middle road and praying with the author of Proverbs: "give me neither poverty nor riches" (Prov. 30:8). Of course, human beings today, wishing to become rich, "fall into temptation and are trapped by many senseless and harmful desires that plunge people into ruin and destruction. For the love of money is a root of all kinds of evil" (1 Tim. 6:9-10).

*This excessive acquisitiveness in today's world is greatly responsible for a large part of the ecological destruction of our planet, and in the final analysis this destruction proves to be at the expense of all humanity, including those who desire to enrich themselves.* For deficiency and poverty necessarily follow exploitation and luxurious living, because the goods that were to be used by the many were greedily used up by the few. Thus *poverty is not caused by an objective lack of resources but is the result of exploitation and the wasting and improper use of certain resources.* Therefore, human greed and acquisitiveness cause ecological destruction on the one hand and the irresponsible and unequal division of goods on the other. Humankind bears the responsibility for both of these ills, and we must help people understand this if we are to work actively toward the reasonable use of the earth's resources, the preservation of ecological balance, and the safeguarding of our planet's ability to yield and produce life, so that poverty may be abolished or at least greatly diminished.

This is the goal and the objective of this year's ecological seminar, whose commencement we proclaim today. We have among us His Beatitude, our greatly loved and distinguished Brother, Archbishop Christodoulos of Athens and All Greece. We welcome all the participants to this seminar, and we pray wholeheartedly for the success of your work and deliberations. Amen.

# FRAGMENTATION AND ISOLATION

*Foreword to the published proceedings of the fifth and final
summer seminar at Halki held in June 1998, composed
in June 2000 in preparation for publication*

The deterioration and, in certain parts of the planet, destruction of the environment constitutes an undoubted reality for our contemporary world. The Ecumenical Patriarchate follows with grave concern this deterioration of the ecological crisis, as well as the development of a tendency of an isolated and exclusive response on the part of various scientific branches and specific efforts to control this problem. As we have repeatedly underlined, *the fragmentary examination of this problem succeeds only in a partial consideration and response.*

In order, therefore, to examine and encounter comprehensively the environmental crisis that we are facing, in relation especially to the problems of poverty and social injustice, the fifth annual summer ecological seminar was held June 14-20, 1998, in the Holy Patriarchal and Stavropegic Monastery at Halki on the theme: "Environment and Poverty: Legal Dimensions and Moral Responsibility." Representatives of Churches and other religions, environmental and governmental authorities, as well as scientists and scholars presented their views, participated in fruitful discussions, and produced common documents that comprise valuable material for a comprehensive approach to the issue at hand.

## Poverty and Environment

For, as one of the more serious ethical, social, and political problems, poverty is directly connected to the ecological crisis. A poor farmer in Asia, in Africa, or in South America will daily face the reality of poverty. For these persons, plastic is not simply harmful to the environment; rather, it endangers the very survival of themselves and their families. Terminology such as "ecology," "deforestation," or "overfishing" is entirely unknown. The "developed" world cannot demand that the developing poor protect the few earthly paradises that remain, especially in light of the fact that less than 10 percent of the world's population consumes over 90 percent of the earth's natural resources.

The present situation reminds us of the poor widow in the Gospel, who made her small offering in the treasury; yet, this contribution was the equivalent of her entire possessions. "For all of them have contributed out of their abundance; but she out of her poverty has put in everything she had, all she had to live on" (Mark 12:44). Therefore, we are not justified in demanding that the poorer nations offer huge sacrifices, when in any case these contribute far less than the developed nations to the pollution and crisis of the environment. Instead, *we ought to assume our own responsibilities and contribute to the solution of the environmental crisis in accordance with our possibilities as financially stronger nations in order to wipe out poverty as well.*

# THE ORTHODOX CHURCH AND CONTEMPORARY ISSUES[5]

*Message of the Synaxis of Hierarchs of the
Ecumenical Patriarchate, September 1, 1998*

The Holy and Mother Church of Christ, in its characteristic affection and responsible care for the issues that today concern the people of God, has convened at the Phanar, at the initiative of its Primate and Ecumenical Patriarch Bartholomew, a Synaxis of the Hierarchs of the Ecumenical Throne in order to study how the Orthodox faithful can be consciously Orthodox within a world of radical confusion and continual social changes.

Therefore, the Hierarchy has gathered and has decided to address a message of love, consolation, and responsibility toward its faithful clergy and laity in the Lord, in recognition of the hope that is within us. Through this message, it seeks to instruct its faithful children, in the midst of a global but unsociable society, to struggle fervently against the prevailing spirit of self-sufficiency and selfishness and anthropocentrism, in order to live in faith and patience the life of the Church.

We welcome with gratitude the new year of the Lord, the first day of the ecclesiastical calendar, which has been established by our sacred Ecumenical Throne also as a day of prayer and supplication for the protection of the nat-

---

5. Although this message is not an address by Patriarch Bartholomew, it was drafted on September 1st in response to his invitation and invocation.

ural environment, which is threatened in manifold ways. We offer thanks to the Creator of all, who is worshiped in Trinity, for His rich blessings bestowed upon humanity through the material world. As you know, our environment groans in travail as a result of the irrational abuse by humanity. Therefore, we observe so many terrible things today throughout our planet. This is why *we persistently beseech you to love the creation of the almighty God, because every harm that is wrought upon it, even out of negligence, constitutes not simply an evil, but a grave sin.*

We address blessings and praise to all those who, in good conscience, work toward maintaining the integrity of divine creation; we address our paternal consolation and exhortation to the governments of every nation, to those who administer their economies and technologies, to scientists and technologists who move in certain daring areas of research, and especially those areas which can have negative consequences in bioethics as well as, more generally, for the future of life and the world; we also address blessings to those who cultivate the earth, that each of them may perform their duty in order to avoid further destruction to our planet, its environment, and the various forms of life that exist in it. For in the last few years our environment has been exposed to a whirlpool of experimentation previously unheard of, which promised much but also threatened great dangers.

As Orthodox Christians, we are obliged to participate in the occurrences of this world and its history. However, we should also be aware of the truth in regard to what is happening, constantly remembering the will of God and unceasingly praying for the life and salvation of the world.

## In the World, Not of the World

We live in the world, since we are human; yet, at the same time, we look to the kingdom of heaven, which is not of this world. We recognize the power of sin and evil, and we perceive "the mystery of lawlessness" (2 Thess. 2:7) performed in all places and at all times. Nevertheless, our faith remains unshakeable; for it has conquered and ever conquers "the world." This faith is in the incarnate, crucified, risen Lord Jesus Christ, who trampled upon death. Moreover, through the power of the Holy Spirit, we are moving toward the glory of God the Father.

The world offers us fear, and it provokes great distress. Nevertheless, we remain steadfast in love, which "casts out fear" (1 John 4:18). In spite of recent political changes and the exodus from the bonds of State and ideological atheism, Orthodoxy remains in difficult circumstances. We Orthodox, too, endure the temptations of "secularism," of seeking to live in and to conform to this world without God. We, too, endure the plots of false brothers and the enticements of vain "saviors." We endure numerous trials from without and from within, "danger from [our] own people, danger from Gentiles, danger in the city, danger in the wilderness, danger at sea, danger from false brothers and sisters" (2 Cor. 11:26).

# 1999

Media workshop at the Halki Ecological Institute (1999)

# GLOBAL VALUES, FINANCIAL TRADE

*Address at the annual Davos Meeting, February 2, 1999*

We should first like to express our joy that this meeting of distinguished and dynamic economists, political figures, and other eminent dignitaries has included on the agenda of its discussions the human dimension of globalization of the economy, as well as non-economic values. There is no doubt that, when ranking values, the human person occupies a place higher than any economic activity. Neither is there any doubt that *economic progress, which is present when there is growth in economic activity, becomes useful when — and only when — it serves to enhance the non-economic values that make up human culture.* This is the reason that justifies our presence at this illustrious gathering, even though we bear no direct relation to economic matters.

Humanity's advance toward globalization is in fact arising primarily out of the private sector; I am referring in particular to the desires of multinational economic giants. This fact finds support in the incredible development of communications. Already the role of governments is being constantly downgraded, with few exceptions, whereas the role of the economically powerful is growing in magnitude, even among the larger nations.

As the Primate of the Ecumenical Patriarchate, and as the first bishop of the Orthodox Church throughout the world, we assure you that the Orthodox Church has experienced and cultivated the idea of spiritual ecumenicity. This is a form of globalization that proclaims that all human beings of every race and language and of all cultures should be united by bonds of love, goodwill, and cooperation. It is true that the Church invites all to one faith, but its desire for unity and its love and concern for people are not contingent upon their joining this faith. For as the Church embraces everyone, it also experiences the unity of humankind to its fullest.

From this point of view, Christian ecumenicity differs substantially from globalization. The former is based on love for one's brother and sister and respects all human persons and also seeks to serve them. The latter is primarily motivated by a desire to enlarge the market and to merge different cultures into one, in accordance with the convictions of those who are in a position to influence the worldwide public. Unfortunately, though globalization may begin as a means of bringing the peoples of the world together as brothers and sisters, it tends to turn into a means of expanding economic dominance of the financial giants even over peoples to whom access was previously denied as a result of national borders and cultural barriers.

## Spiritual Values, Human Faces

It is neither our intention nor our responsibility to suggest ways and means by which this danger may be contained or eliminated. However, we do feel an obligation to point out and proclaim that the highest pursuit of humanity is not economic enrichment or economic expansion. The Gospel saying, "One does not live by bread alone" (Matt. 4:4), should be understood more broadly. We cannot live by economic development alone, but we must seek the "word that comes from the mouth of God" (Matt. 4:4), namely the values and principles that transcend economic concerns. Once we accept these, economy becomes a servant of humanity, and not its master.

We believe that all, independently of religious conviction, can understand this. For *economic development in itself and the globalization that serves it lose their value when they cause deprivation among the many and an excessive concentration of wealth into the hands of the few.* Moreover, evolution in this direction is not without limits, because beyond a certain limit the person dealing with financial matters receives the response well known from ancient times: "You cannot take from one who has not." Consider this example from ancient Athens: Solon, the governor, decided that Athenian society was not functioning properly because of the excessive indebtedness of the majority of its citizens to the few; and so he declared what was known as *seisachtheia,* namely, the writing off of all debts. Although this seemed at first to be to the disadvantage of the rich, in the end it benefited the entire Athenian community because it allowed all of its members to act as free, creative, and self-motivated citizens and not as each other's slaves. Equally well known is the decision of that pioneering American industrialist, the inventor of the assembly line, to raise his workers' wages so that they would be able to purchase his products. We are referring to the automobile manufacturer Henry Ford, who based his ideas on Taylor's views on the rationalism of labor. These examples, and so many others, show that economic progress is morally justifiable and successful only when all the members of the global community participate in it.

Globalization sets before us new problems for economic morality on a global scale. Nevertheless, although we are speaking of new challenges here, we are dealing essentially with an aggravated form of ancient problems. The ancient Athenians excelled, "not by bestowing any advantage on the rich, but by the poor sharing equally with the rich" (Euripides, *Suppliants* 407). Then, when Athens fell into an anarchic democracy controlled by demagogues, its former glory was eclipsed, just as is the case in those societies which Aristotle called "oligarchies," the presupposition of which is the possession of wealth (*Politics* IV.8).

## The Ethos of Respect

It is a fact that as soon as respect for the human person is abandoned as an inviolable presupposition of our ethos and economic principles, power and the ability to influence the masses are turned into idols and worshiped as such, and there arises an insatiable desire for more. This inevitably leads the "haves" to go to great lengths to increase what they possess, whether it be wealth, or political or military power, or the power to shape ideas, or generally the power to influence the world. Thus it is vitally important to preserve all the cultural values that pertain to humanity, without, of course, putting up unnecessary barriers to useful economic development. We must also be aware that globalization is morally justified only when accompanied by the global distribution of the benefits that flow from it.

Globalization thus proves to be a new vision for some and a renewed threat for others, a vision that promises much to a few and very little to many. It is a vision impressive to some extent in its conception and in its realization. At the same time, however, it is also frightening to the degree that the dynamic of globalization breaks free from customary moral limits as well as legal regulations. The almost automatic globalization of information, for example, is impressive. Yet, at the same time, the potentiality for intentional misinformation is alarming. The globalization of knowledge, from the farthest reaches of the macrocosm to the innermost depths of the microcosm, is impressive; but the threat posed by the possible misuse of this accumulated knowledge is also fearful.

The visions, the dangers, the threats, and the dilemmas rise up before us. The achievements of international cooperation in the sectors of economy, commerce, telecommunications, and trade in general, to which the phenomenon of globalization is primarily attributed, are wonderful. What, however, is the true gain for humanity as a whole if the economy, in succumbing to the sickness of elephantiasis, devours the other sectors of culture — namely thought, artistic creativity, and the contemplative side of human life? What is the true gain for humanity if economic globalization causes a culture's creative powers to wither and enfeebles the fundamental principles of coexistence and survival, such as justice, reciprocity, solidarity between individuals and peoples, and respect for the human person, all of which form the unshakeable bedrock of our existence and coexistence?

As a representative of the Orthodox Church, we are not opposed to economic progress that serves humanity. Nor are we bigoted toward or timorous in the presence of other faiths and ideologies. Our desire, rather, is to safeguard the possibility for the members of every religious or cultural minority to maintain their distinctiveness and the particularity of their culture. We are in absolute agreement and are prepared to move ahead when globalization opens doors for the cooperation of all peoples. The Ecumenical Patriarchate and we personally have already frequently invited adherents of divided faiths, ideologies, and interests to put aside their differences and to reconcile and work together on a practical level. *We are opposed, however, to globalization as a means of making humanity homogeneous, of influencing the masses and causing only one unified mode of thought to prevail.* We also regard the use of globalization exclusively for the enrichment of the few to the detriment of the many as something impermissible and to be avoided. And we invite all, rich and poor alike, to cooperate for the improvement of the standard of living of all people. For, this too is in the interest of the "haves," more so than the one-sided increase in their economic worth.

May God enlighten us all to be able to understand this truth.


# ENVIRONMENT, PEACE, AND ECONOMY

*Address at a gathering of banking representatives*
*in Athens, Greece, May 24, 1999*


I am truly overjoyed with the present gathering. We are assembled here in love, in a meeting that extends beyond our regular professional obligations, and this reality adds great sensitivity to the atmosphere that is created among us, something that already constitutes a spiritual environment. For we are not standing opposite one another in order to exchange some professional agreement or contract; rather, we are standing together as co-workers in a common good.

The first part of this common good is getting to know one another and establishing an inviolable bond of friendship, a presupposition for any harmonious cooperation. The second part of this common good is the study of our mutual interests in order to examine how we might successfully achieve our goals. We are deeply grateful for your invitation to this gathering in order to contribute whatever we can to your goals. We are also grateful for your evident love, which reveals feeling hearts and thinking minds.

## Exchanging Money and Serving People

If one considers matters superficially, one might say that we share little in common, for you work in the sphere of material things, money in particular, while we work in the sphere of the spirit. Nevertheless, a deeper study of matters persuades us that things are not quite this way. Indeed, we are bound by a fundamental common element — namely, our interest in the human person. Let us develop what we mean by this.

The literal sense of the word for "money" in the Greek language implies its inner meaning, that is, something that can be used. However, whenever we speak of usage, we are implying both someone who uses and a goal for this usage. Human beings do the using, and their aim in this usage is to meet material and (more rarely, when these are related to material goods) spiritual needs. Therefore, *money is a tool in the hands of human beings, and its purpose is to serve human needs. This means that, inasmuch as you are occupied with money and preoccupied in dealing with money, in the final analysis you are — or should be — serving humanity.* For money is surely not an end in itself. Nor is money the object of some lifeless hoarding. Rather, money is a catalyst that facilitates exchanges; it is an ever-moving catalyst, which, when properly used, offers a sense of satisfaction to the persons through whose hands it is exchanged. This happens even in the case of someone who painstakingly counts it out; for it is also a matter of reward for that person. Consequently, in meeting material human needs, you are ultimately serving human beings.

From a different perspective, and with quite different means, we too serve human beings, seeking to meet their spiritual needs. Nevertheless, we know that the human person is a psychosomatic being, comprising spirit and matter, and that physical needs must be met in order for a person to stay alive and enjoy spiritual needs. Therefore, if a person's material needs are not being met, then we are required to assume responsibility for their needs voluntarily and charitably. The Gospel command is very clear in this regard: Give to those who do not have; take care of the orphans and the widows; feed the hungry; heal the sick; help the helpless. The Church does not ignore material needs, but it incorporates these within an appropriate hierarchy, wherever necessary giving priority to the primary and ranking lower the secondary, in order to meet the basic needs of those who are lacking in material and spiritual things.

Bearing this in mind, when we notice our fellow human beings lacking even that which is given freely by God to all, namely life-giving oxygen and clean air, simply because other human beings consume the available oxygen and pollute the atmosphere with harmful waste, we come to the conclusion that the abuse of our resources is morally impermissible. It is wrong because it deprives some people of their basic needs while it enriches others financially. Thus, measures must be taken. Just as it took many years to establish free shipping trade — that is, to accept that the seas are open for the use of all humanity — in the same way efforts are required to establish people's right to breathe clean air and to inflict proper penalties on those who pollute the air. Since clean air and the preservation of the natural environment in general are necessary for the healthy existence of each person, each person is morally obliged to refrain from pollution and destruction of the environment.

Unfortunately, people have not yet become conscious of this obligation, and so we have mobilized ourselves out of the above-mentioned sense of charity to assume responsibility to enlighten everyone — for we all consume air and water — concerning the harmful consequences of our pollution on humanity. For the attitudes and actions that result in pollution also conceal an ethical insensitivity. Our efforts aim at sensitizing people's consciences, so that they will voluntarily refrain from polluting — particularly so that they will stop large-scale acts of pollution in industry, for example — for the sake of social obligation. Indeed, sensitizing people's consciences constitutes an important first step if we are to stop actions that destroy the natural environment.

Therefore, we propose that we might spend a little more time on this critical issue. The aim is not to idolize the environment but to serve humanity. In particular, we would like to address the impact of war on the environment. For if ecological issues are acute even during times of peace, when the protection of human beings is perceived positively, then how much more critical are these issues during times of war, when the extermination of others and the destruction of their environment are the unfortunate objective?

If we study in detail the conditions of war described in the epics of Homer, and then proceed to compare these to contemporary situations, we will be surprised at the insignificant impact of war at that time on the environment, at least by comparison with the tragic effects that we witness today. Indeed, if we consider the consequences of war at different historical periods, then we shall also observe the sad reality that, the closer one comes to our period, the more dramatic the effects of military clashes have been on the natural environment.

### An Environmental Decalogue of the Impact of War

An enumeration of the precise impacts and effects of war on the environment is not easy for someone who is not a specialist or scholar in the field. However, this is a rough outline of the most obvious effects:

- Obviously war results in a very significant number of fatalities, leading to the disruption of families and sometimes even of societal structures in communities.
- A vast number of injuries also result, which also disrupt families and society; these casualties also require medical care and support, which are costs subtracted from other areas of society.
- An unknown number of people succumb to illnesses as a result of military pollution of the environment by means of chemical gases, radioactive substances, fire, and decomposition.
- An indeterminable number of spiritual wounds result from the cruelty of war in numerous communities, which thereafter foster anti-social feelings and disturb the human environment.
- There is long-term pollution of the region by the wastes from military machinery. For instance, huge amounts of air pollution are caused by military planes flying over a given region for thousands of hours, the shooting of jet-propelled rockets, the sailing of navy ships, and the movement of army and administrative vehicles. All these pollutants affect not just the specific region of the war but the neighboring regions as well, some even reaching distant territories where they affect good and evil people alike.
- A particularly grave type of pollution affects not only the region where the conflict occurs but also surrounding areas: namely, the by-products of explosives, charged and diffused, in the form of radioactive shells of ammunition, rockets, bombs, and other modern weapons of mass destruction. This pollution travels throughout the region, conveyed by air and water, thereby affecting areas that are not even involved in the conflict.
- Equally tragic is the destruction and pollution that occurs when storage tanks filled with chemical products and the factories that produce and

use these products are bombed. If one considers the detailed, strict, and careful measures in place for the safe transfer, storage, and use of these dangerous products until they are transformed into inactive and harmless products for general consumption, and then one considers how all of these products are exploded into the air together as a result of military bombing, then it is impossible not to be overwhelmed by a sense of sorrow. It should be noted that the involuntary recipient of these pollutants is not just the military opponent; indeed, it is not just the noncombatant civilians among the enemy (which in any case, according to international regulations of war, should not be the target of military attacks). Rather, these pollutants also affect populations beyond the borders of the country at war, whether in neighboring or more distant regions. Indeed, the soldiers themselves who are causing the destruction are also affected! The unforeseen effects of the heavy pollution caused by war may even reach the other side of the planet, including the citizens of the country instigating the military attack! For the interconnections and mutual influences within nature are vast and often inscrutable. It is sufficient to recall the example sometimes mentioned by scientists, that the fluttering of a butterfly's wings in Japan can cause rain in America.

- Still more tragic is the radical and often irreparable destruction wrought upon local ecosystems, which suffer as a result of the effects of war. Ecosystems in the oceans, rivers, and lakes are destroyed by explosions of bombs and mines; terrestrial ecosystems are annihilated not only by explosives but also by fires. This destruction affects human habitats as well. Homes are leveled by bombs or fires; infrastructure such as road systems are destroyed; and human lives regress to the conditions of the past.

- In addition to all this, cultural monuments are destroyed or damaged, so that civilization itself suffers a lasting blow, as the organization *Europa Nostra* has declared through its resolution dated April 29, 1999.

- Finally, the spiritual atmosphere is inundated by boundless falsehoods of propaganda; passions are cultivated in people's souls; hatred and violence are justified. The effects of this spiritual "pollution" are manifested everywhere in the world, irrespective of distance — for example in a school where a young child learns to develop racist attitudes toward invisible enemies or even toward visible schoolmates. This psychological pollution, which adversely affects the human environment, is especially important for us to note, although it is usually overlooked by those who deal with environmental issues.

## The Irrationality of War

This list of environmental effects that result from contemporary warfare clearly shows the irrationality of military conflict, which can only be explained as a paranoid act. For, while war is instigated supposedly in order to protect certain people who are provoked by their unjust treatment by other people, nevertheless warfare ensures that unjust treatment is extended to include numerous others. Moreover, often the injustice against which people seek to protect themselves is connected to some financial or territorial gain, and yet vast amounts are expended in war for the destruction of the enemy, and in the end only minimal amounts of money are left to repay the aggrieved parties. Perhaps reversing the expenditures — spending little on military action and much more on reparation — might have successfully resolved many conflicts.

Therefore, *the irrationality of war is evident from its effect on humanity and on the natural environment.* It is our duty to intervene, wherever possible, to persuade those who are responsible for making decisions to seek peaceful resolutions to human problems. With goodwill and the proper effort, such solutions can be found. The choice of military violence as the sole method for resolving conflicts betrays a lack of imagination and intellectual laziness, as well as misplaced confidence in the erroneous notion that evil can be corrected by evil.

As heralds of the Gospel truth, which is the only complete truth, we repeat the words of the Apostle: "Do not be overcome by evil, but overcome evil with good" (Rom. 12:21). We conclude with this exhortation, adding only our fervent prayers that irrational wars may cease as soon as possible and that the almighty and beneficent Lord may grant everyone the wisdom to understand that war is an impasse. May the same Lord decrease as much as possible the dark consequences of military attacks and grant peace to all peoples. As for you, my beloved listeners, may He grant you the grace to struggle for the happiness of all your fellow human beings, so that you may be filled with divine joy.

# PRINCIPLES IN PRACTICE

*Address during the official opening of the inaugural session*
*of the Halki Ecological Institute, June 13, 1999*

It is with sincere joy and profound paternal satisfaction that we address you, the esteemed facilitators, participants, and staff of this unique initiative, the Halki Ecological Institute. It is our fervent prayer and hope that this venture will indeed prove to be the seed of a fruitful cooperative effort for the preservation and improvement of the environment of the Black Sea.

This beautiful sea, around which so many renowned ancient civilizations flourished, constituted a very useful channel of communication between peoples and cultures throughout the centuries. Even more, it is also a biotope, a living habitat, which for thousands of years existed under balanced conditions that allowed for the preservation of life both under the waters and on the surrounding shores, life that nourished the human inhabitants as well.

The linkage of the Black Sea with the Mediterranean via the Bosphorus also allowed the Mediterranean peoples to travel by sea to the north and, conversely, for those in the north to sail south. Even though there have been many military conflicts in this region, today we see that this mode of communication contributed to the cultural development of neighboring peoples. By means of the mighty flowing rivers, in particular the Danube, the Black Sea allowed interaction among the peoples living inland; the Black Sea thus constituted a center of communication, the significance of which continues even until today. Unfortunately, the fact that many rivers of Europe, Asia, and Asia Minor flow into the Black Sea make it the recipient of the pollution that these rivers carry from the surrounding regions and even from more remote areas.

Regrettably, people today do not subscribe to the ancient wisdom of the peoples described by Herodotus who believed the rivers to be sacred and considered polluting the rivers a sacrilege. Too many people today believe only that which is "rational," refusing to consider spiritual reasons for such a principle and belief. Holding up "reason" as the only criterion of truth, and denying the pedagogical power of the myth with its higher rationality found hidden in its message, has led modern human beings to a shortsighted, selfish, and pettily opportunistic state. We experience the consequence of this state as a foretaste of our biological death, which unexpectedly comes upon us and for which we prepare ourselves by our own so-called rational energies, which are, in fact, foolish and irrational.

The overproduction and overuse of toxic substances in both industry and agriculture — not to mention war — puts those non-degradable substances into the rainwater; these toxic substances then find their way into the rivers and finally to the oceans.

The Black Sea, which is relatively small in size, is the recipient of a disproportionate quantity of pollutants. As a result, it is constantly and intensely being overburdened, even more so than are the great Pacific and Atlantic Oceans. This is apparently due to industrialization, over-consumption, and overall changes in conditions of life of modern society.

### Causes and Cause

These causes do indeed contribute to the pollution of the Black Sea, but we insist on characterizing them as "apparent causes," because we consider the "true cause" to be, not the evil that can be carried by the rivers, but the destruction of religious piety within the human heart.

This piety that Herodotus described certain ancient peoples as having elevated them to a level of spiritual civilization higher than our own, inasmuch as we do not have the delicacy of feelings and the sense of responsibility toward our fellow human beings that these ancestors possessed. Thus, our claims that our higher logic does not allow us to consider a natural thing such as a river as sacred are revealed to be egotistical pretensions. In this, we prove ourselves to be foolish and small-minded. We cling to our "reason" and refuse to acknowledge that the rivers and all of creation are indeed sacred, just as are the human beings whom nature itself is ordained to serve. All that was created "good" by the All Good Creator participates in His sacredness. Conversely, disrespect toward nature is disrespect toward the Creator, just as the arrogant destruction of a work of art is an insult to the artist who created it.

*Consequently, if we desire to improve the situation, we must restore in the hearts of the members of our society the sensitivity that was held in the hearts of our ancestors* whom Herodotus mentions. In other words, we must restore respect for the truly existing sanctity of life, which is in peril because of our shortsighted and egotistical polluting actions.

Those who live near rivers and waterways are so numerous and so greatly dispersed that there is no possibility of fully monitoring them. The successful way to avoid river pollution, instilling respect for the sacredness of the rivers, is not a useful lie but a very profound truth; yet this truth is denied and rejected by modern demythologizers and secularists, who think that it confuses the supernatural with the one-dimensional nature of the world, according to our deluded perception. The result is that we have allowed selfish individualism to lead us to act in a very shortsighted way; the transfer of pollution far away from us satisfies us, and we feel secure. Yet we do not consider the fact that we are thus setting into motion a vicious circle of mutual transfers of pollution, followed by a vain struggle to heal the damage, when in fact only prevention can save the situation.

Such prevention can be achieved only if all members of society regard it as their moral and, above all, religious obligation not to cast their waste upon their fellow human beings. This is understood and socially accepted as an obligation of one's daily life. Yet it must also be expanded to include our broader economic and industrial moral conduct.

## The Wonder of Creation

We are therefore obliged to recall and accept the sacred in our daily life, and especially in areas where we would not normally recognize its place, namely in our commercial and professional activity. This is why the Ecumenical Patriarchate, which has a purely religious mission, is mobilizing and sometimes initiating efforts for the protection of the environment that at first glance might seem to refer only to the material world.

*However, this superficial evaluation is not correct. On the one hand, for us the protection of the environment is not simply a matter of adoration of creation, but the veneration of the Creator. On the other hand, concern about the environment is an invitation for all of us to accept the sacred and the holy in our life.*

In this sense, all of our theologians and clergy, who have recently admired the beauty and diversity of our natural environment, must become conscious of the fact and convey the message that the moral life of our faithful should not be limited to dealing justly with those around us but should be extended out of love to avoiding harmful, long-term consequences that may affect our fellow human beings who live hundreds of miles from us.

Our Lord has taught us that our righteousness must exceed the righteousness of the scribes and the Pharisees. In this respect, we should consider the reverence of the ancient Persians described by Herodotus, who neither spat into nor washed their hands in the river, and who also encouraged others to follow their example, out of great respect for the rivers (*Kleio*, par. 138).

We are certain that the Halki Ecological Institute will offer you the opportunity and the motivation to study more deeply, not only the technical and humanitarian parameters of the problem of the pollution of the Black Sea and the rest of the natural environment, but also its Christian and theological perspective. This will enable you to become interested in and more deeply conscious of your mission to work with love and piety, and to cooperate with all those who are dealing with the subject of the environment, to protect nature from actions that create pollution and destroy habitats. This sensitization of ourselves and of those around us, especially those who control major sources of pollution, together with encouragement of members of our society voluntarily to avoid ecologically destructive lifestyles and to exert their influence over those who do not accordingly conform, constitutes the most fruitful path to environmental preservation and restoration for the Black Sea and every burdened ecosystem.

We repeat once again our invitation and challenge to all of you — the Orthodox and other Churches, and the religious leaders of the faiths in the neighboring regions, as well as all leaders in the regions of Europe, Asia, and Asia Minor whose rivers transfer pollution and especially toxic wastes into the Black Sea — to convey to all peoples the need to raise their awareness about such pollution.

We thank all those who seek along with us to reintroduce the sense of sacredness as the guideline for our life, as well as all those who from whatever position carry on the struggle for the preservation of life in the Black Sea, thereby contributing to and assisting our neighboring peoples.

We congratulate all of you who responded to our invitation through your participation and contribution to the success of the deliberations of this Institute. Its success is due to you all, and to the commendable and generous sponsorship of the most honorable benefactor and Archon of the Holy and Great Church of Christ, Mr. Theodoros Papalexopoulos, whom we thank personally for his tireless contribution and work. We are certain that your participation here is a new beginning and an inspiration by which the Creator will lead you to continue work in your countries, so that you may protect the beautiful environment that was created by Him, and so that you may challenge other people as well to accept this obligation as a divine command, given for the sake of humanity. Amen.

# CROSS AND ENVIRONMENT

*Meditation before the Exalted Cross at the outset of the*
*third international symposium on the Danube, October 17, 1999*

## The Crux of the Matter

Standing before the cross, we are called to enter deeply into its great mystery. "For the word of the cross is folly to those who are perishing, but to us who are being saved it is the power of God" (1 Cor. 1:18). However, crucified power, power given to those who seemed to be annihilated, is a scheme not easily acceptable to human logic, which is accustomed to recognizing as stronger the one who avoids personal humiliation. However, in this case the grandeur and power of God is revealed in that it remains truly invulnerable to those who attempt to destroy it, in spite of the fact that it appears to be annihilated through the death of the divine Word on the cross. The *Logos* remains untouched by death and by every threat. In this way, the cross, which was formerly a symbol of defeat and shame, is now turned into a symbol of power and glory, because the Crucified One is untouchable by the cross. In other words, the cross is proven powerless to touch the Word of God. Christ was subject to the greatest trial and was found stronger than it. To Him be the glory and honor.

In Christian societies, the cross is venerated as a symbol of the voluntary passion of the divine Word and His victory over death. Although He who first carried the cross calls His followers to carry their own cross, only few joyfully accept the call to undergo this trial. For *the cross is equated with the death of the ego and yet also raises the transfigured ego through its sacred identification, out of love, with every "thou" of the human race and the heavenly communion of personal spirits.*

Nevertheless, the road of life passes through voluntary crucifixion and the road of eternity lies through the acceptance of death. The mystery of the cross, while difficult to fathom and to accept, therefore stands before us demanding a response. It provokes our conscience and enters it as a living experience and as a challenge, not convinced beforehand by wise and persuasive human words, but "strong as death" (Song of Songs 8:6) in faith and love, when the demonstration in the Spirit and power of God will come (1 Cor. 2:4).

*Before each noble high achievement there is sacrifice. And the symbol of such sacrifice is the cross.* If we want our efforts to succeed, as we begin our study and prayer concerning the Danube's environment in order to make the Danube a river of life, each of us must undergo some sacrifice. This sacrifice is the demonstration of our strength and brings upon itself the blessing and the synergy of God, which can overthrow every obstacle and achieve results that we are unable to characterize in any other way than as miracles. Departing, now, for the miracle of Christ's resurrection, a symbol of our own resurrection and of the restoration of all nature, we stand uprightly before the cross of Christ, in the power of which we wish to triumph. Amen.

# THE DANUBE: A RIVER OF LIFE

*Introductory address at the opening session of the third international symposium, October 17, 1999*

The international symposium on the subject "The Danube: A River of Life" forms part of the broader program on religion, science, and the environment and also constitutes the continuation of our symposium held two years ago on the subject "The Black Sea in Crisis." I would like first of all to address my heartfelt greetings and warmest welcome to our dear participants and all others attending this inaugural session. I also feel a genuine obligation to address whole-hearted thanks to the ecclesiastical, municipal, and political authorities of this historical and most picturesque city of Passau, which is offering us its hospitality. My special thanks go to the Most Reverend Dr. Eder, Bishop of Passau, the Most Honorable Lord Mayor of the City, and all those who have contributed to our hospitality and to the flawlessly organized inauguration of the symposium here.

Passau is built at the confluence of the Inn, Ilz, and Danube rivers and is situated on the frontier between Austria and Bavaria, now one of the federated states of Germany. Thus, Passau constitutes an ethnological and physical boundary point, as from this point on traveling on the Danube becomes easier. However, although boundaries serve in general as points of separation, it seems on the contrary that this city has had the historical mission of uniting. As we all know, it was here that, in the year 1552, peace was reached between Roman Catholic and Evangelical Protestant Germans, while its significance as a center of trade underlines the peaceful cooperation between peoples, a cooperation that benefits all of them, as is the case with every healthy commercial activity.

*The Danube itself is, as we know, a natural border, which divides peoples and states into many sections. It is also a water route that unites and brings into contact all those whom it separates and, through them, even those who live beyond its banks.* However, in addition to being a communications artery, which, through international treaties, has been declared free for shipping, it is also a bearer of enormous quantities of water from continental Europe toward the Black Sea, as well as mud and toxic wastes. This is why the Danube is in danger of becoming an easy dumping ground for pollutants and toxic substances from areas along its banks and carrying them to the Black Sea.

It is well known that the Danube empties 6,000 to 7,000 cubic meters of water per second into the Black Sea. From this point of view it is a very important supplier of water to this sea, helping to revitalize it. However, the growth of industry in all the regions along the banks of the river, as well as in regions of the interior that communicate with the Danube by means of tributaries, has polluted the waters, transforming the Black Sea into a second Dead Sea, as was pointed out during the symposium of 1997.

## Human Impact and Influence

Hence, it is the duty of all persons of good faith to contribute, each according to his or her position and ability, not only to maintaining the Danube as a river with free shipping, so that goods can be freely transported from one region to another, but also to preserving it free from toxic substances, in order to maintain the ecological equilibrium of the physical areas surrounding it and the Black Sea.

At this point, *I cannot fail to express my deepest distress at the recent bombing of Yugoslavia, which also affected the waters of the Danube and caused ecological damage that will be difficult to correct.* The expression of my distress is not, of course, confined exclusively to the ecological effects of the bombing. I have repeatedly expressed my deepest sorrow over the fact that this bombing was responsible for killing people; destroying cultural monuments, monasteries, and churches; incapacitating factories; contaminating human communities, animals, plants, and nature in general with toxic substances; and generally causing material and moral damage on a massive scale. However, the object of the present international scientific symposium obliges us to focus our attention on the ecological consequences of this bombing and to point out that its adverse effects are manifested not only in regions neighboring the areas directly affected but also throughout all the regions down the length of the Danube, as well as those lying on the Black Sea coast.

Of course, we could say, without going beyond the bounds of realism, that human acts have repercussions far beyond our expectations. Even small actions in one place may have significant effects far away. This means we know with certainty — even if we never know exactly when or how — that the pollution of our environment will have consequences for the polluters themselves, regardless of how far away they are from the point at which the pollutants have been dumped. The fact that the effects of pollution also travel upstream from the direction in which the river waters flow must make us all think.

## Sensitivity and Foresight

At this point, allow me to remind you of certain details that we have received from Herodotus, according to whom there existed in his time a people that considered rivers sacred and polluting them to be sacrilege. Perhaps those who demythologize ancient beliefs may regard such faith as superstitious. However, even this superstition is socially preferable to the unscrupulous and irresponsible dumping of harmful substances into the rivers, temporarily re-lieving those who selfishly pollute the river, but substantially harming the next generation of their fellow human beings who are going to use it.

Therefore, we must acquire a moral code higher than the selfish and short-sighted one used by such crude people and learn to respect humanity, accepting as a basic principle of our behavior that it is morally unacceptable to burden others with our wastes. This is the only way to help ensure that the Danube, the longest river of this region, as well as other nearby rivers, be-comes a road of life for all. Otherwise, all of these rivers will end up being bearers of death, a death that is sown by many selfish people to the detriment of their fellow human beings and nature as a whole.

This is the deeper reason why, even though our primary mission is the Christian education and sanctification of the Orthodox faithful, we have wholeheartedly adopted the present series of international ecological sympo-sia. The reason is that, *as the Church Fathers also teach, the root of all evils that plague humankind is selfishness, and the highest expression of virtue is selfless love. It is, therefore, not permissible for faithful Christians who are seeking sanc-tification to remain indifferent to the effects of their acts on their fellow human beings.* The sensitivity of their conscience must be increased so that they are not indifferent even to the indirect consequences of their acts. As Abba Isaac the Syrian observes, the sensitive and charitable heart "cannot stand even to hear of sorrow, even the slightest such sorrow, in creation. That is why the heart of such a person grieves for the creatures not endowed with reason, as well as for enemies of the truth and even for those who harm one. Such a person addresses to God a prayer for them in tears, that God may spare them and have mercy on them; and, similarly, one prays for the reptiles, since one's heart is full of mercy, similar to the mercy that fills the heart of God" (Homily 81). This saintly sensitivity is, of course, possessed by very few. But this does not mean that we should go to the other extreme, to a complete lack of sensitivity. For, as Saint John Climacus says: "The hardened person is a foolish philosopher" (*Ladder of Divine Ascent,* Step 17).

In the context of our pastoral concern to raise everybody's awareness of the effects of ecological catastrophe on humankind, we have been active in a variety of directions, among which is participation in the present symposium, the organization of annual seminars, and the formation of an educational institute at Halki. In all these, the altruistic importance of protecting the environment is emphasized, together with the pleasure God takes in creation. In other words, it is stressed that our motives are not simply inspired by our love for nature — although those who have such inspiration have nobler motives than those who are indifferent to nature and to its destruction — but are human-centered, just as in fact all of creation is anthropocentric. Our Christian faith teaches us — and the modern scientists also accept — that the world was created for the sake of humankind and that everything is regulated so as to contribute to our survival. Of course, not everything in this world works together in such harmony for our sake, but this is the consequence of our revolt against the harmony of God, which brought with it a partial revolt of nature against our rule over it.

## Ecological Curse and Divine Providence

The Old Testament words "Cursed is the ground because of you; . . . thorns and thistles it shall bring forth for you" (Gen. 3:17-18) were spoken by God to Adam after his disobedience; they express, according to the Law of God, the relationship between an act and the consequences of the act. Nonetheless, these words have given rise to much misunderstanding concerning the goodness of God and the condition of the natural world. At first sight, we might have the impression that God is cursing creation. Yet, if we look deeper into the spirit of the Holy Scripture, especially as our Lord Jesus Christ in the New Testament developed it, then we realize that this was not a punishment imposed by God on the transgressor. Rather, it is God's communication to humanity about the new ontological interaction that was created because of our disobedience. Instead of a situation where humanity was in communication with God and accepted the favorable influence of divine grace and love on humankind and on the world, a new situation was created because humankind tried to become independent of God, rejecting communion with Him and the influence of divine grace. From that point onward, humanity was therefore evolving independently, refusing the divine grace in the midst of a world whose initial harmony was now damaged.

The love of God never fails and never will fail (1 Cor. 13:8). Yet, humanity rejected God's love and its gifts and tried to create an independent path. As Abba Isaac says: "Those who feel that they have failed in love" feel such sorrow in their hearts that it is as if they were in the midst of the worst hell. "For the sorrow that hits the heart due to failing in love is sharper than the one that results from any hell" (*Ascetic Treatises*, Homily 84).

The love of God never fails. And the new situation in the world that resulted from Adam's refusal to comply with God's loving plan — namely, the plan of developing a perfect and constant loving relation between God and humanity — was disagreeable only because it fell short of love, because love is the personal relationship that offers true beatitude and happiness. Because of the love of God, Adam was created with a dual nature, composed of matter and spirit; and because of this love of God, Adam was given an opportunity to enjoy the infinite treasure of God's material and spiritual gifts.

God's love never abandoned humanity, even when humanity followed its own independent path. God's love has given to us nature — namely, this earthly and broader cosmic space in which we live — which is good in itself, so that from this space we may draw everything we need to live, and, at the same time, we can practice virtue, a part of which is the use of nature responsibly and with gratitude. *Unfortunately, some people do not use creation in a moderate way but abuse it and create problems for others and for the natural world, damaging the harmonious functions in the physical world that remained in place after the Fall.* Although nature changed ontologically after the Fall, nevertheless it has not ceased to function according to the divine plan and the divine laws embodied within it.

## Human Response and Ascetic Struggle

Within the framework of this rebellious and partly dysfunctional nature, humanity must fight both for its physical survival and for its spiritual improvement. "All our life must be a struggle full of pain," St. John Chrysostom warns us (*PG* 47.453), as do all the Church Fathers. Yet, the purpose of this struggle is not to strip us of our physical body, which some philosophers have wrongly considered the prison of our soul. Instead, it is to lead to the Aristotelian middle road of developing the spirit and preserving the body, for the body is perceived as a useful tool under the guidance of the mind that governs it. Christians living on earth and having their city in heaven *(Letter to Diognetus)* reject neither earth nor heaven. They neither completely attach themselves to earthly goods nor completely reject the earth, even though they have espoused, as they say, the heavenly life. *This life is a place to exercise self-control, not a place of helpless resignation; the aim is to destroy selfish passion rather than to destroy the body, as one early ascetic once told someone who was trying to become perfect through excessively ascetic discipline.* We keep constantly before our eyes what the Apostle Paul wrote to Timothy: "everything created by God is good, and nothing is to be rejected, provided it is received with thanksgiving; for it is sanctified by God's word and by prayer" (1 Tim. 4:4).

Thus, according to St. John Chrysostom, our struggle in the present life consists of becoming virtuous in the right way, so that God, in His great glory, will raise our bodies (*PG* 54.636). Life thus becomes a joyous and creative struggle, full of good works and accepting the whole of the creation of God as very good. That is why the Church prays continuously for the success of all good human works, for the blowing of favorable winds and for the rich harvest of the fruits of the earth. And the Church continually expresses its admiration for the beauty of God's creation, saying with the Psalmist: "O Lord, how manifold are your works! In wisdom you have made them all" (Ps. 104:24).

It is, therefore, in this atmosphere of exuberance, joy, thanksgiving, and creativity that the Christian practices a rational use of material goods and natural resources, always retaining a sentiment of awe and sensitivity toward the whole of creation. Like a wise administrator, the Christian obeys the commandment to work and keep the earth so that it will remain capable of providing humanity with food and pleasure, to the glory of the all-wise and benevolent Creator. In spite of humanity's disobedience, in spite of the ontological alteration of the world as a result of the interruption on our part of God's loving relationship, the Creator has never ceased to do everything for our sake and for the sake of readmitting us into the beatitude of love, the fullness of which constitutes the infinite perfection of happiness.

Therefore, the Church says yes to God's creation, while at the same time inviting everybody through this affirmation to reach out to the Creator and accept His invitation into a relationship of love. We do this, not as ungrateful recipients of the gifts of God, but as grateful and noble receivers, expressing our thanks and our love to Him and thus helping to bring about the eternal and indestructible relation of love, which includes eternal life.

Keeping before us, then, the fact that our final goal is to serve the human race by maintaining our natural surroundings in a healthy state, I salute with satisfaction the symposium that has just begun. I wish with all my heart for every success in its proceedings, and I welcome our dear participants whom I know well and whose wise contributions I appreciate, thanking our hosts once more and invoking upon all the grace and eternal mercy of God.

## SCIENCE, SCHOLARSHIP, AND THE STATE

*Greeting during the visit to the Academy of Sciences in Austria,*
*third international symposium, October 19, 1999*

I would like to express my deep gratitude for the invitation to address you from this distinguished podium. Allow me first of all to express my warmest greetings to all of you and especially to His Excellency the Minister of the Environment of the friendly country of Austria, in whose competency lies the subject of this third international and interreligious symposium on religion, science, and the environment, focusing this year on the theme "The Danube: A River of Life." As we all know, "The teaching of the wise is a fountain of life" (Prov. 13:14), and to know this law is a privilege of a good mind.

Therefore, this temple too, in which the best minds of your dear and hospitable country are sheltered, constitutes a source of life, the starting point for laws inspired by the wisdom concentrated here. Decrees passed by Parliaments are not the only laws governing people's minds; there are also the ideas and arrangements proposed by wise individual men and women. It could be said that citizens may be more easily convinced to comply with what the wisdom of the scientist and scholar recommends than to obey the commands of the constitutional legislator. This is why this symposium, although possessing no state authority whatsoever, is seeking to convince citizens by means of knowledge and faith, not by authority, to cooperate in the effort to keep the Danube clean and to maintain a balanced and undisrupted environment. We certainly consider the cooperation of the authorities both necessary and useful, but their efforts may be inadequate in the face of an unenlightened public whose reactions may therefore be negative.

*We believe that the convergence of efforts by science and the State, on the one hand, and by ordinary citizens, on the other, is the most effective way to proceed; and invoking the cooperation of all of you, we anticipate that the aims of the symposium currently taking place will be achieved. But at the same time, we are doing everything in our power to raise the consciousness of each and every citizen to the problem of the endangered environment.*

I am convinced that you, as preeminent representatives of science, who, in the words of the wise Solomon,

> know the structure of the world and the activity of the elements, . . . the alternations of the solstices and the change of the seasons, . . . the natures of animals and the temper of the wild beasts, the powers of the spirit and reasoning of human beings, the varieties of plants and the virtues of roots (Wisdom 7:17-20),

will use your knowledge to contribute to our effort. And, for this noble intention on your part, I congratulate you, commend you, and thank you, invoking upon you all the grace and the infinite mercy of God. Amen.

# TRADE AND NATURE

*Greeting during the reception with the Lord Mayor
of Bratislava, Slovakia, and representatives of the civil authorities,
third international symposium, October 20, 1999*

It is with much delight and great emotion that I find myself once again visiting beautiful Bratislava, a city so dear to me, in the context of the international symposium on religion, science, and the environment, this year focusing on the more specific subject "The Danube: A River of Life." I recall the beautiful moments I spent last year during my official visit to Slovakia and this delightful city, and I am very happy that God has given me the privilege of being here again, even if only for a short while.

I bring to you the blessing and the love of the Mother Church of Constantinople. I address to you my wholehearted greetings in the Lord, and would like to express my affection to you and my gratitude for all the love and honor you have directed toward the Mother Church and myself. I wish all of you every support and assistance from the Lord for all your various efforts and good works.

I am sure that in the list of these good works you have included support for the effort represented by this floating congress. This effort aims at cleaning up the Danube to remove all pollutants, so that it may be a road of life and not a bearer of death. For, as you well know, the great Danube River is not merely a trade route, used as such for millennia, but also a riverbed over which 6,000 to 7,000 cubic meters of water flow each second toward the Black Sea. This water, and that of all the other rivers that flow into it, renews the water of the Black Sea and contributes greatly to preserving life in its ecosystem. In addition, over its long course, the Danube contributes to many ecosystems of its own, which serve human life in their own way. All these ecosystems are in grave danger of being seriously disrupted, or even completely destroyed, due to the thoughtless dumping of wastes and toxic substances into the Danube. The damage this pollution causes is not limited to areas right on the river banks but extends to the interior of the countries through which it flows, and even to more distant regions.

The object of this present symposium is to study the environmental problems thus created as well as to contemplate practical and affordable solutions to them. It is taking place on the river in order to sensitize public opinion in all the countries involved.

*My personal participation aims at emphasizing the moral character of this entire effort. For, in truth, this is a humanitarian effort; and its success depends on the contribution of all our fellow human beings. The only motive that may concern us all — and, indeed, I believe that it does — is the moral obligation, the duty toward our fellow human beings, to our children, and, more generally, to future generations.*

As Christians, but also as civilized people, we know and accept that social coexistence is based on some generally accepted rules, many of which are formulated or amended to address some specific situations, but which are based on eternal principles. In this case, the eternal principle, as our Lord expressed it, is this: "Do to others as you would have them do to you" (Luke 6:31). We do not want other people's wastes and garbage dumped on us; therefore we in turn are obligated to find ways of not imposing our wastes on others. I am sure that your goodwill and moral sense will contribute to finding and applying the best possible solutions, so that the Danube remains a river of life and does not become a bearer of death.

# NATURE AND HISTORICAL CONNECTIONS

*Address before the Lord Mayor, the political authorities,*
*and the people of Budapest, Hungary, third international*
*symposium, October 21, 1999*

It is with great pleasure and emotion that we have come to the historic and beautiful city of Budapest, capital of the ancient Hungarian people, who next year will be celebrating the one-thousandth anniversary of the foundation of the Hungarian state. I come from the See of the Holy Mother Church, the Great Church of Constantinople, which has very close ties with the Hungarian people. It is a well-known fact that it was through this Church that the Hungarian people became acquainted with Christianity, and that very close ties were developed between the Christian kings of the Byzantine Empire and the Hungarian kings who converted to Christianity, resulting even in blood ties being formed. Allow me to cite the example of the princess Anna, daughter of the Hungarian king Stephen V, who married the Byzantine emperor Andronicos II Palaeologos. Moreover, Mary, daughter of the Byzantine king Theodore I Laskaris, became the wife of the Hungarian king Bela I. Let me mention also Irene, daughter of the Hungarian king Ladislav I, who married the Byzantine emperor John II Comnenus and was mother of Manuel I Comnenus. Yet even beyond these numerous examples, many other Christian Greeks settled in Hungary during the Byzantine period, and their descendants are now Hungarian citizens.

To all of you, then, dear citizens of Hungary, and relatives in spirit and by blood, I bring warm greetings, affection, and the blessing of the suffering Mother Church of Constantinople. I am the bearer of a message of peace, brotherhood, and cooperation among all people for the well-being of humankind.

My visit is taking place in the context of the third international scientific symposium on religion, science, and the environment, whose specific theme this year is "The Danube: A River of Life." This symposium is taking place on a ship sailing on the Danube and on the two rivers, the Buda and the Pest, on which the beautiful city of Budapest was built. The aim of this symposium is to make the responsible authorities in each country and city, as well as ordinary citizens, aware of the dangers to humanity entailed in the thoughtless pollution of the environment. For *it is not only the major industries that pollute our natural surroundings; ordinary citizens do so as well.* Measures must therefore be taken, not only by the state and local authorities, but also by every citizen, to stop this pollution. In addition, responsible and concerned ordinary citizens can put pressure on rulers and scientists, obliging them to study the situation and take the necessary measures.

## Natural Damage, Human Danger

God created the world as something beautiful. Of course, after the original sin of our forebears, nature became subject to corruption and humanity subject to sin. Nevertheless, through our Lord Jesus Christ, God renewed His covenant with humanity, and nature awaits its liberation from the "bondage to decay" (Rom. 8:21). All of us, but especially we Christians, who consider love to be our fundamental duty and an element of our very being, have an obligation to make sure that our actions do not result in harm for our fellow human beings. Pollution, and all harmful influences on our environment more generally, has an adverse effect on the lives of our fellow human beings and must be avoided.

Until a few years ago, the dangers threatening the environment were of no particular interest to the public. Yet now many adverse effects are already becoming evident and many dangers to humanity are already imminent; for this reason, it is imperative that we all become mobilized. We have placed the program of this particular symposium under the Church's blessing. First, because this is a further sign of our true love for human beings and our desire to help them to improve their standard of living. Second, because *we believe that the Church should not be interested solely in the spiritual life of Christians,* but also, according to its abilities, in all their needs; this represents both the express commandment of the Lord and the long tradition of the Church. And third, because interest in our fellow human beings and their various problems is a basic element of higher spirituality, given that it draws people out of their shell of individualism and selfishness and turns them toward their fellow human beings.

I am sure that the Hungarian people who reside along the banks of the Danube have become fully conscious of the importance of keeping the Danube clean both for themselves and for the peoples living around the Black Sea into which it flows. Therefore, I am certain that you will take all necessary means proposed by modern science and technology in order to eliminate its pollution.

# ONE SONG, ONE CONCERN

*Address at the luncheon in Novi Sad,*
*third international symposium, October 22, 1999*

We continue the journey of the third international symposium, and it is with great joy that this morning we find ourselves in the beautiful and hospitable country of Serbia. Today we are once again experiencing the hospitality of the Serbian people, having as our beloved, gracious host the local bishop of Novi Sad, Metropolitan Iriney; all of the delegates thank him for his warm hospitality.

We have found here a community whose people are of one mind, relating to one another in a friendly manner. By this I mean the vision we all are beholding here: Christians of all confessions, Jews, and Muslims living together in peace and concord, in love and mutual respect. This fills us with deep satisfaction. This fraternal spirit can be seen in the fact that the monks of the local monastery have learned chants in the Arabic language and songs dedicated to the Jews, who have suffered over the centuries, songs we heard just a few moments ago.

Speaking in my own right, on behalf of my own religion, as a Christian, I can say that this is our ideal; this is the teaching of our Christian Church. Indeed, all other ways of behaving are outside the spirit of the Christian faith. They constitute a deviation from the authentic Christian and certainly from our Orthodox faith.

It is for exactly this reason that the Ecumenical Patriarchate has, for many years now, not only held dialogues with our other divided Christian brothers but also held academic dialogues with the other monotheistic religions, namely Judaism and Islam. We believe that, through these dialogues, through the attempt to come to know one another better and through the cultivation of mutual respect, we not only fulfill the will of the founder of the Christian faith but also contribute toward the peace of the whole world, which is of common interest to us all.

## Many Words, One Dialogue

Moreover, we also have an ongoing dialogue (Greek: *dia-logos*) with nature, even though it does not have reason (Greek: *logos*). We consider the protection and preservation of nature from further catastrophic exploitation as our sacred obligation, an obligation that concerns all people in general and without distinction.

The initiatives that the Ecumenical Patriarchate has taken for several years in the field of ecology are, we have been happy to see, well and widely received by many people. This can be seen in the fact that this third international symposium is being attended by so many distinguished personalities, religious ministers, journalists, scholars, as well as scientists from various religions and countries.

As we spend a few hours in Serbia, all of the delegates extend a heartfelt salutation of love and honor to all the people of all faiths and ideologies of this country without distinction. Without having any intention to speak in a political way, but simply out of sincere and great love toward the Serbian people, we express our wish for the greater democratization of this country and for its dialogue with the rest of the international human community, as well as for the broader community's greater understanding and receptivity of the Serbian people. This is because we believe that *isolation is of no benefit — either to those who isolate or to those who are isolated.*

As we find ourselves on the threshold of the third millennium, distances have become as nothing; the entire world is becoming, as it should, a single, universal human family. It is our duty, therefore, to bring all people closer together in fellowship. Finally, it is our prayer that the world of the third millennium, which shall commence shortly, may become a single, large community.

In conclusion, we fraternally embrace His Beatitude Patriarch Pavle of Serbia, we warmly embrace all the members of the hierarchy of the Serbian Orthodox Church, and we fervently pray for every blessing and grace from God for all. We thank once again the Bishop of Novi Sad for his warm hospitality. We also warmly thank the political and municipal authorities of Voivodina, the President of the Parliament, the president of the local government, the mayor, and the inhabitants of the area, and we express the gratitude of all the delegates for their warm, brotherly, and heartfelt hospitality.

# WAR AND SUFFERING

*Address during the prayer for peace in Novi Sad,*
*third international symposium, October 22, 1999*

We are here, in beloved Serbia, in conjunction with the third international scientific symposium on religion, science, and the environment. This symposium, planned long before the recent tragic events, is dealing with the specific theme "The Danube: A River of Life." As we encounter the mournful faces of those of you who, together with your people, have been subjected to these air assaults, we do not know whether we should express our joy for this meeting or our sadness over what has occurred. We find ourselves weeping with those who are weeping. We would, however, prefer to express our joy, so that the evil one will not gloat excessively that he has succeeded in removing from our hearts that joy which the Lord of truth, life, and victory over death has assured us that no one can take away from us. Therefore, even in the midst of a myriad of hardships, we always rejoice and are triumphant over the sad things in life, inspiring in those who are injured an optimism and faith in the help that comes from God. For He alone can increase twofold and further bless the last things of the faithful more than the first, just as He did with Job (Job 42:10-12).

However, this applies to a suffering people and not to those who have acted with violence. After all, for suffering people to have the last things more abundantly blessed than the first, in spite of all that has happened to them, they must not sin against the Lord, as Job himself did not, and must not return impudence to God (Job 1:22).

*Those who are responsible for these deeds must be held accountable, whoever they are, and from wherever they may come.* Yet we who, in the spirit of God's love, have time and again condemned the imprudence of war, just as we have condemned racism and nationalism, now wholeheartedly pray that the tempest of war has passed and that the Lord will show compassion both upon those who are to blame and upon the blameless, upon the victims and upon the oppressors alike. We further pray that God will grant everyone repentance and prudence in all things, so that, even in this dreadfully tormented region of the Balkans, beloved peace will prevail again, "something that is sweet in name and in essence," according to St. Gregory the Theologian (Homily 20.1). We pray that the disasters will be rectified, the land restored to health, and the river of life, which overpowers death, will continue to flow and perform its peacekeeping role in this region. Furthermore, we pray that the Danube, which has been disastrously wounded, will never cease to be a peaceful "river of life."

## War and Violence

War and violence are never means used by God in order to achieve a result. They are for the most part machinations of the devil used to achieve unlawful ends. We say "for the most part" because, as is well known, in a few specific cases the Orthodox Church forgives an armed defense against oppression and violence. However, as a rule, peaceful resolution of differences and peaceful cooperation are more pleasing to God and more beneficial to humankind.

*War and violence breed hatred and revenge, leading to an endless cycle of evil* until opponents completely annihilate each other. For this reason St. Paul exhorts us: "Do not be overcome by evil, but overcome evil with good" (Rom. 12:21). We certainly know that each of us is able to determine our own behavior. However, many people, acting together, form another mode of behavior determined either by some authority or by the more dominant group. Nevertheless, we Christians must never forget the example of our Lord Jesus Christ and the beatitude blessing for the peacemakers. Neither must we forget the continual prayer for peace of the whole world. Christians by conviction are lovers of peace and silence. We are not, however, idle or meddlesome. We adopt all good deeds and learn to assume leadership in these, in accordance with the apostolic exhortation (Titus 3:14). The fact, however, that we wish to lead peaceful and serene lives in a situation of international calm does not imply that we do not participate in the concerns of life. Rather, insofar as it is possible, we do not participate in conflicts, according to the apostolic words: "If it is possible, so far as it depends on you, live peaceably with all" (Rom. 12:18).

It is true that serious dilemmas sometimes confront us. Yet Christians are directed toward a solution, both by the teaching of the Gospel and by divine grace, when they seek divine illumination through hard and heartfelt prayer. In this regard, we may underline three basic principles:

"Put your sword back into its place; for all who take the sword will perish by the sword." (Matt. 26:52)

Never avenge yourselves, but give way to wrath. For, it is written, vengeance is mine; I will repay, says the Lord. (Rom. 12:19)

"Render therefore to Caesar the things that are Caesar's, and to God the things that are God's." (Matt. 22:21)

## The Sign of the Cross

From these guiding principles are derived many others, which, combined with the other well-known Gospel commandments, comprise an alternative attitude toward life, one fundamentally different from the prevailing secular perception. *The Christian perception is that cross and crucifixion, martyrdom and sacrifice are followed by resurrection — a resurrection invisible to many, but an actual and genuine resurrection for those who are able to see things more deeply and more clearly. Finally, Christians know that the victor is not the one who has tyrannically imposed his or her views, but the one who has justice on his or her side.* Consequently, our main concern is not to impose our will on others, but to walk together with justice and not to act unjustly. In the long term, this will prove to be more advantageous, because whatever is built on injustice collapses with the passage of time. This is the reason why wars keep recurring, because after each war things are not regulated on the basis of right, but on the basis of might.

As Christians who study history, we know — for we see it proved in the rules of human logic as well as through faith — that the above is true, that justice and truth prevail in the end, so long as there is someone to seek after them. It is for this reason that we always seek truth and justice, which give birth to peace, preferring to be treated with injustice ourselves rather than to do injustice to others, as did the philosopher Socrates, who lived before Christ.

In this way we pursue peace, as the Psalmist also recommends: "Seek peace, and pursue it" (Ps. 34:14). Yet this peace is well grounded on the firm foundation of justice. And we always hold before our eyes the notion that, being crucified, we expect resurrection. By loving the Risen Lord, we overcome fear, forgive our enemies, pray for all, and live in this world the reality of the world to come, which this world does not comprehend.

Thus, again, and repeatedly, and unceasingly, we invite all the faithful with the words of our liturgy: "Let us pray to the Lord; for the peace of the whole world; and for the stability of the holy Churches of God." Standing at this sacred place, we pay tribute to and express gratitude for the sacrifice of all the victims of World War II and of all wars — whether these victims be Jews, Christians, Muslims, people of any faith or no faith at all. We call to memory the environmental wounds of the region, the natural devastation, and the destruction of cultural and religious monuments — synagogues, churches, and mosques alike. We pay tribute to and express gratitude for the victims of every ethnicity or ideology whatsoever, the victims of war and violence in general, without discrimination. We pray for the repose of their souls, that their unjustly shed blood will continuously water the tree of peace. Amen.

# THE SUPREME WORD

*Address before the Minister for the Environment of Bulgaria and His Eminence Metropolitan Vidin on board the symposium ship in Bulgaria, third international symposium, October 23, 1999*

Welcome to this ship of peace. It is a great pleasure for me to address to you my own heartfelt greetings as well as those of all our fellow participants, and to welcome you to the third international scientific symposium on religion, science, and the environment. The theme of the symposium this year is "The Danube: A River of Life," which is why it is taking place on a ship sailing along the Danube. Our subject is clearly of interest to all countries situated along the Danube, of which your own country is one.

Without a doubt, science has important things to say on this subject, because it observes and records the actual situation, determines its causes, predicts their effects, and recommends measures to address it. The government administration and political leaders have an equally important voice in these matters, since it is up to them to decide on the necessary measures and to ensure that they are implemented. *Within this whole process of scientific, technical, and administrative activities, it may appear at first glance that the Church and religion have nothing to contribute. In fact, they contribute the most essential element: namely, belief in the moral necessity of these measures, and upholding the moral justification of the entire effort. Moreover, they contribute their blessing and the blessing of God, without which nothing good can be achieved.*

I say "the most essential element" because, as we all know, without belief in the effort we are making, without good "morale" among those who fight, the initial zeal will soon wear off, intensity will slacken, and the aim will not be achieved. And we are all well aware that the goal we are pursuing —

namely, to clean up the Danube so that it remains a river of life and does not become a river of death — requires that all people be mobilized. Otherwise, anything that one person tries to build, another tears down. However, mobilization in a struggle whose utility is not obvious to the ordinary citizen may be achieved only if that citizen believes that this is a commandment of God, which it certainly is. And it is the commandment of God because He commanded Adam and Eve — and through them, the whole human race — to work and to protect the Garden of Eden as the earthly environment in which He placed them. So this concept of protection includes safeguarding the environment from all manmade forms of destruction. Unfortunately, we are today witnesses of the daily indifference and even deliberate damage to the environment by our fellow human beings, either individually or collectively.

## Commitment and Solidarity

This is why we have adopted and launched an effort to sensitize individuals and entire peoples, governments and nongovernmental organizations, to the present cause.

I would like to convey to you our commitment to this effort to improve the living standard of your people and of all peoples. I also convey to you the affection and blessing of our Holy Mother, the Great Church of Christ, and also my own personal love and blessing. And I convey to you the message that God is pleased when, acting out of love, we do everything in our power not to burden our neighbor and fellow human beings with our own waste, which is so destructive to human life. If such an attitude is generally accepted, this will also mean that we ourselves will not be burdened with others' wastes.

The Danube, like all rivers, is God's gift to humanity. Within His all-wise organization of and dispensation for the world, God offers humankind a wide variety of services. We must not transform this world into a garbage dump; and where this has already happened, we must take all the necessary measures to restore the ecological balance.

I should also like to express my satisfaction that this message, a message of genuine solidarity and universal cooperation in the field of peace, has met with good response and acceptance. Rejoicing in this, *we shall continue to propagate the same message until it has become generally received and understood and contributes to improving the entire situation.*

Once more, please allow me to express to you my pleasure and gratitude for your visit to us on this ship and for your good intentions toward our common effort. I ask that you kindly convey my warmest greetings and our message today to His Beatitude Patriarch Maxim of Sofia and All Bulgaria, as well as to the President and Prime Minister of our dear Republic of Bulgaria and all the Bulgarian people.

# BYZANTINE HERITAGE

*Address at the House of Parliament in Bucharest, Romania,*
*third international symposium, October 24, 1999*

Having entered this very beautiful hall of the House of Parliament of the representatives of the glorious and pious people of Romania, we are overwhelmed by the weight of historical memory that unfolds before us like a vision of the indissoluble spiritual bonds between the ecclesiastical and spiritual leadership of the much loved Romanian people, not only during times of fortune, but also in times of trial. In the brightness of your faces we see reflected in an exceptional way the communion of faith in the bond of love, which springs from our common experience of all the Orthodox peoples.

The Holy and Great Church of Christ of Constantinople and all the local Orthodox Churches have a common tie to the spiritual heritage of Byzantium. This heritage has maintained the anthropocentric philosophy of classical Greek antiquity by transcending it with the anthropocentric teaching of Christianity. Such transcendence did not imply the rejection of all the achievements of ancient Greek thought but the selective acceptance and application of all good elements therein. We see this selection imprinted in a superb manner in the literary work and theology of the great Church Fathers, particularly in their employment of the terminology and methodology of the Greeks, which they imbued with Christian concepts and aims. Thus the Byzantine Orthodox Church was able to express successfully, by means of the advanced Greek language and the elaborate Greek logic, the Christian principles and convictions concerning the God-Man, God, and the world, which were new and revolutionary to the Greek world. At the same time it contributed auspiciously to the spiritual life of the Orthodox Church as a whole, by excluding all Judaizing and Hellenizing heresies and remaining firmly attached to the Christian truth of the cross and of the salvation that springs from it. It did this even though this truth was foolishness to those possessed purely of the Greek spirit and a scandal to those animated with pure Judaic spirituality (1 Cor. 1:23). Thus, the Mother Church of Byzantium formulated the specifically Orthodox proposition concerning our liturgical relation to God and to the world. It is this formulation that inspires even today Orthodoxy's approach to the contemporary problems of humanity and the world.

## Liturgy and Life

The spiritual heritage of Orthodoxy has had a profound effect over the centuries on the public and spiritual life of the Orthodox peoples, defining in an impressive way their particular ethos. This is the case not only with respect to the liturgical experience of the faith, but also with respect to the extension of this experience to the secular realm. In the Orthodox tradition and understanding, the world was initially very good but subsequently became rebellious; within this fallen creation humanity is called to achieve, through divine grace and personal willingness and endeavor, assimilation to God and deification by grace. Through the Orthodox Church, the sanctifying and restoring divine grace of God is extended to the entire cosmos. This is the grace that springs from the Holy Altar, on which the mystery of the divine economy in Christ is constantly celebrated and the sacredness of the divine creation is praised through unceasing thanksgiving and doxology to the all-wise Creator. This doxology has in sight God's manifold gifts to humanity, but especially the saving sacrifice on the cross of the God-Man, God's Son and Word, which reveals the incomprehensible efficaciousness of the cross as the way of transforming and improving the world.

In this way, *the natural world acquires deep significance, because it participates in the plan of divine economy. It is not a place of exile and imprisonment of the spirit, but an instrument and garment that is being sanctified and is participating in the divine economy.* The natural world is destined to partake of the renewal and glorification that encompass the body of the Lord that ascended into heaven. Consequently, preoccupation with nature does not contradict Christian interests or militate against Christian duties. This presupposes, of course, that such preoccupation is given its rightful place within the context of the rest of the Christian duties, such as the ministry of the word, the ministry of the table, the active engagement in good works, and so on. Having all these things in mind, the Mother Church does not refrain from concern with the problems of the natural environment, knowing that this environment should be of good service to humanity and fulfill the purpose for which it was destined. It is, then, in the context of this interest that we have initiated and now participate in this third international symposium on religion, science, and the environment, whose specific theme this year is "The Danube: A River of Life."

## The Gift of a River

The Danube is a superb gift of God to the peoples of Central and Eastern Europe because it has been indeed a source of life for all the peoples of Europe. In Roman times, the Danube marked the limit of the civilized world; and in Byzantine times, it was the natural bridge of communication between the peoples of that region and the civilized world. At all times the Danube has been the means by which material goods and spiritual and cultural ideas have constantly been transported among the peoples of North and South, East and West.

Indeed, when the capital of the Roman Empire was transferred from Rome to Constantinople, the great commercial artery of the Danube connected the highest civilization of Byzantium with the greatest commercial market of the then known world, that of Constantinople. Thus, through the richness and natural flow of its waters, the Danube served for centuries — and still serves to this day — both the physical and the spiritual dimensions of the life of the peoples of Europe and of the East. This was particularly the case during the Christian period, but the river still remains a source of hope and life for the people living beside it and for the people of Europe as a whole.

As a consequence, indifference toward the vitality of "the river of life" on the part of those near to it or farther away could be described as a blasphemy against God the Creator and a crime against humanity. This is because a threat to its life is a threat to the life of all. The dumping of industrial, chemical, or nuclear waste into the flow of the river of life constitutes an arbitrary, abusive, and certainly destructive interference in the natural environment on the part of humanity. For *pollution or contamination of the waters of the river damages the entire ecosystem of the broader region,* which receives its life from the unceasing flow of water through the river's surface and subterranean arteries.

## Laws for Nature

It is obvious, then, that the constantly increasing interest of the European peoples, not only in developing greater use of the river, but also in more direct intervention to preserve its purity, constitutes their supreme duty. This is based on the fact that the life of the Danube is a divine gift that contributes to the life of several European nations. If the pollution and contamination of the waters of the river of life continue, the peoples of Europe will destroy a source of their own life for the sake of insignificant and short-lived economic or other interests.

In light of this, it is clear that the international and interreligious symposium on religion, science, and the environment has rightly included in its mission the study of the problem of the Danube and has rightly conducted this study while sailing down the river of life. *The sensitivity of the Orthodox peoples in general concerning this problem is self-evident; but it has to become a matter of consciousness and personal responsibility for each of us, if it is to be resolved more quickly.* In His perfect wisdom, God has laid down the aims and laws that pertain to the operation of the entire divine creation and has provided for the self-sufficient protection of its life. Therefore, He designated the human person as a steward, not a destroyer of the divine creation. He did this because humanity is the finest member, the king, of the entire divine creation. Consequently, if humanity's stewardship is unfaithful to the divine commandment to work and maintain the creation within which it was placed, then humanity is unfaithful to itself, destroying God's house that sustains its own life.

The Ecumenical Patriarchate and the local Orthodox Churches — among whom the Most Holy Church of Romania is included, under the inspiring leadership of Your beloved Beatitude, our most honorable brother Patriarch Teoktist of Romania — and the entire pious people of Romania, from His Excellency the President of the Republic to the last citizen, are conscious of their mission for the protection of the natural environment. They also know that indifference toward the divine creation would be considered today an unacceptable moral stance. This is because the Orthodox Church cannot afford to show lack of concern for the natural world, which was included by God in the plan of the divine economy in Christ. The Orthodox Church knows full well that the renewal of the entire creation was envisaged in Christ. Thus, the social realism of the Orthodox faith and the Orthodox dogmatic stance in regard to the creation easily lead to the conclusion that every Christian is both able and obliged to contribute actively, not only to the salvation of the river of life, the Danube, but also to the protection of the entire ecosystem of humanity and of other related ecosystems.

# CONCERN FOR NATURE, CARE FOR PEOPLE

*Greeting at the official reception in Galati,*
*third international symposium, October 25, 1999*

It is with great joy that we arrive in the famous city of Galati, whose patron saint and protector is the Apostle Andrew. We feel that we are in familiar and fraternal surroundings, inasmuch as you lie under the protective care of the "first-called" of the Apostles, who is also the paternal protector of our Mother Church of Constantinople.

We are sincerely moved and feel deeply grateful for this honor and reception, as well as for your kind words, which confirm that we are of one soul with each other, and that we share a very close and unbreakable bond of faith and love that already unites our sister Churches.

As you know, we have initiated and are participating in the third international and interreligious symposium on religion, science, and the environment, which this year is dealing with the theme "The Danube: A River of Life." This subject is of direct concern to all peoples who live along the Danube, but also to the peoples of the Black Sea region. For the Black Sea is the receptor of the waters from the Danube and of all the substances in those waters. *Our participation in this symposium is a result of our paternal interest in the welfare and peace of humanity, which largely depends on the plenitude of natural resources and the preservation of ecological health and balance.* In this regard, we believe it is the obligation of all Christians to show respect toward our neighbor, whose life would otherwise be negatively affected by pollutants and by our destructive actions. This is why we preach this message of love and solidarity, and of respect for nature and humanity. The aim is for all of us to be sensitized in regard to this problem, and to work toward its resolution, each in our own field, from our particular position and abilities.

# GRATITUDE FOR EFFORTS IN THE PAST

*Message of thanks at the closing ceremony of the*
*third international symposium, October 25, 1999*

With the grace of God, we have successfully concluded the third international symposium on religion, science, and the environment, which focused in detail this year on the specific theme "The Danube: A River of Life." In our express desire to sensitize all the peoples living along the banks of the Danube to the urgency of this problem, we have held this symposium on board ship and traveled through all the states along this river. It was a rewarding experience to ascertain that all responsible parties are already aware of the problems and intend to take measures to address them.

We have heard the conclusions and recommendations formulated by the specialists among the distinguished participants in the symposium. I express my profound gratitude to all the eminent delegates who have shed light on all aspects of the subject in their well-documented papers. I also thank all the government authorities, as well as the people of the countries through which we have traveled, for their warm welcome, understanding, and support for our endeavor. In particular, I would like to thank the members of the Religious and Scientific Committee of the symposium, and all those who have contributed to assuring its excellent proceeding and successful outcome, for their tireless efforts and concern to ensure its smooth flow and harmonious progress, assuming the responsibility of the proceedings on land and on board. I would also like to thank and congratulate in advance all those who will adopt the conclusions and work toward the implementation of the decisions of this symposium.

I express my joy in the fact that the foundation this year of the Halki Ecological Institute was a direct result of the decisions of our second international symposium, which took place on board a ship two years ago on the Black Sea. I hope that the greater awareness of environmental problems will lead progressively to more and more successful measures that aim to preserve ecological equilibrium and natural harmony. *The general public has almost universally become aware of the fact that a problem exists and that it is possible to take measures to deal with the threat and restore the natural balance of our world, which has been so severely disturbed.*

## Decrees for Nature in the Future

Until societies have been sensitized to such a degree that they are themselves able to initiate and maintain this awareness, thereby keeping alive their sense of responsibility for the protection of the environment and for the assumption and application of the necessary measures, we shall continue to proclaim everywhere the necessity of addressing environmental problems for the sake of all humanity.

We have all agreed that we are not permitted to harm our fellow human beings. This principle is usually understood and applied with respect to direct harm, for which, in any case, the law provides restitution. Consequently, those members of society who transgress this principle are obliged by law to comply, with any necessary penalties also imposed. *We now need to go one step further and agree even to pass appropriate laws (where such laws are not already in place) decreeing that indirect damages are also unacceptable. That is to say, those damages are also unacceptable which have been caused by activities far removed from their effect, whose consequences are cumulative, or are manifested in time, so that the cause-effect relation may not be immediately visible. These causes include pollution of all types, which are cumulative and thus frequently cover both long periods and long distances. The more scientific observation consolidates our knowledge about the harmful effects of pollution, the more frequently and efficaciously will measures be taken in order to avoid such harm.*

Our struggle, then, is not in vain, and our effort is not without benefit. This symposium has offered knowledge and increased moral sensibility, and therefore it has provided the spiritual infrastructure required to assume and apply the necessary measures.

Bidding farewell, with much affection and sincere emotion, to our dear fellow delegates and to all those who have assisted us by serving throughout this symposium, I would also like to express my warm thanks to our experienced captains and their attentive crews, and to all those whom I have thanked earlier.

My heartfelt wishes accompany you as you depart, and I invoke on all of you the grace and the infinite mercy of the almighty God, the giver of all good things. Amen.

# 2000

Patriarch Bartholomew with a small child in Ethiopia (1995)

# YOUTH BEFORE THE THIRD MILLENNIUM

*Excerpts from the keynote address at the Millennial Youth Congress*
*in Istanbul, Turkey, June 18, 2000*

> *We praise and bless the Lord!*
> *Let all the earth praise His Holy Name.*
> *Blessed is Christ our God!*

We are gathered here today in the name and by the grace of our God. We have come together because two thousand years ago "the fullness of time" (Gal. 4:4) occurred and a "new child" was born to us who was "the God before all ages," "the one who opened the heavens and descended on earth for the life of the world." We have come together, also, because on the great and holy day of Pentecost the promise of our Risen Lord was fulfilled, and He comforted the disciples with the words, "I will not leave you orphaned" (John 14:18). In the name of Christ, God the Father sent the Comforter, the Spirit of Truth. And He continues to send the Comforter forever to renew our life and our world. The same Spirit raises up and leads human beings to each other in the life of the Church. In His name, as well, have we gathered here today. To Him be the glory, honor, and thanksgiving to the ages of ages! . . .

Our intent and fervent desire is to speak about the youth, but also to speak with the youth, that is, yourselves. You represent worthily the young people of our Orthodox Church throughout the world. To all the Orthodox youth, we convey our paternal prayer and Patriarchal blessing, as well as the message of hope, courage, conviction, and unshakable faith, "for God is with us!" . . .

Directing our gaze to the past, we certainly do not forget, as well, the myriads of young people who became the innocent and tragic victims of wars and holocausts, particularly in the twentieth century that is drawing to an end. However, the theme of this conference calls us to turn our gaze mainly to the future in order to sketch a vision for the young people in the Church based on our hopes for the coming third millennium.

The content of the third millennium is unforeseeable today. Humankind, for the first time in world history, is subject to a suffocating perplexity about what tomorrow will bring. Many things that were self-evident are now disputed and crumbling. Expectations are being dashed. Unforeseen things take us by surprise. Paradoxical things claim acceptance. What is beyond imagination becomes reality. What was unseen a little while ago becomes conspicuous. What was brighter than the sun becomes darkened. The order of all things is troubled. *Nature's forces are being explored and exploited in ways unsuitable to the harmony of the natural order. Nature is assaulted as a result of egocentric human will.* The uniqueness and sanctity of the human person is directly threatened. And all of the human race, coerced by misplaced belief in the powers of reason and by incurable weaknesses of moral and spiritual conduct, is moving along the precipitous edge of a yawning abyss.

In view of such developments as we move toward the unforeseeable future, it is necessary to seek out the prophetic charisma of the Church through the invocation of the Holy Spirit, the Comforter of our life and of the entire world. Moreover, this is not in order for us to disclose whatever human beings may be planning, or to forecast their consequences, or to make known what only God has set by His own authority (Acts 1:7). Rather, it is in order to remember and recall what the Lord and Almighty God has promised and commanded, so that we may speak and promote "upbuilding and encouragement and consolation" (1 Cor. 14:3). . . .

Having yourselves become partakers of the charismata through your holy baptism and your spiritual life in general, you are called to increase your given talents in order that you may become worthy of more abundant divine grace. In this way you will be inspired by divine grace to participate consciously and boldly in the prophetic mission and witness of the body of the Church, and thus you, yourselves, will be able to speak and promote "upbuilding and encouragement and consolation." Moreover, conducting yourselves in this God-pleasing manner, you will prepare for future generations the example and prototype of the athletes of Christ and of the servants of peace, love, and hope. . . .

## Unemployment

We know that in many countries unemployment is rampant, while at the same time there is an abundance of profits for the few. This situation occurs despite the sincere efforts of many. The marginalization and disillusionment of young people because of unemployment comprise the most glaring economic and political failure even among the most developed societies. This extremely deplorable phenomenon presents an added reason for despair on the part of less developed countries. The phenomenon of unemployment is the result of many factors. One factor is workers' difficulty in adapting to the changes in vocational enterprises due to technical developments. Another is workers' reluctance to engage in certain types of work below their level of education. Still another is the inability of the social system to provide jobs for all, even though available positions of work exist or could be created.

Young people can successfully respond to these negative factors in two ways. The first is at the individual level — that is, by personal versatility, adaptability, ongoing education, and diligent search. The second is at the social level — that is, by promoting ideas, programs, and various solutions in general, which will increase job opportunities, as young people themselves successfully reach higher positions of leadership in society. There are many things to be done for humanity, and the resources are available. What is needed are goodwill, ideas, love for the unemployed, coordination of efforts, and vigilant zeal. Since the assumption of our responsibilities as head of this Church of the First Throne, we have in various ways emphatically conveyed to many national leaders and other appropriate persons the conviction that the problem of unemployment cannot be effectively resolved without mutual social trust and above all without a community of justice and social responsibility. The young people must become agents of such a mobilization for the benefit of all humanity.

## Social Justice and Human Rights

The word of God commands: "Learn justice, you who dwell on the earth" (Isa. 26:9). God's command envisions social justice, which is secured by respect for human rights. The correlative sensibilities connected to this profoundly serious issue at the local, national, and international level are well known. Known, too, are the complex causal factors behind both social injustice and the violation of human rights. Over against this deplorable reality, Christian young people hold fast to the incomparable value of the human person, including the least of the Lord's brothers. The Christian teaching concerning the value of the person constitutes a pioneering historical principle of universal validity, which serves as the foundation of legislation concerning human rights. However, Christian young people do not limit themselves to the claim of respect for human rights. They also advocate another aspect of what is right — namely, human responsibility and duty, for without human responsibility the exercise of human rights proves just as inhuman as their violation. Christian young people also advocate the notion of justice as mercy, as well as the restoration of all things to a condition of harmony, that is to say, the transcending of transactional justice with a justice that combines collectively all virtues.

## War and Peace

Beautiful is that verse of the Psalmist which speaks of the meeting of mercy and truth, and the embrace of righteousness and peace. "Mercy and truth are met together; righteousness and peace have kissed each other" (Ps. 85:10). Neither social justice nor human rights are ultimately comprehensible without mercy and truth. And without the latter, there can be no true peace. Young people, who are the first victims of war, have a right to a peaceful life in truth, justice, and love. Anxieties about the planet's future, which arise out of the potential destructiveness of modern weapons, as well as out of the greed and ambition of certain leaders, necessitate that the young people should remain always alert and enlightened, and thus not be swayed by war-loving sirens.

## Ecology

In addition, the young people and coming generations have a right to a peaceful enjoyment of the natural environment, the integrity of which is cruelly violated to the great detriment of humanity. Ecological disasters, biological changes due to pollution and other causes, and many other forms of humanity's abusive conduct toward the divine creation menace the survival of both humanity itself and of the animal and plant kingdoms. For this reason, our own Ecumenical Throne has long assumed a variety of initiatives pertaining to the ecological realm with the purpose of disseminating information and alerting those who are primarily responsible. In this task we also include the young people, who, when informed about the seriousness of the issue, call others to respect the creation out of love and respect both for God and for our fellow human beings.

# SACRED GIFTS TO A LIVING PLANET

*Address during the international ecological symposium*
*held in Kathmandu, Nepal, November 2000*

Representing at this meeting the Ecumenical Patriarchate, namely the First Throne among the worldwide Orthodox Christian Churches, we address to all of you a heartfelt greeting of honor and love.

The purely religious and non-administrative character of the ministry that we exercise also determines the framework of our potential intervention and contribution for the protection of the natural environment. We have no authority to impose necessary measures. Nor can we react with force against those who negatively influence the environment. We are simply in a position to address free and conscientious people in order to suggest to them what is right according to our faith, so that they may be persuaded to conform freely and willingly to what their conscience dictates in regard to this matter.

Therefore, what we shall say here follows first from our human perspective, since we, along with all the rest of humankind, are responsible for the future of our planet and for human life on this planet. So our words should be acceptable to all people of goodwill, irrespective of their religious conviction, since they are surely, in our opinion, the proper conclusions of rational thought. Furthermore, what we shall say also flows from the tenets of our Christian faith and from our worldview according to the perspective of this faith — that is to say, according to the way in which we regard the world, humanity, creation, and history. We recognize that there are numerous and diverse beliefs and philosophies about the world. However, we believe that the foundation of our practical conclusions, reflected in our personal and collective behavior, can assist all people of goodwill to conform their behavior to the suggested ethical model. This should be the case even if the religious origin of the suggested ethic does not coincide with certain people's opinions about particular details.

We are obliged to clarify the fact that, for us, the demands of our faith are of primary value. Yet we begin with the more general human demands, because we are also addressing distinguished delegates who do not share our religious convictions, and for whom the weight of any argument does not lie in its religious connection but in its rational cohesion.

## Fundamental Data

Before setting forth our arguments on this matter, we consider it necessary to focus your attention on certain data, well known of course to everyone, but nevertheless still worthy of particular emphasis.

(1) *The planet earth, on which all of us necessarily live, constitutes only a minute part of the universe.* No matter how great its dimensions appear to us by comparison with our own size, it is truly very small when compared to the rest of the universe.

(2) *This planet is not separated by natural boundaries into airtight compartments. The legal borders of nations are unknown to nature.* The winds that blow and transfer particles and gases from place to place do not seek anyone's permission to go where they will. The same also applies to the waters, to temperatures, and to every form of radiation.

(3) *The effects from every occurrence have a very wide range — they are worldwide, even in a sense universal. This means that if pollutants are dumped in one spot on the earth, the effects are felt throughout the world.* Of course, the effects may not be perceived immediately in the case of a small trace of pollution, while they are much more apparent in the case of extended pollution. Yet the effect is the same. For example, scientists expect that in the coming decades the average temperature on the surface of the earth will increase by several degrees. This will result in the melting of ice, the raising of the sea level, greater rainfall and floods in colder regions, and more drought and deserts in warmer regions. Such effects are not the result of actions occurring in the affected areas alone, but in any and every part of the world. For as a result of the natural law of entelechy and entropy, of the equation of differences, warm temperatures in any part of the world, and derived from any source at all, are added to temperatures resulting from other sources. Accordingly, these temperatures are conveyed all around the surface of the earth. Similarly, any incident of pollution in one region of the atmosphere is shared throughout the world. It may take up to two years for air pollution in a particular place to spread throughout the atmosphere, according to specialists, but the important thing to note is that it does indeed spread everywhere around our globe.

(4) *The consequences of a polluting action eventually will affect every person equally throughout the world, including the responsible perpetrator, as well as a boundless number of innocent victims.* It is impossible for perpetrators to protect themselves from the consequences of their actions, and it is also impossible to know who will ultimately be the victims of such actions. It is certainly a fact, however, that humanity as a whole is damaged by every such action. Certainly, the density of pollution, and therefore the risk of damage, is

greater at the time and place that the pollution occurred. Nature does have ways of purging contaminants, but these natural functions cannot keep up with human pollution, and the effects are diffused throughout the entire planet.

(5) In ancient Roman law, a property owner had the right to do whatever he wished on his property, irrespective of whether this disturbed or harmed his neighbor. Yet, before long, certain qualifications had to be made to this absolutely individualistic principle. For example, certain dangerous *immissiones* were forbidden. Over time, various social obligations and restrictions were gradually related to the ownership of property as the use of land increased, and as a result many places today have well-established regulations for property use that are socially acceptable and desirable. This means that *the individualistic principles formerly pervading civil law are today becoming more social,* that is, more concerned about the effects of property use on society as a whole. As a result, international law is also becoming more social through our influence as members of societies.

We have already noted that our planet is so small and so free of compartmentalizing boundaries that every act that damages the environment bears worldwide consequences. As we have likewise noted, civil law is developing in ways that stress the responsibilities of property owners. Similarly, we would like to emphasize the worldwide effect of every change in the spiritual attitude and conduct of each and every citizen in regard to the environment; we must conclude that every effort to change the attitude of citizens, even if it appears to have only limited efficacy, has profound significance for the environment.

### Mutual Relationship with Nature

Let us now turn to the environmental imperatives that derive from our human nature. *Herodotus mentions that in some region of the classical world, the people regarded it as blasphemy, as contradicting the very will of the gods, to pollute the rivers.* Some moderns might consider these people culturally underdeveloped in comparison with our advanced technical civilization. Yet their spiritual sensitivity and refinement, when compared with that of contemporary "civilized" people who pollute the rivers with tons of poisonous substances as they sail through them, must be considered exceptional and excellent, whereas we would surely fail by their standards. The specific religious basis of their behavior may not be accepted today, but that does not undermine the fact that their behavior was particularly commendable in this regard.

It has also been observed with great conviction that the majority of deserts, and especially those in Mesopotamia and other formerly inhabited regions, are the result of human actions, such as deforestation for the sake of cultivation, fires caused by arson, the desalination of the earth, and the abuse of nature.

It is well known that acid rain, which comes from sulfur dioxide produced in the mining station of Sudbury in Ontario, Canada, has from 1888 to this day destroyed two million acres of surrounding coniferous forests. The nearby region does not have even a trace of vegetation.

Nevertheless, it is not only the nearby regions that are affected by any source of pollution. We know that air pollution produced in England affects communities in Sweden; pollution in the Great Lakes affects the residents of Canada and the United States; and the radioactive substance strontium 90 has been found in the bodies of distant Eskimo peoples to a far greater extent than in populations living much closer to the points of emission. This is due to the fact that the radioactive element was absorbed into the lichens consumed by the caribou that constitute the primary source of food for the Eskimos. Furthermore, we are all aware of the terrible effects caused by the accident at the nuclear power station in Chernobyl; scientists predict that cancer rates will increase even in populations at a significant distance from this source.

These are but a few of the many possible indications that any change in the environment is a matter concerning all people and all regions in the world. And so *all of us ought to become conscious of our collective obligation to conform to everything demanded for the sake of the protection of the environment.* Each of us has this twofold obligation: first, we should take care not to destroy or pollute the environment and should take action to restore it and improve it; and second, we ought to avoid the use of products whose production burdens our environment, or at least to strictly limit the use of these products, using them only if absolutely necessary. We could also add a third obligation — namely, to make all people aware of these responsibilities. For, although the potential influence of each individual may appear to be limited, the collective influence of all people together is limitless.

This environmental ethic is a clear result of rational thinking and must be embraced even from the point of view of self-preservation.


## Model of Behavior

Now we come to what the Orthodox Christian Church believes and teaches. Let us begin by mentioning a characteristic commandment of the founder of the Christian Church, our Lord Jesus Christ.

Multitudes followed the Lord into the desert in order to hear His teaching and receive healing for their illnesses. Christ blessed five loaves of bread and two fish, instructing His disciples to share these among the five thousand men, together with their wives and children. All of them ate, as we are told, and were filled. Even if the narrative stopped at this point, it describes a miracle. Yet it goes on to say that the Lord said to His disciples: "Gather up the fragments left over, so that nothing may be lost" (John 6:12). *The commandment to gather up the remainders "so that nothing may be lost," especially as it comes from the mouth of their Creator, constitutes a model of behavior that is most useful for our time when the refuse of certain large cities, rejected as garbage, could suffice to nourish entire populations.*

You are undoubtedly familiar with the charitable commandment of love and mercy, which is taught by the Orthodox Church. You are perhaps even aware that the Ecumenical Patriarchate, as the first throne among the worldwide Orthodox Churches, has, at the dawn of the third millennium from the birth of Christ, placed at the center of its attention the urgent problem of our times, namely the preservation of balance in the natural environment of our planet. We are absolutely convinced that an effective approach to this problem requires not only the intervention of governments but also the cultivation of an ethic based on an understanding of the relationship between humanity and nature, which, beyond this ethic, derives from the coexistence of all human beings.

For us, this ethic stems from our faith in God and, as we believe, from the event of creation. We accept that God created the universe out of nothing and out of love. As the crown of this creation, God formed Adam, whom He established in the Garden of Eden, the earthly paradise. The delight in the goods of Paradise was not an end in itself. Adam's pleasure in Paradise was not simply due to the enjoyment of the material goods therein; it was not an animal satisfaction of instincts. God fashioned Adam into a physical and spiritual being, created out of two elements. One element was drawn from the material creation made by Him, "dust from the dust" of the earth, which therefore constituted the human body. The other element was a created spirit, similar to the uncreated spiritual essence of God, and so Adam was created in the image and likeness of God, endowed with all the good attributes of the Persons of the Triune God. These attributes include personal being, mind, freedom, love, judgment, will, and so forth. And the delight of humanity in Paradise was founded on a personal relationship with the Creator, a relationship of love and full trust in God.

## Commandment to Care, Not to Consume

Although created a spirit in the image of the Spirit of God, the human person was not made perfectly divine. Rather, the human person was created with the possibility of becoming like God through gradual progress derived from personal and voluntary asceticism, as well as through the intervention of divine grace, that is, the uncreated energy of God. This ascetic discipline embraced three things: first, working in Paradise; second, the keeping of Paradise; and, third, obeying a commandment to refrain from consuming one fruit. The basis of the desired human behavior was love, and God's desired goal was the preservation and increase of humanity in personal love. This communion of humanity with God would render us partakers of divine nature and blessedness, divine by grace although not in essence.

Insofar as the human person also participates in created, material nature by means of the body, humanity would be called to assume responsibility for the material creation within which they were established as crown. And so, by preserving and nurturing the harmony of material creation, humanity would raise it up in thanksgiving to God, from whom everything was received. Nature was planned by God to produce on its own, and especially through its cultivation and protection by humanity, everything that is necessary for the preservation and pleasure of humanity. However, the relationship of humanity and nature was not that of an owner to a possession. Rather, it was a relationship of a person to a gift, and that relation implied a deeper relation with God, the giver of all good.

Therefore, humanity must remember at all times that it holds this gift only within certain boundaries established by the Giver, and that within these boundaries there are two conditions. *First, humanity is required to protect the gift, that is, to preserve nature unharmed and to consume only its fruit. Second, humanity must not willfully consume every fruit, but must be self-restrained and abstain from certain fruits. Both the protection and the self-restraint, which in ecclesiastical terminology is called ascesis, were not imposed as authoritative commandments with appropriate punishment in the case of their transgression. Instead, they were offered as suggestions of love that ought to be preserved out of love.* In this way, love is preserved alive, as a personal relationship and mutual communion between God and humanity. For the true nature of God is love; and the original nature of the human person was also endowed with love, seeking to be established in love so as to become divine by grace. Therefore, that which would most liken humanity to God was precisely the establishment of humanity in love in the same way as God Himself is stable and unchanging in this love.

The first-created human being, however, misused the God-given freedom, preferring alienation from God and attachment to God's gift. Consequently, the double relationship of humanity to God and creation was canceled; the relationship between humanity and God was lost, leaving humanity preoccupied with creation alone. In this way, the human blessedness derived from the love between God and humanity ceased, and humanity sought to fill this void by drawing from creation the blessedness that was lacking. *Instead of a thankful user, the human person became a greedy abuser. Humanity sought to take from creation what it could not satisfy, namely the blessedness that was missing.* The more humanity feels dissatisfied, the more it also demands from nature. Yet the more it demands of nature, the more humanity recognizes that the goal has escaped its grasp. The soul's emptiness cannot be filled with the world's fullness. Nor can it be achieved by the acquisition of material goods, for it does not result from lacking these goods. The soul's emptiness results from a lack of love and familiarity with God. The lost paradise is not a matter of lack of created goods, but a deprivation of love toward the Creator.

Christ came into the world in order to restore — and He did in fact restore — the possibility of our love toward God. For, as fully human (and divine), He fully loved God (the Father), becoming an example of the loving relationship between humanity and divinity. Those who sincerely and correctly believe in Him and love God also practice keeping the original commandments of God. They practice the commandments to work, to keep the natural creation from any harm, and to use only its fruits, indeed, only those fruits that are absolutely necessary to use, taking proper care "that nothing is lost," and becoming conscientious models of environmental care.

An Orthodox Christian ethic therefore emanates from the worldview of humanity, creation, and God that we have very briefly presented. *All other Christian exhortations about the proper way of life stem from the conscious effort of human beings to cease hoping in creation and to turn their hope to the Creator of all.* When this attitude is adopted, humanity will be satisfied with much fewer material goods and will respond with greater sensitivity to the nature that sustains us. Humanity will then be concerned about loving all people rather than seeking to satisfy individualistic and egotistic ambitions.

The Orthodox Church's teaching penetrates the reason of every being, namely the origin and purpose of every created thing, discerning the complete plan of God from the first moment of creation to the end of the world, considering this as an expression of absolute love and offering. The world was created "very good" in order to serve the mind of God and the life of humanity. However, it does not replace God; it cannot be worshiped in the place of

God; it cannot offer more than God appointed it to offer. The Orthodox Church prays that God may bless this creation in order to offer seasonable weather and an abundance of fruits from the earth. It prays that God may free the earth from earthquakes, floods, fires, and every other harm. In recent times, the Church has also offered supplications to God for the protection of the world from destruction caused by humanity itself, such as pollution, war, over-use and exploitation, exhaustion of waters, changes in environmental conditions, devastation, and stagnation.

## More than Mere Prayer

The Ecumenical Patriarchate does not, however, rely only on supplication to God to improve the situation. Starting from God, as it is always proper to seek His blessing, the Ecumenical Patriarchate works intensely in every possible way to alert everyone to the fact that the greed of our generation constitutes a sin. This greed leads to the deprivation of our children and future generations, in spite of our desire to bequeath to them a better future.

Among other things, the environmental activity of the Ecumenical Patriarchate has involved the convocation of international ecological seminars in the historic Holy Monastery on the island of Halki, in which participants have undertaken systematic theological study of the ecological crisis. We have also participated in numerous conferences convened to discuss these matters. Our environmental initiative is further reflected in the organization of three floating symposia attended by scientists from all over the world. In admirable harmony of spirit, we advanced from the study of general themes to the examination of particular problems. In September of 1995, together with His Royal Highness Prince Philip of Edinburgh, we organized a floating symposium in the Aegean, starting from the island of Patmos, in order to celebrate the nineteen hundredth anniversary of the book of St. John's Revelation. In this symposium, faith and understanding, religion and science, spirit and word all approached, from different perspectives, one and the same purpose, namely the protection of the environment.

The success of this symposium inspired and encouraged us to organize a second international floating symposium on the Black Sea, in light of the ecological destruction of that region. The deliberations of the Black Sea symposium made it abundantly clear that the pollution of this sea largely depends on the pollutants transported there by the rivers. The warm hospitality and fervent reception of the inhabitants of this region toward the delegates of our symposium was deeply moving. Having studied the existing problems, we decided to continue our research by organizing yet another symposium, in the context of which we traveled by ship along the Danube.

Beyond the study of pollution and the search for a solution to the dangerous conditions and contaminations, the pain and the poverty all along this great river, a further concern of this symposium was the healing of this region of Europe that has been plagued with terrible ordeals. As far as we were able, we proposed to affirm the principles of free communication, of mutual respect, and of peaceful coexistence among the people of this region.

In the aftermath of the symposium, it is important for us to look at its practical results, including, we hope, a rise in interest in the environment. At the conclusion of the Black Sea symposium, concerned clergy, journalists, and teachers from the Black Sea region created a network for systematic environmental education. Today, an initiative to create a similar environmental network is gaining ground in the countries along the Danube, with the participation of various Churches, in conjunction with the Danube Carpathian Program of the World Wide Fund for Nature (WWF). This network will support the ecological initiative and strengthen the cooperation among the peoples of the region.

A further symposium is scheduled to study the Baltic Sea. This symposium will direct its attention to one of the more burdened coastal environments of our planet. The Baltic Sea has suffered both from the development and wealth of some countries in the region and from the poverty of certain others. This symposium will endeavor to underline the importance of a common effort and formation of a common ethic. It will remind the world that the sacred creation is not our property, and so we do not have the right to use it however we like. It is the gift of God's love to us, and we are obliged to return His love by protecting everything embraced by this gift.

We would like to conclude by expressing our prayer and hope for the future of humanity. *We fervently pray that peace and harmony will prevail, not simply as an absence of conflicts or as a temporary truce in confrontations, but as a stable condition for the future of our planet. To this purpose, however, all of us are required to work, and to work together, irrespective of religious convictions.*

Therefore, *we fraternally call upon all religious leaders to adopt the effort for the protection of the natural environment* and to inspire and impress upon their faithful the religious and humanitarian obligation to participate in this endeavor, both actively and passively.

We also call upon all of the distinguished and beloved delegates, that together we may honor with our profound gratitude His Royal Highness Prince Philip, with whom we have enjoyed over the past years a warm personal friendship and close collaboration, for his very significant role in the struggle for the protection of the environment, for his initiative in the World Wide Fund for Nature, and for gathering us here in Nepal to offer — each in accordance with his or her own tradition — our "Sacred Gifts to a Living Planet." We especially thank him for his gracious invitation to this historic conference, the "sacred gift" of this particular effort for the creation of cooperation among religions and all those interested in the preservation of the environment.

We also thank Their Majesties the King and Queen of Nepal for the gracious hospitality offered to us. Furthermore, we also thank the honorable government of Nepal for its facilitation and full support of the conference. We thank the WWF–The Danube Carpathian Project, for the exceptional cooperation and initiative in this endeavor. We also thank the King Mahendra Trust for Nature Conservation for the coordination and organization of the conference on behalf of Kathmandu. Special thanks are also due to the particular organizers of the conference, the WWF and the ARC (The Alliance of Religions and Conservation), whom we also congratulate on its success.

## AN AWARD FOR THE PAST

*Toast during the luncheon organized by Scenic Hudson*
*in New York, November 13, 2000*

Distinguished guests, I greet all of you with great joy. For whatever reason you may be present, because you work together with Scenic Hudson or because you are connected with Orthodox Christianity, you share a love for and respect toward God's creation. I assure you that the Church loves and respects you and your work on behalf of the environment.

In events such as this, one clearly speaks on behalf of those bestowing the award, but also on behalf of the award's recipient. The Scenic Hudson organization, well known for its efforts to protect Storm King Mountain, was one of the first voices of environmentalism in this land. Thirty years later, it remains one of the most efficient organizations of its kind. We wish you many years of fruitful service in this critical and vital issue for all humankind.

For many years now, the Orthodox Ecumenical Throne has devoted itself to the service of the protection of the environment. With great interest and sincere anxiety, we have followed the efforts to address the destructive side-effects of humanity upon the world of nature. These effects have also had a negative influence upon human beings themselves. With much trepidation, we now realize the dangerous consequences of human apathy concerning the survival of creation, which also means the survival of humankind itself.

It is for this reason that I am accepting this award in the name of my illustrious predecessor, Patriarch Demetrios. He is the one who invited the entire world to offer, together with the Holy Great Church of Christ, the Ecumenical Patriarchate, prayers of thanksgiving and of supplication for the protection of God's gift of creation. Thus, beginning in 1989, the beginning of the new ecclesiastical year, commemorated and celebrated September 1st, has been designated for all Orthodox Christians as a day of prayer for the protection of the environment.

## The Contribution of Orthodoxy

In what way can Orthodoxy contribute to the movement for the protection of the environment? By the grace of God, there is one concrete response. We believe that through our *unique liturgical and ascetical ethos*, the spiritual teaching of the Orthodox Church may provide important theoretical and deontological direction for the care of our planet earth.

The spiritual root of our pollution, and our sin against the world, consists in our refusal to face life and the world as God's gift to humankind, which humans have to utilize with discernment, with respect, and with thanksgiving. In the Orthodox Church, we call this the Mystery (or, the Sacrament) of the Holy Eucharist, in which we return the entire creation in thanksgiving to Christ. We do this out of gratitude to Him who was crucified on behalf of the world; we do this in the framework of the eucharistic celebration, during which His sacrifice on the cross is repeated in a sacramental way. "We offer Your own gifts from Your own gifts," we exclaim as we offer the bread and wine, basic elements of the natural creation, in order to be changed by the Holy Spirit and become the Body and Blood of Christ, the gifts of our continual communion with God.

Thus, we believe that our first duty is to sensitize the human conscience so that people realize that, when they utilize the resources and the elements of our planet, they should do this in a devout and eucharistic way. Ultimately, to the benefit of our posterity, we should consider every act through which we abuse the world as having an immediate negative effect upon the future of our environment, as assaulting the prosperity and well-being of our world.

The heart of the relationship between humans and their prosperity is found in the relationship between humans and their environment. The way in which we treat our environment reflects upon the way we behave toward one another; more specifically, it reflects upon the way in which we relate to our children, to those born and those who are yet to be born.

## A Seamless Garment

*Human beings and the environment compose a seamless garment of existence,* a multicolored cloth, which we believe to be woven in its entirety by God. Human beings are created by God as spiritual beings, reflecting the image of God (Gen. 1:26). However, human beings are also created by God from material nature, from the dust of the earth. Consequently, we are called to recognize this interdependence between our environment and ourselves. This interconnectedness between ourselves and our environment lies in the center of our liturgy. St. Maximus the Confessor, during the seventh century, described this liturgy as being beyond a divine or a merely human liturgy. We cannot avoid our responsibility toward our environment and toward our fellow human beings, who are negatively affected as well by its deterioration.

In the Orthodox Church, there is also the ascetical element, which involves voluntary restraint regarding the use of material goods, and which leads to a harmonious symbiosis with the environment. We are required to practice "restraint" (the theological term in Greek is *enkrateia*). When we curb our own desire to consume, we guarantee the existence of treasured things for those who come after us and the balanced functioning of the ecosystem. Restraint frees us from selfish demands, so that we may offer and share what remains, placing it at the disposal of others. Without this restraint, we are characterized by avarice, which has its roots in lack of faith and the worship of matter, which we consider idolatry. Restraint is an act of humility and self-control, of faith and confidence in God. It is also an act of love. There are Christians who voluntarily deprive themselves of their due portion and exercise restraint in order to share with those who have a greater need. This ascetical spirit gives us an example of living simply, satisfied with what is needed, without collecting needless things, without the consumerism that leads to exploiting and lording it over nature.

This voluntary ascetical life is not required only of the anchorite monks. It is also required of all Orthodox Christians, according to the measure of balance. Asceticism, even the monastic form, is not negation, but a reasonable and tempered use of the world.

## Redressing an Imbalance: The Impact of an Orthodox Monk

It was correctly stated that a human being who has lost the self-consciousness of the divine origin, of humanity created in the likeness of God, has also lost the sense of divine destiny. In a word, such a person has lost self-esteem as a human being reflecting the image of God and has tried to make up for this loss by increasing material goods, over which one may have control. *When one's "being" is decreased, one's need for "having" is increased.* Consequently, the consciousness that a Christian has of his or her own existence makes superfluous the need for consumerism and the accumulation of material goods. For this reason the seventh-century hermit on Mt. Sinai, St. John of the Ladder, said: "A monk without possessions is master of the entire world." And St. Paul recommends the avoidance of avarice, when he writes: "if we have food and clothing, we will be content with these" (1 Tim. 6:8).

Therefore, the Orthodox ascetical life is not an escape from society and the world, but a way of self-sufficient social life and behavior that leads to a reasonable use and not an abuse of material goods. The opposite worldview leads to consumerism; consumerism leads to increased production, which overburdens the ecosystem; this upsets the balance of the ecosystem and leads to its destruction. In the long run, such destruction will lead to the end of the world's ability to survive as an environment and our own ability to survive as a race. *The Orthodox ascetic attitude seems to be passive; it appears not to impose any method of dealing with and solving the environmental problems of our time. However, just as the individual actions of tens of thousands of members of society produce great pollution, so the voluntary restraint of one Orthodox monk is of great benefit for all.*

Repentance for our past mistakes regarding the environment is indispensable and useful. Unfortunately, humanity has become intoxicated by its technological possibilities and behaves tyrannically toward the environment. Humankind ignores the fact that silent nature will take its revenge — perhaps slowly, almost unnoticeably, but inevitably and surely.

## Environmental Rights

Unfortunately, avarice and excessive exploitation, with no regard for the consequences, are a common phenomenon. *If we were to treat the possessions of our fellow human beings the same way we treat the environment, we would suffer legal sanctions and expect to pay compensation for damages.* We would have to repair the damages and return the stolen property to its legitimate owner.

Such behavior would be characterized as anti-social, and we would offend our fellow human beings.

From human rights declarations, we gather on the one hand that most of the environmental goods — like air, water, and the like — cannot become private property; on the other hand, there are legal and social obligations concerning their use that cannot be ignored. Any use that contradicts the social obligation and damages the usefulness of this good is prohibited as abusive and is subject, or should be subject, to legal sanctions.

The imposition of such sanctions does not belong to the realm of the Church, which addresses itself to the human conscience and calls for voluntary compliance. This call for compliance is accompanied by the obvious alarm that disrespect toward nature constitutes a sin against the love of God and humanity as well as against God's creation. According to Scripture, "the wages of sin is death" (Rom. 6:23). The truth of this is confirmed by our everyday experience of the chain reactions resulting from environmental damage: changes in the climate, deforestation, torrential rainfalls, floods, mudslides — the consequence of all these is death. Atomic explosions, radioactivity, cancer — again, the consequence is death. Toxic wastes; pollution of the air, water, and ground; introduction of toxic substances into the cycle of life — once more, the consequence is death. Dispersion into the atmosphere of gases that damage the ozone layer, augmented infrared radiation that damages human health — this, too, leads to death.

For all these causes of death, which are the direct result of our own doing, and of which we are not even conscious that we are the cause, we ask for God's forgiveness. Our responsibility for whatever happens around us is an unavoidable given. We are not only destroying the beauty of created nature but are also bringing harm and death to our fellow human beings. To remedy the situation, we should become conscious of this great sin; we should allow it to become an important motivation to change our behavior toward the environment. Then the goal of our common ecological responsibility will also become increasingly socially acceptable. Then perhaps we will begin to live responsibly as individuals with conscious choices, whether in the context of the environment or in the context of our souls.

## Ecumenical Imperative: A Common Responsibility

For all these reasons, we address ourselves to the leaders of the world and pray that they will take the necessary measures so that the catastrophic changes of climate caused by human activity may be reversed. We must propagate an ecological ethic that reminds us that the world is not ours to use as we please. It is a gift of God's love to us. It is our obligation to return that love by protecting it and using it responsibly.

This common purpose unites all of humanity, in the same way as all the waters of the world are united. In order to save a sea, we must save all the rivers and oceans. *God created heaven and earth as a harmonious totality; consequently, we also have to see creation as a harmonious and interdependent whole.* For us at the Ecumenical Patriarchate, the term "ecumenical" is more than a name: it is a worldview and a way of life. The Lord intervenes and fills His creation with His divine presence in a continuous bond. Let us work together so that we may renew the harmony between heaven and earth, so that we may transform every detail and every element of life. Let us love one another. With love, let us share with others everything we know, and especially that which is useful in order to educate godly persons so that they may sanctify God's creation for the glory of His holy name.

As a symbol to remind us of this responsibility — that each of us must do our part so that we may keep our natural environment as it has been handed down to us by God — we present you with this parchment with the inscription from Holy Scripture of God's commandment to the first-created people placed in the Garden of Eden. It is the commandment to "work and keep the earth" of the garden. This is also the theme of our message, addressed to every human being: Let everyone work to produce material goods from nature; but also, let everyone preserve its integrity and keep it unharmed, as God commanded human beings to do.

# 2001

Patriarch Bartholomew feeding an injured bird in Evros, Greece (2001)

# PRAYING FOR THE EARTH

*Foreword for the English translation of the Vespers*
*for the Protection of the Environment composed by Monk Gerasimos*
*of the Community of Little St. Anne on Mount Athos*
*and translated by Rev. S. Kezios of California*[6]

God is blessed because He is love. When we live out of love, we broaden our existence; it becomes something without end, for "love never ends" (1 Cor. 13:8). There can never be too much love; there is no over-saturation of love nor a turning away from love. A person who loves gathers all things together under the shelter of that love. If sinners or self-centered persons can feel even a limited love, then surely they are also able to comprehend how much greater that happiness would be if they broadened that love which brought them so much joy.

God, being the very essence of love, could not possibly be a single-faceted entity because love is a feeling directed to another entity of identical essence. Literally, it is a feeling expressed only between persons. Thus, the very nature of God as love unavoidably leads to the begetting of the Son, by the Father, before all ages, and also the emanation of the Holy Spirit. These are personal hypostases able to love the Father and one another and to be loved by the Father.

Love turned inward on the self, without loving another, is not really love and does not give the true, precise meaning of the word. The love of God the Father, and the other two Persons of the Holy Trinity with Him, could not be limited even to the limitless bounds of love between them. This does not mean that God is dependent on others (for this would be blasphemy against God, who in the fullness of His blessedness is self-sufficient). Expressed in terms of human understanding, the meaning is that the overflowing of His love could not possibly take on a form of existence unless directed toward something capable of accepting this overflowing of His love. *The quintessence of this overflowing love of God, capable of giving and receiving love, was the boundlessly abundant, personal, spiritual, and body-spirit creation of angels and people, and the infinite creation of the whole universe to serve them.*

---

6. The foreword was prepared during June 1997 but was published in 2001.

## God's Love for the World

The angels, spiritual beings composed of a spiritual essence different from that of God, are in a more immediate relationship with Him. Their exultation is expressed through the wondrous and incomprehensible majesty of their life, in that they are loved by the Triune God. In turn, they love Him by their unending glorification of Him and their immediate conformance to His will.

Somewhat lower than angels, people were created by God in His image and likeness and were crowned by God with glory and honor. As such, they are capable of both receiving and returning His love, resulting in their true happiness. Indeed, the breadth of God's love for us is manifested in terms of the limitless number of persons we are able to love and be loved by in turn. People experience a taste of this love (the breadth of God's love) when, irrespective of their religious credo, they realize the joy of loving and being loved by many.

*God's love for humanity is unsurpassed and cannot be equally reciprocated, since humanity turned its face from Him and from His love, whereas God continues to love us.* This love is even more unrivalled because God expressed the infinite richness of His love by the creation of a material world of incomprehensible beauty, variety, and expanse. This was done for the sake of humankind, who is comprised of both matter and spirit. When one considers all that is offered to human beings for their enjoyment through sight, sound, taste, smell, and touch, it is more than enough to put us in awe before the benevolence of God.

The first-to-be-created human being was placed by God in a beautiful garden on planet Earth. But, indeed, the whole of Earth was adorned by such splendid things that the psalmist, citing but a few, concludes in total wonder: "O Lord, how manifold are your works! In wisdom you have made them all" (Ps. 104:24). Today we can better see the infinite richness of the visible universe through the aid of scientific instruments. We can begin to understand the grandeur of the indescribable celestial universe whose dimensions we measure in millions of light years.

"Those who say, 'I love God,' and hate their brothers or sisters . . . cannot love God" (1 John 4:20). However, those who love God and their neighbor become resplendent because of this love, love "for all creation, for people, and birds, and animals, and demons, and for every creature . . . and one cannot bear to hear or behold any harm whatever or any minor affliction occurring in nature. For this reason, this person offers a tearful prayer in every hour of every day for the animals (irrational beings), for the enemies of truth, and for those who would harm him, that they may be protected and receive expiation; and out of the great, immeasurable mercy, motivating the heart in imitation of God, prays as well for the reptilian species" (Abba Isaac, *Ascetic Treatise* 81).

If these feelings toward the whole of creation are nurtured by a monk who has abandoned the world and its cares, then what should a person who lives in the world feel as a sense of duty to creation? Obviously, one's first sentiment should be to give thanks and glorify God who granted us the whole of creation for our use and enjoyment. This is especially so for the part of creation that forms our immediate surroundings, which we call the environment. St. Paul gives us this charge when he writes: "Pray without ceasing, give thanks in all circumstances" (1 Thess. 5:17-18).

In fulfillment of this charge, the Holy Great Mother Church of Christ has designated the first day of September as a world day of prayer for the environment, for the creation granted by God to humankind, which instead of being protected, as commanded by God (Gen. 2:15), is often abused.

Wherefore, expressing our great pleasure and our paternal and Patriarchal blessings, we pray to the Lord that He may graciously renew all of creation in Christ, that all who shall receive, chant, and hear this Holy Office may find rest from their labors and, with thanksgiving, exult in the gifts of God both in this present life and in the life hereafter.

# 2002

Patriarch Bartholomew addressing the Adriatic Sea symposium (2002)

# CREATIVITY AND CREATION

*Greeting during a musical reception on the occasion*
*of the Sunday of Orthodoxy, March 24, 2002*

## Truth and Beauty

The Sunday of Orthodoxy appears at first sight to be a religious feast that exclusively concerns those Christians who belong to the Orthodox Church. A closer examination, however, persuades us that it is essentially a universal feast during which truth — as the supreme desire and ambition of the human spirit — is honored. Naturally, the variety of human conceptions of truth is such that we cannot say that we are approaching a unified and universal understanding of truth. Nevertheless, we are able to proclaim with conviction that the appreciation that all of us, and almost all people, have about truth is common, given, and established. In this respect, Christ's words, that "you will know the truth, and the truth will make you free" (John 8:32), are universally accepted, irrespective of the particular religious faith or philosophical stance of each person.

*Even skeptics and all manner of agnostics, and in general all those who deny the human potential to approach and experience truth, cannot deny the Aristotelian assertion that humanity naturally thirsts for knowledge. They cannot deny the fact that such a natural attraction toward knowledge reflects or depicts a deeper and innate universal desire to achieve perfect and infallible knowledge of all things. This desire is what we otherwise call the knowledge of truth.*

Behold, therefore, we are celebrating today a feast of Orthodox Christians, the feast of Orthodoxy. It is a feast of true opinion, or rather of true knowledge. It is not simply a feast concerning the secular triumph of one segment of people who believe in certain truths. Rather, it is a universal feast, which emphasizes that any prevalence of a true opinion, or of true knowledge, is universally profitable and worthy of more general celebration.

More particularly, the widespread understanding that tangible reality can be perceived and described is not just a narrow Christian perspective but a universal possession. For the transmission of knowledge and the progress of science are not possible today without a form or picture or realistic representation of the natural world that is shared by everyone. Of course, we respect and even agree with the religious prohibitions against depicting the invisible Divinity, for we do not permit imagination to replace tangible perception.

Rather, we are celebrating today the possibility of depicting this tangibly perceived reality, for through such depiction we are able to communicate with one another and to convey knowledge and sentiments to each other.

It is precisely this purpose that is fulfilled by today's musical reception. Through the universally accepted means of the musical harmony of notes and rhythms, the select composers and performers of the musical creations that we will hear today are conveying to us the truth that all of us share a potential for the common enjoyment of cosmic harmony. We can all enjoy and be grateful for this music. All people are able to delight together in common. Therefore, the conception that the joy or wealth of one must correspond to the sorrow or deprivation of another is a delusion that is far removed from truth.

## Music and Beauty

Narrow-minded and greedy people will not comprehend how participation in joy only increases this joy, while the sharing of sorrow only diminishes the sorrow. Yet, the present musical enjoyment confirms that the joy of one person among us can never constitute a hindrance in the joy of another. Indeed, our joint participation in this enjoyment extends the pleasure that we experience, inasmuch as it strikes chords deep within the heart. These chords produce sounds of interpersonal harmony and love, which also reveal the deeper and archetypal truth that all people are created to coexist, to share in joy and gladness, to live in peace and harmony.

Consequently, *the feast of Orthodoxy reveals to us its universal significance as a celebration of truth. Furthermore, this feast celebrates the affirmation of creation as being very good, inviting us to an understanding of the world that shares in the overall divine harmony,* but that avoids the dissonance and lack of harmony that result from an extreme and partial emphasis on only certain isolated elements. A natural and environmental balance is necessary for the survival of the world's ecosystems; but it also leads to a moral balance between individualistic and communal ambitions, a balance that is necessary for the smooth development of social systems.

The truth that sets us free indicates, through this music, that the harmony of our individual spiritual chords and rhythms is a necessary condition for the delight of social, spiritual, and universal harmony. It is for this harmony that we were created and intended. The Great Regulator of this universal harmony, according to whose rhythm the myriad of enormous galaxies as well as the boundless multitude of minuscule cells move, invites us to join in the harmonious unity of peace, love, and truth that it suggests.

Let us obey in order to hear ineffable otherworldly words on earth, words heard only by the chosen that ascend to the heavens.

# A SEA AT RISK, A UNITY OF PURPOSE

*Introductory remarks at the inaugural proceedings*
*of the fourth international and interreligious symposium*
*on the Adriatic Sea, June 6, 2002*

First, we thank God, the Creator, Provider, and Governor of the universe, for the joy of this auspicious gathering, motivated by our common and vivid interest in the environment granted to us by the Creator. We address a heartfelt, friendly greeting to all of you and wish you a pleasant stay, inspiring thoughts, creative deliberations, and a positive outcome in this sea-borne symposium, as well as a good harvest of profitable conclusions.

The present conference constitutes part of a series of similar symposia, during which the environment, and especially the aspect connected with rivers and seas, is examined from the points of view of its present as well as its ideal conditions, based on both religious principles and scientific precepts. This year our exploration probes more deeply into the environmental ethos that determines our attitude toward the environment.

Our position as the first among equal bishops of the Orthodox Christian Church obliges us to offer a brief exposition of our faith concerning the environmental ethos in order to contribute to the formulation of a commonly acceptable environmental ethos, which may serve as a guide to further action.

## The Term "Environment"

It is a fact that the term "environment" presupposes the presence of someone to be encompassed. The two realities involved include, on the one hand, human beings as the ones encompassed, and, on the other hand, the natural creation as that which encompasses. In our discussion, then, of our environmental ethos, we must clearly retain this distinction between nature as constituting the environment and humanity as encompassed by it.

We underline this point because *it is widely held among certain ecologists that humanity is classified within the natural ecosystem, inasmuch as humanity is considered of equal significance with every other living being.* This demotion of humanity, sometimes characterized as humility, constitutes a reaction of anthropocentric arrogance — due either to a complete rejection of God and the corollary divinization of humankind, or else to a misunderstanding of the divinely ordained relation of humanity to the rest of creation, whereby humanity lords it over creation unrestrainedly and abusively. In both cases, the attitude toward nature is criminal and destructive, because humanity regards nature myopically and selfishly.

It is, therefore, appropriate and imperative to respond to and react against this attitude and ethos, especially when the wide-ranging and universally destructive consequences resulting from them have become so well known. *Yet it is not proper for the distinction between human beings and created nature (between the ones encompassed and the environment that encompasses) to be abolished in a way that equates humanity with the rest of the created beings.*

The various proposals of this "deep ecology" have — whether this is admitted or not — no religious basis and lead to a passive attitude with regard to human disasters, which are explained as natural consequences of the ecological equilibrium. In this case, creation is rendered divine as a whole, and humanity's unique position therein is not recognized, except with regard to the Creator's action upon the environment.

## The Bible as Starting Point

*The Orthodox Church assumes as its starting point the teaching of the Bible, accepted by the three great monotheistic religions, which introduces a third factor into the relationship between humanity and the environment. This factor is the Creator of both humanity and the environment,* who provides for all and has laid down the laws of harmonious coexistence of all elements in the universe, both animate and inanimate, endowing humankind with the mandate to serve as king of creation and the command to cultivate and preserve it.

Cultivating the environment implies collecting from nature all that is required for our material survival and spiritual growth. Preserving the environment involves the obligation to respect this divine gift and not to destroy it, using it responsibly and reasonably so that it may fulfill its purpose of serving humankind.

## Biblical Principles

Let us concentrate on certain elements of this biblical account of the divinely ordained relationship between humanity and the rest of creation. *The first noteworthy point is the restriction placed on the first-created not to consume a certain fruit.* Beyond serving as a basis for Christian asceticism, this commandment is a clear indication that the authority granted to humanity over nature is not absolute. While humanity was created to rule over the earth and all therein, that rule is subject to restrictions ordained by the Creator. Trespassing against these restrictions results in fatal consequences. The profound symbolism and extensive implications of this fact for an environmental ethos are apparent. Today we witness death approaching because we have trespassed against limits that God placed on our proper use of creation.

*A second noteworthy point is that the gift of the paradise of delight to the first-created was accompanied by the commandment and responsibility of humanity "to work in it and to preserve it."* Working and preserving constitute a duty of active responsibility. Therefore, any principle of passivity or indifference toward environmental concerns cannot be regarded as sufficient or proper.

*A third point, equally worthy of our attention, is that the consequences of the transgression of the first-created also had cosmic implications,* rendering the earth cursed on account of their actions and producing thorns and thistles in the environment (Gen. 3:17-18). This rebellion instigated the gradual corruption and ultimate destruction of the ecological balance, which continues to this day whenever we violate the commandment of preservation and abstinence and proceed instead to misuse and abuse the earth.

*Finally, we should observe that the Creator also took special care during the great flood, so that, through Noah, the plants, the clean animals that were directly useful to humanity, and also the unclean ones that appeared to be of no consequence should all be preserved from extinction.* This divine concern constitutes a clear foundation for our interest in the survival of those living species that are nearing extinction.

Contemporary scientific research underlines the wide-ranging environmental consequences of human behavior in a particular time and specific place. This constitutes an experiential recognition of the religious truth that Adam and Eve's act of transgression wrought an important change and a fatal corruption for the entire world. This is not the result of a legal-ethical responsibility bequeathed to future generations; rather, it is an irreparable disruption in the natural harmony. In a musical symphony, a single note of dissonance can destroy the entire performance; the only possible remedy is the repetition of the concert. In ecclesiastical terminology, this is called regeneration.

Roman law recognized owners' absolute authority over property. Yet it stipulated certain restrictions concerning the disposal of unwanted materials, determined according to their usefulness and effectiveness. These principles should also govern the disposal of modern industrial wastes according to their detrimental impact on others.

The entire universe constitutes one community, and the actions of any single member affect every member of the community. The traditional Christian doctrine, both concerning the destructive evil committed by Adam, whereby corruption was introduced into the world, and the restorative good enacted by the new Adam, whereby new life was introduced into the world, provides a critical basis for the formulation of a new environmental ethos. Such an ethos is clearly warranted by the global impact of every behavior, both proper and improper.


## The Way of the Saints

The saints have always taught that no one is saved alone and, therefore, that no one should strive for individual salvation but for the salvation of the whole world. Such a teaching is affirmed in the environmental field and confirmed by science. This conviction constitutes an essential aspect of the environmental ethos, required both of believers who rely on the precepts of faith and of those who wish to establish an ethos based on reason alone.

This concern for the salvation of all humanity and the preservation of all creation is translated into the merciful heart and sensitive spirit so characteristically described by the seventh-century ascetic, Abba Isaac the Syrian. *We are responsible not only for our actions, but also for the consequences of our actions.* After all, no responsible ruler leaves the growth of the people unplanned and to the mercy of fate. Rather, a wise ruler assumes appropriate measures for the people's growth in accordance with specific goals. As ruler of creation, then, humanity is obliged to plan for nature's preservation and development. This requires the recruitment of scientific knowledge, and it also involves respect for all life, especially the primacy of human life. It is precisely such a vision that also constitutes the fundamental criterion for any environmental ethos.

# SACRIFICE: THE MISSING DIMENSION

*Closing address during the concluding ceremony
for the fourth international and interreligious symposium
on the Adriatic Sea, June 10, 2002*

As we come to the close of our fourth symposium on "Religion, Science, and Environment," we offer thanks to God for the fruitful proceedings as well as for your invaluable contribution. We recall the prophetic words of our predecessor, Ecumenical Patriarch Demetrios I of blessed memory. In his historic encyclical letter of 1989, urging Christians to observe September 1st as a day of prayer for the protection of the environment, he emphasized the need for all of us to display a "eucharistic and ascetic spirit."

Let us reflect on these two words, "eucharistic" and "ascetic." The implications of the first word are easy to appreciate. In calling for a eucharistic spirit, Patriarch Demetrios was reminding us that the created world is not simply our possession; rather, it is a gift — a gift from God the Creator, a healing gift, a gift of wonder and beauty — and that our proper response, on receiving such a gift, is to accept it with gratitude and thanksgiving. This is surely the distinctive characteristic of ourselves as human beings: humankind is not merely a logical or a political creature, but above all a eucharistic creature, capable of gratitude and endowed with the power to bless God for the gift of creation. Other creatures express their gratefulness simply by being themselves, by living in the world in their own instinctive manner; but we human beings possess self-awareness, and so consciously and by deliberate choice we can thank God with eucharistic joy. *Without such thanksgiving, we are not truly human.*

## A Spirit of Asceticism

However, what does Patriarch Demetrios mean by the second word, "ascetic"? When we speak of asceticism, we think of such things as fasting, vigils, and rigorous practices. That is indeed part of what is involved; but *askesis* signifies much more than this. It means that, in relation to the environment, we are to display what *The Philokalia* and other spiritual texts of the Orthodox Church call *enkrateia*, "self-restraint." That is to say, we are to practice a voluntary self-limitation in our consumption of food and natural resources. Each of us is called to make the crucial distinction between what we *want* and

what we *need*. Only through such self-denial, through our willingness sometimes to forgo and to say "no" or "enough," will we rediscover our true human
place in the universe.

*The fundamental criterion for an environmental ethic is not individualis-
tic or commercial.* The acquisition of material goods cannot justify the self-
centered desire to control the natural resources of the world. Greed and avarice render the world *opaque*, turning all things to dust and ashes. Generosity
and unselfishness render the world *transparent*, turning all things into a sacrament of loving communion — communion between human beings, and
communion between human beings and God.

This need for an ascetic spirit can be summed up in a single key word:
*sacrifice*. This is the missing dimension in our environmental ethos and ecological action. We are all painfully aware of the fundamental obstacle that confronts us in our work for the environment. It is precisely this: how to move
from theory to action, from words to deeds. We do not lack technical scientific
information about the nature of the present ecological crisis. We know, not
simply *what* needs to be done, but also *how* to do it. Yet, despite all this information, unfortunately little is actually done. It is a long journey from the head
to the heart, and an even longer journey from the heart to the hands.

### Repentance and Sacrifice

How shall we bridge this tragic gap between theory and practice, between
ideas and actuality? There is only one way: through the missing dimension of
sacrifice. We are thinking here of a sacrifice that is not cheap but costly: "I will
not offer burnt offerings to the Lord my God that cost me nothing" (2 Sam.
24:24). There will be an effective, transforming change in the environment if
and only if we are prepared to make sacrifices that are radical, painful, and
genuinely unselfish. If we sacrifice nothing, we shall achieve nothing. Needless to say, with regard to both nations and individuals, so much more is demanded from the rich than from the poor. Nevertheless, all are asked to sacrifice something for the sake of their fellow humans.

*Sacrifice is primarily a spiritual issue and less an economic one.* In speaking about sacrifice, we are talking about an issue that is not technological but
*ethical.* Indeed, environmental *ethics* is specifically a central theme of this
present symposium. We often refer to an environmental crisis; but the real
crisis lies not in the environment but in the human heart. The fundamental
problem is to be found not outside but inside ourselves, not in the ecosystem
but in the way we think.

The root cause of all our difficulties lies in human selfishness and human sin. *What is asked of us is not greater technological skill but deeper repentance, or metanoia,* which in the literal sense of the Greek word signifies "change of mind." The root cause of our environmental sin lies in our self-centeredness and in the mistaken order of values that we inherit and accept without any critical evaluation. We need a new way of thinking about our own selves, about our relationship with the world and with God. Without this revolutionary "change of mind," all our conservation projects, however well intentioned, will remain ultimately ineffective. For we shall be dealing only with the symptoms, not with their cause. Lectures and international conferences may help to awaken our conscience, but what is truly required is a baptism of tears.

### The Biblical View of Sacrifice

Speaking about sacrifice is unfashionable, and even unpopular, in the modern world. But if the idea of sacrifice is unpopular, this is primarily because many people have a false notion of what sacrifice actually means. They imagine that sacrifice involves loss or death; they see sacrifice as somber or gloomy. Perhaps this is because, throughout the centuries, religious concepts have been used to make distinctions between those who have and those who have not, as well as to justify avarice, abuse, and arrogance.

Nevertheless, if we consider how sacrifice was understood in the Old Testament, we find that the Israelites had a very different view of its significance. To them, *sacrifice meant not loss but gain, not death but life. Sacrifice was costly, but it brought about not diminution but fulfillment; it was a change not for the worse but for the better.* Above all, for the Israelites, sacrifice signified, not primarily giving up, but simply giving. In its basic essence, a sacrifice is a gift — a voluntary offering in worship by humanity to God.

Thus in the Old Testament, although sacrifice often involved the slaying of an animal, the whole point was not the taking but the giving of life; not the death of the animal but the offering of the animal's life to God. Through this sacrificial offering, a bond was established between the human worshiper and God. The gift, once accepted by God, was consecrated, acting as a means of communion between Him and His people. For the Israelites, the fasts — and the sacrifices that went with them — were "seasons of joy and gladness, and cheerful festivals" (Zech. 8:19).

An essential element of any sacrifice is that it should be willing and voluntary. That which is extracted from us by force and violence, against our will, is not a sacrifice. *Only what we offer in freedom and in love is truly a sacrifice. There is no sacrifice without love.* When we surrender something unwillingly, we suffer loss; but when we offer something voluntarily, out of love, we only gain.

When, on the fortieth day after Christ's birth, His mother the Virgin Mary, accompanied by Joseph, came to the temple and offered her child to God, her act of sacrifice brought her not sorrow but joy, for it was an act of love. She did not lose her child, but He became her own in a way that He could never otherwise have been.

Christ proclaimed this seemingly contradictory mystery when He taught: "Those who want to save their life will lose it" (Matt. 16:25; cf. 10:39). *When we sacrifice our life and share our wealth, we gain life in abundance and enrich the entire world.* Such is the experience of humankind over the ages: *kenosis* means *plerosis;* voluntary self-emptying brings self-fulfillment.

All this we need to apply to our work for the environment. There can be no salvation for the world, no healing, no hope of a better future, without the missing dimension of sacrifice. Without a sacrifice that is costly and uncompromising, we shall never be able to act as priests of the creation in order to reverse the descending spiral of ecological degradation.

### The Liturgical View of Sacrifice

The path that lies before us as we continue on our spiritual voyage of ecological exploration is strikingly indicated in the ceremony of the Great Blessing of the Waters, performed in the Orthodox Church on January 6th, the Feast of Theophany, when we commemorate Christ's Baptism in the Jordan River. The Great Blessing begins with a hymn of praise to God for the beauty and harmony of creation:

> Great are You, O Lord, and marvelous are Your works: no words suffice to sing the praise of Your wonders. . . . The sun sings Your praises; the moon glorifies You; the stars supplicate before You; the light obeys You; the deeps are afraid at Your presence; the fountains are Your servants; You have stretched out the heavens like a curtain; You have established the earth upon the waters; You have walled about the sea with sand; You have poured forth the air that living things may breathe. . . .

Then, after this all-embracing cosmic doxology, there comes the culminating moment in the ceremony of blessing. The celebrant takes a cross and plunges it into the vessel of water (if the service is being performed indoors in church) or into the river or the sea (if the service takes place out of doors).

The cross is our guiding symbol in the supreme sacrifice to which we are all called. It sanctifies the waters and, through them, transforms the entire world. Who can forget the imposing symbol of the cross in the splendid mosaic of the Basilica of St. Apollinare in Classe? As we celebrated the Divine Liturgy in Ravenna, our attention was focused on the cross, which stood at the center of our heavenly vision, at the center of the natural beauty that surrounds it, and at the center of our celebration of heaven on earth.

Such is the model of our ecological endeavors. Such is the foundation of any environmental ethic. The cross *must* be plunged into the waters. The cross *must* be at the very center of our vision. *Without the cross, without sacrifice, there can be no blessing and no cosmic transfiguration.* Amen.

# COMMON DECLARATION ON ENVIRONMENTAL ETHICS BY POPE JOHN PAUL II AND ECUMENICAL PATRIARCH BARTHOLOMEW I

*Signed by Ecumenical Patriarch Bartholomew I*
*during the closing ceremony at the Palazzo Ducale in Venice,*
*fourth international and interreligious symposium, and co-signed by*
*Pope John Paul II via satellite connection from his library in*
*the Vatican, Rome, June 10, 2002*

We are gathered here today in the spirit of peace for the good of all human beings and for the care of creation. At this moment in history, at the beginning of the third millennium, we are saddened to see the daily suffering of a great number of people from violence, starvation, poverty, and disease. We are also concerned about the negative consequences for humanity and for all creation resulting from the degradation of some basic natural resources, such as water, air, and land, brought about by an economic and technological progress that does not recognize and take into account its limits.

*Almighty God envisioned a world of beauty and harmony, and He created it, making every part an expression of His freedom, wisdom, and love* (cf. Gen. 1:1-25). At the center of the whole of creation, He placed us, human beings, with our inalienable human dignity. Although we share many features with the rest of the living beings, Almighty God went further with us and gave us an immortal soul, the source of self-awareness and freedom, endowments that make us in His image and likeness (cf. Gen. 1:26-31; 2:7). Marked with that resemblance, we have been placed by God in the world in order to cooperate with Him in realizing more and more fully the divine purpose for creation.

At the beginning of history, man and woman sinned by disobeying God and rejecting His design for creation. Among the results of this first sin was the destruction of the original harmony of creation. If we examine carefully the social and environmental crisis the world community is facing, we must conclude that we are still betraying the mandate God has given us: to be stewards called to collaborate with God in watching over creation in holiness and wisdom.

God has not abandoned the world. It is His will that His design and our hope for it will be realized through our cooperation in restoring its original harmony. In our own time we are witnessing a growth of an ecological awareness, which needs to be encouraged so that it will lead to practical programs and initiatives. An awareness of the relationship between God and humankind brings a fuller sense of the importance of the relationship between human beings and the natural environment, which is God's creation and which God entrusted to us to guard with wisdom and love (cf. Gen. 1:28).

Respect for creation stems from respect for human life and dignity. It is on the basis of our recognition that the world is created by God that we can discern an objective moral order within which to articulate a code of environmental ethics. In this perspective, Christians and all other believers have a specific role to play in proclaiming moral values and in educating people in ecological awareness, which is none other than responsibility toward self, toward others, toward creation.

*What is required is an act of repentance on our part and a renewed attempt to view ourselves, one another, and the world around us within the perspective of the divine design for creation.* The problem is not simply economic and technological; it is moral and spiritual. A solution at the economic and technological level can be found only if we undergo, in the most radical way, an inner change of heart, which can lead to a change in lifestyle and a change of unsustainable patterns of consumption and production. A genuine *conversion* in Christ will enable us to change the way we think and act.

First, we must regain humility and recognize the limits of our powers, and most importantly, the limits of our knowledge and judgment. We have been making decisions, taking actions, and assigning values that are leading us away from the world as it should be, away from the design of God for creation, away from all that is essential for a healthy planet and a healthy commonwealth of people. A new approach and a new culture are needed, based on the centrality of the human person within creation and inspired by environmentally ethical behavior stemming from our triple relationship to God, to self, and to creation. Such an ethics fosters interdependence and stresses the principles of universal solidarity, social justice, and responsibility, in order to promote a true culture of life.

Second, we must frankly admit that humankind is entitled to something better than what we see around us. We and, much more, our children and future generations are entitled to a better world, a world free from degradation, violence, and bloodshed, a world of generosity and love.

Third, aware of the value of prayer, we must implore God the Creator to enlighten people everywhere regarding the duty to respect and carefully guard creation.

We therefore invite all men and women of goodwill to ponder the importance of the following ethical goals:

1. To think of the world's children when we reflect on and evaluate our options for action.

2. To be open to study the true values based on the natural law that sustains every human culture.

3. To use science and technology in a full and constructive way, while recognizing that the findings of science have always to be evaluated in the light of the centrality of the human person, of the common good, and of the inner purpose of creation. Science may help us to correct the mistakes of the past, in order to enhance the spiritual and material well-being of the present and future generations. It is love for our children that will show us the path we must follow into the future.

4. To be humble regarding the idea of ownership and to be open to the demands of solidarity. Our mortality and our weakness of judgment together warn us not to take irreversible actions with what we choose to regard as our property during our brief stay on this earth. We have not been entrusted with unlimited power over creation; we are only stewards of the common heritage.

5. To acknowledge the diversity of situations and responsibilities in the work for a better world environment. We do not expect every person and every institution to assume the same burden. Everyone has a part to play, but in order for the demands of justice and charity to be respected the most affluent societies must carry the greater burden, and from them is demanded a sacrifice greater than can be offered by the poor. Religions, governments, and institutions are faced by many different situations; but on the basis of the prin-

ciple of subsidiarity all of them can take on some tasks, some part of the shared effort.

6. To promote a peaceful approach to disagreement about how to live on this earth, about how to share it and use it, about what to change and what to leave unchanged. It is not our desire to evade controversy about the environment, for we trust in the capacity of human reason and the path of dialogue to reach agreement. We commit ourselves to respecting the views of all who disagree with us, seeking solutions through open exchange, without resorting to oppression and domination.

It is not too late. God's world has incredible healing powers. Within a single generation, we could steer the earth toward our children's future. Let that generation start now, with God's help and blessing.

Rome and Venice, June 10, 2002

## SCIENCE, ETHICS, AND SACRIFICE

*Toast during a dinner hosted by His Excellency*
*the Ambassador for Greece in Norway, June 11, 2002*

As you know, we have arrived here following a week-long sea-borne symposium, the fourth international and interreligious symposium on religion, science, and the environment, whose theme this year concerned the Adriatic, a sea at risk and in need of preservation. The next sea-borne symposium will take place the following year, much closer to this country, on the Baltic Sea.

Beyond the technological and scientific dimensions, our symposium widely discussed the ideological perspective of an appropriate environmental ethic. In brief and in summary, we may say that there exist two tendencies. The first of these tendencies demotes humanity and equates it with all other beings in our ecosystem, regarding human survival as equivalent to the survival of any other life-form. The second accepts the superiority of humanity over the rest of creation and regards humankind as a responsible steward looking to preserve creation for the sake of future generations.

Naturally, we believe that the second view is more correct than the first. This is the view that we accept as Christians. However, this view conflicts with the harsh reality that many of those with power pollute the environment, either because of their ecological insensitivity or because they do not want to assume the cost of protective measures for the environment. This is precisely why *we are working to sensitize nations, so that the necessity to assume such measures and to discover ways of meeting such costs may be commonly accepted as the moral obligation of all.*

In our concluding address during the symposium, we emphasized that the essential requirement for every good deed is a sense of sacrifice, without which no good may be gained. It is our hope that people will widely embrace an attitude toward the natural environment summed up in Euripides' statement about the human body: "We do not possess this as our own, but we dwell in it during our lifetime." It is our further hope that we will care for the environment with the same degree of concern that we do for our children.

# THE SOPHIE PRIZE

*Address during the official Sophie Prize
presentation ceremony, June 12, 2002*

Please accept our humble and sincere gratitude for the honor bestowed on us with the presentation of the 2002 Sophie Prize. We would like to stress from the outset that we consider this honor as belonging to the Ecumenical Patriarchate, which we serve as Primate.

All of our efforts to cultivate a sense of environmental responsibility and to promote genuine reconciliation among people comprise the immediate responsibility and initiative of the Ecumenical Patriarchate, which has served the truth of Christ for some seventeen centuries. Our Church regards the sensitization of its faithful in relation to the natural environment and in regard to the development of interreligious dialogue as a central and essential part of its ministry of solidarity and peaceful coexistence.

We thank you wholeheartedly for the gracious invitation to address this auspicious assembly on one of the most critical global issues of our time: namely, the ecological crisis that we face. We recall the recent news in regard to government representatives who did not come to an agreement about measures to be taken. This means that *those nations which have the privilege of freely choosing their rulers have not yet reached the level of environmental sensitivity demanded of their governments in regard to the cost involved.* Therefore, having voluntarily assumed the effort of sensitizing people's conscience in the face of this crisis, we readily admit how much work still remains.

## The Beauty of the World

*We must stress that it is not any fear of impending disasters that obliges us to assume such initiatives. Rather, it is the recognition of the harmony that should exist between our attitudes and actions on the one hand, and the laws of nature that govern the universe, on the other hand.* These laws have been established by the supreme personal Being, a Being that we call Trinitarian God, who loves and is loved.

From the outset, we should state that we reject outright any dualist opinions claiming that the world is the creation of evil and is consequently evil. Furthermore, we also reject the notion that material creation preexisted and was simply fashioned by God, or the notion that the body is the prison of the soul, which seeks to be liberated from its physical bonds. Finally, we reject any opinions that demote humanity into a fragmented part of our earthly ecosystem, rendering it equivalent to every other part and undeserving of any greater protection than that afforded to other species.

It is our conviction — and the truth of our conviction has been experientially confirmed — that both the material and spiritual worlds, visible and invisible things alike, are, according to the Nicene-Constantinopolitan Creed, a "very good" creation by the good and loving God. On the basis, then, of such a conviction, we are able to articulate the fundamental principles of our worldview.

## An Environmental Creed

We believe that the human person constitutes *the crown of creation,* endowed with the sacred features of self-consciousness, freedom, love, knowledge, and will. Such a teaching is part and parcel of our creation "according to the image and likeness of God."

We believe that the natural creation is *a gift from God,* entrusted to humanity as its governor, provider, steward, and priest, in accordance with the commandments "to till it and keep it," as well as partially to abstain from it.

In this way, we admit the limitations as well as the responsibilities of humanity with regard to the natural environment.

We believe that the universe comprises *a single harmony or "cosmos,"* according to the classical Greek significance of this term, which implies a harmonious coordination of human will and human action on the basis of natural and spiritual laws established by the discerning, loving, and perfecting will of the divine Word.

We believe that *humanity did not wish to coordinate personal will and universal harmony* in accordance with the divine plan. Instead, it preferred to pursue independence, resulting in the creation of a new order and different pattern within the natural environment — commonly referred to as anthropocentrism, but more properly identified as anthropomonism.

We believe that *a New Man, the God-Man, Jesus Christ,* appeared in the world, demonstrating perfect obedience to the original plan of the Father with regard to the relationship between humanity and the world. Jesus Christ reconciled the world to the Father. Henceforth, the world functions harmoniously through Him and in Him. He commanded us to use the world's resources in *a spirit of ascetic restraint and eucharistic sacrifice,* to transform our way of thinking from egocentrism to altruism in light of the ultimate end of the world. In the Greek language, again, the word for "end" *(telos)* implies both conclusion and purpose.

These brief principles describe our attitude and concern for the natural environment. We are all endowed with freedom and responsibility; all of us, therefore, bear the consequences of our choices in our use or abuse of the natural environment. Yet, we also have the capacity to repent and the ability to reduce the damage of our actions in the world. We know, however, that the complete reconciliation and ultimate renewal of the world can only occur through Jesus Christ at the end of time.

Until then, God's unceasing love allows us only glimpses of that total reconciliation, to which we partially contribute when we abandon the abusive violation of nature and accept it as a divine gift of love, treating it reasonably, gratefully, and fruitfully. Such is our dutiful response to the loving Creator, as well as to all those with whom we share this divine gift.

To imagine a world that functions in beauty and harmony, balance and purpose, in accordance with the overflowing love of God, is to cry out in wonder with the Psalmist, "O Lord, how manifold are your works! In wisdom you have made them all" (Ps. 104:24).

## Original Sin and the Environment

Our original privilege and calling as human beings lies precisely in our ability to appreciate the world as God's gift to us. And *our original sin with regard to the natural environment lies, not in any legalistic transgression, but precisely in our refusal to accept the world as a sacrament of communion with God and neighbor.* We have been endowed with a passion for knowledge and wisdom, which open before us the boundless worlds of the microcosm and the macrocosm and present us with great challenges for creative action and intervention.

However, the arrogance that destroyed the Tower of Babel, through the misuse of power and knowledge, always lurks as a temptation. The natural energy wrought by the sun as a blessing on the earth can prove perilous when profaned by the hands of irresponsible scientists. The interventions of geneticists, the potential benefits of which arouse such enthusiasm, have not been exhaustively explored with a view to their negative effects.

We are not opposed to knowledge, but we underline the importance of proceeding with discernment. We also stress the possible dangers of premature intervention, which may lead to "the desire to become greater than the gods" (Euripides), which the classical Greeks described as *hubris.* Such discord destroys the inner harmony that characterizes the beauty and glory of the world, which St. Maximus the Confessor called "a cosmic liturgy."

## All-Embracing Love

Our prayer and purpose join the priest who chants these words in the Divine Liturgy: "In offering to You, Your own of Your own, on behalf of all and for the sake of all — we praise You, we bless You, we give thanks to You, O Lord, and we pray to You, our God." Then we are able to embrace all — not with fear or out of necessity, but with love and joy. Then we care for the plants and for the animals, for the trees and for the rivers, for the mountains and for the seas, for all human beings and for the whole natural environment. Then we discover joy, rather than inflicting sorrow, in our life and in our world. Then we are creating instruments of life and not tools of death. Then creation and humanity — the one that encompasses and the one that is encompassed — cooperate and correspond; they are no longer in contradiction or in conflict. Then, just as humanity offers creation in an act of priestly service and sacrifice to God, so also does creation offer itself in return as a gift to humanity. Then everything becomes an exchange, an abundance, and a fulfillment of love.

It is our sincere hope that our hearts may receive and return the natural environment to the Divine Creator with gratitude. It is our fervent prayer that our hands may minister to this divine gift of the environment in a celebration of thanksgiving.

## SCIENCE AND THEOLOGY

*Toast during the luncheon hosted by the Minister*
*of the Environment in Oslo, Norway, June 12, 2002*

*The primary purpose of our interest in the protection of the environment is our concern for humanity in our own time and in future generations.* Of course, we are not indifferent toward the preservation of natural elements that are endangered. Indeed, we see in them God's love and wisdom. Therefore, out of respect for God, we consider it a duty of our love toward Him to preserve His creation, which bears witness to His goodness.

Our attitude toward the whole of creation is influenced by our faith in God and our love toward Him and His works, and especially toward our fellow human beings. *We see the entire world as an expression of the goodness that characterizes the Supreme Being.* We know that everything that exists has a reason for its existence. Nevertheless, we also believe that the original harmony of every being in the universe has been disrupted through the intervention of the human will, which has rebelled against the divine plan. The only way in which a complete harmony can exist in accordance with the original divine plan is if the human will embraces and voluntarily submits to this plan.

Science concentrates all of its attention on one object. It is, of necessity, analytical. Therefore, the understanding of general principles that regulate the universe — which many of the Church Fathers, and especially St. Maximus the Confessor, describe as the "inner principles" — constitutes a philosophical task. In the theology of the Church, which delves into the revealed truth and appreciates human knowledge, this is described in this way: "the heavens are telling the glory of God" (Ps. 19:1). Consequently, any effective resolution to the contemporary environmental crisis requires a theological basis that will result in an appropriate environmental ethos.

# HUMAN ENVIRONMENT AND
# NATURAL ENVIRONMENT

*Toast during a dinner with the board and staff
of the Sophie Foundation following the awarding
of the Sophie Prize, June 12, 2002*

Interpersonal relationships are among the more significant capacities of human nature. Indeed, we could say that human communication — especially with God and also with one's fellow human beings — constitutes the primary element of human existence. For it is not possible for us to conceive of humanity without personal relationships; just as God is inconceivable as an impersonal Being, but only as Trinity.

A human being exists as a part of humanity, that is, in relation to other human beings. Therefore, in addition to speaking of the natural environment, we should also speak of a human environment. The latter is no less significant than the former. The present banquet reminds us of the warmth and joy of this human environment. *Unfortunately, in contemporary societies, this human environment is no less problematic than the natural environment.*

It is our duty to improve both environments, introducing elements of love, understanding, reconciliation, tolerance, communion, dialogue, and respect for one another, in order to render human life more humane.

PART III

# INTERVIEWS AND COMMENTS

# A COMMON VISION

*Address at a seminar of Greek, Turkish, and German journalists*
*sponsored by the Konrad Adenauer Foundation, October 25, 1996[1]*

We are pleased to welcome you here, at the very heart of Orthodox Christianity. You have taken time out of your schedule to visit us and this venerable and historic Ecumenical Patriarchate and we are honored by your presence. Here, in the great city of Istanbul, the meeting place of Europe and Asia, people from all walks of life and from every corner of the world gather to enjoy the mystery, the history, and the majesty of this city. Although for some of you this may be your first time in Turkey, you surely are not strangers to the legacy given the world by the diverse civilizations and cultures that have blessed these sacred lands.

Here, you are standing at the crossroads of civilizations. Look in any direction and you will see the descendants of some of the greatest of those civilizations: the Greek, the Ottoman, the Armenian, the Jewish, the Levantine. Open your minds and hearts and you will be inspired by some of the greatest world faiths: Christianity, Islam, and Judaism, which for centuries have coexisted here, and which, at the threshold of the third millennium, are determined to coexist here for many more.

Among these great world religions is our own Orthodox faith, which has been rooted here since apostolic times, when St. Andrew, the first-called by our Lord, brought the gospel of Jesus Christ to these seven hills and founded the Church on this hallowed soil. The Holy Great Church of Christ, now housed in these humble but friendly surroundings, remains the beacon of Orthodoxy and the Mother Church to Orthodox Christians throughout the world. The Ecumenical Patriarchate continues to be held in special honor and today opens her loving arms to welcome you to her bosom.

Gathered here today are four — you might say — "unlikely" groups: Turkish journalists, Greek journalists, German journalists, and the Ecumenical Patriarchate. Of course, as journalists you all have your industry in common, but your viewpoints often vary. Sometimes they agree; sometimes they

1. This address to the media is included here as an introduction to this section, which comprises segments from selected interviews with the Ecumenical Patriarch. Although there is little direct reference to the environment in this address, it nevertheless reveals the openness and readiness of the Ecumenical Patriarch to work with people of all disciplines and experience in confronting ecological issues.

intersect at certain points; sometimes they are maverick and shoot off in different directions. For serious journalists, such as those of this distinguished body, the main objective each time is NOT sensationalism, NOT to flirt with politics, NOT to undermine peace, but to print the truth.

And just how do we fit in? We are a religious institution, a Church. We are in the world but not of the world; and, as such, we too are bearers of truth and are obliged to communicate it to all humankind. So there are common threads uniting us, but are there enough to support the fabric? Obviously, we all believe that there are, because we have all gathered here today under this common roof, a place symbolizing truth, love, dialogue, and understanding — you, as professional journalists with a mandate to report life as it develops from day to day in the world around you; we, as men of God also with a mandate to bear a message of salvation and eternal life to the world around us. Each from their own vantage point agrees that their message of truth must not be captive, but must reach our audience — for you, your readership; for us, our faithful believers.

## A Single Communication

Therefore, we are all communicators, each in his or her own way. You communicate with hard facts and convincing or controversial arguments; we communicate by faith and by revelation from God. You attempt to reach your public intellectually and rationally, from mind to mind; in the hope that the public will understand what you have spoken or written in the way that you have meant it, you are careful how you word your scripts or texts. We, on the other hand, attempt to reach our public spiritually, from heart to heart, since neither faith nor revelation can be definitively rationalized or verbalized.

Nevertheless, in order for your work to be successful and meaningful, you must draw from us, you must give it soul, or else what you are trying to communicate is dry and uninspiring and the message falls on deaf ears. Likewise, we must see things in a historical and cultural context as well, a context relevant to our lives, or else the message we are trying to communicate can seem mythical or even ridiculous.

So what is our purpose in hosting you here today? We believe the answer is really quite simple. We must look into each other's eyes and see that we are all struggling for the same common end: to make this world a peaceful one, to elevate men and women and inspire them to reach new heights, to leave this world a better place than we found it. We work in different ways, but toward the same goal — you, through journalism, through the stroke of a pen, through your insight, open-mindedness, talent, and objectivity; and we through faith in God, through the gospel, the written word of God, through prayer, tradition, and continuity.

It is our strong belief that the Orthodox Church has a significant spiritual role to play in the world today — first, by living its faith and perpetuating it from generation to generation; and second, by making its contribution in encouraging rapprochement between East and West and incorporating into Europe the renewed ideas that the Orthodox East, rich in tradition and history, has to offer. Europe is not merely a geographical entity but a mosaic of cultures, faiths, and traditions. Our Orthodox faith and tradition shares in this diversity. Recently, the overall process of civic reform in Europe has contributed to the revival of many of our Orthodox communities, in particular our sister Churches in Eastern Europe. Our role as Orthodox Christians is to help in the development of open, tolerant, and spirit-filled societies within our local parishes and communities, regardless of religion, race, language, or culture.

In your field, you are also contributing to the mission of this great revival both in Europe and in your communities. We hope this occasion will offer you the opportunity for further dialogue that will lead to better understanding and fruitful cooperation. Your industry, like our Church, can make an enormous difference. We commend the German journalists, and in particular the Konrad Adenauer Foundation, for the inspired idea of inviting Turkish and Greek journalists to join them in what can be a meeting of the minds and souls of those connected with one of the most powerful tools of communication in the world today.

We fervently pray that your pilgrimage to this sacred center will be spiritually filled with the inspiration and inner peace that these hallowed walls and grounds have brought to so many. We further pray that you will grow from your experience here and that a new dimension will be brought to your work as journalists. In closing, beloved friends, we should like to say how much we appreciate this time together; we ask you to join us — each in your own way, using the talents and faith God has given you — in bringing peace and understanding to every corner of the world, so that our ever smaller planet will be a place of peace, dignity, justice, and freedom for all humanity. May the grace and peace of God go with you always.

# THE HOUR OF ORTHODOXY

*From an interview with Nikolaos Manginas*
*for the journal* Eikones, *January 24, 1992*

Our age is the age of Orthodox witness. The hour of Orthodoxy has come. Today, orthodoxy is respected and welcomed more so than at any other time in the past. The responsibility, then, of its Church leaders is greater than ever before. Wherever Western Christianity and Western civilization have left a vacuum, Orthodoxy is called to transfigure the face of the earth and renew its youth like the eagle's (Ps. 103:5), to fill that emptiness with its spirituality and apophaticism, and in general with its inexhaustible spiritual treasures, which belong to the whole world and which for this reason must be spread as widely as possible.

The contemporary and critical issue of the environment justifiably concerned our predecessor of blessed memory, Patriarch Demetrios. We, too, cannot but continue our interest in this matter. The Ecumenical Patriarchate has always endeavored to show its concern in people's lives of every period and to express an interest in human problems and needs in order to assist and support them as it should. Only a few days ago, the Ecumenical Patriarchate convened a special inter-Orthodox conference on environmental studies at the Orthodox Academy of Crete, chaired by the distinguished hierarch and university professor, Metropolitan John of Pergamon. Furthermore, next year, the Duke of Edinburgh will visit the Phanar in his capacity as Chairman of the World Wide Fund for Nature, and we shall then surely have occasion to exchange views and initiate plans for the protection of the natural environment from human exploitation, which also implies the protection of human life itself.

# AN INITIATIVE, NOT A NOVELTY

*From an interview for the student magazine*
*of Columbia University, March 3, 1998*

The Orthodox Church has always embraced the entire creation and indeed prays daily "for favorable winds, the abundance of the fruits of the earth, for those who labor and those who are sick, for those who are traveling by sea or road or air," and, in general, "for the unity of all in Christ." This is a prayer for reconciliation with God, not only of estranged humanity but also of the rebellious nature, which "sighs and suffers with us," desiring to be liberated from subjection to decay (cf. Rom. 8:19-23). Therefore, it should not be considered a novelty that we are asking our fellow human beings not to despoil nature, on behalf of which we are praying daily to God. However, it is not true that we assign the highest priority to ecological questions alone. We are simply giving these questions their proper place among many other, equally or even more serious, problems to which we call the attention of our fellow human beings. Such problems deserving our close attention are peaceful coexistence and collaboration, reconciliation, support for the weak and the needy, respect for the human person, the correct practice of our faith, the return of all things to God, and so on.

# ORTHODOX SPIRITUALITY IS MAXIMALIST

*From an interview/message broadcast by Granada Television,*
*in its series* This Sunday, *on the occasion of*
*Orthodox Easter, January 18, 1993*

The teaching about the creation of the world and the doctrine in general about the natural environment provide the overall parameters within which anyone interested is called to study all the contemporary "ecological" or "environmental" problems. This is why it would constitute an unbearable and unjust "minimalism" if one were to judge the relative stance of the Orthodox

Church solely from the perspective of an occasional document at a particular event or from the establishment of September 1st of each year as the day of prayer for the whole creation and environment. The entire lifestyle of the Orthodox faithful at every moment of every day is indicative of the sacredness of every created thing. By way of reminder, it is characteristic that the monks of Mount Athos will make the sign of the cross in a gesture of gratitude even before drinking a mere glass of water.

## SOUNDING THE ALARM OF DANGER

*From an interview with Alexi Tsolakis and Panagiotis Christofilopoulos in the educational journal* Athinaios, *January 1996*

The interest of the Ecumenical Patriarchate in matters concerning the protection of the environment, as in all contemporary issues, is taken for granted. All of us here at the Phanar believe that the burning issue of the environment must be addressed at its root. And the root of this problem, as of so many other problems, is humanity. Human beings exploit their identity as the only rational beings and act on their selfish attitudes, inflicting significant and irreparable damage on nature. You see, we are given the opportunity to use creation, but instead we have preferred to abuse it.

The Orthodox Christian Church must sound the alarm of danger. We must work and walk with all those persons who see the great risk and contribute to the restraint of this evil. We too must contribute as a Church by raising the awareness and awakening the conscience of all those who remain indifferent. I am certain that, when humanity in its entirety becomes truly conscious of the fact that its existence depends on the environment, the ecological problem will disappear. However, the world must be mobilized now. Appropriate measures must be taken in timely fashion, because we have already delayed somewhat. Should we delay still further, then the dangers for humanity will become greater and we shall no longer be able to turn things around.

The Orthodox Church is working diligently in this direction. Already in 1989, Patriarch Demetrios had formally established September 1st as the yearly day of prayers for the protection of the natural environment. In turn, in March of 1992, in a gathering of all the leaders of the Orthodox Churches held here at the Phanar, I established it for the Orthodox Church worldwide. Every September 1st, the Patriarchate issues an official message, an official encyclical related to the environment. Only a month after my election, a Pan-Orthodox ecological conference was organized at the Orthodox Academy of Crete. In early June of 1992, together with Prince Philip the Duke of Edinburgh, who is the Chairman of the World Wide Fund for Nature, I organized a conference in the halls of the former Theological School of Halki, a seminar about the environment. One year later, in November of 1993, at the invitation of Prince Philip, I visited Buckingham Palace, where we had the opportunity of exchanging opinions and ideas concerning the ecological problem.

Now we are preparing an international ecological symposium on the island of Patmos, which will be combined with the celebration of the nineteen hundredth anniversary of the Revelation of St. John. Next spring, an environmental congress in two parts is being organized, first in Japan and subsequently in England. I shall also participate in this, as a representative not only of the Orthodox but of all Christians. These activities are indicative of the Patriarchate's concern for the environmental crisis and of its contribution toward the preservation of the natural environment.

# AN ECUMENICAL VISION

*From an interview for the journal* Aerodromics
*of Air Greece Airlines, October 9, 1999*

From the moment of its foundation to the end of the ages, the purpose and perspective of the Ecumenical Patriarchate's contribution and service to humanity remain constant: the proclamation of truth, the teaching of the gospel, the coordination of and ministry to the Orthodox Churches, the sanctification of the faithful, and the transfiguration of the whole world. Within these general aims and fundamental perspectives are included the more particular goals, such as the insistence on tradition, the evasion of secularism, and the mobilization of all people in regard to preserving the environment.

The Ecumenical Patriarchate has taken the initiative to remind all Christians that the protection of the environment is a divine command and a human obligation, for the destruction of the natural environment bears dangerous consequences for all of humanity. So the Ecumenical Patriarchate seeks to sensitize everyone, because even the small actions of individuals contribute to ecological destruction.

## SPIRITUAL ROOTS OF A MATERIAL PROBLEM

*Interview with Prof. Bruno Forto*
*for Italian Television, January 6, 1999*

What people refer to as "genuine human problems" have a spiritual root and cause, stemming as they do from the human heart and soul. Consequently, in order to solve these problems satisfactorily, what is required is a change of lifestyle, a conversion of mind-set and attitudes of the heart — what in ecclesiastical terminology is called *metanoia* (or repentance). So the Orthodox Church attributes great value to spirituality, acting precisely like a good physician, who does not seek to heal an illness by simply eliminating the particular symptoms but by addressing the causes of the disease.

All contemporary "real" problems have a spiritual cause, and the Orthodox Church is right in focusing its attention on the spiritual dimension. And it is not the first to do so. The historian Thucydides claimed, many centuries before Christ, that it is impossible for any change to occur in society and in social matters without a change first of all in individuals. And of course a change in the character of individuals comes about only through a change in their spirituality. This change is wrought by the wealth of Orthodox worship. For without the grace of God, which is invoked through the liturgy, no human change for the better is possible.

# RELIGION AND HUMAN SUFFERING

*Question by a representative of the United Nations*
*following an address at the annual Davos Meeting, February 2, 1999*

Q. We have come a long way, Sir, from the Karl Marx comment about religion being the opium of the masses, to your wonderful remarks today, and also the Pope's speech not so long ago in Mexico, about the necessity for globalization to develop a human face. I am curious, however, about the traditional critique of religion, that it essentially requires of its people, and itself becomes, an escape from the need to do something about the predicament of their political situation. How do you see religion today in the context of the old charge that it is an instrument that reconciles people with their suffering rather than a tool that helps them to conquer it?

A. If I have understood your question correctly, I must qualify that it is important to try to help people, that is, people who are suffering, because they are our brothers and sisters. We cannot live in peace, and we cannot sleep in peace, when we feel that some — or many — of our brothers and sisters among us and around us suffer because they do not have food or they do not have clothing, and so on. If poverty and suffering continue to exist in our society, it means that we are not fulfilling our sacred responsibility toward our fellow human beings. We are not fulfilling our obligation to preserve the sacredness and the uniqueness of every human person. If we see people around us simply as people, then poverty and suffering will most certainly continue to exist. However, if we see them as persons created in the image of God, as our fellow human beings — that is, as people with whom we must be in communion every day in all aspects of life — then we shall fulfill our obligation toward them. And if poverty and suffering continue to exist, this means mainly that we, religious leaders, have not succeeded in teaching our people, our flock, the necessity of respecting every human being.

The other day, I was sitting at the same table with the Greek author and intellectual, Mr. Samarakis, who said to me, "Your All Holiness, we are all United Nations." All human beings on earth are connected to one other by the same anxieties and at the same time by the same hopes.

So we have to cooperate. As we leave Davos in a few hours, later today or tomorrow, we all have to take with us — along with our luggage and the fresh air of Davos — the firm decision to promote a globalization of love, instead of one based on hatred and hypocrisy. We must promote a globalization of communion and cooperation, instead of one based on conflict and competition.

# HUNGER AND POVERTY

*Interview on Greek radio Sky 100.4, April 9, 1999*

The root of the problems of hunger and poverty is human lifestyle, not the insufficiency of material goods to support human needs. It is well known that vast amounts are expended for the production of destructive military weapons. It is also well known that a vast majority of wealth and resources are concentrated in the hands of few, as we recently stated in Davos. If these resources were used for peaceful and productive purposes, they would be able to transform our planet into an earthly paradise.

Of course, we are not a political leader and therefore are not in a position to propose or impose solutions. Yet we are obliged in the name of our faith and of truth to proclaim the need to change people's lifestyles and attitudes, to preach that which in ecclesiastical terms is called *metanoia* (or repentance), in order for human conditions to improve. The word "repentance" is misunderstood today, calling to mind a sense of guilt for sins that some people consider unimportant. By "repentance," however, we imply those things that are more important than the transgression of law — namely, discernment and mercy, justice and compassion.

The lack of a sense of justice leads to greed, domination, the exploitation of the weaker by the more powerful, the abundance of wealth for the strong and the extreme poverty of the weak. The lack of a spirit of compassion renders the soul indifferent to another person's pain and prevents the development of those things that kindle a sense of justice. Therefore, in calling for a change of attitude, we are offering a compassionate service to humanity and indicating a way of solving problems of poverty and hunger. Nevertheless, we are not naively optimistic.

At the same time, there are numerous signs that a significant — and, it is our hope, a growing — portion of human societies is conscious of need for repentance, although we are not ignorant of the fact that the abundantly wealthy minority will continue to increase in wealth. However, as a religious leader, and especially as a leader of the Orthodox Church — the Church of love, justice, compassion, and service — we have no other way but that of proclamation and persuasion.

Our efforts in particular for the protection of the natural environment must also be intensified. Yet we must broaden the notion of the natural environment to include the human and cultural environment. For it would be a paradox to be concerned solely for the natural environment, and yet be lacking in interest in humanity and our cultural heritage. Our human environment also deserves our love, just as our natural environment deserves our respect. Likewise, our cultural heritage is a monument of the human journey that is deserving of our respect and protection.

# THEOLOGY AND LIFE

*Interview with Anders Laugesen, January 2, 2001*

The knowledge of the truth about creation, as well as of the purpose of the world and humanity, contributes to the correct response toward the ecological problem. The Church reveals the truth, and in this way contributes toward the solution of every problem, including the environmental one.

The problems of humanity derive from the inner world of the human person, which defines human behavior. As a Christian hierarch, as a person who does not exercise worldly power, we propose the perfect way of human holiness as the solution of all human problems. It is clear that not everyone will follow this way, and so it is also clear that the problems will continue to exist. The powerful and aggressively greedy person creates the poor person, just as the lazy person also creates his or her own poverty.

There are no purely theological matters that do not also have practical implications for life. The content of each person's faith creates the psychological presuppositions that define his or her conduct. Thus theology and life are intertwined. Even the alienation of one's life from theology is a theological act, albeit a negative one. We pray that everyone will come to know the truth that sets us free.

# THE CHALLENGE FOR THE FUTURE

*Interview for the periodical* Premin-Pass Over *of Skopje, January 3, 2001*

Q. In the past, but also in the contemporary world, we are witnesses of the existence of religious and other intolerance. Does the Orthodox Church do enough to initiate and develop theological and other dialogues between other churches and confessions?

A. Never is any one attempt alone sufficient, when the sought result has not been achieved. We must continue and intensify our efforts.

Q. Your All Holiness, you are known as a preacher of love, peace, and reconciliation for humanity. You did your best, for example, to stop the military conflict in former Yugoslavia. Where and how do you see the ways of achieving these principles in a world of hatred, despair, and military conflicts?

A. We do not consider the world to be a place of general hatred, despair, and military conflicts. A large portion of humanity are people of love and hope, who can be mobilized to influence their leaders. This is something achievable in democratic nations.

Q. You are also known as a "green" Patriarch. Are you satisfied with the mobilization so far of the world's moral and spiritual forces to achieve harmony between humanity and nature?

A. A good number of steps have been taken toward a general mobilization of communities, but there still remains so much to do, and we must continue our efforts. We shall indeed continue these with the utmost sense of responsibility.

Q. What are the most important and crucial challenges of the Orthodox Church in the future?

A. No greater challenge is expected for Orthodoxy in the future than has already occurred in the past. This is the challenge of "evil," which in ecclesiastical language is called "the world" — namely, the world of evil, the root of which is egoism, and the consequent rejection of the divine harmony and order that renders the world "very good." Christ, then, came into the world/creation and overcame the world/evil, that is, the world that had corrupted its "very good" nature. And Christ did this through His ultimate humiliation of death on the cross, an act that wipes away the root of evil, namely egoism. Thus He declared that "in the world you have tribulation; but be of good cheer, I have overcome the world" (John 16:33). Therefore, for the Orthodox Church, whose head is Christ and which constitutes the Body of Christ, the great challenge of evil has already been overcome. Of course, each faithful person must struggle to become incorporated into the Body of Christ. And when this occurs, every challenge in the world is overcome for the faithful. So for each person, the great challenge is self-deification, that is, the deification of the ego, and the right way is deification through the divine-human person of Christ. This way comprises the eternal and divine order of the world. Any other order is in reality disorder, because the order of God alone is perfect.

# A COLLECTIVE RESPONSIBILITY

*From an interview for the Norwegian newspaper* Tagbladet, *April 2002*

Q. In your opinion, how significant are the ecological problems for contemporary society?

A. The Orthodox Church has always been conscious of the unity of humanity with the natural environment. Such awareness derives from the universal concept of the world and the inviolable interdependence of the parts with the whole, and vice versa. The Ecumenical Patriarchate has long ago said, and often continues to repeat, that God entrusted to humankind the supreme mission of performing a "priestly" role within sacred creation. The disruption of this relationship that we have observed for many years, but especially in the most recent years, as well as the burdening of the natural environment, explains and justifies the increased significance that we attribute to ecological issues. For these are not simply local and regional but in fact concern the entire planet and its immediate environs, threatening the regular function of our natural environment as well as the very survival of humanity and the other living organisms.

Q. Which is the most significant ecological problem today?

A. We do not have — nor do we claim to have — the qualifications to determine the most important ecological issues. This is a task that belongs to the specialists, whose knowledge and opinion we should all seek, heed, and respect. The Ecumenical Patriarchate systematically and consistently seeks to achieve this by organizing — among other things — interdisciplinary scientific dialogues on an international level in order to promote mutual information, an unprejudiced concentration on real issues, and the recommendation of appropriate solutions wherever this is possible.

People seem to be increasingly conscious of — or else they are obliged to become more conscious of — the fact that the environmental problem is an ethical issue. Usually, the more visible issues are the ones brought to people's attention. Nevertheless, it is wrong to ignore the spiritual, ethical, or deontological issues. For the ecological problem is primarily a matter of each person's attitude or conduct toward that part of sacred creation which has been divinely appointed as the dwelling place of humanity. Attitude and conduct are of course first of all individual matters. However, they are also collective matters that concern life and action in local communities, nations, international coalitions, and even the global community.

The respect or violation of such contexts is a matter of moral concern. From our own ecclesiastical perspective, we wish to highlight this essential dimension of the entire issue, as well as the urgent need to confront any indifference, wherever this may appear. For indifference entails inaction, which in turn encourages further abuse, increasing the causes that originally provoke and preserve this indifference.

Q. In what way is the Church able to contribute, whether on the local or the international level?

A. In what we have stated above, a partial response has already been given to your question. We believe that the responsibilities are many, just as the potential of the local ecclesiastical and in general the religious communities is great. Within our own Orthodox Church, each time we celebrate the eucharistic Divine Liturgy, we chant with thanksgiving to God, saying: "Your own of Your own, we offer to You." That is to say, we confess that the elements of Holy Communion, the bread and the wine, which are offered by the faithful for sanctification, represent the entire creation that belongs to God and is offered to Him in thanksgiving. When these elements are transformed through the Holy Spirit into the Body and Blood of Christ, they are distributed to those who participate, for the forgiveness of sins and life eternal. What is of special and creative significance is the spiritual exercise among the faithful of introspection and intense understanding of the unity between the mystery of creation, the mystery of life, and the mystery of salvation. We feel that it is only from the depth of such a spiritual contemplation that humanity is able to behold the beauty of nature, to become sensitive to the harmony therein, and to wonder humbly and obediently at the sacred laws, which govern the function of the microcosm and the macrocosm. This humility, which comes from a sense of wonder and awe, has always inspired poets, hymn writers, and artists. It is also perhaps the only source of power that can enable humanity to confront its egocentrism, ugliness, greed, and arrogance.

Moreover, the cooperation among churches on a broader, international level is also necessary and capable of making a substantial contribution. For example, the Orthodox Church has for years cooperated with the World Council of Churches (WCC) and European Council of Churches (CEC) in promoting programs of environmental study, research, information, and awareness in the world. Personally, we are also grateful for the opportunity that we have had of presenting the ecclesiastical position on environmental issues, among other matters, before the members of international organizations such as the European Council, the European Parliament, the Commission of the European Union, and other bodies of international constitution and responsibility.

It is our conviction that the disappointments sometimes created by the meager results that come from international environmental endeavors, such as those by the United Nations, should not lead us to surrender, but on the contrary to greater vigilance and persistence. This is especially so because, as we know, the greater ecological problems know no national boundaries. No person, in any part of the world, is able to feel secure in the face of climate and other changes, which we have already experienced or which are particularly threatening, as a result of the corrupt, egoistic, insatiable, irresponsible, and deeply sinful conduct of humanity toward our natural environment. We believe that the Church is obligated to coordinate still more its resources and activities on an international level, in cooperation with everyone who has the good intention and commitment to protect the natural environment on an individual as well as on a collective level.

Q. Did the award of the Sophie Prize surprise you?

A. We were gladly surprised, for in our time people do not usually place great hope in the Church, especially concerning issues that are considered "secu-

335

lar." This is why we regard the award of this prize as constituting a partial correction of this image. Moreover, our joy upon hearing this gracious decision offers us encouragement and a renewed starting point for further concern for the protection of our natural environment.

Q. Is this your first visit to Oslo? And how does Your All Holiness intend to use the prize money?

A. We visited Norway several years ago on the occasion of the Faith and Order Commission of the World Council of Churches and later returned to Norway to participate in the events organized to commemorate the millennial anniversary of the first proclamation of the Christian gospel in that country. We shall distribute some of the prize money to the needy children of Africa, through UNICEF, and to the "street children" in Istanbul and Athens, and some will be used for the support of ecological initiatives.

## ORTHODOXY AND THE ENVIRONMENT

*From an interview with journalists in Oslo, Norway,*
*immediately before the awarding of the Sophie Prize, June 12, 2002*

It may surprise you that the first among hierarchs of the Orthodox Church is profoundly concerned with environmental issues. The reason for this is that the Orthodox Church believes that the creation of God, both natural and spiritual, is "very good," and that humanity is obliged to cultivate and to preserve this beautiful world, within which God placed us as rulers and providers, but not as unreasonable and abusive tyrants.

Naturally, we distinguish the position of humanity from that of other created beings. We do not equate human beings with the other members of our ecosystem. This is why we regard humanity as being responsible for the rational regulation of the ecosystem and invite our fellow human beings to assume the necessary measures recommended by science for the improvement of the environment.

In addition to this, the Orthodox Church does not regard the material creation as evil (as the Gnostics did), nor the body as the prison of the soul

336

(as Plato did). The Orthodox Church believes that humanity in its entirety, body and soul alike, is destined for eternity and is therefore sanctified and resurrected with the body, which is transfigured into a different form, yet still remains a body.

Therefore, the Orthodox Church is also concerned for the material needs of the world, exercising charity and healing illnesses (just as Christ did), caring for those who are hungry and naked, praying for seasonable weather and an abundance of the fruits of the earth. It is a Church that embraces the whole of creation.

Indeed, the Orthodox Church also feels compassion for inanimate nature and is unable to tolerate any harm that comes upon it. Therefore, within the context of recognizing nature as God's creation and humanity as nature's sustainer, with particular limitations that safeguard against the abuse of creation, we have assumed the responsibility of raising people's awareness on environmental issues.

In this regard, we have held five successive summer seminars at the Ecological Institute of Halki; we organize, jointly with the European Union, seaborne symposia that explore the environmental problems of particular marine ecosystems (such as the Aegean, the Black Sea, the Danube, the Adriatic, and — next year — the Baltic); and we participate in international environmental conferences as well as other events (such as those in Japan, Nepal, and the United States of America).

There is no need to emphasize the global consequences of local actions for the environment; this is familiar to everyone. There is also no need to underline that, in our environmental endeavors, we do not seek to worship nature but to serve humanity; this is clear to everyone.

We simply wish to stress that it is our responsibility — according to the commandment of God and the voice of our conscience — to face the environmental crisis with discernment, knowledge, love, and sacrifice. We are losing time; and the longer we wait, the more difficult and irreparable the damage will become.

# ECOLOGY AND MONASTICISM

*Message for the opening of the seminar on the natural environment*
*on Mount Athos, September 29, 1997*

Inspired as we are by the will to love one another, we wholeheartedly embrace the concern for the natural environment as a way of overcoming or at least restraining the prevailing individualism. Indeed, love for one another and the whole world constitutes a fundamental teaching and command of the gospel of Christ. . . .

There are numerous regions throughout the world where, for the general benefit of all, even when this contradicts the narrowly conceived interests of certain inhabitants, particular environmental prohibitions have been imposed. Therefore, by way of example, roads may not be constructed and motor traffic is not permitted on the Greek isle of Hydra and the Princes Islands of Turkey. We might also consider the example of a monk mentioned in *The Sayings of the Desert Fathers,* who deliberately built his cell far away from the water source in order to increase the labor involved in his transportation of necessary resources.

Perhaps, then, it would not be farfetched to demand of those who have voluntarily espoused the monastic life to be less concerned about their personal comfort and more concerned about the preservation of the natural beauty and the dimension of silence on Mount Athos, the Holy Mountain, particularly because it is this aspect of silence that attracts those who renounce worldly cares. Therefore, these persons are also obliged to preserve the cultural and natural environment of Mount Athos by sacrificing certain material and mundane benefits for the sake of the more significant and spiritual benefits that are to come.

Abba Isaac the Syrian, who is so beloved among the monks of Mount Athos, observed that no one ascends to heaven by means of comfort. Indeed, to extend our paternal recollection of this same Abba, we might remind you that he also says that God and the angels rejoice in heaven at the sight of ascetic labor, while the devil and his cohorts rejoice in hell at the sight of bodily comfort. Abba Isaac adds, however, that every sacrifice for God leads to and results in everlasting gladness.

# THE PRIEST AND THE SCIENTIST

*Message for the conference entitled "Orthodoxy and the Environment,"*
*held in Kavala, Greece, September 7, 1993*

The priesthood does not have exclusive responsibility for the theological aspect of environmental concern; nor should science and technology feel self-sufficient in their scientific analysis of the subject. The analysis of scientific data should be informed by theological understandings if a proper evaluation and appreciation of the ecological crisis is to be reached. However, the opposite holds true as well: theologians are called to cultivate a more comprehensive picture of scientific principles and demands in environmental issues. Indeed, we are convinced that such a mutual and common examination and exploration of theological and scientific methodology will result in the necessary foundation for particular recommendations and a more successful cooperation on the subject.

As we have stressed elsewhere, the Orthodox Church has always — from the fourth- and fifth-century thought of the holy and God-bearing Fathers and Teachers of the undivided Church — emphasized cosmology together with, and never separated from, anthropology. The classical thinkers of the Orthodox Church, such as the Cappadocian Fathers, never ignored the fundamentally eucharistic dimension of creation, which is returned to God in an act of thanksgiving and glorification. Material creation is good, both beautiful and blessed, expecting its eschatological transformation and the recapitulation of all in Christ, the eternal Word.

# POPULATION AND ENVIRONMENT

*Message to the conference in Thessalonika on the subject of population*
*development in relation to the environmental crisis, June 4, 1995*

The Most Holy and Patriarchal Ecumenical Throne . . . expresses its satisfaction inasmuch as the Society of Population Studies [in Greece] has opportunely related the environmental crisis with the crucial and difficult subject of demographic explosion throughout the world.

Indeed, as specialists, both environmentalists and others, agree, the breathtaking increase in our planet's population will create great difficulties for future generations, given that, in the wise words of the Swiss philosopher Denis de Rougemont, "a cancer cannot be larger than the body that it possesses."

# FAITH AND SCIENCE

*Message to the delegates of the international conference organized in Constantinople by the Ecumenical Patriarchate and entitled "The Creation of the World and the Creation of Humanity — Challenges and Problems Before the Twenty-first Century," September 1, 2002*

Orthodox theology has traditionally avoided, at least as much as possible, the conflict between faith and science on account of the double gnosiological methodology of the Church Fathers, whose thinking was based on the ontological distinction between Creator and creation.

Therefore, the Church rejoices in the scientific success of humanity. It stands with a sense of profound awe, attention, and also caution before the various means of research and application presented by contemporary genetics and mechanics, biomedicine and biotechnology. It seeks to establish an essential dialogue with these, acknowledging that the Church shares a common responsibility with the sciences for the healing of a suffering and burdened world.

Nevertheless, the Church also reminds the world that whatever abolishes a sense of respect before creation as a miracle of divine love and freedom also distorts the biblical and patristic criterion of moral truth, disturbs human relations, restricts human freedom, and undermines personal uniqueness.

Scientific achievements that soothe human pain, promote human health, extend human life, and generally improve the human condition truly constitute divine gifts for the world. However, they are not ends in themselves. Nor are they excuses for an arrogant transcendence that reduces the soteriological perspective of the human person. The role of the Church is not to eliminate scientific progress but to realize human salvation and to promote moral values.

The expected life in the age to come is life in the kingdom of God. It is a life that begins "in time" and is fulfilled "in eternity." Historical time becomes a place of encounter with eternal reality. The salvific "now" of the kingdom is found in the Church, while the "always" of the Church exists in the heavenly kingdom. This life is not merely a preparation for the expected kingdom, but actually shares in this reality through faith in the kingdom, through the sacraments of the Church, and through the commandments of God.

## SAINTS AND THE WORLD

*Message on the occasion of Earth Day, June 1997*

Our Church supports an attitude of thanksgiving toward creation, rather than an attitude of egoism that results in abuse of the natural resources and life of the world. It condemns greed, avarice, limitless acquisition, and uncritical consumerism, which sometimes reach the point of insanity.

In contrast, we can look to the luminous examples of the saints, who respected life and humanity, who befriended the animals and the birds, who positively influenced their environment and community, and who lived with simplicity and self-sufficiency.

Therefore, we call upon everyone — government officials, clergymen, educators, artists, and journalists — to work together in withstanding the captivity of overconsumption. "It is for freedom that Christ has set us free. Stand firm, then, and no longer submit to any yoke of slavery" (Gal. 5:1).

# Select Sources

**Books**

Ascheron, Neal, and Sarah Hobson, eds. *Danube: River of Life.* Athens: Religion, Science and the Environment, 2002.

Bartholomew, Ecumenical Patriarch. *Conversations with Ecumenical Patriarch Bartholomew I,* by Olivier Clément. New York: St. Vladimir's Seminary Press, 1997.

Belopopsky, Alexander, and Dimitri Oikonomou, eds. *Orthodoxy and Ecology: Resource Book.* Bialystok, Poland: Syndesmos, 1996. [This publication includes articles by Ecumenical Patriarch Demetrios, Ecumenical Patriarch Bartholomew, Metropolitan Paulos Mar Gregorios, Dr. Elizabeth Theokritoff, Fr. K. M. George, and the editors. It also contains liturgical services for the creation, workshops, and activities.]

Chryssavgis, John. *Beyond the Shattered Image: Orthodox Insights into the Environment.* Minneapolis: Light and Life, 1999.

Chryssavgis, John, with G. Ferguson. *The Desert Is Alive: Dimensions of Australian Spirituality.* Melbourne: Joint Board of Christian Education, 1990.

*The Churches and the Ecological Problem in Europe: The Proceedings of the XIV International Orthodox Postgraduate Conference (1993).* Geneva: Foundation of the Orthodox Centre of the Ecumenical Patriarchate, 1993.

*The Environment and Ethics: Proceedings of the Summer 1995 Seminar on Halki.* Istanbul: Melitos Editions, 1996.

*The Environment and Religious Education: Proceedings of the Summer 1994 Seminar on Halki.* Istanbul: Melitos Editions, 1995.

Gillet, Lev. *The Burning Bush.* London: Fellowship of St. Alban and St. Sergius, 1976.

————. *On the Invocation of the Name of Jesus.* London: Fellowship of St. Alban and St. Sergius, 1950.

Hobson, Sarah, and Jane Lubchenko, eds. *Revelation and the Environment,* AD *95-1995.* World Scientific, 1997.

Hobson, Sarah, and Lawrence Mee, eds. *Religion, Science, and the Environment: The Black Sea in Crisis.* World Scientific, 1998.

Kallistos of Diokleia, Bishop. *Through the Creation to the Creator.* London: Friends of the Centre Papers, 1997.

Lang, D. M. *Lives and Legends of the Georgian Saints, Life of St. David of Gareja.* London and Oxford: Mowbrays, 1976.

Limouris, (now Metropolitan) Gennadios, ed. *Come, Holy Spirit, Renew the Whole Creation.* Brookline, MA: Holy Cross Orthodox Press, 1960.

———, ed. *Justice, Peace, and the Integrity of Creation: Insights from Orthodoxy.* Geneva: WCC Publications, 1990.

———, ed. *Orthodox Visions of Ecumenism: Statements, Messages, and Reports on the Ecumenical Movement 1902-1992.* Geneva: WCC Publications, 1990, 1994.

Lossky, Vladimir. *The Mystical Theology of the Eastern Orthodox Church.* New York: St. Vladimir's Seminary Press, 1976.

Nellas, Panayiotis. *Deification in Christ: Orthodox Perspectives on the Nature of the Human Person.* New York: St. Vladimir's Seminary Press, 1987.

Nikodemos, Metropolitan. *Service for the Protection of the Environment.* [In Greek.] Patras, 1994.

*Orthodoxy and the Ecological Crisis.* Ecumenical Patriarchate assisted by the World Wide Fund for Nature, WWF International, Switzerland, 1990.

*The Orthodox Church and the Environment.* Athens: Ekdotike Athinon, Ministry of Foreign Affairs, 1992.

*Orthodoxy and Ecology: Orthodox Youth Environmental Training Seminar Resource Book.* Conference in Neamt, Romania, 1994. World Wide Fund for Nature and Syndesmos, 1994. [See also the Resource Book under Belopopsky.]

Ouspensky, Leonid. *The Theology of the Icon.* New York: St. Vladimir's Seminary Press, 1992.

Paulos (Verghese), Mar Gregorios, Metropolitan. *Cosmic Man: The Divine Presence.* New Delhi: Sophia Publications, 1980. [This book has appeared in various editions.]

———. *Enlightenment, East and West: Pointers in the Quest for India's Secular Identity.* New Delhi, 1989.

———. *The Freedom of Man.* Philadelphia, 1972.

———. *The Human Presence: An Orthodox View of Nature.* Geneva: WCC, 1978; Park Town: Christian Literature Society, 1980. [Later published as

*The Human Presence: Ecological Spirituality and the Age of the Spirit.* New York, 1987.]

———. *A Light Too Bright — The Enlightenment Today: An Assessment of the Values of European Enlightenment and a Search for New Foundations.* New York, 1992.

———. *Science for Sane Societies.* Park Town: Christian Literature Society, 1980.

*The Problem of Ecology Today: The Proceedings of the XIII International Orthodox Postgraduate Conference (1992).* Geneva: Foundation of the Orthodox Centre of the Ecumenical Patriarchate, 1992.

Schmemann, Fr. Alexander. *For the Life of the World: Sacraments and Orthodoxy.* New York: St. Vladimir's Seminary Press, 1973.

Sherrard, Philip. *The Eclipse of Man and Nature: An Enquiry into the Origins and Consequences of Modern Science.* West Stockbridge: Lindisfarne Press, 1987.

———. *Human Image, World Image.* Ipswich: Golgonooza Press, 1990.

———. *The Sacred in Life and Art.* Ipswich: Golgonooza Press, 1990.

*So That God's Creation Might Live: The Orthodox Church Responds to the Ecological Crisis.* Proceedings of the Inter-Orthodox Conference on Environmental Protection, Crete 1991. Bialystok: Ecumenical Patriarchate assisted by SYNDESMOS, 1991. [This publication includes articles by Metropolitan John of Pergamon, Prof. Elias Oikonomou, Bishop Irineos Pop, Fr. Makarios, Sr. Theoxeni, Fr. Ignatios Midich, Fr. Stamatios Skliris, and Kostas Stamatopoulos.]

Stefanatos, Joanne. *Animals and Man: A State of Blessedness.* Minneapolis: Light and Life Publishing, 1992.

Vasileios, Archimandrite. *Ecology and Monasticism.* Montreal: Alexander Press, 1996.

Vischer, Lukas, ed. *Churches on Climate Change: A Collection of Statements and Resolutions on Global Warming and Climate Change.* Geneva: WCC, 1992.

## Articles

Anthony of Sourozh, Metropolitan. "Body and Matter in Spiritual Life." In *Sacrament and Image.* London: Fellowship of St. Alban and St. Sergius, 1987.

Bartholomew, Ecumenical Patriarch. "The Orthodox Faith and the Environment." *Sourozh* 62 (1995).

Basil (Osborne) of Sergievo, Bishop. "Beauty in the Divine and in Nature." *Sourozh* 70 (1997).

———. "Preaching the Gospel to All Creation." In his *Speaking of the Kingdom.* Oxford: St. Stephen's Press, 1993.

————. "Sermon on the Sunday of Orthodoxy." In his *The Light of Christ*. Oxford: St. Stephen's Press, 1992.

————. "Towards 2000: The Transfiguration of the World." *One in Christ* 3 (1997). Also in *Sourozh* 72 (1998).

Brock, Sebastian. "Humanity and the Natural World in the Syriac Tradition." *Sobornost/ECR* 12, no. 2 (1990).

————. "World and Sacrament in the Writings of the Syrian Fathers." *Sobornost* 6, no. 10 (1974).

Chryssavgis, John. "A Doxological Approach to Creation." *On the Move* 68 (1990).

————. "Essence and Energies: Dynamic Anthropology and Cosmology." In *Human Beings and Nature,* ed. G. Moses and N. Ormerod. Sydney: Sydney College of Divinity, 1992.

————. "Giver of Life, Sustain Your Creation." *WCC Pre-Assembly Report,* 1990.

————. "Reflections on Church and Environment." In *Crosstalk: Topics of Australian Church and Society,* ed. P. Henman. Brisbane: Boolarong Publishers, 1991.

Clapsis, E. "Population, Consumption and the Environment." In *Boston Theological Conference Papers.* Boston, 1996.

Evdokimov, Paul. "Nature." *Scottish Journal of Theology* 18 (1965).

Guroian, Vigen. "Ecological Ethics: An Ecclesial Event." In *Ethics after Christendom: Towards an Ecclesial Christian Ethic.* Grand Rapids: Eerdmans, 1994.

Harakas, Stanley. "The Ethics of the Energy Crisis." In *Contemporary Moral Issues.* Light and Life, 1982.

Ignatius IV, Patriarch of Antioch. "Three Sermons on the Environment: Creation, Spirituality, Responsibility." *Sourozh* 38 (1989).

John of Pergamon, Metropolitan. "The Book of Revelation and the Natural Environment." *Creation's Joy* 1, nos. 2-3 (1996).

————. "Ecological Asceticism: A Cultural Revolution." *Our Planet* 7, no. 6 (1995). Also in *Sourozh* 67 (1997).

————. "Man: The Priest of Creation; A Response to the Ecological Problem." In *Living Orthodoxy in the Modern World,* ed. A. Walker and C. Carras. London: SPCK, 1996.

————. "Orthodoxy and the Problem of the Protection of the Natural Environment." In *So That God's Creation Might Live: The Orthodox Church Responds to the Ecological Crisis.* Proceedings of the Inter-Orthodox Conference on Environmental Protection, Crete 1991. Bialystok: Ecumenical Patriarchate assisted by SYNDESMOS, 1991.

————. "Preserving God's Creation: Three Lectures on Theology and Ecology." *King's Theological Review* 12 (1989). Also in *Sourozh* 39-41 (1990). Summary in Elizabeth Breuilly and Martin Palmer, eds., *Christianity and Ecology.* London and New York, 1992.

Kallistos of Diokleia, Bishop. "Lent and the Consumer Society." In *Living Orthodoxy in the Modern World,* ed. A. Walker and C. Carras. London: SPCK, 1996.

————. "The Value of Material Creation." *Sobornost* 6, no. 3 (1971).

Khalil, Issa J. "The Ecological Crisis: An Eastern Christian Perspective." *St. Vladimir's Theological Quarterly* 22, no. 4 (1978).

Limouris, (now Metropolitan) Gennadios. "The Church as Mystery," in his *Church, Kingdom, World: The Church as Mystery and Prophetic Sign,* Faith and Order Paper no. 130. Geneva, 1986.

————. "Creation — Kingdom of God — Eschatology," in *Creation and the Kingdom of God.* Church and Society Documents no. 5. Geneva, 1988.

————. "New Challenges, Visions and Signs of Hope: Orthodox Insights on JPIC." In *Between the Flood and the Rainbow,* ed. D. Preman Niles. Geneva: WCC, 1992.

Makarios, Monk. "The Monk and Nature in the Orthodox Tradition." In *So That God's Creation Might Live: The Orthodox Church Responds to the Ecological Crisis.* Proceedings of the Inter-Orthodox Conference on Environmental Protection, Crete 1991. Bialystok: Ecumenical Patriarchate assisted by SYNDESMOS, 1991.

Mouzelis, Nicos. "Religion, Science, and the Environment: A Synthetic View." *Sourozh* 70 (1997).

Muratore, Stephen. "Earth Stewardship: Radical Deep Ecology of Patristic Christianity." *Epiphany Journal* 3, no. 2 (1992); 3, no. 4 (1993).

Oikonomou, Elias. "Holy Scripture and the Natural Environment." In *So That God's Creation Might Live: The Orthodox Church Responds to the Ecological Crisis.* Proceedings of the Inter-Orthodox Conference on Environmental Protection, Crete 1991. Bialystok: Ecumenical Patriarchate assisted by SYNDESMOS, 1991.

Oleksa, Michael. "Icons and the Cosmos: The Missionary Significance." *Sourozh* 16 (1984). Also in *Sacred Art Journal* 5, no. 1 (1984).

Paulos (Verghese), Mar Gregorios, Metropolitan. "Christology and Creation." In *Tending the Garden: Essays on the Gospel and the Church,* ed. W. Granberg-Michaelson. Grand Rapids: Eerdmans, 1987.

————. "Science and Faith: Complementary or Contradictory?" in *Faith and Science in an Unjust World,* vol. 1: *Plenary Presentations,* ed. Roger L. Shinn. Geneva, 1980.

————. "Science and Faith." *The Ecumenical Review* 27 (1985). [Also appeared in Emilio Castro, ed., *Church and Society: Ecumenical Perspectives. Essays in Honour of Paul Abrecht.* Geneva, 1985.]

―――. "Six Bible Studies," in *The New Faith-Science Debate: Probing Cosmology, Technology, and Theology,* ed. John M. Mangum. Geneva, 1989.

―――. "Theological Trends: Mastery and Mystery — Spirituality within Humanity's Mediating Role." *The Way: Contemporary Christian Spirituality,* October 1986.

Rossi, Vincent. "Inspiration: Who Comes out of the Wilderness?" *GreenCross* 2, no. 2 (1996).

Theoxeni, Sister. "The Orthodox Monastic Tradition and Our Relation to the Natural Environment." In *So That God's Creation Might Live: The Orthodox Church Responds to the Ecological Crisis.* Proceedings of the Inter-Orthodox Conference on Environmental Protection, Crete 1991. Bialystok: Ecumenical Patriarchate assisted by SYNDESMOS, 1991.

Staniloae, Dimitru. "Christian Responsibility in the World." In *The Tradition of Life,* ed. A. M. Allchin. London: Fellowship of St. Alban and St. Sergius, 1971.

―――. "The World as Gift and Sacrament of God's Love." *Sobornost* 5, no. 9 (1969).

Theokritoff, Elizabeth. "Eucharistic and Ascetic Ethos in Parish Life." *Creation's Joy* 1, no. 2 (1996).

Theokritoff [Briere], Elizabeth. "Creation, Incarnation, and Transfiguration: The Material World and Our Understanding of It." *Sobornost/ECR* 11, nos. 1-2 (1989).

―――. "Orthodoxy and the Environment." *Sourozh* 58 (1994).

# *Index*

349